Zapotec Women

LYNN STEPHEN

Zapotec Women

Gender, Class, and Ethnicity

in Globalized Oaxaca

SECOND EDITION

REVISED AND UPDATED

Duke University Press   Durham & London

2005

© 2005 Duke University Press

All rights reserved

Printed in the United States of

America on acid-free paper ∞

Designed by CH Westmoreland

Typeset in Monotype Garamond by

Tseng Information Systems, Inc.

Library of Congress Cataloging-in-

Publication Data appear on the

last printed page of this book.

I DEDICATE THIS BOOK

to the people of Teotitlán del Valle;

to my sons, Gabriel and José Angel;

and to my partner, Ellen Herman

Contents

Maps, Illustrations, and Tables

Acknowledgments

ACKNOWLEDGMENTS, FIRST EDITION

This book represents a seven-year period of my life beginning as a second-year graduate student at Brandeis University. In the seven years that I have dedicated to this project, family, friends, mentors, and colleagues both in the United States and in Mexico have contributed immensely and provided me with a rich and supportive context.

When I was a graduate student in the Anthropology Department at Brandeis University, Robert Hunt provided inspiration, support, and encouragement for this project from its very beginning until its completion as a book. The careful attention of Sutti Ortiz in the conceptualization and analysis of the larger effort this book represents was also invaluable. Judith Zeitlin was the first person to open the doors of ethnohistory to me and I thank her for her example and her encouragement in better integrating local and regional history into the project.

While I was teaching at MIT, Martin Diskin and James Howe provided intellectual and collegial support, spending many hours discussing various aspects of the book. They have remained important colleagues.

While working in Mexico during the past seven years, I have been fortunate to have shared my fieldwork, graduate school, and "new faculty" status with Jonathan Fox, who has provided unending support, encouragement, and intellectual inspiration, resulting in exciting collaborative research. Jeffrey Rubin has also been an invaluable Mexicanist colleague.

Since I began teaching at Northeastern University in 1987, my colleagues have shown tremendous support and encouragement. Christine Gailey, in particular, has provided me with inspiration, challenges, friendship, and critical feedback on several sections of this book. Debra Kaufman, Michael Blim, Alan Klein, Carol Owen, and Pat Golden have provided intellectual and collegial support for this project. My students have also provided challenges and encouragement. The Women's Studies Program and its executive board members at Northeastern have also provided support.

Other scholars in the United States have provided encouragement, criticism, and inspiration, including Stefano Varese, Karen Sacks, and Art Murphy. June Nash has provided critical intellectual and editorial feedback and suggestions. Friends and colleagues who have proved invaluable in supporting this project include Carol Zabin, Sylvia Maxfield,

Nicole Sault, and Helen Clements. I would like to thank Judith Hellman, Fran Rothstein, Michael Kearney, and anonymous reviewers for the University of Arizona Press and the University of Texas Press for their careful comments and suggestions, which helped to make this a better book.

Funding for field research was provided by the Inter-American Foundation, the Wenner-Gren Foundation for Anthropological Research, and the Damon Fellowship of Brandeis University. Time for additional research and writing was funded by the Center for U.S.-Mexican Studies, University of California, San Diego.

My six months at the Center for U.S.-Mexican Studies resulted in a wonderful intellectual experience in a superb physical and academic environment. I wish to thank Wayne Cornelius and my colleagues Teresa Korack, Neil Harvey, Maria Cook, Ilan Semo, and Enrique Semo for making this a particularly interesting and productive time.

In Mexico, I have many people to thank for their contributions to this work. In Oaxaca I would like to thank Cecil Welte, resident anthropologist and director of the Oficina de Estudios de Humanidad del Valle de Oaxaca for advice and use of his wonderful library. The Oaxaca office of the Instituto Nacional de Anthropología e Historia was extremely generous in assisting me to secure permission to work in Oaxaca, particularly Lic. María de la Luz Topete, Dra. Alicia Barabas, and Dr. Miguel Bartolomé. Colleagues at GADE (Grupo al Apoyo del Desarrollo Etnico), including Gary Martin, Alejandro de Avila, Teresa Pardo, and Pedro Lewin, were particularly helpful. Jorge Hernández and Josefina Aranda of the Instituto de Investigaciones Sociológicas de la Universidad Autónoma Benito Juárez de Oaxaca provided great assistance in making resources and data available and offering opportunities for intellectual interchange with students. Dr. Manuel Esparza, director of the Archivo del Estado de Oaxaca, was very helpful in locating historical information. Kate Raisz provided critical support and encouragement during the longest stretch of fieldwork for this project.

In Oaxaca, my personal and intellectual friendships with Margaritas Dalton Paloma and Guadalupe Musalem have been invaluable. They were the first people to open their homes to me there. Michael Higgins, whom I associate more with Mexico than with the United States, has also been an important friend and colleague, as has Julia Barco.

My family has provided me with comfort, support, and inspiration throughout this project, often visiting me in the field and encouraging me through the more difficult parts of writing. Suzanne Brown, Bruce Stephen, and Rachel Goldman have backed me through the entire pro-

cess. Ellen Herman has provided unending daily support, encouragement, and critical intellectual feedback throughout the writing of this
book and the dissertation that preceded it.

A special group of friends in Boston always made it a wonderful place
to come back to after being in the field.

More than anyone, the people of Teotitlán are to be thanked for opening their homes, hearts, and minds to me for over seven years. I would
like to thank the González family for sharing their home with me, my
family, and friends for so many years, particularly Paco, who has served
as one of my primary teachers, guides, and friends, along with Cristina.
To Petra I owe many wonderful insights into local culture and history.
María Chavez has also been a valuable friend and research assistant.
Many other people in the community who prefer to remain unnamed
have been important friends and collaborators in this research.

ACKNOWLEDGMENTS, SECOND EDITION

Acknowledging my debts for the new edition of *Zapotec Women* is an occasion to think over the twenty years that I have been working in Teotitlán.
The bulk of the fieldwork done for this edition was completed during
the summers from 2001 to 2004. In 1998 my family moved from Boston
to Eugene, Oregon, where I have been teaching since that time. I want
to acknowledge the support of Terry O'Nell, Sandra Morgen, Madonna
Moss, Jon Erlandson, Bill Ayres, Carol Silverman, and John Lukacs in
the Department of Anthropology at the University of Oregon. They have
supported me as colleagues, some as critical readers, and as friends. I
have been very happy at the University of Oregon and the Department
of Anthropology has proved to be a stimulating, friendly place to work.
I also want to thank and acknowledge the important work of María de
la Torre, a graduate student in the Department of Sociology at the University of Oregon, who worked with me in Teotitlán during the summer
of 2001. Jonathan Fox, a close friend and colleague, provided ongoing
important intellectual exchange on the West Coast. I thank Analisa Taylor and William Warner Wood for their close readings of and excellent
suggestions for Chapter 5. Jean Jackson and Kay Warren provided important support and conversations during the research and writing of
this edition.

The University of Oregon has provided me with research support that
allowed me to complete the fieldwork necessary for this book. I am

grateful to the Center for the Study of Women and Society for a research grant in 2002 and to the University of Oregon for a Summer Research Award for Faculty in 2001. In 2003 I was named a Distinguished Professor of Arts and Sciences at the University or Oregon, and I am grateful for the accompanying funds that furthered my research in 2003 and 2004.

Several new friends in Mexico City and elsewhere with passionate interest in questions of indigenous autonomy and indigenous women's organizing in Mexico have provided invaluable intellectual conversations and inspiration, among them Rosalva Aída Hernández Castillo, Shannon Speed, and María Teresa Sierra.

Some of the lasting friendships I made in Oaxaca in the 1980s have been crucial in helping me to bring this work up to date. Margarita Dalton Paloma and Julia Barco have continued to be wonderful friends, comadres, and sources of knowledge and insight. Layla Musalem, Paola Sesia, Teresa Pardo, Stefano Varese, and Carlos Moreno all continued to be important local friends and intellectual colleagues in Oaxaca. The loss of my dear friend Guadalupe Musalem in 1995 is a sadness I never forget, but I still encounter her friendship and zest for life in many of the corners of Oaxaca I frequent. Lucero Topete, the first person who welcomed me to Oaxaca in 1983, continues to play an important role in the life of my family. As director of the Instituto Cultural de Oaxaca, she has provided warm friendship and a wonderful learning environment for my older son, Gabriel, as well as assistance in finding housing in Oaxaca. Juana Rodríguez Ramírez and her son, Gustavo, have been wonderful friends to my family during our summer visits to Oaxaca. Fidel Morales has also been an important family friend and support during our time in Oaxaca. Matt Gutmann — a longtime friend whom I now see more in Oaxaca than elsewhere — has been a valuable colleague in Oaxaca, a research site we now share.

I continue to cherish my old friendships and relationships in Teotitlán. Paco González has continued to be a valuable research collaborator, friend, and compadre. Petra Bautista Vicente continues as a close friend, confidante, research collaborator, and comadre. My compadres Andrés Gutiérrez and Margarita Alavez opened their home and hearts to me and my family as always. Efraín Gutiérrez Alavez and Aurora Lazo González have become good friends and I thank them for sharing their home and good food with me and my family. I am particularly grateful to a group of women active in the cooperatives for their invitation to carry out this new project and for their enthusiasm and support. They include Aurora Bazán López, Aurora Contreras, Reina González Martínez,

Isabel Hernández, Pastora Gutiérrez Reyes, Josefina Jiménez, Guadalupe Ruiz Sosa, Francisca Ruiz García, and Violeta Vásquez Gutiérrez. Moisés Lazo González offered very helpful perspectives on his and other cooperatives' histories and challenges. Arnulfo Mendoza and Mary Jane Gagnier were particularly generous with their time and I enjoyed our developing friendship, discussions, and personal and intellectual passion in all things Teotitlán. With Francisco Sosa, who was *presidente municipal* (mayor) during three of my summers in Teotitlán, I enjoyed many delightful conversations. I thank him and the other *autoridades* for granting me permission to work in the community and to observe community assemblies.

Alejandro de Avila, father of my two sons, has provided boundless support, encouragement, and friendship throughout the time I researched the book. As a family member rooted in Oaxaca, he has helped us all to enjoy and cherish our time there. To my sons, Gabriel and José Angel, who accompanied me on my research trips, I thank you for your love and patience, and for the good times we enjoyed in Oaxaca. To Ellen Herman, my life partner, who shared time in Oaxaca and in the trials of writing and daily living and loving, I thank you for the gift of our family and life together.

Finally, I thank my Duke editor Valerie Millholland for her support and encouragement of this project. I gratefully acknowledge the permission of University of California Press Journals and the American Anthropological Association to reprint parts of "Negotiating Global, National, and Local 'Rights' in a Zapotec Community" in *PoLAR: Political and Legal Anthropology Review* 28 (Spring 2005), copyright © 2005 by the American Anthropological Association. I also thank *Critique of Anthropology* for permission to reprint parts of "Women's Weaving Cooperatives in Oaxaca: An Indigenous Response to Neoliberalism," appearing in spring 2005. Thanks to the University of Texas Press for permission to base the two maps of Oaxaca included here on maps that appeared in the first edition.

Introduction

> We really like speaking Zapotec. We speak it because it is our
> language—the language that our parents and their parents spoke.
> Even though they teach us another language in school and other
> kinds of customs and traditions, we like being Zapotec. We can be
> modern and Zapotec at the same time.—Carlota, age 17

Zapotec Women was originally published in 1991, based on fieldwork carried out between 1983 and 1990. This updated edition contains several new chapters. The idea of publishing a new version came from the women of Teotitlán. A Spanish version of the first edition, *Mujeres zapotecas*, was published in Mexico in 1998 by the Instituto Oaxaqueño de las Culturas. In August 1999 we followed the wonderful Mexican custom of holding a party and forum when a new book appears. When a book is launched in the United States, authors usually talk about their own works, but in Mexico colleagues of the author, experts, and persons who have a distinct perspective on the book's topic offer comments and analysis. At the launching of *Mujeres zapotecas* speakers included Margarita Dalton, a historian and philosopher who at that time was Oaxaca's minister of culture; Josefina Aranda, a rural sociologist and expert on indigenous movements and politics and gender; Francisco González, my compadre and research collaborator from Teotitlán; Isabel Hernández, one of the founding members of Teotitlán's first cooperative of women weavers and president of the Asociación de las Mujeres Antiguas de Teotitlán del Valle; and Juana Pérez González, a member of Mujeres Que Tejan, a continuation of the first women's cooperative.

The women from Teotitlán offered praise for the first Spanish edition of the book, saying it was interesting and accurate, but they had two critical comments as well. First, the woman pictured on the jacket had married into the community; she was not from Teotitlán, so how could she represent them? Apparently a photographer from the Oaxaca Ministry of Culture had been assigned to go and take a picture of a woman weaving and didn't think to ask who she was. For the women from the weaving cooperatives, this was a problem that needed to be corrected. Second, the book ended too soon; it said nothing about the developments of the 1990s, especially the flowering of women's weaving cooperatives in the community. Isabel, Juana, and other women from Teotitlán declared that

I needed to produce another book, one that would bring readers up to date on the women's cooperatives and women's increasing participation in local politics. I made a public promise to do just that. I hope that this new incarnation does justice to the accomplishments and aspirations of the multiple generations of women from Teotitlán who inspired it.

SCENE 1

Soledad sits surrounded by the four oldest women at the wedding fiesta. Before them are the roasted carcasses of four pigs. The older women and Soledad work quickly to divide up the meat, putting large chunks into bowls to be served to the guests. They make sure that the largest portions are given to the most important people. This is the second meal of the day. A more elaborate meal will be served tomorrow to the two hundred men and women assembled in the courtyard. Outside, groups of younger women, some married with small children, are making tortillas. They comment on the recent improvements in Soledad's house. Soledad's family has six good-sized looms and a new pickup truck. A new wing has doubled the size of their house. And just in time for the wedding, they built a bathroom, complete with a flush toilet. Some of the women fantasize about adding rooms to their one-room homes. Others describe beds, refrigerators, and new dishes they hope to buy someday.

SCENE 2

Petra steps inside as her neighbor Gloria opens the door. Petra solemnly crosses to the altar at the center of the room. She kisses the altar, greeting the saints, and then turns to Gloria and her husband, Pedro, and explains that she and her family are going to sponsor a *posada*, a three-day celebration involving several large meals and drinking when the statue of the Christ child is brought from the church to their home just before Christmas. She requests that they return the turkey she lent them two years ago when their youngest son was married. Pedro and Gloria pull out a small blue notebook and find the entry recording the loan of Petra's turkey. They nod and agree to deliver a turkey of equal or greater weight one week before the Christmas posada.

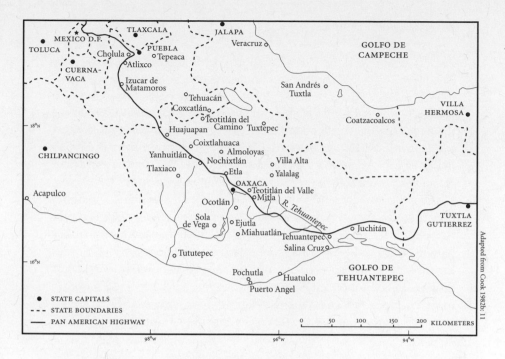

Map 1. State of Oaxaca.

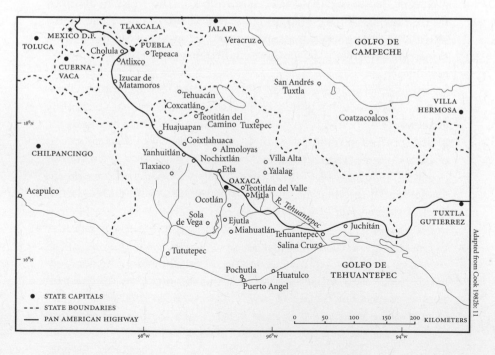

Map 2. Teotitlán and surrounding communities.

SCENE 3

Fourteen-year-old María is alone in the house. Her parents are across town, celebrating the baptism of the new son of their compadres. Outside, a white Nissan four-door sedan has pulled up in front of María's house. The driver gets out and knocks at the door. María opens it to admit Susan, an American who owns an importing business in Santa Fe, New Mexico. She has come to pick up an order of 200 weavings. She hopes they're ready, she says, because she's flying back to the United States in two days. Perplexed, María gives her a hot tortilla, explaining that her parents are not at home. She knows they haven't completed the order because of the invitation to the baptism. She also knows, however, that Susan is a very important client. She quickly sends her younger brother to give a message to her parents. Half an hour later, María's father arrives; her mother has remained at the compadre's house to help with the cooking.

These scenes represent common events in the Zapotec-speaking community of Teotitlán del Valle, Oaxaca, Mexico. Known internationally for its wool textiles, Teotitlán has become an economic success story in a state that is distinguished by having one of the lowest per capita gross domestic products in all Mexico. In conjunction with the successful weaving industry, people continue to devote a significant amount of time and energy to ritual activity. Looking at the impact of textile commercialization on Teotitlán, we might expect to find a community that was rapidly abandoning its links to the past and was completely absorbed into the global capitalist economy. We might also predict a rapid advancement of class differentiation and an increase in the status of women as they began to work as weavers and were paid at rates equal to those of men. These were the predictions I made during my first two months of fieldwork in the summer of 1983.

After investigating several Zapotec communities in the central valley of Oaxaca as possible field sites, I was attracted to Teotitlán by three factors. First, I discovered that, contrary to everything I had read about treadle loom weaving and about Teotitlán in particular, a significant number of the weavers were women. This seemed to signal an important change in the gendered division of labor, which could have major consequences for the status of women not only in production but in other areas as well. Second, it was abundantly clear that economic development was taking place in the community, at least for some families. New homes were being constructed and everyone was busy producing or selling wool textiles. There were many signs written in English to attract tourists. During my first days, most of the people I met tried to sell me a serape or asked if I had an importing business in the United States. Yet despite the evidence of rapid economic development, a strain of traditionalism could be seen there. Everyone spoke Zapotec and every day someone somewhere was having a ritual ceremony that disrupted the rhythm of weaving production. I decided to stay in Teotitlán precisely because what I saw happening was not what was predicted. It seemed to be a place caught between a rapidly advancing future in export production and a long-entrenched past of ethnic uniqueness anchored in ongoing institutions.

Most of my first two-month fieldwork stint was spent trying to understand the basic social structure of the community, the daily routine of households, the agricultural cycle, and the gendered division of labor. Because I knew very few people, like most anthropologists I became expert in initiating conversations on any pretext. One of my most successful techniques was to inquire about fine-looking cows, pigs, and chickens. Most women and men were interested in talking about animal production—when I was able to communicate with them.

While well prepared to speak Spanish, I soon discovered that much of life in Teotitlán was carried on exclusively in Zapotec. Because my first place of residence was with a largely monolingual Zapotec-speaking family, my first efforts at conversation were painful, but I pressed on out of necessity. My first friends turned out to be either monolingual elderly Zapotec women or younger married men who were interested in talking about agriculture and politics. Because I wanted to include gender as a major category of my research, it became clear that my monolingual elderly female friends were critical in helping me to gain an understanding of women's lives in Teotitlán. I credit them with providing many of the insights I gained as time went on.

Another way of learning Zapotec was to exchange Zapotec lessons for lessons in English appropriate for selling textiles. I finally got so many requests for English terms for color, size, design, counting, and descriptions of the basics of making a sale that I produced a small document that I gave to people as a study aid. Eventually I also began to work consistently with one young man, who became my Zapotec tutor and most consistent research collaborator. Later several young women in the community also began to work with me.

My longest stint of fieldwork began in November 1984 and ended in January 1986. I lived the entire time with an extended family, an experience that proved to be critical in teaching me about the basics of life as well as providing emotional and intellectual support for my work. I spent many evenings reflecting with them on what I had seen or discussed during the day. As I began to participate in the heavy ritual cycle of the community, they trained me in appropriate behavior and ritual speech and incorporated me into their cycle of ceremonial participation.

During 1985, 1986, the summer of 1987, and shorter visits in 1988 and 1989, I began to see my initial ideas about gender and economic development challenged by the complexity of recent history in Teotitlán. As my knowledge of Zapotec improved and I began to delve into twentieth-century community and regional history through exploring local archives and carrying out oral history interviews with the eldest members of the community, my ideas changed. My thoughts about the logical trajectory of economic development were challenged by the contradictory and dialectical consequences of the gradual commercialization of treadle loom weaving in Teotitlán and surrounding communities during the twentieth century.

Because I chose to focus on women, I began to see the varied consequences of textile production for export first in the category of gender. What I came to see as a basic contradiction between a kin-based ideology of community solidarity linked to local Zapotec ethnic identity and a class-based ideology emphasizing wealth and employer status in the relations of production alerted me to potential differences among women. The consequences of textile commercialization could not be generalized to all women in Teotitlán. To understand how changes in textile production affected women, I also had to explore how class and ethnic identity have changed over time. This investigation allowed me to see how women are differentiated in the process of commercialization regardless of gender and shed light on the consequences they share precisely because of gender. The primary lesson I learned from working in Teotitlán in the mid-1980s was that indigenous communities are not homogeneous.

I returned to Teotitlán in the summers of 2001, 2002, 2003, and 2004 to do in-depth fieldwork again after more than a decade of more sporadic contact limited to annual visits with friends, compadres, and my goddaughters and godsons. My Zapotec was rusty at first, but by the end of the summer of 2002 I was speaking reasonably well again and had entered that wonderful space of being able to feel the world differently because of the language in which it is captured. As I told friends in Oaxaca, "I can joke with the old women again. I think that means I am back on track with my Zapotec." Indeed, being able to have meaningful conversations with older monolingual Zapotec speakers in Teotitlán was the one of the most important and pleasurable parts of my research in the 1980s and again in the twenty-first century. The beauty and meaning of a place reside in language and conversation, and I felt blessed to be able to enter that world again.

In contrast to the more general ethnographic work I carried out in the 1980s, my fieldwork from 2001 to 2004 was focused on the histories of the women's cooperatives while at the same time I tried to understand the broader context out of which the cooperatives had emerged. The larger context that affected the emergence of the cooperatives is tied to several key factors: the intensification of competition between local merchants and the lowering of prices paid to pieceworkers by larger exporting merchants, whose exporting activities were facilitated by the North American Free Trade Agreement (NAFTA) in 1994; active encouragement of cooperatives by both nongovernmental organizations and various branches of the Mexican government; and increasing migration of women out of Teotitlán into circumstances where they came to see themselves as more independent.

I greatly enjoyed carrying out this new research, especially since I was doing it at the request of women of the community. I spent much of my time talking with women, individually and collectively, and with the few men who had joined the cooperatives that had formed, their families, and others linked to them. I also caught up with many old friends. Migration emerged as a major theme in the lives of some of the key players in the formation of the cooperatives and of others as well. In appearance the community had changed significantly. Many more people were bilingual in Spanish and Zapotec, new houses were going up everywhere, and people's level of consumption seemed to have accelerated.

At the same time, the community was unchanged in many ways. Rituals went on in much the same way, weddings were just as grandiose as before, and community assemblies continued in Zapotec, with the one difference that they were now attended by some women as well as men. The class stratification between merchants and weavers seemed more fixed and exaggerated than before, yet the cooperative movement and the members' efforts to link directly to consumers suggested an alternative kind of economic model for the production and marketing of Teotitlán's beautiful textiles.

This updated and significantly revised version of *Zapotec Women* was written first and foremost for the women weavers who requested it as well as for the many other readers who enjoyed the first edition of the book and have taken an ongoing interest in the community. It offers readers the chance to view one community over a span of twenty years through the eyes of one anthropologist. The anthropologist has changed as well as the community.

The first edition of this book, based in part on my doctoral dissertation, was punctuated by the need to show "I know the literature," was objective, and was steeped in both quantitative and qualitative methods of investigation; now I no longer feel the need to prove myself along many dimensions. While I still appreciate and value quantitative and qualitative methods and efforts to understand problems and stories from their many sides, I am also interested in meaning, interpretation, and the ways in which individual experience through time can collectively alter local institutions and human relationships, producing multiple layers of identities.

During the past fifteen years my work came to be strongly informed by cultural studies as well as work on cultural politics (see Alvarez, Dagnino, and Escobar 1998; Babb 2001), social movements (see Escobar and Alvarez 1992), studies of nationalism and transnational communities (see Kearney 1995b, 1996b; Levitt 2001), flexible citizenship (Ong 1999), and cultural citizenship (Flores and Benmayor 1997; Rosaldo 1997). Scholarship on women and social movements in Latin America has also been influential in my thinking (Alvarez forthcoming; Eber and Kovich 2003; Montoya, Frazier, and Hurtig 2002; Molyneux 2003), as has the proliferation of excellent research on gender in Mexico (see, for example, Gutmann 1996; Hernández-Castillo 1997, 2001a; Rodríguez 1998, 2003). In other words, the themes of culture and politics have come to occupy a central place along with my analysis of gender and political economy.

Because I have been working in Teotitlán for so many years, I have a strong historical and broad-based general understanding on which to build my more recent research. For that reason I was able to concentrate my recent research on the specific circumstances that contributed to the rise of the cooperatives and to women's challenges and gains in that process. Being known and invited back to work in the community made most of my conversations relaxed and fun.

A final difference between this version of *Zapotec Women* and the first is the nature of the relationship between me and the women who worked with me in Teotitlán. This was a much more collaborative project than my earlier research. The process of updating and revising this book involved discussions and interviews with the members of each weaving cooperative, the submission of transcripts to people whose interviews I had tape-recorded, the giving of photographs to each group, and in some cases the creation of bilingual (Spanish–English) brochures or other pieces of literature for the cooperatives. I was able to connect other groups with people who could help them create Web pages. Finally, I translated most of the new material in this book from English to Spanish (and occasionally to Zapotec) so that I could discuss and debate it with the women's cooperatives. Their suggestions have been incorporated in the final draft.

I offer one more scene to illustrate the differences among women as well as some of the roles they share. The rest of the book elaborates on this theme, focusing on gender relations in ritual, weaving production and marketing, local politics, and families.

SCENE 4

Ritual space is segregated by gender: men eat, drink, lounge, and sit apart from women. Within this segregated space a ritual order of respect and prestige is evident, based on ritual experience and age. Those men and women with the most ritual experience have leadership roles. In this context an elderly woman, Gloria, discusses how the dance should be structured with the male host, the *mayordomo*. Later she instructs a young merchant woman to serve shots of mescal to all the women present.

The next week Gloria visits the young merchant woman's house to pick up yarn for several rugs she has agreed to weave on a piecework basis. The young woman, who is probably repeating her husband's specifications, tells Gloria what size to make the weavings, what colors to use, what design to copy, and when they should be ready. Gloria will be paid when she delivers the weavings.

That evening Gloria is at home finishing up a day of weaving. She talks with her husband, who is preparing to go to the town hall for a community assembly. Gloria gives her opinion on how difficult negotiations with the state-run yarn factory have been and urges him to push for community control. When he leaves, she continues to weave. Gloria does not go to community meetings because, she says, it is not the custom for women of her age to attend.

When her husband arrives at the community assembly, however, he finds eight women sitting together, the youngest 18, the eldest 50. They are from one of the women's weaving cooperatives in Teotitlán. They vote in the assembly and one of them offers her opinion. He makes a note to tell Gloria about the women at the assembly. She probably won't approve of their presence here, he thinks.

As this example indicates, an elderly woman who holds the highest authority in a ritual event may have little or no control over the style, color, or dimensions of what she weaves. In contrast, a young merchant woman who has little authority in a ritual event has some authority in production relations, particularly in comparison with women who are working for her and her husband. Women like Gloria structure their political participation through discussions with other women in the market, at ritual events, and at community water sites, through subtle protest actions, and through efforts to influence their husbands, who do attend community assemblies. Other women, however, are beginning to attend community assemblies themselves. Some of their toughest critics may be other women, but they feel they have a right to equal participation with men.

The shifting dynamics of ethnicity and class frame and define the daily world of women in Teotitlán and other indigenous communities, as well as their possibilities for changing it. For this reason, gender does not function as a separate analytical category. Rather than simply being about women as differentiated from men, this book attempts to clarify the way in which gender takes on specific meaning in relation to particular economic and cultural arrangements — in this case, in relation to global capitalism, the class system it engenders, and formulations of ethnic identity influenced by local aspects of indigenous Zapotec culture and state-promoted images of "Mexican Indians." In contesting the idea that world markets alone determine local social and economic relations, this book shows that the changing positions of women in Teotitlán are not simply the products of increased demand for woven goods. Rather, the lives of Zapotec women have been shaped by the intersection of regional, national, and international markets with education, changes in the local and national gender ideology, migration, changes in the local and national political systems, and local, national, and international processes of ethnic labeling and identity construction.

The chapters that follow emphasize the multiple representations of gender, class, and ethnicity and how they are used, particularly by women, to achieve goals and agendas.

Chapters 1 and 2 discuss key concepts used in the book (culture, ethnicity, class, and kin-based institutions of solidarity and exchange such as ritual kinship and reciprocal goods and labor exchanges) and outline how these institutions function in relation to the social reproduction of laborers and social actors. The concept of social reproduction is discussed as an alternative framework to the public/private model of gender relations, but is also critically reexamined in relation to how globalization, transnationalism, and migration have significantly altered the terrain on which social reproduction occurs.

Chapter 3 explores the arenas of weaving production, ritual, and politics through the life histories of six Zapotec women—merchants and weavers, young and old. These life histories provide concrete illustrations of many of the analytical and descriptive points made in the book.

Chapter 4 introduces the Zapotecs and the community of Teotitlán, offering current and historical information on agriculture, the division of agricultural labor, occupations, land distribution, economy, migration, geography and climate, political ties, markets, religious institutions, education, and health.

Chapter 5 documents Teotitlán's transition from a community of subsistence farmers and part-time weavers laboring under a system of mercantile capitalism to a town of artisans producing for export under a system of commercial capitalism. It contrasts local constructions of economic history to those of the state, focusing on women's roles in the labor force, state constructions of indigenous women, and the impact on women of the large-scale migration of men to the United States during the bracero program and afterward.

Chapter 6 continues this discussion, describing the commercialization of Zapotec textiles in relation to several local, national, and global processes, including the disappearance of local and regional markets for hand-woven blankets; the promotion of *arte popular*, or folk art, as a part of Mexican nationalism beginning in the 1920s; government promotion of tourism; development programs to improve the quality of craft production and distribution; and Teotitecos' own efforts to gain control over the marketing and distribution of their products. The chapter includes a discussion of the debates about political economy and intellectual property rights in relation to Zapotec and Navajo designs. Finally, the chapter highlights the creation of Teotitlán's community museum as a local strategy for reclaiming Teotiteco Zapotec history and culture as a counterweight to external constructions of Teotitecos and their textiles by the government, exporters, and tourists.

Chapter 7 explores how class differentiation distinguished between merchant and weaver women in the arenas of weaving production and marketing and politics in the mid-1980s and how the emergence of women's weaving cooperatives in the late 1980s and 1990s has partially challenged the economic marginalization of women weavers, often with significant roadblocks to their participation in the cooperatives thrown up by male and female family members.

Chapter 8 lays the historical basis for a discussion of women's changing participation in ritual and political life in Teotitlán. Focusing on the divorce of civil from religious offices in local government beginning in the 1930s and the gradual phasing out of most sponsorships of ceremonial activities, this chapter examines the changing structural conditions that decreased women's roles in formal politics until the late 1980s.

Chapter 9 documents how the content and form of religious ceremonies have been transferred to life-cycle rituals and how women use these rituals and the traditional idea of respect to continue to influence the community.

Chapter 10 explores the varied dimensions of women's political participation during two distinct time periods. It first documents how women were shut out of most formal political institutions and how their age and class status influenced their ideas about themselves as political actors and their strategies for political participation in the mid-1980s. Then it shifts to the 1990s, when both internal and external factors led to an increase in women's participation in the formal political system. The emergence of the movement for indigenous autonomy in the wake of the Zapatista rebellion of 1994 was a significant factor in developments in Teotitlán and other indigenous communities (see Stephen 2002). Both the Mexican government and a wide range of nongovernmental organizations developed programs emphasizing the importance of women's political participation. A national indigenous women's network was created for the first time in 1997. The National Indigenous Women's Council/Coordinadora (CNMI) was founded in Oaxaca. Changes in Oaxaca's constitution and state laws that confirmed the right of indigenous communities to elect officials according to their own customs and traditions sparked debate on the role of indigenous women in local and statewide politics. The emergence of more than a dozen weaving cooperatives (eight of them women's) and their formal incorporation into Teotitlán's political structure increased women's participation in community assemblies and led to leadership roles for a few both inside and outside the community.

In "After Words" I look at the implications of this historical and ethnographic material for the political, economic, and cultural participation and creativity of other indigenous women in contemporary Mexico, particularly under the policy of economic neoliberalism, which has characterized Mexico and much of the world since the 1990s. Mexico's entrance into a neoliberal model began in the mid-1980s and was consolidated under NAFTA. Most people in Mexico lost ground in the 1990s, particularly the rural poor—a significant part of the indigenous population. The emergence of women's cooperatives in Teotitlán and other organizational efforts to improve the standard of living of the poorest parts of Mexico are important to document. Such movements to improve the lot of persons disenfranchised by the neoliberalism of the 1990s can offer concrete insights into alternative ways of earning a living, working, and participating in community and national life that offer dignity, respect, and recognition for cultural distinctiveness and artistic skill. Finally, the chapter suggests that indigenous women's organizing is providing a new model for incorporating ethnic and gender rights into Mexican society.

Unless I have indicated otherwise, all translations are my own.

CHAPTER I

Ethnicity and Class in
the Changing Lives of
Zapotec Women

We are all united here. This is a very quiet town where no one
causes any problems. We aren't like other towns where people are
divided. We are all just one community. No one is better than
anyone else. — Jorge, age 50

Of course some women have more status than others. The ones
who are older, who have given a lot of fiestas, they are always the
most distinguished. — Marina, age 26

There are some really big merchants here in the community. There
are five or six families that make all of the money. So the rest of the
families are just workers for these people. — Angela, age 48

In the course of the twentieth century the economic base of Teotitlán del Valle went from mercantile to commercial capital to full
incorporation in a global economy. Within this economy, women and
men came to occupy an ever-shifting and globally competitive niche associated with the production of folk art, crafts, and high art that required
the commoditization of Zapotec ethnicity and put the weavers of Teotitlán in direct competition with other indigenous producers of ethnically
identified products. By 2004, a wide range of production arrangements
could be found in the community. While it is tempting to label both the
relations of textile production and the dynamics of identity formation
as parts of one type of system — for example, post-Fordist capitalism,
characterized by outsourcing and subcontracting around the world in
efforts to find the cheapest and most efficient source of labor, which then
subsumes all other aspects of identity — this is not the case. For most
of the twentieth century, textile production in Teotitlán involved multiple markets and types of relations of production. Thus it is important
to recognize the changing and continued complexity of systems of textile production and the different kinds of labor, kin, ethnic, and gender
relationships that crosscut them. As Fran Rothstein observed in respect

to rural women workers, "differences need to be the starting point, not the end point of our analyses" (1999, 579).

Workers in Teotitlán's textile industry employ a variety of strategies and systems of production:

a. Piecework production for local merchants who resell in other parts of Mexico and the United States.

b. Increased direct control over production and distribution by businesses in the Southwestern United States that market Zapotec and knockoff textiles from Mexico and around the world (Wood 2000a).

c. Weaving cooperatives that produce primarily for the tourist market in Oaxaca.

d. Establishment of households and small businesses in Oaxaca, on the U.S.-Mexico border, and in the United States by independent merchant and producer families struggling to maintain control over family businesses (somewhat similar to the "flexible citizenship" strategies described by Ong 1999; see Wood 2000b).

e. Subcontracting of weaving in Teotitlán and surrounding communities by several powerful local merchant households, who deal also in a wide range of other folk art and ethnic crafts.

While U.S. textile designers, importers, and entrepreneurs have been important forces in shaping the relations of work in the age of neoliberalism, kin networks also continue to be crucial in helping people to "access material and cultural resources and labor within and beyond the household," as Teotitecos struggle to improve their lives (see Rothstein 1999, 587).

As in much of the world, being part of a global economy has reinforced tension between economic stratification and ethnic identity, which has evolved to accommodate Mexico's focus on the self-determination of its indigenous peoples and the search for ways of maintaining cultural difference in an interconnected world. The tension between class differentiation and ethnic identity formation and reformation often works to create differences among women as well as among households. Differences among women must be related to the structural dynamics of economic neoliberalism, which affected women not only in Teotitlán but elsewhere in Mexico as well.

CULTURE AND THE CONCEPT OF ETHNICITY

In an ongoing battle to determine the analytical primacy of class or ethnicity as the major motor of social relations in rural communities from the 1960s through the 1980s, both Mexican and U.S. anthropologists often reduced ethnicity to class or class to ethnicity without really looking at the ways in which the two intersected. This strategy reflects a larger problem that emerges in anthropology and other social sciences when a static concept of culture is used to analyze social class formation and transition, usually in the guise of acculturation. When culture is defined as a set of shared values or rules for organizing social life, and thus is assumed to be equally shared by all, understood the same way by all members of the group that "shares" the culture, and passed on intact from one generation to the next, it is unlikely to be used in analyses of change. Culture either becomes derivative, "an attachment of more basic political-economic processes," or becomes "independent of the realities of social class" (Sider 1986, 5). If a more flexible definition is used, culture can be helpful and indeed essential in discussing social and economic change. Sally Engle Merry argues that in more recent years, anthropology has developed a complex way of understanding culture by focusing on its "historical production, its porosity to outside influences and pressures, and its incorporation of competing repertoires of meaning and action" (2003a, 4). Her reading of Jean and John L. Comaroff's *Of Revelation and Revolution* bolsters her optimistic assessment of the value of the culture concept for understanding rapid change, colonization and decolonization, human rights, and other more contemporary phenomena. She writes:

> Anthropology is now struggling to think of culture in more flexible ways, as unbounded, changing, contested, and as rooted in practices and habits as well as ideas and values. Not only are there always flows of new ideas, perspectives, and practices, but there are also, within any group, contests over meanings and action. Those in power may use claims of cultural authenticity to force their ideas on others. Subordinated groups may seize other cultural arguments to contest those claims—arguments derived either from contradictions within a society or provided by newcomers or those who have traveled elsewhere. Such processes of reformulation, argumentation, and change are fundamental to any social group, although the rate and extent of contestation may vary. (Merry 2003b, 466)

If culture is not shared and is unbounded, what is it? How does it function and where is it located? The Comaroffs (1992, 21) define culture as "the space of signifying practice, the semantic ground on which human beings seek to construct and represent themselves and others — and hence, society and history." It is located in individual consciousness as well as in the ways historical change promotes new relations of power that are contested, accepted, and taken for granted (Merry 2003b, 466). Thus culture is in everyone's head, but not in all heads in the same way or even necessarily always in the same head in the same way through time. As individual consciousness, interpretations, and ideas change, so can one individual's interpretation of culture. One way to think about culture (as in any kind of group identity formation process such as ethnicity, gender, nationalism) is: What are the key contested areas or questions that appear in a particular site or group of linked sites? In other words, what specific pieces of contested representation are being debated, by whom, and for what purpose?

Anthropologists' past attempts to define ethnicity or specific ethnic groups have often suffered from some of the same problems as models of culture. All too often ethnic identities were assumed to be constituted in the same way for all who held them and to be identifiable according to a set of objective characteristics. Historically, anthropologists often divided people into discrete units — cultures, tribes, ethnic groups — based on the fact that they spoke a particular language, shared common ceremonies and material artifacts, and lived in similar areas. This time-honored approach was taken up by anthropologists in Mexico in relation to particular ethnic groups as well as by the government census office, where it continues to this day. Multilingualism and migration, among other things, have led most anthropologists to conclude that ethnic groups cannot necessarily be distinguished by objective empirical traits such as the language they speak or the territory they occupy. Instead, ethnicity is seen as a subjective, dynamic concept through which groups of people determine their own distinct identities by creating boundaries between themselves and other groups through interaction (Adams 1988; Barth 1969). The cultural theorist Stuart Hall writes that identities (including ethnicity) are constructed through difference — through the relation to what is not, to what is lacking, to what has been called "the other" or the "constitutive outside." Identities "can function as points of identification and attachment only because of their capacity to exclude, to leave out, to render 'outside,' abjected" (Hall 1996, 5; Butler 1993).

The form of unity, of closure that they exhibit is constructed and discursive—and, as the Comaroffs argue, contested.

While Barth's (1969) discussion of ethnicity is situationalist, in that he views ethnicity as constructed in relation to a particular situation and contingency, his discussion does not directly take on situations of conflict or the larger political context in which ethnicity is asserted. More recent theorists such as Brackette Williams (1989) insist that ethnicity be conceptualized as a category of identity within the political unit of the nation-state. My view coincides with hers: ethnic groups often are competing not only among themselves but also in relation to the state as they seek political recognition, which may bring access to resources. (Velasco Ortiz 2002 offers further discussion of this point.)

Ethnicity is a concept used by a group of people in particular situations where they are trying to assert their status vis-à-vis another group of people, often for political, economic, or social reasons. A self-chosen ethnic identity is usually based on a claim to historical autonomy and perceived cultural or physical traits that are emphasized as a primary source of identity and recognized internally as well as externally (Stephen and Dow 1990). Ethnic identities are articulated and mobilized not only in response to the need to stake political and economic claims in relation to states, but also in relation to the global economy.

Steve Stern (1987, 15–16) has pointed out that presumed physical and cultural traits draw social boundaries that may or may not coincide with economic class boundaries. Depending on the context in which a specific ethnic identity is used, by whom, and to what end, ethnicity may be used to link classes together in opposition to a perceived common threat or to reinforce the dominance of one class over another. When mobilized in a global economic context, ethnic identities are linked to both international and national political and economic structures and situations.

The above discussion is meant to clarify the way in which ethnicity can be understood as an analytical concept, which is distinct from the particular way in which Teotitecos and other groups culturally construct ethnicity for themselves. I argue below that Teotitecos' construction of ethnicity has two dimensions: an ethnic identity for outside consumption, which emphasizes community solidarity and a common claim to being the originators of treadle loom weaving in the Oaxaca Valley, and an internal version of ethnic identity, which, although it emphasizes common language, participation in local social and cultural institutions, and weaving production, also allows the contradictions of class differentiation, age, and gender to slip through in subtle ways. It is here that the key questions and debates of ethnic identity are manifested: What is at the core of local Zapotecness? Who has a claim to it? How do differences of power and prestige that are rooted in economic strength push back at local ideas of respect, kin obligations, and reciprocity? These dimensions are part of the same cultural construction, but demonstrate the ways in which indigenous peoples have consciously built ethnic identities to serve their needs in a variety of contexts.

Scholars point out that socially constructed categories such as race and ethnicity can become perceived as impassible symbolic boundaries that become fixed and take on the appearance of an autonomous force capable of determining the course of social and economic life (Appadurai 1996, 15; Comaroff and Comaroff 1992, 60; Hall 1988, 2). That is why it is necessary to closely examine their construction through time, the ways they are contested, and how they change. The specific construction of Teotitlán ethnic identity also has important historical and processual aspects. Rather than proposing that the specific content of Teotiteco ethnic identity be characterized as a protective defense of "traditional" local institutions against outside intervention, I try to demonstrate that Teotitecos, particularly merchants, have been actively engaged with the discourses of state officials on "Indian tradition" and "folk art" and for quite some time have incorporated pieces of hegemonic national culture in their own construction of what it means to be from Teotitlán. William Roseberry (1989, 75–76), following Raymond Williams (1977), notes that tradition is selective. People create alternative, oppositional cultural forms out of the dominant culture, as Teotiteco merchants have done with official versions of Mexican "Indian tradition." Because the process of Teotiteco ethnic identity construction takes place within a community that is neither homogeneous nor egalitarian, differentiation that has existed within the community (according to wealth, gender, and relative ritual and economic status) is reflected in the ways in which ethnic identity is formulated and expressed within Teotitlán as well as in the tales told to outsiders (see Wood 2001). As increasing numbers of Teotitecos have migrated to the U.S.-Mexican border, the Los Angeles area, Chicago, and elsewhere, the context in which Teotiteco ethnic identity is displayed and reformulated has also broadened and shifted.

ETHNICITY, RESISTANCE, AND HEGEMONIES
IN THE FORGING OF INDIGENOUS IDENTITIES IN
POSTREVOLUTIONARY MEXICO

A critical discussion of the idea of resistance is also in order here if we are
to understand how Teotiteco ethnic identity has been constructed and
manifested. As many Gramscian scholars have suggested (see Field 1999,
Mallon 1995, R. Williams 1994), resistance does not imply complete iso-
lation from and rejection of the dominant culture. Teotitecos addressed
postrevolutionary ideology by emphasizing the creation of a national
subject incorporating both Spanish and "Indian" heritage as *la raza cósmica* (Vasconcelos 1979). Resistance to cultural domination is an incom-
plete and dialectical project in which ongoing local processes of identity
creation along several dimensions (class and gender in particular) produce alternatives to hegemonic ideology precisely because of their local
specificity and content. For example, the fact that Teotiteco weavers have
continued to produce textiles in an economic system that included reciprocal exchanges of labor and goods, as well as commoditized labor,
has affected the way in which they have formulated their identity as indigenous craft producers. They have not simply absorbed outside designations of themselves as weavers unchanged by time, using the technology of their ancestors, but have developed an identity commensurate
with their place in both global capitalism and local reciprocal exchange.

The Zapotecs of Teotitlán have created their own locally defined ethnic identity in partial opposition to, but also incorporating elements of,
the commoditized Indian identity promoted first by the postrevolutionary Mexican state and later by U.S. and Mexican textile entrepreneurs.
The incorporation and reinterpretation of elements of imposed culture
is raised in Edward Sapir's (1956) idea of genuine and spurious culture.
Sapir distinguishes between the creation of an oppositional, internally
generated culture that may exist within the confines of larger oppressive
social relations and an external or spurious culture that does not "build
itself out of the central interests and desires of its bearers" (93; see also
Jackson 1995 and Gailey 1987b, 36–37). Stanley Diamond (1951) points out
that genuine culture includes the creation of new cultural forms that
combine the structure and content of older forms with new social and
political reality—an insightful perspective in the 1950s.

Gerald Sider's later work, incorporating the Gramscian concept of hegemony and the problematic concept of culture, provides further insight into the larger processes at work in the forging of indigenous ethnic identities in postrevolutionary Mexico. His work in Newfoundland emphasizes the possibility of creating an assertive and autonomous life for one class out of the cultural hegemony of another (1986, 119). As used by Sider, William Roseberry (1989), Stefano Varese (1988), Raymond Williams (1977), and others, the concepts of hegemony and counterhegemony suggest that cultural and economic patterns of expression and consumption involve a dialectical dynamic in which the marginalized sectors of a national population absorb and rework material conditions, ideology, and culture imposed on them by dominant classes. "Hegemony, I suggest, is not opposed by protesting elite values in the abstract —simply as values—but by opposing the conjunction of these values with appropriations. . . . Rather, opposition to hegemonic domination advances values that are, or become, rooted in the ties people have to one another in daily life and in production. The fragmentation of these ties in Newfoundland shaped both the hegemonic assertions and the capacity of fisherfolk to resist" (Sider 1986, 122).

The dominant culture that is reworked by marginalized groups in the routines of daily life and through social reproduction can emanate from the state as well as from dominant economic classes. While Antonio Gramsci initially separated the state from civil society, he later argued that the two were inseparable (D. Harvey 1989). Power is expressed by the state as government and carried out through coercive means. But power is also diffused through state ideology in institutions linked to civil society, meaning that the state is integrated with and not separate from civil society (Nagengast 1990). Gramsci (1971, 242) identified the characteristic institutions of civil society as newspapers, schools, public buildings and spaces, national symbols, and churches.[1] It is through these institutions that the state and the dominant classes deliver their cultural messages. Such institutions serve the state's educational interests by helping to create new types of civilization that link the national productive system to a shared sense of morality.

Yet these same symbols can also be redefined and recast from below by movements that seek to change the state and alter power relations; consider the appropriation of the figure of Emiliano Zapata by the Zapatista movement in the 1990s after decades during which he had been an icon of the Partido Revolucionario Institucional (PRI), Mexico's ruling political party until 2000 (Stephen 2002). Such hegemonies may be called unstable and are not absolute, as Williams writes; they are lived processes and coexist with new competing hegemonies that come to compete with established hegemonies. "While by definition [a particular hegemony] is always dominant, it is never either total or exclusive. At any time, forms of alternative or directly oppositional politics and culture exist as significant elements in the society" (Williams 1994, 599). This formulation suggests that local ethnic identity formations are likely to incorporate elements of dominant hegemonies, but contain oppositional elements as well.

Gramsci's model of the integral state is appropriate for examining the historical creation and dissemination of dominant ideology concerning what it means to be "Indian" in Mexico.[2] Through a battery of state-linked institutions—schools, cultural missions, newspapers, development projects, local systems of government—the PRI made "Indian" an identity to which all Mexicans could lay claim as they sought to build a nationalist consciousness to support continued domination of the political system. Promoting Indianness as part of Mexican national identity was a political strategy for incorporating indigenous communities into the political system and also provided a national racial distinction to separate Mexico from its dominant northern neighbor.

While general Indianness became acceptable, chic, and even desired in some social circles in urban capitals (Friedlander 1975, 165–88), the Mexican government encouraged local ethnic identity as a strategy to promote tourism. In many Latin American countries indigenous ethnic groups have been encouraged to maintain and reproduce certain outwardly picturesque characteristics, in particular dress, ritual, and craft production, which make them identifiable as Indians to tourists (S. Cook 1984a; García Canclini 1982; Graburn 1982). Such external characteristics stand in contrast to internally defined characteristics and social relations used by a particular ethnic group to distinguish itself from others.

Richard Chase Smith (1985) discusses the basic distinction between a self-chosen ethnic identity and that of an imposed Indian identity. While he is speaking largely of foreign colonial powers in the Andean republics, his characterization of Indian identity as a "political and racial label imposed on the indigenous population irrespective of tribal identity marking a hierarchical relationship" (9) could also be applied to outside appropriation and definition of specific ethnic identities. When the state and private business market "Indian culture," whether or not the culture is specified, they invoke the same relationship as the colonial designation of *indio*, indicating the subordinate position of indigenous peoples (Bonfil Batalla 1981; R. C. Smith 1985).

Most discussions of ethnicity in Mexico, while they are critical of the colonial meaning attached to *indio*, nevertheless indirectly embrace a similar paradigm by keeping discussions at the level of two large racial or ethnic groups in Mexico, mestizos and *indios*. The category of *mestizaje* as a new claim to national authenticity "denies colonial forms of racial/ethnic hierarchy and oppression by creating an intermediated subject, interpolating him/her as 'the citizen'" (Mallon 1996, 171). This new subject in the case of Mexico—the mestizo as the supposed biological product of Spaniard and Indian—continued the marginalization of indigenous people and also left out the substantial presence of blacks, Chinese, and others. During the three hundred years when Mexico was a colony of Spain, approximately 200,000 slaves had been brought from Africa (Lewis 1997, 2). Colonial society contained even fewer Spaniards than blacks. With the elimination of caste designations from the census after independence, the new national ideology of mestizaje completely erased blacks from the Mexican imaginary. They were simply to vanish as the new mestizos were created. As Laura Lewis notes (1997, 2–5), African-descended immigrants were discouraged from settling in Mexico. Areas of Mexico that clearly had significant black populations descended from runaway slaves, such as the ports of Acapulco, Huatulco, and Veracruz, were simply no longer seen as part of the Mexican nation. Only in the past decade have Afro-Mexicans begun to assert their presence politically.

The late 1920s and early 1930s in Mexico were marked not only by major campaigns to assimilate Indians but also by a vigorous anti-Chinese campaign launched from the state of Sonora. Groups with names such as the Comité Pro-Raza y Pro-Salud (Committee for Race and Health) decried the defilement of the Mexican "race" and blamed the Chinese for forcing chaste Mexican women into the underworld of prostitution and drugs. In 1925 a Sonoran state survey of the Chinese business community "demonstrated the Chinese monopoly of the small commercial sectors, to the practical exclusion of Mexicans" (Hu-DeHart 1995, 247). In 1929 the governor of Sonora, supported by Mexico's former president Plutaro Elías Calles, instituted a series of discriminatory work, health, and marriage codes designed specifically to harass the Chinese. Local groups organized vocal protests against the Chinese, and by late 1931 most of the Chinese had been driven out of the state, after they quickly sold their property at a large loss. The General Population Law passed under President Lázaro Cárdenas in the 1930s continued this nationalist anti-Chinese sentiment. It was aimed at encouraging mestizaje and imposed marriage restrictions on syphilitics and other individuals who were deemed "diseased" or "abnormal" (A. Stern 1997, 464).

Mexico's obsession with the mestizo/*indio* dichotomy also downplays the significance of the reappropriation and reworking of indigenous ethnicities. While the situation of the Teotiteco Zapotecs is certainly less desperate and dramatic than that of the Tojolabal, Chol, Tzeltal, Tzotzil, and other ethnic groups that rose up in armed rebellion in 1994 and now form the Zapatista movement for indigenous autonomy, Teotitecos' specific claim to local Zapotec ethnicity and a right to control weaving production and distribution has been critical to the community's struggle for autonomy in relation to the larger political economy of Mexico and increasingly of the world. As Zapotec textiles compete against other globalized indigenous commodities, including imitations of their work, Teotitecos' Zapotec ethnicity becomes a key element in the economic claim they stake with their textiles in a global market. Teotitecos' struggle for political, cultural, and economic autonomy is consistent with that of other indigenous communities and groups in Mexico, including the well-documented case of Chiapas. Evidence of a desire for autonomy was found first in the community's efforts to circumvent documentation of its growing textile industry by the state and later to avoid involvement in development programs that put the government in the role of middleman peddling Indian crafts and folk art. It is seen more recently in the efforts of women and some men to organize cooperatives in order to circumvent the increased influence of foreign textile designers and entrepreneurs as well as the hold of local merchants.

CHANGING CONSTRUCTIONS OF TEOTITECO ZAPOTEC IDENTITY: FROM LOCAL TO PAN-ETHNIC ZAPOTECNESS

Through time, Teotiteco Zapotec identity has been maintained and perhaps strengthened by an indirect opposition to pressures of assimilation. This opposition has taken the form of a multidimensional ethnic Teotiteco Zapotec identity that has two faces: an external face shown to consumers of Teotiteco Zapotec and other indigenous cultures (such as importers, state agencies, and tourists and other foreigners who purchase indigenous crafts) and an internal face that is accessible to persons who are members of the community by virtue of their participation in community networks and institutions, now scattered from Oaxaca across the U.S. border into several locations in the United States (Wood 1997,

2000a, 2000b). This internal dimension not only emphasizes the common heritage of Teotitecos as weavers but also subtly accommodates the tensions that threaten community solidarity. The insider definition of Teotiteco Zapotec ethnicity is an alternative to the commoditized version of ethnic identity promoted by the state and textile importers and tourists.

While we can no longer refer to a literally "local" Teotiteco Zapotec ethnicity, now that the "community" has become transnational and can embrace a variety of local bases (Teotitlán, Tijuana, Ensenada, Santa Ana, Oxnard, Moore Park) in both Mexico and the United States (see Velasco Ortiz 2002, 35–36), it is important to understand the significance of place-based local identity in the history of Teotitlán. The relative autonomy maintained by indigenous populations in Oaxaca and the political atomization of the area before and after the coming of the Spaniards are important parts of the construction of Teotiteco Zapotec identity through time.

The growth of Teotitlán and other valley communities as population centers is closely linked with the rise and fall of Monte Albán. Located about thirty-eight kilometers from Teotitlán, Monte Albán was the capital of a valley-wide Zapotec political state that had broad regional influence in matters of religion and military offense and defense, but did not seem to interfere directly in local production and trade. Local populations continued to play important administrative and economic roles.

The population of Monte Albán reached a high of 30,000 to 60,000 (Blanton 1978, 108; Flannery and Marcus 1983, 183) between A.D. 400 and 600 and probably exerted its greatest influence on surrounding communities at this time. Monte Albán was largely abandoned after A.D. 700; its main plaza was finally abandoned around A.D. 800. Richard Blanton (1978) speculates that the downfall of Monte Albán is related to the collapse of Teotihuacán during the same period, but others have since argued that there were no strong connections between Monte Albán and Teotihuacán (Winter 1977; Miller 1995, 42–46). With the decline of Monte Albán, local ceremonial centers seem to have taken over the political leadership of the Zapotecs and perhaps some of the population lost from Monte Albán (Flannery and Marcus 1983, 184). Such centers included powerful local polities such as Zaachila, Lambityeco, and Cuilapán. This is often referred to as the "Balkanization of Oaxaca." During Monte Albán Period V (A.D. 950 to 1500), the Oaxaca Valley was divided into numerous small states that were hostile to one another.

As Michel Oudijk has noted, it is interesting to observe that although the concept of "Balkanization" has been widely accepted as characterizing this period in Bènizàa or Zapotec history, "one of the consequences of this acceptance should be a rejection of general terms like 'Zapotecs' and 'Mixtecs' as these could not have been a determinant factor in a Balkanized Postclassic Oaxaca. The acceptance of 'Balkanization' should undeniably lead to a determination and denomination of local political entities rather than regional ethnic ones" (2000, 10n). In fact, until quite recently many ethnographers have argued precisely this point—that ethnic identity in Oaxaca has been constituted not at a regional level—as "Zapotec," for example—but at a much more localized, even community level. In the 1970s, 1980s, and 1990s—particularly in the wake of the Zapatista rebellion and a national movement for indigenous autonomy and in certain other historical locations where the state has promoted a pan-indigenous identity through specific institutions—"Indian" identity and broader pan-ethnic identities have come to the fore. The ways in which the archaeological and ethnohistorical records are interpreted, of course, relate to the political context and moment in which the interpretation occurs.

Many have read the archaeological record in relation to sixteenth-century historical sources such as the *Relaciones geográficas* and Fray Francisco de Burgoa's *Geográfica descripción*, written in 1674. The *Relaciones geográficas* are a survey of political, economic, and social conditions in New Spain conducted between 1579 and 1585 at the command of Philip II. According to historical information presented in the Oaxaca *Relaciones*, just before the arrival of the Spanish small city-states were warring with one another and alliances changed rapidly. Oudijk suggests that because there is no archaeological information to confirm or contradict the accounts in the *Relaciones geográficas*, it is possible that they are actually "compressed oral histories in which events from a large period are clogged together into a relatively short period, which therefore appears as a tumultuous time" (2000, 10). Thus he recommends that readers take the "Balkanization" description with a grain of salt.

Oudijk's translation of the Genealogy of Maquilxóchitl (a Zapotec community next to Teotitlán) contains information about a lineage of fourteen consecutive ruling couples up to one generation after the Spanish conquest. The genealogy provides clear pictures of how female and male rulers dressed and some descriptive information. The male rulers in the Maquilxóchitl genealogy wear a loincloth or *maxlatl* and a cloak or *tilmatli* tied over the right shoulder with a large knot. Female rulers wear long blouses or *huipiles* similar in style to those still worn in the Zapotec sierra, with a knot at the neck. As Oudijk notes, the last couple looks quite distinctive. "The man is dressed in Spanish clothes, has a beard, and is seated on a European chair set on a mat (*petate*). He holds a plant and faces a woman who sits on the mat in front of him, dressed in the huipil also holding a plant" (2000, 116). The drawing of each couple is accompanied by a brief description in Zapotec, noting their names, titles, and sometimes a birth-order marker, personal name, or calendar name.

Information about the women includes their places of origin, allowing readers to understand the political alliances formed by marriages. According to Oudijk, five of the women who married into the dynasty at Maquilxóchitl were from places situated in the Tlacolula Valley (2000, 279–82, fig. 18). His analysis shows that the second and fourth marriages of the Maquilxóchitl lineage were with women from Teotitlán del Valle, an indication of a political alliance with noble lineages there (282). The Zapotec gloss in the genealogy describing where the women are from uses the Zapotec name Xaquiya (282) for Teotitlán, the name still in use today.

Here are the glosses from the genealogy describing women from Teotitlán who married into the second and fourth generations of the Maquilxóchitl lineage (Oudijk 2000, 282, with my English translations):

II.
Alatii xonaxi xilla tinelo ça toa[a]
Vatee xaquiya
Aquí está la señora Algodón 8 Mono
Que sale [de] Toa[a]va yee [de] Teotitlán.
Here is the Señora Cotton 8 Monkeys
Who comes from Toa[a]va yee [de] Teotitlán.

IV.
Alatii xonaxi pechite çaa quiavao
Xaquiya
Aquí está la señora Pechite que sale
[de] Quiavao [de] Teotitlán.
Here is the Señora Pechite who comes from
Quiavao [de] Teotitlán.

Later marriages of men in the Maquilxóchitl genealogy were with women from the *cacique* lineages of Zaachila and Cuilapán (Oudijk 2000, fig. 18). Maquilxóchitl's incorporation in the Zaachila *caciazgo* (kingdom) through marriage was confirmed by its obligation to pay tribute to the *coqui* of Zaachila. Oudijk states that the incorporation of Maquilxóchitl into the Zaachila caciazgo is described in the text of the "Mapa de Maquilxóchitl" that accompanies the *Relaciones geográficas* published in 1580 (Acuña 1984, 340). The Nahuatl gloss on the map has been somewhat differently translated by John Paddock (1982, 345), René Acuña (1984, 340), and Oudijk (2000, 130–32), but all agree that it indicates the incorporation of Maquilxóchitl into the Zaachila caciazgo and that at that time there were three lords who held lands from Teotitlán and Tlacochaguaya as well. The earlier marriages of Maquilxóchitl elites with women from Teotitlán and this later reference to a lord with lands from Teotitlán (with no specific date really discernible) confirms the importance of elite lineages from Teotitlán in the political alliances and battles of the Valley of Oaxaca before the arrival of the Spaniards.

Teotitlán, Maquilxóchitl, Mitla, and Tlacolula all came under Spanish control in 1521. As the ethnohistorian William B. Taylor has noted, one of the things that distinguished the experience of indigenous people in Oaxaca from the experience of those elsewhere was "the retention of substantial landholdings and high status by the hereditary native chieftains" (1972, 35–36). The Spaniards' recognition of indigenous rights and privileges based on descent from an important ancestor enabled indigenous rulers in Oaxaca to defend their land and status rights in Spanish courts. In fact, most of the land in Oaxaca remained in the possession of indigenous communities for the first part of the colonial period, because indigenous communities and nobles held more land grants than the Spanish did through the sixteenth century (Romero Frizzi 1988, 137). Because the crown insisted on respecting the rights of indigenous rulers and their descendants, only lands that were royal Spanish patrimonies were officially granted to Spanish immigrants. The "Mapa de Maquilxóchitl" confirms in pictorial and written form in a Nahuatl gloss the lands that belonged to the nobles of Teotitlán (see Oudijk 2000, 131–32). While Teotitlán is described as a "barrio" or part of Maquilxóchitl in the 1580 map, as the colonial period advanced, it increased in influence and political power until it became the sole administrative unit in the Tlacolula arm of the valley.

Teotitlán and other communities were put in varying combinations of local administrative units called first *corregimientos* and later *alcaldias mayores* (regional administrative offices of the crown). In 1531 Teotitlán and Maquilxóchitl were formally delegated to the Spanish crown and became a corregimiento, as did Mitla and Tlacolula. These two corregimientos were under the alcalde mayor of Antequera (Gerhard 1972, 190–

91). In 1680 the two jurisdictions of Teotitlán del Valle/Maquilxóchitl and Mitla/Tlacolula were combined to make one administrative unit, an *alcaldía mayor* administered from Teotitlán (Gay 1881, 23; Gerhard 1972, 191).

From 1680 until Mexican independence in 1821, Teotitlán was head of a large administrative unit as a district seat. Community archives from this period reflect the growing influence of the town as people came from all over the region to take care of their administrative affairs. The town's political advantage brought economic advantages as Teotitlán made trade connections with other towns. After independence, Teotitlán reverted to being a *municipio* (the seat of a township), one of 570 in the state of Oaxaca. Almost half of the municipios in all Mexico are located in Oaxaca. Through the continued colonial and postindependence actions of the state, the political atomization of Oaxaca probably resulted in a high level of very localized allegiance and sense of ethnic identity tied to a sense of community. A tendency to conflict is often seen between communities that share a language and are defined by the state as belonging to the same ethnic group (Barabas and Bartolomé 1986, 29; Dennis 1987). While this pattern cannot be generalized to all of Oaxaca's linguistic groups, such as the Triquis, Mixes, and Chatinos, all of whom have extracommunity levels of political organization, it applied to most communities. Because Teotitlán was a center of political and administrative power from 1680 through 1821, its dialect of the Zapotec language, customs, and culture may have had broader influence than those of most other communities.

In the twentieth century, the sense of community was reinforced by Mexican anthropologists and bureaucrats who structured programs aimed at integrating the indigenous population with the national polity at the level of the community. Colonial and modern state policy of isolating communities and reinforcing the importance of locality has limited the possibilities for regional movements of ethnic autonomy (Medina Hernández 1983). The result in places such as Teotitlán is a high level of ethnic identification with the community. This strong sense of locality operates in relation not only to the state and outside textile entrepreneurs but also to surrounding Zapotec communities, from which Teotitlán seeks to distinguish itself on the basis of producing high-quality weavings, maintaining an elaborate ceremonial system, and speaking a unique form of Zapotec. The strong locality of Teotiteco identity also operates as an ongoing dynamic of resistance to incorporation by dominant national ideologies that homogenize Oaxaca's fourteen distinct ethnic groups into "Indians."

As we shall see in more detail in chapter 9, however, regional and national movements for indigenous autonomy in Mexico since the 1970s have changed this tendency to extreme localism in the construction of ethnic identity in Oaxaca. Perhaps the best public example of this development in Teotitlán is the discourse captured in the community museum in 1995 (discussed in chapter 6), which works back and forth between claiming local distinctiveness and linking the community to such archaeological sites as Monte Albán and uses the Zapotec language and Zapotecness as a part of its message, implying that the community is a part of a larger pan-Zapotec ethnic group. Local leaders such as Aurora Bazán, who was elected to the national congress, have participated in regional and national political meetings, events, and organizations that are based on a pan-indigenous identity. Increasingly, people from Teotitlán and other communities in Oaxaca are reclaiming a wider Zapotec identity and even a pan-indigenous identity as part of social and political movements.

THE MULTIPLE FACES OF TEOTITECO ETHNIC IDENTITY
AND THE CULTURAL POLITICS OF AUTHENTICITY

Critical to an understanding of Teotiteco ethnic identity is the way the dimensions of its construction work in different contexts. The version of Teotiteco identity projected to people outside the community emphasizes community solidarity, particularly in laying claim to the fruits of Zapotec weaving. An important piece of the Teotiteco claim on textiles is a continuous link to the past as the originators of treadle loom weaving in Oaxaca. Superficially, this type of identity creation may seem to be consistent with the identity created by the promotional imagery of foreign textile wholesalers, entrepreneurs, and designers, as discussed in chapter 5 and in the work of William Warner Wood (2000a, 2000b). Successful commercialization of Teotiteco weavings for both foreign entrepreneurs and Teotiteco weavers and merchants is partially dependent on the creation of an identity that obscures the complex field of interactions between the consumer and the artisans, merchants, foreign wholesalers, designers, and resellers. The identity of weavers must appear as traditional, indigenous, and simple. The complexities of their identities and the power relations within which they are embedded need to be deemphasized.

Michael Kearney has accurately captured the essence of what at first may appear to be the collaboration of Teotiteco weavers and merchants with foreign wholesalers and importers in the creation of an essentialized Teotiteco Zapotec identity. Yet he suggests that this collusion, like the differentiation of the people of Teotitlán, is not what it appears to be:

> And here at the point of the commercial creation of cultural difference, the aims of the subaltern producer and the impresario coincide, such that the subaltern collaborates in the creation of his or her cultural distinction, and therefore the strategy of containment elaborated from above has a complementary creation of difference actively elaborated from below. Thus, containment is achieved not only by the images of the subaltern other produced by and for consumption by elites, but it may also be engendered by the active, creative collaboration of the subaltern others themselves in what amounts to a sort of hegemony from below but that obviates the necessity of hegemony, for in such creative work subalterns create and inscribe their own difference. In so giving the ersatz indigenous artifact a more portent "authenticity," the artisans also occult their own complex identity behind a synthetic tapestry of tradition. (Kearney 1996a, 167)

The promotion of what appears to be essentialized cultural difference by both Teotiteco weavers and merchants and foreign entrepreneurs must not be permitted to obscure the agency and intentions of Teotitecos in the active creation of their own ethnic identity. Writing on the cultural politics of identities in the production and reproduction of carnival in Trinidad, Phillip Scher warns that theorists of cultural constructivism must be careful not to denigrate what may be seen as "invalid" cultural forms such as art for tourists and government-sponsored festivals by going overboard in an effort to be anti-essentialist in their quest for authenticity (2003, 8–9). If we were to see the constructed Zapotec identity that Teotitecos project to the outside world as an invalid, unreal tradition, then we would devalue this identity and the motivations behind it as well as run the risk of working against the stated goals of anti-essentialism, "extend[ing] and legitim[izing] scholarly control over the discourses of others" (Briggs 1996, 463, cited in Scher 2003, 9). Scher suggests that we distinguish between "(a) an understanding of culture as constructed through social processes that include the mobilization of primordial notions of identity and (b) those primordial notions themselves as evidence of a kind of false consciousness of essentialism against which cultural constructivism labors" (2003, 8). Ultimately the content of ethnic identities includes a set of specific cultural differences (in the case of Teotitecos language, place, production of textiles, ritual elements, and more) that have been naturalized as a way of articulating group identity for particular purposes (see Appadurai 1996, 15; Scher 2003, 19–20). The meaning of a particular set of cultural differences — even if there is overlap between, for example, U.S. merchants and Teotiteco weavers and merchants — is hinged to the purposes of the group of people mobilizing the set of naturalized differences. Thus the economic, political, and social motivations of various Teotitecos in mobilizing a set of cultural differences as cultural identity are often quite different from those of U.S. wholesalers and importers. That is why it is so important to look at class and ethnicity together.

Teotitecos have been engaged in the creation of an "authentic" identity since early in the twentieth century, both in relation to the government of Mexico and with tourists, folk art collectors, artists, and foreign textile wholesalers and importers. It is irrelevant to Teotitecos that the technology and materials that they used to produce the first wool weavings were brought by the Spaniards. The people who penned the official correspondence for Teotitlán in the twentieth century worked self-consciously to maintain an aura of mystique about the community, reproducing stereotypes of indigenous artisans and protecting the interests of merchants by deemphasizing their activities. They created and recreated a picture of simple precapitalist relations of production, describing "humble weavers working at simple looms," creating unique blankets "adorned with designs and idols that signify the history of Mitla and Monte Albán" (Archivo Municipal de Teotitlán del Valle 1938).

The commercial version of the identity that Teotitecos maintain for outsiders emphasizes a united community of kin producing unique textiles and participating in an elaborate ceremonial life; internal representations of that same identity are more contradictory. Riddled with subtle tensions, the picture of local history and identity painted by older men and women suggests a more complex reality. According to them, while community members did have a common history of weaving production and a rich ceremonial life, there were also differences among people in what they wore, what they ate, the kind of houses they lived in, the number of godchildren they had, the number of fiestas they were able to sponsor, and the material conditions of their lives. On the one hand, these histories offer a strong image of community identity and emphasize the importance of how things were done by *bɛ:n(i) lo'getš* (Teotiteco Zapotec for "people of the town"). On the other hand, they also focus on the diverse realities of that history for a population with varied levels of wealth, ritual status, and distinct gender roles. Today Teotitecos still use the language of kinship and solidarity to manipulate each other toward specific ends. For example, merchants use the language of kinship and *compadrazgo* to recruit their godchildren as pieceworkers. Merchant women may use the same language and the implication of equal relations in order to leave early from a ritual commitment. Weaver women use the same language to pressure a ritually superior comadre to purchase some clothing for a child's school graduation. This internal expression of Teotiteco identity in daily productive, ceremonial, and political relations provides a complex and sometimes conflicting reality for Zapotec women.

THE CHANGING NATURE OF CLASS RELATIONS IN TEOTITLÁN: FROM MERCANTILE TO COMMERCIAL TO GLOBAL CAPITAL

Class analysis has fallen out of fashion in anthropology. Instead of analyzing class, we talk of globalization, transnationalism, and post-Fordist models of production, in many cases suggesting that the category of class be reexamined in relation to forces that splinter classes and crosscut class identity with other types of identities so that class is no longer a useful primary category of analysis. While class is an important analytical element in this book, my specific interest is in how class interacts with ethnicity and gender. Changes in the way class was theorized in the 1990s are important to consider in order to understand how class operates in Teotitlán in conjunction with gender and ethnicity—particularly as the textile-producing economy of Teotitlán competes more directly with producers around the world and Teotitecos establish multisited communities that link the United States, the Mexican-U.S. border, and their home community in Oaxaca.

The model of economic class used here describes Teotitecos in relation to one another vis-à-vis the relations of production or what might better be called the relations of work. Ritual authority or respect is also examined in relation to kin-based notions of status, which, although they coexist with class differences, are not the same. Nevertheless, kinship is an important mediator of class and vice versa. Kin-based notions of status are part of a distinct system of differentiation that interacts with class

and is affected by it under the various conditions of capitalist development, such as mercantile, commercial, and global capitalism.

The concepts of merchant capital and commercial capital are important not only for understanding how Teotitlán fitted into the wider political economy of Mexico from the Mexican Revolution until about 1985,
but also for understanding a further shift from the mid-1980s to 2005,
when the textile economy became more deeply integrated with transnational capital through subcontracting by U.S.-based businesses that
provided designs, raw materials, and small capital to local merchants.
As documented by Kate Young (1976, 1978), economies in the Oaxaca
sierra region were characterized by the intervention of two kinds of capital during the late nineteenth and twentieth centuries. The period from
1870 to 1930 was marked by economic activities dominated by independent merchant capital—local capital not directly tied to a larger systemic
process of industrialization. This domination was broken, and a new in-
flow of commercial or circulation capital resulted in the monetization
of the economy and increasing social and economic differentiation after
1930 (Young 1978, 135). While the timing and structural alignments of this
transition were somewhat different in Teotitlán than in the higher sierra
communities Young analyzes, her general description is also applicable
to Teotitlán.

Before 1931, a shifting group of six or seven merchant households
dominated economic relations in Teotitlán through trade and an indirect
hold on labor through debt connected to obligatory *mayordomías*, sponsorships of ceremonial activities to honor the saints.[3] Cult sponsorship
was obligatory, and it was expensive. Sponsors were designated, often
against their will, by ritual elders. In the poor economic conditions that
prevailed during and after the Mexican Revolution, many men and
women had to sell their land and their own or their children's labor to
local merchants in order to cover ritual expenses.

As exemplified by Teotitlán in the late 1920s, merchant capitalism does
not produce a system of differentiation that corresponds to categories
of labor and capital. Rather, labor relations of dominance and subordination are indirect and often mediated by local cultural forms that are
controlled by local leaders and may also provide mediums of community
solidarity (Sider 1986, 34). In Teotitlán, the mayordomía system, which
sometimes resulted in debt peonage and cheap land for merchants, also
pulled together large sectors of the community in celebrations that trig-
gered reciprocal exchanges and symbolically united everyone with protective saints.

Class relations under merchant capitalism have two outstanding features: capital appropriates labor not directly, by buying and selling it, but rather through other mechanisms that may be political or cultural; and communities are not internally stratified in accordance with permanent differences in wealth and private appropriation of land and wage labor (Young 1976, 127, 133).

Under conditions of mercantile capitalism, labor was not directly and overtly exploited by Teotitlán's merchants; instead it was appropriated indirectly through the mayordomía system. Community elders who had already served as mayordomos sanctioned the desperation of men and women who sold whatever was necessary to finance their ritual obligations. Because the mayordomía system was intertwined with the cargo system of civil offices, the authority of elders was also political. While many elders had been poor themselves and were victims of the same system of obligatory mayordomía, they indirectly supported the interests of merchants, who in return gave them their political support and legitimized their ritual and political authority in the civil-religious hierarchy.

Merchants began to lose their hold over the population in the 1930s as a consequence of both state intervention and the penetration of commercial capital into the community. Beginning in the 1920s, some weavers in Teotitlán received recognition as folk artists through exhibits in Mexico City, Los Angeles, and other U.S. cities. While Mexico's industrial sector received a boost as it produced for the U.S. market during World War II, with peace, commercial capital made major inroads into the internal areas of states such as Oaxaca in search of new markets (Young 1978, 139). The completion of the Pan American Highway in Oaxaca in 1948 facilitated the further integration of Oaxaca's periodic markets with the Mexican national economy and brought folk art collectors, tourists, and others directly to the community. And weavers and merchants of Teotitlán began to sell their wares in tourist locations such as Acapulco and Mexico City.

The inauguration of the second U.S.-Mexican bracero program in 1942 was a major factor in the penetration of commercial capital into communities such as Teotitlán. When large numbers of men migrated from Teotitlán to the United States to work for wages during the late 1940s and 1950s, women supported themselves and their children by taking on additional chores, often labor previously considered men's work. When the men returned home, they invested their savings in land, animals, and the means of production for weaving (looms and wool). The labor of women thus helped men to accumulate capital, which later enabled some households to move into merchant activity. As the tourist and U.S. market for Teotiteco weavings opened up in the 1950s and 1960s, local entrepreneurs began to reinvest in weaving production and to employ nonhousehold laborers, paying them initially with money earned in the United States. Local wage labor relations were initiated first by men who paid others to do their farm labor while they were in the United States and then through piecework weaving production. As the need for weavers grew with U.S. demand for Teotiteco textiles, women supplied the labor. Beginning in the 1970s, women and girls began to weave in large numbers.

Whereas labor relations had been mediated by the civil-religious hierarchy until the 1930s, in the 1960s and early 1970s they were characterized by the direct appropriation of surplus labor through sale and purchase. Economic necessity obliged some people to sell their labor and the need to accumulate capital for reinvestment obliged others to buy it (Young 1978, 128). Under commercial capitalism, the dynamics of class were altered significantly in Teotitlán along multiple dimensions. Class relations under commercial capitalism beginning in the 1960s were characterized by a direct appropriation of labor by merchants and indirect appropriation by foreign businesses that subcontracted by buying up finished textiles at a piece rate below the value of labor embodied in the weavings (S. Cook 1988, 11). The capitalist merchant class was reproduced through inherited wealth, and the presence of multiple classes can be documented, not only those of merchant and weaver but also such intermediary and overlapping classes as independent producers who sold to tourists and galleries but did not employ nonhousehold wage laborers.

Class relations in Oaxaca under commercial capitalism were scrutinized by anthropologists during the 1970s. Scott Cook and Martin Diskin took a conventional Marxist approach: "Valley of Oaxaca society would be viewed as a dual class (bourgeoisie/proletariat) structure of multiple levels (medium and small bourgeoisie, proletariat proper, semi proletariat, subproletariat, and lumpenproletariat) and sectors (e.g., industrial, commercial, agricultural, artisan)" (1976, 22). Following this line of inquiry in a later work, Cook quoted Lenin's description of socioeconomic strata identified by their relation to the means of production, by their role in the division of labor, and consequently "by the dimensions of the share of social wealth of which they dispose and the mode of acquiring it" (Lenin 1967, 213–14, as quoted in Cook 1982b, 71). Cook's 1982 book concludes with a discussion of the primacy of class versus ethnicity as a tool of social analysis in Oaxaca. His later work (1984b, 1988) takes on the issues raised by an analysis of social differentiation based on the thinking of A. V. Chayanov (1966) and looks at the complex process by which petty commodity producers become petty capitalists. Cook's later work, which focuses on the dynamic processes of class formation, provides insight into the dynamics of local capital accumulation in Zapotec communities and suggests the importance of flexible, relational models of class rather than dualistic typologies.

Scott Cook finds strong structural evidence of class differentiation between direct producers and employers or intermediaries of palm articles, metates, wool textiles produced on treadle looms, cotton textiles produced on treadle looms, textiles produced on backstrap looms, embroidery, and bricks. The income ratios of direct producers and their employers or intermediaries range from a high of 1:22 in embroidery to a low of 1.9:1 in treadle loom weaving. "The industries experiencing the most pervasive extension of capitalist relations of production, namely, treadle-loom weaving and brickmaking, are the most likely to display the highest incomes in combination with the lower employer/worker income ratios. This reflects, among other things, the higher capital costs, the stronger market position of labor, and the keen competition among enterprises in these industries." Weavers in Teotitlán, he finds, look at employers "disapprovingly as appropriators of a disproportionate share of the income produced by the weaving industry" (1993, 69, 72).

In the mid- to late 1980s, the increasing presence of transnational capital in the community through subcontracting relationships established between U.S.-based businesses and local merchants acted to solidify the division between merchants and weavers. By 1990, a few merchant households that had achieved the status of petty capitalist employers in the 1970s were passing wealth on to their children, who then used it to start their own businesses. By 2005, the wealthiest merchant families in the community had all inherited wealth from family businesses.

William Warner Wood, who studied what he calls the weaving production complex (WPC) of Teotitlán and several surrounding communities, criticizes earlier studies, among them the 1991 edition of this book and Scott Cook's work, for "creating a sense that Zapotec textiles continued to be produced in the communities making up the WPC independent of the export, wholesale, and retail businesses that ship and sell Zapotec textiles throughout the world." He further states, "More recent research reveals how contractual relations (as well as the movement of capital, labor, and raw materials) have begun to blur the distinctions between, for example, workshops in the communities of the WPC and ethnic art businesses in Santa Fe, New Mexico, that sell Zapotec textiles"

(2000b, 185). Wood suggests that because U.S. businesses have greatly increased their subcontracting with merchants in Teotitlán and are providing wool, dyestuff, and capital to initiate new designer lines of textiles, the Zapotec textile production complex is "better understood as a transnational network of subcontracting relations . . . not regionally based subcontracted relations of production linked to wholly separate and independent retail and wholesale outlets, as was described for the 1980s . . . but a truly transnational productive strategy characteristic of the relations of production under late (or post-Fordist) capitalism (especially the 'flexible' and 'off-shore' varieties)" (2000b, 185). His critique suggests a serious reconceptualization of production, relations of work, and thus class relations in the circuits of what now constitutes the community of Teotitlán. That, however, is not his focus. Like many anthropologists who work in the realm of globalization, transnationalism, and "flexible labor," Wood is more interested in the cultural politics of meaning read into Teotiteco textiles by Teotitecos themselves and a myriad of others (tourists, guides, anthropologists, textile designers, and importers) than in a more grounded and empirical analysis of shifting class relations.

Wood did some excellent work following out very specific links between several wholesalers based in Santa Fe, New Mexico, merchants who supplied them in Teotitlán, and weavers who were subcontracted laborers for those merchants—people who are here called pieceworkers. In addition, Wood followed several Teotiteco households that have tried to retain control of textile production by distributing themselves across a transnational social space in multiple locations. These developments are important and are a part of changes that have taken place in the way textiles are produced in Teotitlán. I do not believe, however, that they describe the totality of situations that people work in. The emergence of cooperatives and the continued presence of six or so powerful merchant families who both work with wholesalers in the United States and run their own businesses with local weavers bound to them through kinship, ritual kinship, and other local relations make me hesitate to characterize the entirety of weaving production in Teotitlán as "a proliferation of outsourcing, subcontracting and the creation and maintenance of a low-cost-temporary labor force" (Wood 2000a, 135) or as an enterprise solely of transnational flexible households. Wood is entirely right to call for ethnographers of petty commodity production to "devise field research strategies that enable the global to be present in the local and be responsive to the global practices of those who have been traditionally thought of as 'locals'" (2000a, 135). The important question here is: How do Wood's findings affect the kind of perspective on class we would advocate for understanding the relations of work in Teotitlán in the twenty-first century?

ADAPTING THE CONCEPT OF CLASS TO A
GLOBALIZED ECONOMY

In *Reconceptualizing the Peasantry: Anthropology in Global Perspective*, Michael Kearney provides some important guidelines for how to continue to use the concept of class in understanding the reformulation of traditional anthropological subjects — particularly those called peasants — in a globalizing world order. After reviewing much of the literature on articulation of modes of production (which is where Kearney situates Cook's class model) and discussing its shortcomings as well as its contribution in pointing out the interdependence of capitalist and noncapitalist forms of production, Kearney looks to literature on resistance and social movements as a way of recuperating the usefulness of class. He suggests that the

> modernist theory of class also points to a general theory of class conceived as a field in which power-value is differentially distributed as a result of physical and cultural strategies of domination and resistance that result in the formations of identities positioned within the field of class. These identities assume cultural-specific forms such as genders, ethnicities, races, and so forth, as shaped by specific historical configurations of the distribution of value-power. And indeed, one of the de facto functions of such refractions of class is to occult the primacy of class in the structuring of difference, a primacy it is the task of theory and ethnography to recover. (1996a, 163)

Kearney suggests that theorists such as Ernesto Laclau and Chantal Mouffe (1985) have gone overboard in concluding that because class consciousness is generally lacking, class does not exist. He points out, however, that they make a compelling case against class-based party politics "in favor of movements organized around other issues." Kearney then asks a key question: "For what do internally differentiated subjects — formed within complex political fields where they occupy multiple, often unconnected subject positions — struggle?" Kearney finds his answer in cultural politics. He suggests we recast the way class functions in the lives of the people who have been called peasants by incorporating the ways in which culture interacts with political economy and is experienced by individual people as they construct and reconstruct the multiple dimensions of their being:

> 'Peasant' and 'proletarian' persist only as reifications of categories whose referents have passed from history. But class as a structuring of subject positions within differentiated fields of value-power is a valid concept. Class so defined is the structure and physiology of social space within which value-power is created and distributed. Class dynamics have to do with the flows—the production, loss, transfer, accumulation, and consumptions, that is the differential distribution—of value-power by persons situated within class spaces. Class so conceived is far too complex and multidimensional for a two-dimensional space—upper-lower—within which class is conventionally defined. And because class is embodied in subjects who collectively constitute the structuring of classes, these subjects are also defined by the multiple dimensions of class that run through them, with this interpenetration of class identities resulting in the internal differentiation of the subject . . . . (1996a, 168)

CLASS AS A CONCEPT IN TEOTITLÁN DEL VALLE

Kearney's discussion of how to conceptualize class fits very well with the project of this book: understanding the ways in which gender, class, and ethnicity interrelate and co-construct one another through the changing political economy and cultural politics of Teotitlán del Valle. By using the analytical category of class as one aspect of an analytical model that also incorporates ethnicity, gender relations, and kinship relations, I am seeking to show how the formation and reformation of these various types of relations and identities operate together within a broadly construed field of power relations. I am not seeking to reduce gender, ethnicity, and kinship to class or to argue that class relations are the only or always the primary factor in structuring power relations in any situation. Quite the contrary.

However, because I am interested in discussing class relations as one of the types of relationships that we need to understand to look at the various constructions of Zapotec women, I need to have a way of talking about it. Rather than discard concrete class categories because they are insufficient to capture the total complexity of possible and contingent positions that Teotitecos have occupied since the 1970s, I have chosen to continue using the broad categories I outlined in 1991. I find that they continue to be an important part of the way all kinds of people in Teotitlán construct difference, particularly in relation to the emphasis people put on fair payment: weavers must be paid the full value of their work.

I suggest an amendment to a class model based on the work of Erik Olin Wright that focuses on the relational aspect of class found in the sphere of work. These ideas can be used to incorporate the inclusion of textile wholesalers, designers, and importers in the United States as well as the independent, transnational, flexible weaving households such as those described by Wood (1997, 2000a, 2000b). In the case of Zapotec weaving production, which forms the basis for contemporary class relations in Teotitlán, class divisions rest not solely on forms of property ownership but also on relations of domination and control in the labor process, understood as encompassing not only the locality of Teotitlán but other sites involved in the production process as well.

In his model of contemporary class relations in industrial society, Wright (1979, 1985) distinguishes between basic class positions that reflect the dichotomy between bourgeoisie and proletariat and contradictory class locations that are positions within the productive process that are characterized by some elements of a two-class system. Households in Teotitlán can and do occupy intermediate positions in the class structure related to the transition from weaver to petty capitalist merchant or as independent weaving households. Both merchant households and weaving households could also be said to occupy somewhat contradictory class locations because their structural positions are not strictly tied to property relations. Ownership of the means of production is not a primary means for measuring class position among the weaving population, since most weavers own their own looms. In the earlier part of the twentieth century, when land was the primary means of production, large landholdings were important in assessing class divisions.

Class relations in Teotitlán are manifested more directly in domination and control over the labor process, both directly in the community and indirectly through the roles played by foreign wholesalers and importers. People experience and talk about class in terms of domination and exploitation in the labor process. It matters whether one is contracted as *mano de obra* (laborer) by *revendador* (reseller) or *hurɛšlat(ši)* (seller of weavings). Who gives orders and sets the parameters for how, when, and at what price textiles are produced? The difference between selling one's labor and hiring the labor of others, either directly or indirectly, continues to be important in the way people articulate difference. Not being paid the full value of their work is a major frustration for most weavers, whether they produce for a high-end art market or for a local tourist market. Foreign textile wholesalers, importers, and designers become an additional layer in the merchant class and are often seen the same way by weavers. Many weavers in Teotitlán would agree with Cook that

> value created by the labor of direct producers is appropriated by the "others" without compensation. The shop proprietor and putter-out accomplish this by paying a piece wage that is below the value of the labor embodied in the commodity produced (i.e. bricks, cotton cloth, wool blankets, shawls) and selling the commodity for a price that exceeds the wage bill (and other production costs); the intermediary [whether living in Teotitlán or Santa Fe, New Mexico, or both] appropriates value by charging high prices for raw materials supplied or high interest on cash advanced and/or paying low prices (i.e. lower than the market value and lower than the reproduction cost of labor contained in them) for the commodities acquired. (1993, 70)

MERCHANTS AND WEAVERS AS CLASS GROUPS

Because of the conceptual importance and local meaning of the difference between the people who produce their own work and those who sell the work of others, I use two primary categories, merchants and weavers, to illuminate the ways in which the relations of work affect gender, ethnicity, and kinship. In relation to changes in gender roles and identities and differences among women, I found these two groups to be the most significant, as articulated by women themselves. While women in the community have common social roles based on their gendered positions as wives, mothers, and daughters, these roles are modified by the position of their household as weavers or merchants. In their discussions of differences among themselves, women particularly emphasized merchant or weaving status, specifically in the role of each in local labor relations. These are not the only categories that operate in the local relations of work, but they are the two that affect the largest portion of the population, and they were the focus of my discussions with women about rituals, economics, and politics. "Merchant" and "weaver" are also class labels that imply one's position in the relations of work, and they were and continue to be very culturally significant in the articulation of inequality and difference by citizens of the community.

While it is difficult to make absolute distinctions between merchant and weaver households,[4] for the purposes of discussion these categories will have to do. The category of weavers includes both self-employed persons who sell their own goods and pieceworkers who work under contract to merchants or U.S wholesalers. In Teotitlán, the linguistic categories of merchant and weaver have political, cultural, and economic significance. A weaver is called *rúnčìlàt(ši)* (maker of weavings). A merchant or *hurɛšlat(ši)* (seller of weavings) is identified by Teotitecos as a person who purchases textiles and, through those textiles, the labor of others. Merchants are viewed, in the words of one weaver, as "buying what someone else labored to make. They didn't sweat for it." "A merchant is someone who makes more money than a weaver. Merchants are those who buy from other weavers. Half of what they make comes from other people; they earn money without working. A weaver only lives from his own work," said Salomon.

A small group of people whom we might call "flexible transnational artists" independently produce textiles for the art market and for galleries in the United States. They do not subcontract other laborers and primarily market their own textiles, though some of them deal in other folk art as well. Such a person is Arnulfo Mendoza, described in chapter 6. Weavers consider independent artists such as Arnulfo "the same as us." Arnulfo has been very successful financially, but still, people say, he earns his living by his own work, not by buying the weavings of others and reselling them. Thus even though independent artists may have accumulated significant capital and built very nice homes and small businesses, local people do not classify them as *hurɛšlat(ši)*, unlike foreign wholesalers and importers such as those described by Wood (2000a, 2000b) and by Andra Fischgrund Stanton (2000). While Teotitecos may not express quite so much animosity toward the foreign traders as against local merchants, subcontractors, and resellers, many people I spoke with from 2001 to 2004 saw them as ripping people off and making huge profits that should have gone to the weavers themselves.

The class position of merchant households is based on the fact that the primary source of its members' income is either woven goods they have purchased directly or textiles produced by weavers for piece rates. While many merchant households continue to produce textiles, they have all reached a level of capital accumulation where they purchase the labor of others and thereby extract surplus value from weavers, which they then reinvest in their businesses.

The class position of weaver is based on the fact that weavers either produce independently and then sell to local merchants at a low price, not receiving the full value of their work reflected in the price the merchant will charge to tourists or importers, or are contracted as laborers by merchants and paid at piece rates, also resulting in an extraction of surplus value. Although some independent weavers who produce for foreign art markets have managed to receive a much greater share of the value of their work for themselves, gallery owners still make a significant profit. If such independent artists can sell directly to consumers—and some do—then they can circumvent the cut taken by a gallery owner. While there are intermediate positions between merchant and weaver, all Teotitecos who participate in weaving production are either merchants or weavers in the eyes of their peers. Such distinctions reflect real differences in control and domination in the labor process and in the distribution of profits and are also reflected in the cognitive classifications Teotitecos devise. When viewed in relation to gender, distinctions between merchant women and weaver women, as well as between merchant men and weaver men, become important in understanding the dynamics of gendered participation in weaving production, ritual, and politics.

In contrast to class relations under mercantile capitalism, class relations from the 1960s to the present are characterized by a direct appropriation of labor by merchants and indirect appropriation by foreign businesses that buy up finished textiles at piece rates below the value of labor embodied in the weavings (Cook 1988, 11); the reproduction of a capitalist merchant class through inherited wealth; and the presence of multiple classes, not only merchants and weavers but also such intermediary and overlapping classes as independent producers who sell to tourists and galleries but do not employ nonhousehold wage laborers. The increasing integration of Teotiteco textiles with competing textiles produced around the world for a U.S. consumer market has taken local class relations and embedded them in a global system of intertwined consumption and production relations, requiring a reframing of class in transnational, cross-border terms and linking the role of U.S.-based businesses to Teotiteco merchants who operate not only in Mexico but in the border region and in the United States as well.

CHAPTER 2

Kinship, Gender, and Economic

Globalization

The sharper differentiation of class relations in Teotitlán under global capitalism has intensified the challenge to the unified community-based ethnic identity that Teotitecos have projected to outsiders since the 1930s and sometimes to themselves as well. As the basis of the economy shifted to commercial and then global capitalism, the merchant/weaver dichotomy became more clearly and permanently articulated and the unity of a community of weavers bound by kinship and ceremonial ties was challenged. At the center of this challenge are women, *benguna*, who throughout the history of the community have been an integral part of its productive, ritual, and political relations.

KIN-BASED INSTITUTIONS OF SOLIDARITY
AND SOCIAL REPRODUCTION

While the changing system of class relations in Teotitlán has provided Teotitecos with individual identities in relation to production, the community's complex ceremonial system has provided another set of identities and statuses that are related to local constructions of ethnicity as well as to the reproduction of legitimate social adults and local citizens. Women's roles in three of these institutions—*respet*, or ritual-based authority; *compadrazgo*, or ritual kinship; and *guelaguetza*, or reciprocal exchange of goods and labor—are a primary source of prestige, leadership, and access to labor and resources both within their households and in the community at large. While the benefits of superior class position as merchants have been contradictory for women, these three institutions continue to provide a basis of power and resources for all women in the community, although relations between women in these institutions are not untainted by their relative class positions.

Respect and Ritual Authority Zapotec ethnographers who have not focused on economic differentiation have often emphasized individual status and the ideas of respect, responsibility, and cooperation, deemphasizing the significance of class stratification in Zapotec communities and focusing on shared cultural concepts. *Respet* (the Zapotec version of the Spanish *respeto*, or respect) has been discussed by ethnographers as a characteristic of social relationships in which "individuals merit respect because of the kinds of relationships they develop and because of the ways they behave toward others in these relationships" (O'Nell 1979, 184). Henry Selby (1974), Carl O'Nell (1979, 1986), and Douglas Fry (1988) have suggested that, while respect relationships are reciprocal, there are also dimensions of asymmetry. These ethnographic accounts signal the multiple meanings of the word *respet*. While all members of a community are accorded respect by virtue of being born into and participating in the community, the amount of respect accorded to someone depends on certain criteria. Thus, while it implies equality because everyone is due it, it is not given in equal amounts to all people in a community. Selby (1974, 27) notes the difficulties in the use of the term for a wealthy villager:

> It is very difficult to show respect for such a man, because respect is based on the subtle manipulation of the symbols of status as to indicate to the other that you feel he deserves a higher status than he actually has. For another villager to say to Joaquin that "every man is equal; we are all poor humble souls" would be effrontery, because it would suggest that the former was "equal" with Joaquin and he would resent this. On the other hand, for Joaquin to say that "all men are equal; we are all poor humble souls" is a mark of great respect, because he has brought the other villager up to his level, and therefore obliterated the status difference.

In Teotitlán, where economic class differences persist, *respet* does not substitute for class differences but signals criteria for social ranking that are rooted in relations of kinship and ritual participation. The concept of *respet* is an emic one that first surfaced in my research in the mid-1980s when I asked six informants, three male and three female of varying ages, including both merchants and weavers, to arrange in rank order slips of paper on which I had written the names of forty household heads. At first they divided people by whether or not they were merchants or weavers and how much wealth they had, but they then mentioned that people could also be ranked according to the amount of respect they had. They discussed in detail what they meant by *respet* and specifically how it was measured. I discussed the concept at length with 100 other people and later worked it into a ranking exercise carried out by an additional six people. The outcome of this exercise and its relation to wealth and class-based occupational rankings are described in detail in chapter 9.

The amount of respet accorded to an individual is based on age, number of godchildren sponsored, number and type of civil cargos the male household head has completed with the support of all household members, and the number of fiestas (mayordomías, posadas, and life cycle rituals) sponsored. These criteria are strikingly similar to those for accumulating prestige that Beverly Chiñas (1973) documents for the Isthmus Zapotecs. She, like Holly Mathews (1985), notes that prestige received for ceremonial activities and sponsorship of godchildren transfers to both men and women as heads of households or cosponsors. The transference of respet to women for ritual participation and compadrazgo sponsorship is discussed in chapter 8. Hugo Nutini and Betty Bell also describe in detail the relationship between respect and sponsorship of godchildren (Nutini and Bell 1980; Nutini 1984).

Respect is reflected in the deference two people demonstrate when they meet (see O'Nell 1981; Selby 1974). If they are not owed the same level of respect, the person who is subordinate is supposed to greet the other with head lowered and hands out, palms up, and say, "*Ščay*." The person of a superior respect level gives the same greeting with head upright and hands extended with palms down. This form of deferential behavior is still taught to most children by their parents, but is slowly eroding as younger people take on other forms of greeting. Many elderly people I spoke with in 2004 named a "lack of respect" as one of the changes they most noted as a consequence of migration. Many young people, they say, no longer stop to greet their elders in the street as they should. Young people counter that they do so with close relatives, but not with everyone.

Respect also determines a person's ability to hold authority and to have an influential opinion. While respect is positively associated with fulfilling community and family ritual and social obligations, disruptive behavior can limit the amount of respect accorded a household, although it tends to reflect more on the individual than on the household. Because the positive indicators of respect, such as ritual participation, civil cargo participation, and ritual kinship ties, are established on the basis of the household unit, the respect and prestige accrued from accomplishments within these institutions is returned at the household level. Disruptive social behavior such as drinking, gossiping, fighting, or being rude on the street is engaged in by individuals. But because the basic indexes of respect are tied to the household, extremely disruptive behavior on the part of one spouse can eventually cause the entire household to lose its respect position. Others feel sorry for household members affected by the deviant member, but they say that the disruptive person prevents the household from functioning well in important social institutions. Because respect continues to be a major avenue of influence and access to resources for women, they often engage in extensive damage control to repair harm caused by deviant household members.

Compadrazgo: Ritual Kinship In contrast to class divisions, ritual kinship ties of compadrazgo bind merchant and weaving families together in lifelong relationships and ritual commitments. As discussed in chapter 8, women are central actors in the compadrazgo system. In Teotitlán, *compadrazgo* refers to ritual kinship ties that are initiated when an individual woman or a married couple acts as godmother or godparents to an unrelated child in respect to a particular life cycle event, usually a ceremonial milestone in the Catholic church: baptism, confirmation, or marriage.

While the word *compadrazgo* is a Spanish import, this system of ritual kinship is similar in form to elaborate sponsorship ceremonies performed among the Aztec and Maya before the Conquest. Compadrazgo today reflects the Spanish system imposed on preexisting indigenous systems of ceremonial sponsorship (Sault 1985a). It remains a distinctive feature of Latin American social structure, particularly in Mexico, where many studies of it have been made (Foster 1953, 1969; Kemper 1982; Mintz and Wolf 1950; Nutini 1984; Nutini and Bell 1980; Sault 1985a, 2001). As Nutini points out, while many ethnographers have documented compadrazgo systems, there is no standardized framework for study. Their insistence on treating compadrazgo as kinship and on focusing on the importance of compadrazgo networks is applicable to Teotitlán.

The importance of compadrazgo in Teotitlán stems from links that are created not only between sponsoring godparents and their godchildren but in the relationship of compadres—the social ties that emerge between a child's biological family and the sponsoring godparents. In addition to kinship determined by marriage and descent, compadrazgo greatly increases the number of people an individual can count on as kin. Because kinship relations are built around a series of reciprocal obligations and responsibilities, the more kin an individual has, the greater access he or she has to labor and resources. In his exhaustive study of compadrazgo in the Tlaxcalan community of Belén, Nutini (1984, 403) states that it is critical to transcend the dyadic, egocentric bias that has permeated the analysis of compadrazgo. He proposes that compadrazgo networks exhibit the permanence, structure, and behavior patterns associated with real kinship units.

The important thing about kinship, as Christine Ward Gailey has ob-

served (1987a, x), is the content of the relationship, rather than its source
or how it is phrased: "kinship relations are many-faceted and encompass
functions that would be housed in separate religious, economic, and political institutions in our own society." Through ritual kinship ties, Teotiteco women are able to extend the range of kin they can count on for
aid in specific economic, ritual, and political projects both in Teotitlán
del Valle and as they increasingly settle into other parts of Mexico and
the United States. Compadrazgo continues to be an important source of
ties for community members, wherever they may be.

Guelaguetza The institution of guelaguetza—the word is a Spanish conversion of Zapotec *xɛlgɛʐ*—is another extension of kin ties; although
more limited than compadrazgo in the kinds of obligations it entails
(particularly in the exchange of goods), it offers an additional institutional setting for reciprocal exchanges of labor and goods. Often referred to as reciprocal exchange, the institution of guelaguetza is well
documented in Zapotec ethnographies.[1] Guelaguetza has been found in
agricultural labor exchanges (Cook 1982b; Martínez Ríos 1964; as *gozona*
in de la Fuente 1949; González 2001, 115; Nader 1990, 242) and in reciprocal exchanges of goods and labor for ceremonial purposes (Beals 1970;
Cook and Diskin 1976; Diskin 1986; González 2001, 114–17). The institution was alive and well in Teotitlán in 2004.

In Teotitlán guelaguetza is a system of economic exchanges in which
long-term interest-free loans of goods, cash, and labor are made from
one household to another. Transactions are usually documented in notebooks, but the many women who are illiterate commit them to memory. In the mid-1980s, I found many Teotitecos who either owed or
could collect guelaguetza loans made by their parents up to fifty years
earlier. As Martin Diskin (1986) found in San Sebastián Teitipac, guelaguetza debts can be inherited. As a rule, guelaguetza of money and goods
is used exclusively for ritual consumption. Labor guelaguetza can be
used for either ritual or production activities. Agricultural guelaguetza
in Teotitlán is detailed in chapter 4. During 2001 to 2004, I found that
guelaguetza continued to be of major importance in Teotitlán and most
women still kept guelaguetza notebooks, primarily in relation to ritual
expenses.

The primary purpose of in-kind guelaguetza is to allow a household,
particularly its women, to prepare for ritual responsibilities in advance.
The idea is to plant debts slowly and then recall them all at once to help
finance major ritual events. They plant loans with other people for what-

ever they will need — corn, beans, tortillas, chiles, pigs, turkeys — so that they can recall them as they need them for a specific event.

The place of guelaguetza exchanges in local economic systems has been debated in the past. As Cook has pointed out (1982b, 115), scholars such as Charles Leslie (1960) have argued that the economic system that embraces guelaguetza differs from one in which the profit motive operates. Cook suggests (116) that guelaguetza transactions function as part of the general production and circulation of commodities in a community and that an individual's decision making in regard to participation in guelaguetza reflects the total economic situation of the domestic unit he or she represents. Diskin (1986, 288–89) argues that participating in guelaguetza transactions necessitates thinking about setting aside for fiestas a portion of what one produces. He suggests that the ceremonial systems of Zapotec communities, along with reciprocal labor exchanges and services, constitute an ethnic mechanism that can slow the formation of capital. While this process does not preclude capitalist activities, for Diskin the existence of guelaguetza suggests that there are ethnic communities where social reproduction is not exclusively capitalist or determined entirely by a capitalist dynamic.

In Teotitlán, guelaguetza does result in the reproduction of some social relations that are not exclusively capitalist in nature, such as kin relations and those of compadrazgo, but these social relations clearly coexist with the accumulation of capital, and in fact can often help to facilitate it. It does so when compadres use their ritual kinship relations with their *ahijados* or godchildren as a way to recruit field laborers or weavers. Guelaguetza clearly operates in relation to the larger political economy. As Roberto González has observed, it is tempting to romanticize guelaguetza as a quaint sharing arrangement, but for most people (particularly the poor) "it is a survival strategy, a heavy obligation that simply cannot be avoided — and a way of guaranteeing *mantenimiento*" (2001, 117).

Inflation has had an interesting effect on guelaguetza in Teotitlán. Guelaguetza books kept before the late 1970s show many entries for loans made in cash. By the time women got their money back, however, its purchasing power had greatly diminished. By the mid-1980s and into the twenty-first century, women preferred to make loans of animals and food, which they recorded by weight down to the ounce. By making in-kind loans, they have kept up with inflation because they reclaim the original value of the loan. This strategy signals a basic flexibility in the exchange system. Guelaguetza is described in greater detail in chapter 9, particularly in relation to the pivotal role played by women, which has remained largely undocumented, and to the impact of migration. Some women who have moved away from Teotitlán have continued to participate in the guelaguetza system, but others have found it difficult to do so.

THE INTERSECTION OF CLASS, ETHNICITY, AND GENDER IN A GLOBAL ECONOMY

The examination of women's roles in a variety of arenas within Teotitlán and as a part of the transnational community that Teotitecos have formed from southern Mexico to the northern United States requires a flexible understanding of gender constructions and the way they interact with other aspects of identity, such as class, ethnicity, nationalism, and age. In the first edition of this book, I proposed using social reproduction as a framework for understanding the complex nature of gender roles in communities such as Teotitlán. I was trying to move beyond the public/private dichotomy that in the mid-1980s and even into the 1990s was a predominant model for understanding gender relations, regardless of their historical, regional, or cultural location. Conceptualizing "social reproduction" primarily as a local concept is problematic in efforts to understand gender relations in transnational communities such as Teotitlán in the twenty-first century. I do believe that my original discussion of why the public/private dichotomy did not work as an explanatory mechanism of gender relations in Teotitlán still holds and that the model of social reproduction can continue to be useful if it is conceptualized as part of transnational space and global connections.

The study of Latin American indigenous women in the 1970s and 1980s (the Zapotecs in particular) was informed by a critical dialogue with the public/private model initially proposed by Michelle Rosaldo (1974). A brief review of that work allows us to see how research in the mid-1980s moved beyond that model to a more dynamic and historical understanding of women's daily lives, setting the groundwork for later analysis that stopped looking at women as part of "communities" and considered how gender, race, and ethnicity are configured in neoliberal economies that are globally connected. Rosaldo's explanation of the cross-cultural subordination of women was based on the existence of two distinct social spheres: a private or domestic sphere associated with institutions and activities organized around mothers and their children and a public sphere of activities, institutions, and forms of association that link, rank, organize, or subsume mother-child groups.

The first explicit study of Zapotec women by Beverly Chiñas (1973) attempted to find hidden sources of female power through the introduction of a concept involving two sets of parallel male-female roles, formalized and nonformalized, which she proposed as existing within a public/private dichotomy. As Holly Mathews has pointed out (1982), while Chiñas concludes that "where formalized roles occur in complementary pairs by sex, the male role of the pair is normally accorded higher status than the female role" (1973, 96), her own data and later work suggest that the Isthmus Zapotecs do not necessarily view female ritual roles as subordinate to those of males. In a later article Chiñas (1987) provides important information on a current trend among Isthmus Zapotecs: the ritual participation of women appears to be increasing, while that of men seems to be declining. As in Teotitlán, women are the primary participants in reciprocal exchanges of labor and goods. While Chiñas's early material lacks an analytical framework consistent with her data, her groundbreaking ethnographic work has drawn attention to the roles of Zapotec women in social reproduction and how women fit into community prestige systems.

A later use of Chiñas's analytical framework is found in the work of Laurel Herbenar Bossen (1984), who compared women's status in four Guatemalan communities: a Maya village, an urban squatter settlement, a middle-class neighborhood in Guatemala City, and a plantation. While her work documented important differences among women in the four communities in terms of "formal public organizations, informal public networks, and the domestic sphere," her reliance on the public/private dichotomy as an explanatory mechanism prevented her from addressing the subtleties of how ethnicity and class are manifested in the spheres she analyzes. Her comparative approach in conjunction with her well-grounded description of capitalist development in Guatemala works best in showing the differing degrees to which capitalism has brought about a "redivision of labor which has relatively penalized women" (320).

Working in a Oaxaca community of mixed Zapotec and Mixtec descent that ethnically identifies itself as mestizo, Mathews rejected the public/private dichotomy, concluding that what appears to be a division between the domestic roles of women and the public roles of men is really a division between the community-oriented religious sphere and the extracommunity-oriented political sphere (1985, 298). Mathews's theoretical orientation leads her to correct earlier views on the institution of mayordomía and to provide new information on women's political participation. She demonstrates that ritual sponsorship of mayordomías is shared by men and women and that both perform important functions and receive equal social status for their participation. She has also found that women's political authority erodes as individual skills more likely to be possessed by men become more important in community decision making, a finding echoed in the work of Kate Young (1978).

While Mathews does not frame her conclusions in terms of economic class and ethnicity, her findings suggest a situation similar to the one found in Teotitlán in the mid-1980s. Her innovative analysis could be strengthened by a definition of class that examines local production relations more closely and explores how they have changed historically and extend beyond the community level. As it stands, her work provides a bridge between studies using the public/private duality and those that emphasize the Marxist feminist framework of production and social reproduction.

Mathews's work also resonates with the response of Jane Fishburne Collier and Sylvia Junko Yanagisako (1987), who strove to avoid analytical dualisms such as the public/private dichotomy by studying gender institutions as social wholes. Emphasizing the cultural meanings of gender relations, they focused on ways in which individual men and women of different social positions act out their relationships. While they stress the inevitability of systems of inequality in all societies, because they do not situate ideological inequalities historically, their model does not clarify why inequalities exist or persist in radically different settings through time. As seen in Teotitlán, where class inequalities became more entrenched through time, in a nuanced analysis of how gender interacts with class, ethnicity, and other systems of inequality and difference through time, it is necessary to move outside of a situational perspective.

Cultural Marxists have tried to explain the historical dimensions of systems of inequality (including gender) in Latin America by exploring how cultural ideology and material circumstances interact and change through time. Such an approach also bridges the public/private dichotomy. The exemplary ethnohistorical work of Irene Silverblatt (1987) looks at the changing relationship among culture, class, and gender during ongoing colonial conflict in the Andes. "The problem of power and its insinuation into cultural forms," Silverblatt writes (xix), "is central to historical process. Accordingly, gender systems—metaphors as well as conduits for the expression of power—stand out as pivotal to the creation of, and challenge to, social class." In her exploration of the interplay between political hierarchy and gender in the Andes under Inca and

Spanish rule, Silverblatt unravels gendered cultural ideology and symbols to reveal how they are used to assert dominance by rulers and how they are reclaimed and manipulated by women as forms of cultural defiance. Her description of how women designated as witches by the Spanish fled to the puna and maintained their native religion provides direct evidence of the importance of gendered ritual institutions in indigenous responses to colonialism. Her emphasis on how religious and cultural forms are inherently political eliminates the necessity to deal with material/ideological dualism. Such a perspective provides a valuable tool for understanding some parts of the multifaceted relations of gender in Teotitlán del Valle.

Kate Young (1976, 1978) was one of the first to explore the historical dynamics of inequality in relation to changing gender roles in Mexico. Her ethnographic work in Oaxaca is organized around the idea of production and reproduction as articulated in a theoretical discussion she coauthored with Felicity Edholm and Olivia Harris (1977). These three Latin Americanists tried to confront Frederick Engels, whose proclamation of a "world-historical defeat of the female sex" virtually ended his discussion on women (Engels 1972, as quoted in Edholm, Harris, and Young 1977, 101). Operating from a theoretical framework stressing the articulation of modes of production, they attempted to unravel the Marxist concept of reproduction. They suggest (105–16) that the subordination of women and the nature of their participation in the labor force cannot be understood unless distinctions are made among biological reproduction, reproduction of the labor force, and social reproduction. "Biological reproduction" refers to childbearing or procreation. "Reproduction of the labor force" refers to both the maintenance of the labor force here and now and the allocation of individuals to positions within the labor process over time. "Social reproduction" refers to the reproduction of conditions necessary for the continued existence of a particular mode of production.

Lourdes Benería (1979, 205) broadens the definition of social reproduction, moving it out of a mode-of-production orientation and rephrasing it as "the reproduction of conditions sustaining a social system."[2] Both in her 1979 article and in a book coauthored with Martha Roldán (1987) focusing on women's response to the economic crisis in Mexico, she sees the reproductive sphere of the household as the primary locus for relations of subordination/domination between the sexes. She proposes (Benería and Roldán 1987, 110–13) that social scientists decompose

the "monolithic household" in order to understand power relations between men and women that stem from control of money and resources,
domestic exchanges, and marital relations.

A broader representation of "reproduction" is also found in Florence
Babb's (1989, 1998) analysis of market women in Peru, where she points
out that, just as housework is essential to the reproduction of a family,
the distributive trades and service occupations in which so many women
engage also maintain and reproduce society. Through work done both in
the home and in the so-called informal sector, women ensure the continuity of society (Babb 1989, 198). Cultural reproduction, however, is not
a part of her discussion.

In the first edition of this book I proposed use of a production/repro-
duction model to analyze gender relations in Teotitlán. Following the
lead of Benería (1979) and a definition proposed by Gailey (1987a), I expanded the definition of social reproduction I used there. While Benería conceptualized social reproduction somewhat vaguely in relation to
the conditions sustaining a social system, Gailey (1985a, 76; 1987a) provided a more detailed definition. She points out that a limited notion
of reproduction such as that proposed by Edholm, Harris, and Young
(1977) does not discuss means of worker acquisition, which is nonbio-
logical (adoption, fosterage, migration, and slavery), and leaves out the
reproduction of social groups that function outside of strict production
activities. Social reproduction "refers to the recreation of an entire set
of social relations, including a division of labor, means of socialization
and preparation for production, means of recruiting or creating future
group members, maintenance of non-producing members, beliefs and
customary behaviors. . . . The concept includes, but is not restricted
to, reproduction in the biological sense" (1987a, 271). In her analysis of
the changing nature of gender and kinship relations in conjunction with
state formation and capitalist development, Gailey formulated a concept of social reproduction that integrated the cultural/ethnic dimensions of social reproduction with changing material conditions. I found
this aspect of the model useful in that it was able to integrate culture
with material production. The shortcoming of the definition is that it
is so broad that it could incorporate virtually the re-creation and maintenance of all aspects of material and cultural life and social relations.
In addition, such a broad understanding of social reproduction doesn't
distinguish among types of contexts for the reproduction of kin, labor,
and ethnic relations at local, regional, and global levels—an important

consideration when one evaluates gender relations in the transnational Teotitlán of the twenty-first century.

What I continue to find useful in Gailey's expanded concept of social reproduction for understanding gender relations in Teotitlán is a focus not only on the maintenance of material relations of production but also on the maintenance and replication of institutions and relationships that define individuals as social actors in their specific ethnic context (see also Parrish 1982). These institutions and relationships often include economic and social relations such as reciprocal exchanges made through extended kin and compadrazgo networks, frequently in the context of ceremonial activity. These kin-based institutions are the backbone of ethnicity; they are also crucial in the reproduction of the labor relations of class. In this sense, the concept of social reproduction specifically includes reproduction and socialization of the labor force, including relationships linked to biological kinship, compadrazgo or ritual kinship, and apprenticeships; and institutions, events, and relationships tied to the socialization and status of individuals, primarily through mayordomías, life cycle ceremonies, and the reciprocal exchanges of goods and labor that support them.

Institutions such as compadrazgo and guelaguetza continue to link people across national boundaries and are among the key ties that make up the web of human connections that holds together the people of Teotitlán, physically dispersed though they be. They are the threads of the web of transnational community. When we think of social reproduction we have to broaden our sense of the local. Any notion of social reproduction that will be useful in the twenty-first century has to be able to incorporate aspects of the reproduction and socialization of the labor force that operate outside the bounds of the original community and extend across national boundaries into the transnational spaces, relationships, and institutions that intersect with gender in what we could call greater Teotitlán. We can continue to use the insights of the model of social reproduction to illuminate how local kin and ritually based social and cultural relations influence and are integrated with global economic and labor relations. While the social reproduction of people as both laborers and social actors suggests a focus on local-level processes and institutions—the basis of much of my previous analysis—it is clearly necessary to move to an understanding of how laborers and social actors are also constituted by the factors of global neoliberalism and a transnational construction of identity and community.

SOCIAL REPRODUCTION IN THE LIGHT OF GLOBALIZED MARKETS AND TRANSNATIONAL COMMUNITIES AND LABOR RELATIONS

If we begin with a focus on the multiple contexts that have influenced women's gender roles and relative power and autonomy in the community of Teotitlán in the early twenty-first century, we will include kinship, ritual kinship, ritual events, institutions, and relationships and the reciprocal exchanges of goods and labor that support them. But we will also include physical migration; experiences living and working in California and elsewhere in the United States; increased levels of education obtained in Teotitlán, elsewhere in Mexico, and in the United States; subcontracting relationships with foreign merchants and distributors originating in the United States; experiences in cooperatives and in classes on design, exporting, and marketing; and to a very limited degree the experience of a few women as cooperative or political leaders representing their communities in other contexts inside and outside of Mexico.

This long list of factors that frame the shifting ways in which women's gender roles have been constructed, as well as the changes in power and autonomy that have gone with these shifts in gender roles, suggests an analytical strategy that allows for simultaneous experiences and realities.

The coexistence of labor relations structured in some cases by kinship and ritual kinship, in other cases by friendship and family bonds through a cooperative structure, and in still other cases by indirect labor subcontracting relations where there are no direct personal connections tells us that the primary characteristic of contemporary labor relations and of social reproduction in Teotitlán is flexibility. David Harvey aptly captures this idea in his pathbreaking analysis of late twentieth-century capitalism, *The Condition of Postmodernity* (1989). Harvey argues that the evidence "for increased flexibility (subcontracting, temporary and self-employment, etc.) throughout the capitalist world is simply too overwhelming" to ignore (191). At the same time, he points out that flexible technologies and organizational forms have not become hegemonic everywhere. This is an important observation in relation to the organization of textile production in Teotitlán since the late 1980s, where the ethnic and gendered relations of production are influenced by multiple forms of organization. Harvey states (1989: 191–92):

The current conjuncture is characterized by a mix of highly efficient Fordist production (often nuanced by flexible technology and output) in some sectors and regions . . . and more traditional production systems (such as those of Singapore, Taiwan or Hong Kong) resting on 'artisanal,' paternalistic or patriarchal (familial) labour relations, embodying quite different mechanisms of labour control. . . . This shift has important implications. Market coordinations (often of the subcontracting sort) have expanded at the expense of direct corporate planning within the system of surplus value production and appropriation. The nature and composition of the global working class has also changed, as have the conditions of consciousness formation and political action. . . . Gender relations have similarly become much more complicated, at the same time as resort to a female labour force has become much more widespread. By the same token, the social basis for ideologies of entrepreneurship, paternalism, and privatism has increased.

Harvey's analysis suggests how market coordination in a globalized economy results in the fulfilling of demand for a particular product through production organized in many ways. Textiles produced in Teotitlán for tourists as well as for export markets can come from a variety of organizational systems of production that rely on a wide range of social, cultural, and kin-based relationships to function. Such relationships and their links to the relations of production are key to the shifting ways in which gender roles are constructed and experienced by individual women as they carry on their lives.

In an analysis of apparel production in San Cosme Mazatecocho in central Mexico, Frances Rothstein (2005) documents several kinds of production workshops, ranging from independent workshops that produce for regional markets and produce and market their own products to maquiladoras where workers sew precut pieces for local or outside brokers who subcontract for domestic retailers and sometimes for export. Women are a significant part of the labor force. "That the residents of San Cosme have been able to endure the volatile market," Rothstein writes, "is due in part to their multiple income strategies and also to their flexibility with regard to production. They change what they produce, how they produce, for whom, and how much they produce very often. Although they cannot control the unstable apparel market, they have adapted to that market to survive its volatility" (2005). In the variety of forms of organization of production the residents use as well as the flexibility in what they produce and how, San Cosme is somewhat reminiscent of Teotitlán.

So what do these findings suggest for an analysis of gender among women in Teotitlán? First, to understand how ethnic identity, kinship, and changing class relations operate in the daily lives of Zapotec women, we have to move outside of physically bound, one-site localized spaces and explore the national and transnational dimensions of women's experiences, including the way ethnic identities are experienced and reconfigured in different contexts. For example, how does working as a maid in Mexico City change a Teotiteca's understanding of her Zapotecness as she navigates the capital city and runs into primary categories of identity that differ from those in her home community and state? Or we might consider what it means to be a Teotiteca in Santa Ana, California, where dozens of hometown associations and federations of hometown associations (Rivera-Salgado 1999a; Kearney 1995a, 1995b, 1996b) are being formed with pan-indigenous names, such as the Oaxacan Indigenous Binational Front, changed to the Indigenous Front of Binational Organizations in March 2005.

Second, because different forms of labor organization link Teotitecas to many individuals and types of social and economic relationships, models of class difference have to be put into a wider frame for visualizing how women are differentially inserted into the global economy. The work of Marxist feminist scholars of the 1980s, such as June Nash (1989), María Patricia Fernández-Kelly (1983), Helen Safa (1983), and Carmen Diana Deere and Magdalena León (1987), drew critical attention to the consequences for women of being drawn into a globalizing economy as low-wage industrial and agricultural workers. Later work by some of the same scholars demonstrates how further entrenchment of a neoliberal economic model in Latin American economies has usually only further marginalized women both in the subsistence sector and in other rural regions, but has also spawned significant new spaces for rural women's organizing, and has produced differential consequences for women depending on local circumstances (Nash 2001, 4, 178–84; Deere and León 2001; Stephen 1997a). Helen Safa's 1995 study, *The Myth of the Male Breadwinner*, provides a detailed analysis demonstrating how the results of women's insertion into the globalized Caribbean economy vary. She suggests that "paid employment only empowers women under certain specific conditions, which vary with state policy, access to resources, and the nature of the household economy" (182). Recent research on what happens to women as they are inserted into the global economy as workers suggests the importance of looking at local and regional histories of gendered labor relations as well as at the other kinds of ethnic, class, and age relations that co-construct women's gendered experiences on a daily basis. This kind of localized understanding and conceptualizing of gender/class/ethnic relations can then be linked to wider analysis of how state economic policy, migration, changes in law, and so on affect women on a broader level. While some women may be working under contract to local merchants who in turn are under contract to U.S. distributors, so that the women do not know who their real employers are, others spend at least part of the year working with other women in cooperatives and selling to tourists in Mexico. Other women may be working as both subcontracted laborers for part of the year and in cooperatives the rest of the year. Such complex forms of production organization defy efforts to categorize all women in respect to their insertion into the global economy.

Third, because most women in Teotitlán have continued to have responsibility for procuring basic household goods and for basic health care and child care, and at least partial responsibility for administering household budgets, we have to take a look at the range of strategies they have employed to take care of their families. The strategy of forming or joining a weaving cooperative suggests that women have more ways of caring for their families than those that have been called their "individual responses" to economic hardship (González de la Rocha 1994; Benería 1992). Highlighting the pivotal role of the women's cooperatives both as economic strategies and as political and cultural spaces for expanding women's autonomy and influence in a range of arenas builds on other work that has explored women's collective responses to poverty and marginalization (Alvarez forthcoming; Babb 2001; Dore 1997; Jaquette 1994; Jelin 1990; Kumar 2001; Lind 1992; Stephen 1997) and goes beyond it by exploring the consequences for identity construction as well.

Reframing the idea of local social reproduction to incorporate not only the national and transnational dimensions of women's experiences but also the transformative potential of women's participation in new organizational forms and social movements (such as the cooperatives) pushes the discussion of gender away from the idea of fixed roles and spheres and concentrates more on the fluid dynamics of identity construction and reconstruction. Such an effort works inherently against the fixed notion of automatically dichotomous "spheres" (public, private, and other) by emphasizing how differentiated Zapotec women conceive of themselves as workers, women, kin, political subjects, and indigenous peoples in relation to other craft producers, the international market, and global consumers. Such a perspective allows for the inclusion of the structural dynamics that inform and frame women's actions as well as their agency and the potential impact that such agency can have on structures at the local, national, and even global levels.

CHAPTER 3

Six Women's Stories

Julia, Cristina, Angela, Alicia,

Imelda, and Isabel

> If I tell you my story, it is very sad. Maybe you want to talk to
> someone with an easier life. A lot of hard things have happened.
> . . . Even now when things are good I worry. Now my son is gone
> and when he leaves his children suffer a lot because there isn't any
> money to buy them food and the things they need. There is always
> something to worry about. —Julia, age 60

Like women anywhere, Zapotec women share many experiences yet are also distinguished by important differences. For the women of Teotitlán, these differences are most strongly related to age or generation and to the class position of their households. In the 1980s, women often described themselves as divided into two groups: largely uneducated, monolingual Zapotec speakers above the age of 30 who still wore traditional dress and strictly followed local customs, and modern, bilingual, better-educated women younger than 30 who had economic aspirations for themselves and their families. By the early twenty-first century, most of the monolingual speakers of Zapotec were over 50, and the remainder of women were bilingual in Spanish and Zapotec; most 30 and under had completed a primary-level education or at least four to five years of school. Descriptions women gave of themselves in terms of class didn't change in the years from the 1980s to 2004. If anything, I heard more women talking self-consciously about themselves as *mano de obra* or paid laborers as distinct from *revendadores/hurɛ̌lat(ši)*, or resellers of textiles, what I have called merchants. Women readily distinguish between merchants and weavers, but these differences are relative to the life experiences of individual women.

In reality, of course, individual women do not fit neatly into these categories. By 2004, women in their thirties, forties, and early fifties seem to be a bridge generation, reflecting ideas of both younger and older generations. The class positions of their households are far from static: many women, particularly in merchant households, have experienced drastic changes in their standard of living. Older merchant women (such as Julia) spent the first forty years of their lives in extreme poverty, working as weavers from dawn to dusk seven days a week. Even as the economic status of their households has improved, women who are now part of merchant households do not feel that their individual work loads have lightened. While they certainly pursue the business agendas of their households, as individuals they still see their lives as full of hard work. The most optimistic women are those (such as Imelda) who are younger and feel that they are able to run a business and maintain some degree of independence from their families. Education, or a lack of it, has been critical to the abilities of all these women to control and improve their lives.

I collected five of these narratives from 1985 to 1989 in the process of developing ongoing relationships with these women. The stories of Julia, Cristina, and Angela are taken from transcripts of various interviews. Because Julia and Angela would not agree to be tape-recorded, some parts of their narratives are based on copious notes taken during the interviews and immediately transcribed. In the first three narratives the notation "[. . .]" indicates fragments that came from two conversations, not omissions.

The narratives of Cristina, Alicia, and Imelda are direct transcriptions. Those of Alicia and Imelda are based on single interviews. The names of these five women and their family members have been changed at their request to maintain anonymity. Finally, I have added one more story, that of Isabel, who was nineteen years old in 2001, in order to provide a picture of some of the experiences of the youngest generation of Teotiteco women.

JULIA

Julia was born in 1929, just as the effects of the Mexican Revolution were winding down in Teotitlán. She has lived through times of great poverty in the community as well as recent prosperity. She never went to school, but she has learned some Spanish by her own efforts to communicate with customers in a small general store she opened. She prefers, however, to speak Zapotec. She wears her hair in two braids wrapped with ribbons on top of her head and wears a long piece of wool fabric called a *manta* wrapped around her waist and held in place with a bright pink woven sash.

Since the early 1980s, her living situation has improved considerably as the household textile business has developed. Recently she was able to expand her tiny store and install a gleaming glass display case, her pride and joy. She enthusiastically supports her son's efforts to build up their merchant business, yet she has also undertaken to organize a large and seldom-sponsored mayordomía. As part of this effort she has devoted untold energy over the last year to organizing three large parties, each stretching from three to five days. Julia enjoys being in charge and believes that sponsorship of rituals for the local saints is extremely important. She has done it twice before and knows how hard the work is. She has been rewarded with a high degree of respect and is a very influential woman in the community. Recently this respect has been reinforced by her merchant status.

She has not had an easy domestic life. Her husband beat her often throughout their long marriage, and she had to support her children alone for many years. She bore twelve children. Four of them died in infancy, and one was shot and killed in an urban area of Mexico. Three others have lived near Los Angeles for more than six years. She has several grandchildren she has never seen, and her voice becomes melancholy when she speaks of her lost children and those who have moved north. Her one act of self-indulgence is to take an hour-long bath every few days and wash her long black hair, which still falls to her knees. She seems happiest when she is walking around her yard with her hair down, calling out to her chickens, turkeys, and pigs. Likewise, when sitting at the head of a long line of women calling out orders during a fiesta, she seems content and assured of her importance in the life of her family and the community.

When I was a little girl we could buy everything with centavos. You could get half a centavo's worth of coffee or hard brown sugar, and it was plenty. Pesos used to be like dollars. Even when we used to take the serapes to sell them to the rich men we only got a peso or so. I remember that on my street there was a man who was very rich and people sold their serapes there.

[. . .] I was married in the church in 1949, when I was 20 years old. Only three couples came to my wedding. Each of our godparents from when we were baptized came to the wedding along with my husband's sister. I didn't get any presents at all. I remember that I cried a lot after my wedding because I didn't get any presents. Not even my mother gave me a present. No one had any money.

When I first moved in with Juan, before we were married, the lot was divided in half between Juan's father and his uncle. Well, actually, the uncle was dead, but the aunt was still living there. Eventually we bought the land, but at first it wasn't ours. We had nothing. Even the mats we slept on weren't ours.

When we were first living together I worked carding wool. Juan would go get the uncleaned wool in Oaxaca. There was no money around then. He would weave and I spun and he would go to the houses of two merchants and sell the blankets.

When I was first married I never left the house. Never. My husband would go alone to Oaxaca. He sold the blankets and kept the money. At first I didn't even leave the house to buy food. I was too scared. I had never been out alone. He would give the money to his aunt, and she would go to the market. I never left. I didn't know how to buy anything and we only ate tortillas. We didn't eat bread and meat. We didn't go to many fiestas then, and there weren't any. Because we lived with the aunt, I didn't get to say anything. A lot of women who were my age didn't go on the street. You know when we were first living together, we just worked all the time. I just worked in the house. Sometimes I would card wool and spin all night long.

After the aunt died, then I started to do more. Even before she died, my husband went to the United States to work. He went to the States on and off all the time. . . . You know this whole time I worked like a burro. I would card and spin two kilos of yarn in two days as well as doing other work. First I'd get up and make tortillas for Laura and another woman who was a neighbor. I also made *tejate* [a corn drink] for her. Miguel, her husband, had a lot of money. I got paid two centavos for making an *almud* [two kilos of corn]. It was a hard life.

My husband hit me ever since we were married. Once he went to jail for hitting a boy from here with a rock. We got a lawyer then. Maybe I'll go talk with that lawyer. Before, when he was in the United States, he was never here. And when he had all his cargos it was me and the children who worked. I don't see why he has a right to get so mad when we all work so hard. He's like a lot of men who beat their wives here.

A woman's work is never done, they say. Men's, yes. Men just do one thing for most of the day. Women have to run around and do a lot of different jobs. It was easier for me when I had both of my daughters at home. One would make *atole* [morning corn drink] and the other would make tortillas. Both of them know how to weave. My daughter María would start weaving and weave most of the day. When my husband had his cargo of being in charge of communal lands, María worked really hard because my husband wasn't weaving.

[. . .] My husband had a lot of cargos and I had to work too. Even when he was a *sruez* [servant to the mayor], I had to work when the mayor was leaving. I had to make tortillas at the mayor's house for a week. When Juan went to the United States, he paid someone to do his cargos. In 1957 we were mayordomos for the Virgin of Guadalupe. Like many things then, my husband didn't tell me he had made a vow to be a mayordomo. Now I decide these things. But I wasn't afraid then because I had some turkeys ready that I had already given as guelaguetza. I had six years to get ready. I began to get more animals and to make guelaguetza with a lot of people. Men worry about how to get money and women worry about things for the kitchen and animals. I planted forty-five turkeys with people and some cacao too. There were three fiestas for this mayordomía and we were ready for them.

We didn't really have any *mozos* [contracted on-site pieceworkers] until two years ago. All the looms we had were being used by our children. I'd sell an animal each time we wanted to buy a loom. We'd buy a loom for each child when they were big enough. . . . We bought our first loom in 1958 for Eduardo. I sold a pig to pay for it. In 1970 we bought a second loom for Carlos. Then in 1974 we bought a loom for Jorge and in 1976 one for María. In 1980 we bought the last loom. Now we have mozos working for us because none of our children are around anymore.

When my husband came back from the United States he bought about three blankets. He went to Oaxaca to sell them. Since then he always kept the money and had the key. I never knew how much money he made in Oaxaca or what he did. He used to go there all the time to try to sell blankets. He didn't work much and was hardly ever here. About fifteen years ago he started to go to Mexico City and sold the blankets our children made. One year in 1975 when he had another cargo, I started to run the business more. My children were weaving and the youngest was taking care of our oxen. I also started my little store. I learned more about money by running the store. Then my husband stopped controlling the key to the money and now all three of us share it—me, him, and my youngest son.

I don't know how to read and write, and I need it to run the store. There are a lot of people who don't know how to read and write. You know last year I went to the school for adults that they had for one day. When I got home, my husband said, "Why do you want to learn? You're too old." I do want to learn, and I need to know for my family. My daughter doesn't know how to read, she didn't go to school either.

[. . .] My husband doesn't care about my granddaughter going to school either. I told you my husband wouldn't let me go to the school for adults. I think a lot of men are jealous when women learn to read and write and that's

why they don't like it when their wives are educated. I need to learn for the
business and to go to Oaxaca and Tlacolula. I can't read the street signs.

Julia's story is a case study of the transition from weaver to merchant
status. By using the household labor of their children, Julia and her husband were able to accumulate a small amount of capital, and using that,
along with money earned in the United States and by Julia's sale of animals, they were able to invest in a small inventory of textiles to begin
business. Later they were able to hire other kin and neighbors as pieceworkers as well.

Julia's labor was important in the creation of the business, but for the
first two years she was denied any participation in business transactions.
Here we see the contradiction in the lives of merchant women, who may
have control of household labor and resources for fiesta sponsorship but
are denied active roles in business decision making. Her discussion of
fiestas and guelaguetza suggests the importance of these activities in her
life. Finally, her story reveals the domestic violence that is a large part
of many women's lives. Violence against women and their lower level of
education than men's are issues that are shared by merchant and weaver
women and are frequent topics of discussion.

Julia's husband died in 2001. The last two years of his life were very
difficult for her, and her son, like her husband, was very ill and unable to
care for himself in any way. Since she has become a widow, Julia has been
able to relax some because she is free of her husband's abuse and difficult personality. In the early 1990s, she, her husband, and their son were
mayordomos for Teotitlán's patron saint. Julia describes the experience
as the most important thing she has done in her life. She greatly enjoyed
it, and although it cost the family a great deal of money, she has no regrets. Serving God and her community through her sponsorship of the
year-long cult celebration of Nuestro Señor de la Preciosa Sangre (Our
Lord of the Precious Blood) made her feel proud, secure, and important.

The debt from the elaborate mayordomía combined with a decline in
sales for their textiles, however, resulted in a sustained period of financial difficulty. When Julia's husband became very ill, their problems were
compounded by his medical bills. Like most people in Teotitlán, Julia
and her family have no health insurance and must pay cash for all doctor's visits and prescriptions. By the summer of 2002, Julia and her son
had recuperated somewhat financially and were running a new business
based on selling dyed yarn.

In the 1990s, Julia did get to see her grandchildren a few times when they came to visit her in Teotitlán. One of her daughters visited more frequently and came to help care for her husband and for Julia when she had surgery to remove cataracts from her eyes. At one point after her husband died she contemplated going to live in California with one of her daughters, but she decided that she would be happier remaining in Teotitlán. Seeing her chickens and pigs whenever she looks out her door, buying her food every day in the market, socializing with old friends and family —this is how she wants to spend her remaining years. She continues to run her small store and to be a respected elder in the community.

CRISTINA

Cristina was born in 1910, at the start of the Mexican Revolution, and her childhood was marked by war and hunger. She has always had a hard life and has never managed to emerge from poverty. She has been a widow for quite some time. While respected for her age, she often receives charity from her family and neighbors. She benefits from going to ritual celebrations because she is fed at them and receives food to bring home. Her primary source of income is weaving, a skill she recently learned and does very slowly because of arthritis in her legs. She also continues to card and spin wool into yarn for additional income. She produces for a nephew who is a merchant.

She is not particularly bitter about her hard life or regretful about her lack of prosperity. She still sleeps on a mat on the ground because she prefers it and grinds her corn on the metate. She had a few children and feels that motherhood limited her possibilities.

Cristina speaks only Zapotec and does not read or write. When she needs to do something official, she gets one of her grandchildren or children to help her. She never leaves Teotitlán and spends most of her time at home working or going to fiestas. She styles her gray hair in two braids and wears a traditional manta made of polyester because wool is too expensive. She is usually wrapped in a black shawl as she moves slowly down the street. The wind bothers her eyes. Because of her age, she is greeted by everyone she sees, most of whom bow in respect. She has witnessed many changes in the community and has her own theories about them.

I was born in 1910, I think. I don't know how old that makes me. One of the first things I can remember really well was when we went to Esquipulas,

Guatemala [a place of pilgrimage, home of the celebrated Black Christ], when I was young—maybe 13 years old. It took us over a month to walk to Tapachula [close to the Guatemalan border]. Then it took another two weeks to walk to Esquipulas. We were gone more than three months, walking. I guess it was 1923. We had a big fiesta when we came back.

[. . .] When I was a girl, on Monday and Wednesday the merchants would go to the plaza and buy blankets from people. I think there were quite a few. They would buy from people and also leave and go and sell in Oaxaca. . . . My father would buy wool in Oaxaca for weaving because not very many people here had sheep.

I was married in 1940 when I was old [she was 30]. My husband used to go to the *monte* [communal land] with a *χolbats* [hand ax] and plant. He planted corn, beans, and squash over there on that mountain by the cave. No one plants there now—they all left.

You know when my husband went to ask [my parents] for me [in marriage] they only brought one or two candles. There was a little bit of fruit and some bread and chocolate.[1] When I was married it was simple too. We only had one meal for the compadres. I didn't get any presents, only one shirt. I was married in one day and that was it, there wasn't any big ceremony like *sa(ᴾa)χúil(i)* [elaborate five-day wedding ritual].

My husband didn't go to the United States when the others did, but about a hundred men went. A lot of people thought the men who went to the north were being signed up to go to the war. When the men were gone, a lot of women made tortillas to sell and made yarn to sell to weavers. I remember that the gringos came here after the men went to the north. Before there were a lot more poor people than there are now.

They had no money so they borrowed money to live. There were a few rich people who made the loans. People would make blankets to pay them off. Some people were so poor they also had to borrow food. Now it's better. The money goes further. There is work.

Now women weave too. When there was a school and the girls began to go, they knew more so they could begin to learn how to weave. Now a lot of women weave. It's the same as going to school. I learned how to weave from my grandchildren. Before only a few women knew how. Now everyone does.

. . . Now there are also a lot more weavers because there are more children around. Everyone has five or six kids. Before they just died of measles and other diseases. Children don't die anymore. Before up to half of the children would die. People were afraid to go to the doctor. Now the women weave and they have more children who also weave. People aren't so poor now because their families are bigger.

Cristina's story gives us clues about many of the changes that have taken place in the class system, in weaving production, and in rituals since her youth. The pilgrimage to Esquipulas, her first significant memory, was not an unusual event for people of the area. Until the 1960s, many families in Teotitlán, as well as in other Zapotec communities, undertook extensive pilgrimages to sites where the Virgin appeared and miraculous images can be visited. Such pilgrimages, involving months of travel, were attached to some of the mayordomías in the community. While the celebrations attached to mayordomías were quite elaborate, in the 1920s and 1930s life cycle ceremonies such as weddings were much more simple than contemporary ones. Ceremonial life for women was concentrated largely in mayordomías. Only later did life cycle ceremonies become the focus of their energies.

Cristina's story also alerts us to class differences in the 1920s. She refers to some of the merchants who sat in the plaza and bought blankets from people. These were the rich people who loaned money to cover living expenses as well as to cover the costs of mayordomía sponsorship. Cristina grew up among the majority poor, who sometimes had to borrow money and had to work for others in order to pay off debts.

Like Julia, she is impressed by the potential that schooling offers to women. She comments on the change in the division of labor: women are now weaving along with men. She believes that more women are weaving now because going to school has made them more skilled and able. She notes that improved health care has allowed more children to survive, and as a result there are many more weavers in the community. For her the option of weaving is critical—it is her only source of income. She is a poor pieceworker, but the work allows her minimally to support herself. The encouragement of her grandchildren and their belief that even as an old woman she can weave have been important to her survival. As an elderly widow who lives alone, she is among the most economically marginalized people in the community.

Cristina passed away in the early 1990s; *bkwa'a lang Diuz* (God came to take her back), one of her relatives told me. She continued to weave until she died.

ANGELA

Angela was born in 1946 in a family of eight children. She speaks Spanish fluently and also speaks a little English, which she uses regularly with tourists and importers who frequent her house on the town's main street. With a commanding presence, Angela has cut her hair to shoulder length and wears simple dresses of the sort seen in many mestizo communities around Oaxaca City.

Although she went to school until the sixth grade, Angela believes that she really did not receive enough education; she considers herself to be ignorant of many things. She focuses most of her energy on her nonstop work load, which has her overseeing a weaving workshop with up to six workers as well as a big family and managing a large business under her husband's direction. She is determined to move her six children out of the community and into professional jobs. Her oldest son is studying to enter medical school and her oldest daughter is finishing as a business major at a Oaxaca high school. She and her family speak Spanish at home. In 1985 theirs was one of the few houses in the community where Spanish was heard more consistently than Zapotec.

Angela usually downplays how well off her household is and has a strong sense of the limitations placed on her as the wife of a merchant. Her movements are restricted, and she resents the control her husband has over her as well as her ritual obligations, which make her overall work load heavier. Angela's household is one of the few merchant households that has four to six workers weaving daily and also contracts pieceworkers. She has done some weaving and even produced some original pieces that brought high prices. Her favorite moments have been at the loom weaving original designs, but for the most part she has little time for this creative work.

> When I was 14 years old I went with my sisters to the cave on New Year's and asked for some things.[2] I asked to have money, a car, children, and a big house. There at the cave I made a big house with many rooms, a place for a car, and a place for lots of chickens and pigs. I also asked for a husband who would take care of me. See, it came true, that's why I believe in it. When I was pregnant for the first time I went there and asked to have a son. I made a little doll. I wanted to have a son because I thought that if I had a little girl, my mother-in-law would kick me out. When you have a baby people ask you, "*teŋgjuwɛʔɛ́ɲí(ŋ)*?" [Is it a little man?], with a smile

on their face. Women always have this expression. If it's a little girl they say, "*Mmmmm, težapɛʔɛ(nɛŋ)*" [Hmmm, it's a girl]. If it's a little boy they say, "*škalbao teŋgjuwɛʔɛñĩ(ŋ)*" [Lucky you, it's a little man].

We came here to this house after we spent two years in my father-in-law's house. Felipe had money from working in the north. He went there from 1962 to 1969 to work. In 1966 we eloped, and we met at his father's house [she was 20]. In 1969 we got married in the church. We paid for our own wedding because he worked in the United States for seven years. He used the money he earned in the United States to make the little store that used to hold our serapes. [It is now a small general store.] He also used his money from the United States to buy blankets. When we first came here, there was just one little house. It was a one-room adobe house with a dirt floor. We fixed up the yard and built the store, then the porch, the kitchen, and later the other rooms.

In 1969 we had three workers. I was making tejate every day as well as carding wool in the afternoon. He paid the workers with money he earned in the States. It used to be easier to get people to come to your house to work. He had money that he saved. When he was in the United States he was one of the few who came back with money. He told me that when he was there he didn't drink soda pop, but drank water, and that they'd eat the fresh fruit and vegetables they harvested. Anyway, he came home with money. Believe it or not, we started our business with just four weavings.

We don't think about being mayordomos. We think of our kids. We want them all to be educated at the university—that is our mayordomo. [. . .] I left school in sixth grade. I already knew how to card wool and spin wool and make tortillas. My grandparents told me and my parents that I should stop school and help my mother take care of the other kids. I wanted to study more, but I couldn't. My parents wanted me to, but my grandparents have the last word in the house. So I left school. I don't want the same thing to happen to my children. Right now my grandfather still doesn't want my youngest brother to study because he and my grandmother will be left alone in the house. I don't want that to happen to my children.

Now I have to buy what my husband asks me to. He gives me a certain amount of money every day for food. He keeps the key to the money and doesn't let me handle it. He says he knows how to take care of money. Some women take care of all the money. In my parents' and my grandparents' house after my father or grandfather would sell a weaving they would give the money to my mother or grandmother. I don't buy anything. I don't know what to buy. Now I get up every day about five-thirty A.M. and go to bed about eleven P.M. I start out by waking my son up so he can catch the bus to Oaxaca for school. I spend most of the first half hour getting him out of bed and onto the bus. He likes to stay in bed. I have a girl named Lucía who helps me in the morning, and in the afternoon my daughter Catalina comes home from school to help.

[. . .] My husband drives me to the plaza every morning so I don't waste time and so I can't stop to talk to anyone. Today he said I spent too much time buying meat. I didn't think it was very long, barely enough time for them to wait on me and wrap and cut up the meat. But he thought it was too long. I think you should write that down.

We spent three days at a wedding this week. A lot of our mozos also went to the wedding so they are just beginning to work again. While I was at the wedding, this woman teased me for not drinking. I said I had a sore molar and I couldn't because I was taking medicine. Then she said I wouldn't drink with them [the other women], that I only drink when I'm having sex with my husband. I really get angry when women talk to me like that. But she was older than I was so I couldn't really yell at her. I had to respect her. I'm not naive about sex, but I think talking about it at parties is really rude. Some people asked me if I was afraid of her, because she's a witch, but I said I am not. I'm not afraid of witches and I don't believe in witchcraft.

[. . .] You know men here can talk to any girl they want and women aren't allowed to say anything. If women spoke to other men they'd get in trouble. Men are very jealous. . . . Once when my father was in the hospital in Oaxaca, I went to visit him with my sister. We got a ride there in someone's truck. When I got home, they [her sister-in-law and husband] slammed the door in my face. They called me all kinds of names. Imagine me, whose father is dying, I'm very sad, and I come home and they shut the door in my face and call me all kinds of names for going to the city— whore, prostitute—just because I left and got a ride in somebody's truck.

You know, I don't think money makes life easier. Just the opposite. I think I work twice as hard as any poor person. The money makes my life harder—now we have more people working for us and I have to take care of them. Now I have a lot more things to do. For example, I promised some customers I'd make them a serape. They gave me a 10,000-peso advance for my work. Felipe, my husband, put the money away and now I can't finish the work. I have no time. It's difficult.

[. . .] I'm practically not weaving at all anymore. I spend all my time cooking for people who are working here and for my children. I did some work that sold well. I did one design that had a boat and some clouds and mountains. I made it just on the loom, I didn't use a drawing. I want to work again, but now it's impossible. I can't even leave here. When he goes somewhere I have to be here to deal with the clients who show up and might want to buy something. Today I couldn't even get to the market because he left in the morning and went to Oaxaca. I sent two of the boys to the market. When they got there they got a girl to go in because they didn't want to be seen there.

Angela's marriage to an ambitious young man who saved money while working in the United States moved her fairly rapidly into the status of a merchant wife. While she is respected by many people in the community because of the household's prominent business, her story relates her frustration at her lack of physical mobility. She experiences the gendered aspects of her merchant class status as more oppressive than what she believes poorer weaver women experience. She shares all women's work load of food preparation and child care and on top of that must feed and oversee five or six weavers who work in her home on a daily basis.

Angela has a keen consciousness of her position as a woman, both at home and in the community. While she talks about her unique situation as part of a merchant household and complains about her work load because of the family business, she also emphasizes the double standard that she believes all women experience, as in the preference for sons and the inability of a woman to talk to a man without suffering her husband's jealousy. She is able to identify with other women in the community and as a result is quite popular with both merchant and weaver women. While her personal friendships span class distinctions in the community and she feels bound by the traditional requirement to show respect for all older people regardless of their economic status, the formal friendships of the household, which are often initiated by her husband and carried out in public, are primarily with other prominent merchant households in the community.

By 2004 Angela's children had all grown up and married. She had thirteen grandchildren. On any given day at least three or four were hanging around her home playing between the looms and watching cartoons. During the mid-1990s, Angela's husband was mayor of Teotitlán. During that three-year period, they basically shut down their textile business. Angela dedicated herself to supporting his work as mayor. She described her role as the mayor's wife as basically helping the wives of other municipio officials to organize and provide food, entertainment, and support services for a wide range of community public works projects and special events. Any other time she had she spent tending to her children and grandchildren.

Angela went to visit one of her children who was working in Los Angeles. Three of her children spent time working in the United States. Her oldest son dropped out of medical school to become a musician. He spent some time playing in the United States.

Once her husband finished his term as mayor, Angela worked on rebuilding their textile business. Angela felt that there was much more competition among merchants now than there had been in the 1980s. She commented that many merchants now let U.S. importers take away finished textiles on credit, to be paid for once the rugs are sold. She does not like to work this way. Her own designs — she works only with natural dyes and undyed wool — are selling fairly well. Whereas the family used to have about twenty weavers working for them in the 1980s, they now are working primarily with their children. It is a significant change, but Angela seems to be content with it.

She now talks of retiring with her husband and building a small house out in the middle of their cornfields, away from the community. The corn rustling in the wind is what she wants to hear, not the pickups, buses, and cars that run past their house all day long on the main street of town.

ALICIA

Alicia was born in 1953 and raised her five children alone for almost twelve years after her husband left her. Now a grandmother several times over, she has fought hard to support her family. Pulled out of school by her father the first day she tried to attend at the age of 6, she never learned to read and write, but taught herself Spanish while working as a domestic in Mexico City at the age of 19. Like other women her age, Alicia has left Teotitlán several times in efforts to improve her lot, recently even to go to the United States.

Alicia began weaving as a way to support her family after her husband left her, selling first to local merchants and later to family members who opened their own businesses. For most of her life she has been living in other people's houses. As an impoverished single mother, she has had very little control over her life, moving from her parents' house to her in-laws' house and other places to work.

Alicia bridges the older and younger generations in appearance: she wears her hair in two long braids and is dressed in a modern wool skirt and an indigenous blouse. She is acutely aware of the limitations placed on her as a poor woman. Now that her children are older, she is beginning to think about how she can realize some of her own ambitions. Many of her ideas for self-improvement are tied to her efforts to accumulate some savings while working in the United States. She has recently spent eight months in the United States, where the interview took place.

What I remember from when I was young was that I spent a lot of time taking care of my mother's children and I made tortillas since I was really small, since I was 8 years old. I remember they sent me to wash clothes in the river and to wash dirty wool.

My father didn't want me to go to school when I was little. My grandmother went to take me to school. She bought me a notebook and a pencil, and she went to bring me to school. When my father saw I wasn't home, he went to look for me. My grandmother told him she took me to the school. He came to the school to get me. . . . I tried to go again, but neither my father nor my mother wanted me to go to school. They told me I didn't need to go to school because I'm a woman. They said men go to school because they are men. I took care of the babies. Every year my mother had a baby. Maybe that was why they wouldn't let me go to school. I don't know.

I was 14 years old when I got married. I don't know how it was that I met my husband, but I loved him. When he came to get me [*robarme*] we went to his house . . . his uncle's house. I wanted to go because my father got really angry and beat my mother a lot. He beat all of us, my brothers too. I got tired of living there. When I got married I knew what I was doing, but later my husband began to drink. He began to do this in Tuxtla [Tuxtla Gutiérrez, Chiapas]. . . . I went to Tuxtla five weeks after we were married and I didn't speak Spanish. I just stayed in the house. My mother-in-law used to go out with him. They'd go to buy the things we needed.

We went back to Teotitlán because his mother wanted to. When I came back I had to work again preparing wool, making tortillas, making tejate, making all the meals. I had different work in Tuxtla. We made peanuts to sell. We cleaned them, peeled them, and cooked them in oil. . . . They sold them on the street. It's easier to do this than it is to work with the wool.

When I came back, I was pregnant with Luis. I gave birth to Luis in my father's house because my husband didn't want me to be with his grandparents and his mother. His mother got back together with her husband. They were separated for a while.

I also stayed there when my husband left. He went to work first in a circus that was in Oaxaca. When the circus left, he told me he was going to go with the circus and work so he could send me something. I told him yes. He didn't send anything. Since he left, he never sent any money, no letters, nothing. I learned to weave at my parents' house when my second son was three months old so my children would have something to eat.

After that, when my second child was 3 years old, my *concuño* [sister-in-law's husband] came to tell me that we should go to Mexico City because I could find better work there. At the time I didn't know that my husband was with them. So I lived with my husband there for a year in Mexico City while I washed clothes.

The last time I saw him was in 1977. He never beat me, but what I didn't like was that he drank a lot. He was very irresponsible. He left. . . . I felt sad, because I was left with five children who were all young. The oldest was 12 years old, the next one was 9 years old, and then the next one was 7 years, 2 years, and a newborn baby. . . . It was very hard for me to think about how I was going to raise my children. My in-laws helped a little when they could. My oldest daughter began to weave when she was 11 years old and my oldest son when he was 10 years old. They helped some.

Three months ago I got across the border with a *coyote* [person who leads people across the border for a fee] from Teotitlán, a boy from Teotitlán. I came across by the bridge on the border. There was some *migra* [immigration officers] there. We ran for a while, like half an hour. This boy I came with said the migra wouldn't do anything. He said we would go to where my brother-in-law was waiting for us. My brother-in-law and my sister paid him. When we went across the border, there were some apartment buildings there, nearly on the border. We had just gotten to where the apartment buildings were and the migra came. I thought they were far away, but then they were really close to us. When they shined the light on us, they told each other, "Grab them, grab them." But this coyote told me, "Let's go, let's go running through here." We went behind the building, running. . . .

When we got to San Clemente [California] there wasn't anyone there. No one was stopping people. My brother-in-law told me that's where they ask for your papers in the road.[3] . . . We passed without any problems. Some people say they come through the mountains and it's more difficult. A woman who lives with us went through the mountains. They got here at four o'clock in the morning. They had to walk all night before they were safe.

When I first got here I felt a little sad, a little frightened. I was afraid because I didn't know about anything. I'm still afraid to go out, to go anywhere. . . . It's like when they say the cat is guarding the mice. I'm a mouse. That's how I'm living here.

It's not quite as hard here as living in my village. There I was weaving a lot but I couldn't make enough money. There are a lot of customs in Teo-titlán — weddings, engagements, other things where you have to buy a lot of things. They're all expensive. In contrast, here I am working and I'm not spending anything. I'm working with my family. They take care of expenses, for eating.

You know when my daughter got married last year I spent a lot of money. Some people loaned me some as well. I'm going to pay back the guela-guetza I owe and the loans. I spent a lot of money — almost three million pesos [U.S. $1,250 in 1989]. I bought a chest, some dresses, a shawl for my daughter, and also the food, the beer, the mescal. I had to buy all this. And also turkeys. . . . I had about forty of them.

I take care of another little girl who comes here. I get $50 a week for taking care of her, and my sister also pays me $50 a week. My daughter also went to work for two months when she first came here. She worked two months. She got paid the same amount, $50 a week. That's how she earned a little money. After she started in school she didn't work anymore.

In the future I'm going to work to get what I don't have right now. First I'm going to study and work more so I can build a house. I'm always in someone else's house. I already bought that land, a piece of land. Now I'm going to put a house on it so that people won't say the land is abandoned. . . . Now that I have my own adobe bricks, I'll start to build.

Alicia's story, like Cristina's, reveals the difficulties of growing up poor and female in Teotitlán. Unlike Angela and Julia, whose households achieved merchant status, Alicia married into a poor family that relied on a combination of weaving and migratory work to make a living. Many of Teotitlán's poor migrated to Chiapas either to work in small cities or to harvest coffee and sugarcane. Some still go there rather than finance the longer trip to the U.S. border. For Alicia, migration has been a long-standing survival strategy.

In Alicia's story we see some of the difficulties of the steep costs of sponsoring any type of fiesta in Teotitlán. Her daughter's wedding left her with many guelaguetza debts to pay off, which she is doing by earning cash to purchase the turkeys, cacao, and other goods she received as loans.

Finally, Alicia's story also relates some of the experiences shared by all women in Teotitlán, particularly the denial of education to girls. Her very clear memories of being told that she did not need to go to school because she was a girl have stayed with Alicia as she becomes aware of how important it is to read and write, particularly in a new environment. As a result of this experience, Alicia and other women insist that their daughters receive an education equal to their sons'.

Alicia has remained primarily in the United States since she arrived in 1989. With the cooperation of an employer, she gained legal residence, as did her children. All of her children have married, and two of them and their families live in the Los Angeles area. She worked for almost ten years for a professional family in the Los Angeles area, taking care of their children until they entered middle school. She then moved to a similar job with another family. She now co-owns part of her own home in California and is building a home in Teotitlán as well. All of her siblings and their families except one also live in the Santa Ana area. She regularly returns to Teotitlán to visit her parents and to provide assistance to her mother when she needs it. Of all her siblings, Alicia has kept in the closest contact with her extended family in the community. She talks of returning to live in Teotitlán someday.

IMELDA

Imelda was born in 1958 and has two children. In 1989 they were 5 and 7 years old. She has spent more than half her life outside Teotitlán, an unusual situation for a Teotiteca. She wears her hair shoulder length, cut in a shag, and sports a modern polyester dress like those worn by women in Tijuana. She has a watch and carries her money in a purse. She still uses a shawl like those worn in Teotitlán.

Her experiences living in California and in Tijuana are typical for women who have left the community for some period. Many women her age or younger have spent part of their lives working as domestics in other parts of Mexico or have come to the United States. As Imelda says, leaving Teotitlán is one of the few ways for women to achieve some independence and begin to save some money.

After leaving home at age 14, Imelda worked a wide variety of physically demanding jobs. She helped her family and finally was able to open her own small business, as many young women in Teotitlán hoped to do. Imelda's story reflects the changing pattern of migration from the community beginning in the 1970s, when more young women went to Mexico City, the border areas, or the United States.

The sacrifices that Imelda made in order to help her parents and her younger siblings resulted in a lot of hardship for her, but allowed her independence later as a single woman when her family helped her to set up a small business in Tijuana. In 1989 I interviewed Imelda in her store in Tijuana, where she was living and working with her family. Recalling the hardships she lived through as a child and young woman, she felt that she had finally begun to achieve some of her goals and had plans to return to Teotitlán someday.

Since we were little, we suffered a lot. I have two brothers and three sisters — six of us altogether. My grandfather had a business and my parents were living with my grandparents before I was born. Then my parents separated from them.

My parents worked a lot for my grandfather. My grandfather gave us the house. His name was Miguel Gutiérrez. He had a big business at this time and he was the only person who helped everyone in town. He bought weavings from everyone. He was a good person and he helped everyone there by buying their weavings, because before the people were more ignorant. They didn't know how to sell their weavings in Mexico City. They never left town. The tourists only came to my grandfather's house, which was the Casa Gutiérrez.

My mother worked really hard, and she had us help her to spin, card, and wash the wool. We helped her make tortillas and went to the market. In the morning we went to school. I also took care of my brothers and sisters. I had a little brother who was sick and died because of a lack of money, really. And because later my grandfather completely abandoned us.

Almost all the girls went to school. This was when the government demanded that all indigenous children attend school. The mayor fined the parents who didn't send their children to school. My father was also very demanding about school. He made us go to school.

Whether or not girls went to school had as much to do with their parents as with the government. . . . I have some friends who only went until third grade. A lot of them, about half of them, stopped going because they were older and maturing and their parents didn't want them to leave because they had to help their mothers in the kitchen. There are some who did finish and even a few who went to study in Oaxaca. I went until sixth grade. Then I didn't want to go anymore.

Of what they taught me, mathematics is the thing I find most useful right now. I often tell myself that if I hadn't gone to school, then I wouldn't know anything about how to keep accounts or do other things. And still, I'm missing a lot. I should have studied more.

I was 14 years old when I finished sixth grade. When I left school I wasn't thinking about getting married. I wanted to leave. A lot of my girlfriends got married, but I didn't think about this. I wanted to help my parents. I saw my little brothers and sisters, who were really skinny, and saw that we were really poor. My father couldn't really get ahead with his little business of selling what we made in Mexico City.

After I finished sixth grade, one of my cousins came who lived in Ensenada. . . . I ran into her in the market. She said, "Don't you want to come and work? I have a sister-in-law who needs a girl to work in her house." Oh, I was really happy. I said, "Let's go so you can talk with my parents so they'll let me go." We went to talk with my parents to convince them. I asked them to let me go. I convinced them to let me go, and she brought me to Ensenada. I was 14. I was in Ensenada for two months. I worked there for this woman cleaning her house.

At that time I had an aunt who was living in Los Angeles, one of my father's sisters. She's still there. My father wrote to her and told her I was living in Ensenada. I also wrote to her, and she came to see me. I told her I wanted to go to Los Angeles. . . . She found someone, a coyote, who took me across. I think my aunt paid about $200 American to get me across to Los Angeles. But I couldn't find any work because I was a minor. I wanted to go to school, but my aunt couldn't support me.

Then my aunt got me a job working in a house taking care of a little girl. They were people from Texas. I didn't understand any English—nothing, nothing. They only spoke English. They spoke to me and I answered them in Spanish. I was there for three months. During those three months I only ate liver because I didn't know how to ask for food. The man there didn't know how to understand what I wanted. The only thing he knew how to say in Spanish was "Liver? Liver?" So I said, "OK, liver." So for three months it was "liver, liver" every day. When I left there, I couldn't eat it anymore.

After that I went and learned a little English, and one of my father's brothers was working in the fields near Los Angeles, in Oxnard. He said to me, "Why don't you come with us and work in the fields?" Then I started to work, and even though I was younger, I always said I was 17 years old. I was working in the harvests, picking strawberries, tomatoes, squash, string beans. It was really hard work for me. You got paid a dollar for a box of strawberries. You got paid by the piece, not by the hour. Sometimes I'd pick twenty-five or thirty boxes in one day. I saved a little money, but most of it I sent to my parents, $100 a month.

There were a lot of women there from Michoacán and from Oaxaca, but from other towns. Some were from Guelatao—there were Mixtecos and a lot of people without papers. This was a big problem for me. The immigration would show up and everybody would run. Sometimes I didn't run because I would pass as my uncle's daughter. He had papers. . . . A lot of times I hid in cardboard boxes or in garbage cans.

There the women were paid the same as men because it was piecework. . . . A lot of people came from the unions. César Chávez came there a lot. There were strikes, the police came, and the bosses were against all the workers. My uncles and aunts were in the strikes, but I didn't go. They left me at home. They said it was dangerous, that there was a lot of fighting and anger. That was when they raised our wages. Our wages went up even though we didn't have papers.

We all suffered the same because it was hot and there wasn't any water to drink. There was water in the truck for the produce, but the water was hot, as if it had been sitting on a stove. That was where I learned to eat tomatoes. . . . There all the people would grab a tomato and clean it with their shirt and eat it. It was cleaner than the water, which was dirty and really hot. . . . In the winter we would get up and the plants would be white with frost, and we had to go and pick them. Now when I remember, I don't want to do that work again.

Later I began to go to night school for adults. . . . I went there for six months to learn English. During the day I worked. I was really tired when I finished work and had to go to school. . . . During this time I kept sending letters to Teotitlán. My parents wanted me to come back. But when they'd write to me telling me to come back, I'd send them some money, and then they wouldn't tell me to come back anymore. Finally, I wrote asking them all to come and live with me in Los Angeles.

I sent them money so they could all get here. . . . They arrived in Tijuana and I paid a coyote to get them all across. Then they came to Los Angeles. We sent my three younger siblings to school, Celerina, Ernesto, and Miguel. I had a small apartment and we all lived there. We suffered a lot because the money I earned wasn't enough for all of them. There were six of us. It was then that I began to work in a curio store. I knew a little English, and I got to like the job a lot.

When I was 23 I had my first boyfriend, and I got married to someone from Teotitlán. . . . I got to know him because a lot of people from Teotitlán were living in Santa Ana, California. I went to Los Angeles every week to dance or go to the movies. He'd come to my house and ask me to go dancing. I'd go out with him. My parents only let me go with him because they knew him. . . . If I had been living in Teotitlán with them, they wouldn't have let me go. They let me go because I had already helped them a lot. And because I was old enough, I was 23.

We became boyfriend and girlfriend, and then we eloped and I went to his house to live. It was a different life there. I quit working and had my son. After that I couldn't work because of the baby. Only my husband worked. On the one hand it was OK because I rested a lot, which was good, but on the other hand it was really hard. We didn't have enough money. The rent was expensive. I still didn't have any papers. The whole time I lived in the United States, I never had any papers. I was going to work again when I got pregnant again. My other son was born in 1983. It was really expensive to live there with two children. When we were just living in Los Angeles, my parents moved to Tijuana.

. . . After a while it got really hard for us. So my parents said, "Why don't you come here to Tijuana, try to save some money to start a small store? It's OK here." . . . So I came here and my parents helped me with my two children. We all lived together. Me, my children, my brothers and sisters, and my parents. I started to work here again with my sister in her store. I liked it because I liked the work and I could bring my baby to work.

I worked with them for two years. My husband sent some money, but very little. He kept saying he was going to come, but he never came. . . . Now we are totally separated. With help from my father and from all my family, I was able to buy this little store [a stall in the market] in 1987.

It would be very hard to be in Teotitlán alone with the two children. It's hard to have money to dress them and send them to school. My parents have a house there, but I don't. . . . I don't think I'm going to get a piece of land either. It's expensive to live there because there are a lot of fiestas with a lot of expenses. . . . And even though a woman is there alone, she still has to pay a quota or provide food for the men who are doing *servicio* [labor required of townspeople].

I have the idea that one day if I can make some money here in Tijuana, I'll go back there if I have a place to live. I'll go there and set up some kind of business, something they don't have there. Something different, like a restaurant, but a restaurant that's nice, where you can get different things to eat. Or a general store with everything, like in the city. Or a hotel or motel for tourists. . . . But first I have to wait for my sons to get older. When they get out of primary school here, I want to take them to the United States. And because they're U.S. citizens, they have the support of the government to study there, right? That's what I want to do, help them get ahead.

Imelda's story brings together several critical issues that signal several of the transitions in gender roles being experienced by some younger women. While performing household work done by all young women in

Teotitlán, such as washing wool, carding, and spinning as well as making tortillas and taking care of siblings, Imelda did not get married at age 14, like some of her girlfriends. By the time she graduated from sixth grade, a larger percentage of young girls were completing their primary education, and some were leaving the community for other parts of Mexico or the United States. Most stayed for a few years. Some, like Imelda, have not yet returned to the community, but plan to do so eventually.

Imelda's grandfather was one of the wealthiest men in Teotitlán in the 1960s, with a large merchant business. He did not pass his wealth on to his children. This pattern has changed since then, particularly among merchant families that have moved to Tijuana. There, parents help their children to set up businesses and siblings help one another. Imelda's parents did not receive the benefit of inherited wealth, but some of her younger siblings have received family assistance in setting themselves up in business. Perhaps the Teotiteco merchant class is being consolidated as it becomes replicated elsewhere in Mexico.

Like Alicia, Imelda says the multitude of fiestas makes it hard to get ahead in Teotitlán. In Tijuana she is not accumulating guelaguetza debts. She also realizes that the independence she has in Tijuana would not be possible in the village. Imelda has told me that she never would have been allowed to live and work alone as a young woman in Teotitlán, as she did in the United States. She would have been treated as a dependent of her parents. But because she left, she was able to support herself and win her parents' approval of her independence by offering them support. She is aware that her current status as a single mother would make it difficult for her in Teotitlán. She thinks of returning only when she can open her own business there, which would allow her to maintain her independence.

In the mid-1990s, Imelda began a new relationship with a man from the state of Michoacán. She had two children with him and continues to work in the market in Tijuana. She continues with her own business. She remains estranged from her first husband and his extended family and has not returned to Teotitlán. I was unable to contact her directly and got this information from relatives of hers in Teotitlán.

ISABEL

Isabel, born in 1982, is the third youngest of six children. She lives at home with her mother and four sisters, one older and three younger. Her mother is single, and all the girls work together with her; they have always had to struggle to make ends meet. Isabel and one of her sisters belong to a women's cooperative that has periodically shifted between working exclusively with textiles and branching out to other kinds of projects. Isabel has never left Mexico, but her textiles have been sold in the United States through a project organized by a U.S. woman. Isabel is part of a younger generation of women who are better educated, are waiting longer to get married, and are motivated to improve their economic and social position through organizing.

Isabel has kept her hair long, but she often wears blue jeans as she works at home. Her dress resembles that of some returning migrant women who now wear pants regularly. Isabel completed junior high school. She wanted to continue with her studies, but her sense of duty to support her mother and younger siblings brought her home to work full-time as a weaver. She has a strong sense of what women are capable of and the options open to young women of her age that distinguish them from their mothers' generation. Through her experience in the weaving cooperative she belongs to, Isabel already understands the kind of harassment and pressure women go through when they try to move out of their marginal position in formal community politics. She and some colleagues went to some community assemblies and also marched as a group in parades marking national holidays. They faced severe criticism from their families. Her group at one time had the support of the PRI, or Institutional Revolutionary Party. The members of the cooperative were taunted for allying themselves with the president at the time, Ernesto Zedillo. They later became independent of the PRI or any other political party.

Isabel has a trenchant class analysis of what has been happening not only in her community but throughout the world as Teotitlán's textiles have to compete with cheaper knockoffs from elsewhere, much as Navajo weavers have suffered from competition from the Zapotec weavers who produce imitations of Navajo designs. Her view is informed by the continual hardship she, her mother, and her sisters have faced in their efforts to earn a living and to participate in what she sees as the ever more elaborate and expensive ritual celebrations. We talked about what young women were doing at age 14 or 15 when they finished junior high school.

> Because women want to get ahead, they don't get married so young. Like my own case. I'm a young woman and I want to get to know new places, to travel, to enjoy myself, to have new experiences. In contrast, as a married woman I can't do any of this. . . . There are also more single women now

than before because people's mentality is changing. Now young women know what it's like for married women. They know they can be mistreated and all that, so they say, "I don't want this to happen to me." . . . Some young women think, "No, I'm not going to get married now." For example, those that are studying want to finish their education, to work. Those that are single still don't want to get married. They say they're going to wait because they're very young and they don't want to get married so young. Their mentality is changing.

. . . Right now in the community the men are going to say it's only the men who should be given public cargos, not the women. The problem now is that they have the assemblies at night, like at ten or eleven P.M., and they don't finish until one or two o'clock in the morning. A lot of people say it isn't right for women to be out that late. Here women don't really have a voice and a vote, only men, according to the custom. A lot of people still believe that. I don't think that's right. I think women should have the same rights as men. I actually think that if women were to take on cargos in the community, they would do a better job. Often women are more responsible than men. . . . Women do have some small cargos now, like working in the library, distributing milk for a government program . . . maybe one was in the municipal office, but that's very rare. . . .

. . . It's really hard for women to participate in the assemblies right now, even if they're officially invited. It would require a lot of changes, particularly for married women. First they'd have to talk back to their husband and say, "No, I'm going to go to the assembly." I think when they said something like that, their husbands would beat them. The husbands would tell them, "How are you going to go?" Then the women would lose their will and decide not to go. Even for young single women like me, we have to get permission from our mother. Their mothers might say to them, "What are you going to do there among all of those men? You don't have any reason to go." I think if women are ever going to really be able to participate freely in community assemblies, it depends on the older people. Like my mother . . . she wouldn't want me to go. She'd be upset about it. And for the married women, it's their husbands who don't want them to go. Maybe if a group of young women got together and were supported by young men and they said, "We're going to go to the community meeting, we're going to have an opinion, we're going to participate," maybe then it would work. But I don't think that's going to happen quite yet.

. . . Before, when we used to participate in the parades, everyone said a lot of things to us in the streets. They said, "There go Zedillo's women. . . ." They called us Zedillo's women and the men made fun of us. Whenever any one of us from the group would pass a man on the street, they would say, "There goes one of Zedillo's women. How is it that your family lets you walk around in the street, going from one place to another?" "Don't you have work to do at home? Why don't you stay home and clean, make dinner, take care of the kids?" they would say to us. "Women shouldn't be out on the street marching," they told us. . . . I didn't feel good when they said that to me. Other women told me not to pay any attention to them. So after that I didn't pay attention.

. . . Now we don't want to work with political parties. It causes problems. The last time a woman from the PRI came was last month, before the elections. She told us we should work with the PRI. She said the PRI would support our women's group, they'd give us chickens, they'd get us corn mills if we supported the political party and looked for more votes for the party in town. But my sister [who was president of the women's group at the time] said no. She told this woman that we couldn't support the PRI. This woman was unhappy about this and she said OK, but then they kept coming and telling us we had to work with them. . . . The rest of the women in our group don't want anything to do with political parties now. Now we try to work only with institutions that can help us, not parties.

. . . These things we discussed about political parties never change. But what is really changing around here are the customs. They're not the same now as before. My mother says that now the ritual celebrations are much larger than they used to be, and a person who is really poor can't pay for these celebrations the same way the rich can. Then people gossip and say, "Did you see how So-and-so didn't do what that other person did?" . . . So, for example, in the case of a rich person, people from other nearby communities come to make the tortillas for their ritual meals so the people from here who are invited to the meal don't have to do anything.[4] The guests are just sitting watching these other people work. . . .

. . . They come from Maquilxóchitl and other towns near here. They hire them so they come to do all the housework. They come to wash dishes, to make the food, to make tortillas, to make tejate. The people from here don't do anything. At a wedding or any other kind of celebration.

Then another person from here sees this, and when it's their turn to have a celebration like a wedding, they say, "I have to do the same thing." In order to do that, they'll borrow women. So that's what's changing. A poor person will try to do the same as a rich person now, and so everything costs more money . . . now some people are even hiring servants to come and work in their houses from the same towns where they buy weaving from the people, from Santa Ana, from San Miguel.

. . . And right now there are a lot of poor people in this town as well. That part above the town is now all made up of poor people. They all dedicate themselves to making textiles and selling them to the merchants. Then the merchants turn around and sell them at double or triple the price that was paid to the person who made them. If you take a rug to one of these merchants they'll tell you, "I don't have any cash right now. Come back tomorrow." You return the next day, and they give you a little bit of money so you can buy more yarn to invest in a new weaving, but it doesn't work out financially.

. . . The only way poor people can make it or build even a small new house is if they have sons or husbands who are working in the United States and they send money. If they have someone in the United States, then they can send money and they spend it on the house. Then they are still poor. In contrast, those who sell and export textiles keep on being rich. Their money doesn't run out.

. . . We only get by once in a while because we live in the center of town. When tourists come, we go outside our house and say, "Wouldn't you like to buy a rug? Sometimes we sell one or two . . . but as I told my sister, there's going to come a time when our textiles aren't going to sell because there are people in other countries who are making textiles just like ours, but of another quality and with other materials—cotton, for example, instead of wool. These are much cheaper than what we produce here. So now in the United States people are buying a lot of these other textiles, and the tourists and importers come here and they say, "Why are your weavings so expensive? They're much cheaper in other countries . . . like in Chile or in Africa."

. . . We've seen them. They're made of cotton and they have the same pre-Hispanic designs we use here in Oaxaca. That's why I say we have to learn to make other things, because the day is going to come when we can't live just by making rugs. We have to think of other things.

Through her education and the weaving cooperative and the women's group in which she has participated since 1995, when she was 13, Isabel has gained a wide range of experience, reflected in her analysis of local gender relations, the local political system, global competition in textile production for the U.S. market, and increasing class stratification. Her discussion suggests a budding social scientist as she systematically analyzes and reflects on different aspects of economic and political change. Being the daughter of a single mother in Teotitlán has equipped her with a certain toughness as she grew up in a household that was not considered the norm. Isabel has taken advantage of recent opportunities to gain training in other kinds of craft production. She has made floating candles and branched out into woven handbags and pillow covers; she has taught women in nearby communities under the auspices of the Instituto para Capacitación de los Artesanos (Institute for the Training of Artisans), or INCAPET. She hopes to come to the United States to sell her weavings personally.

These women's stories reflect some of the commonalities of growing up female in Teotitlán as well as important differences tied to their ages, class positions as merchants and weavers, and experiences in making the transition from weaver to merchant. Many experienced a childhood of extremely hard work, beginning at the age of 5 or 6 to produce yarn, prepare food, and care for their younger siblings. They have all experienced gender-linked limitations and the double standard of lower expectations for girls, a loss of independence with marriage, and an interest in ceremonial activity. While the older women remember poverty, the three younger women are more familiar with the current prosperity of the community and relate strongly to the kinds of material differences that exist between people. The class differences between merchants and weavers are very real in their lives and inform their perceptions of themselves and others.

All of these women mention education, or the lack of it, as an important factor in their lives. Julia, Cristina, and Alicia all regret the fact that they were not allowed to go to school and feel that their lack of education has significantly limited what they have been able to accomplish in their lives. Imelda and Angela, who completed the sixth grade, recognize that even that was not enough to equip them for running and expanding a business. Isabel completed junior high, and that advantage and her experience in a women's cooperative since age 13 have brought her some experience and understanding of the larger world. Finally, all of these women have a strong sense of themselves as filling female roles; regardless of their current class positions, they recognize the heavy work load that they have in the gendered division of labor, whether in Teotitlán or outside of it.

In order to understand how Julia, Cristina, Angela, Alicia, Imelda, and Isabel have developed their view of themselves and their world, we must begin to unravel the historical, cultural, and economic context they live in and grew up in. As we explore the complex history of Teotitlán, the circumstances that frame the lives of these six women will move into sharper focus. The following chapters document how their identities as individuals and as women have been shaped not only by political, economic, and cultural changes at the local level but also by the changing policies of the postrevolutionary Mexican state and international economics.

CHAPTER 4

Setting the Scene

The Zapotecs of Teotitlán

del Valle, Oaxaca

> This town is called Teutitlan in the Mexican language and in its
> own Zapotec language it is called Paguia: the ancestors gave it this
> name because they say that they had their idols and gods on top of
> a mountain that they worshiped near the town that had this name.
> —Francisco del Paso y Troncoso, *Relaciones geográficas de Oaxaca*

> In 1519 when we came ashore on the coast of Veracruz,
> we all came as Catholics. When we came ashore we gave thanks to
> our Lord Jesus Christ for our faith in him, which let us cross the
> ocean. We went through great pain and today we have arrived.
> We are here in the new land. Each one of us is a Christian and is
> obligated to worship the mysteries, the unity of Christ in the
> Holy Trinity. Our faith states that there is only one God in the
> supernatural world. —Agustín, age 19, in the role of Cortés
> in the Dance of the Conquest

Teotitlán del Valle is an indigenous Zapotec community of approximately 5,000 (including Teotitecos living elsewhere) located in the foothills of the Sierra Juárez 29 kilometers from the state capital, Oaxaca. Buses run between Teotitlán and Oaxaca six to eight times a day. People make frequent trips to Oaxaca to go to the bank, visit the market, or get on connecting buses that take them to the other periodic markets in the central valleys of Oaxaca. By the early twenty-first century, many cars and pickup trucks drove in and out of town each day on their way to Oaxaca or elsewhere. An increase in migration in the late 1980s and 1990s resulted in a significant increase in the number of cars and trucks in the community. As the town stretched out in all directions in the 1990s and some houses were as far as two or three miles from the center, it was not uncommon to see people drive into town to the market as well.

The visitor to Teotitlán is struck by the industry of local residents and by their ability to drive a hard bargain when they sell their weavings. A peek inside any doorway will reveal at least one weaver, male or female, slinging the shuttle across a loom as others wind yarn onto bobbins to keep pace. Visitors are also impressed by the conservation of the Zapotec language and the strong current of tradition found in Teotitlán. On most days, a group of Teotitecos can be seen carrying out a ritual—a wedding, funeral, or celebration for a saint's day. The elements of ritual—candles, copal, band music, a wooden image of the saint or the Virgin, a large feast, and fireworks—are omnipresent.

Early in the morning and again in the afternoon, the local food market is crammed with women dressed in traditional huipiles atop lengths of plaid wool cloth wrapped around their waists as skirts or in print dresses from Oaxaca. They move briskly from stall to stall, filling their baskets with fruit, vegetables, meat, bread, tortillas. . . . Vendors from Teotitlán and surrounding communities come to ply their wares here because most people have some money to spend. Outside the food market groups of women are selling hand-spun yarn, flowers, and alfalfa. By 2005 the market was also distinguished by more than a dozen stands offering prepared foods for women to take home for the next meal—*atole* (a corn drink), tamales, chocolate, various meat dishes, even cooked rice. Women increasingly preferred to purchase some of the food they served to their families rather than prepare it all from scratch. The market also sported many booths offering shoes, clothing, and appliances.

Across from the market, down the hill from the church, some local municipal officials may be leaving city hall to go home for the mid-afternoon meal. Young women who sell textiles in the artisan market for tourists are opening their lunches. Lest they lose a sale, they eat in their stalls, savoring the cloth-wrapped food brought to them by younger siblings. Everyone is busy.

Teotitlán is one of 570 municipios in the state of Oaxaca.[1] The large number of municipios is indicative of the past and present political fragmentation of the state. Teotitlán is a municipal seat that has one other community under its jurisdiction, the *agencia* of Santiago Ixtaltepec, locally referred to as Santiaguito.

The state of Oaxaca has several distinctions in relation to Mexico's other thirty-one states. With 1,120,312 speakers of an indigenous language over the age of 4 in the 2000 census, Oaxaca has the most indigenous people—37.11 percent of the state's total population (INEGI 2000). If children 4 and younger are included, the percentage probably rises to about 43 percent. Fourteen indigenous languages are spoken in Oaxaca: Amuzgo, Chatino, Chinanteco, Chocho, Chontal, Cuicateco, Huave, Mazateco, Mixe, Mixteco, Nahuatl, Triqui, Zapoteco, and Zoque. In

Figure 1. A food market and a sixteenth-century church sit in the center of Teotitlán del Valle. Photo by the author.

Figure 2. The former food market in Teotitlán is now a textile market for tourists. Most of the booths are staffed by women of smaller merchant households or of independent weaver households. Photo by the author.

2000 there were 347,020 Zapotec speakers over the age of 4 in Oaxaca (INEGI 2000).

THE ECONOMY OF OAXACA

Oaxaca is the second poorest state in Mexico (after Chiapas); over 46 percent of the municipalities have a high degree of poverty (Livas and Gamboa 1998, 168). Oaxaca's per capita gross domestic product has long been one of Mexico's lowest (U.S.$1,136 in 1980, when Mexico City's was $5,500). By 2002, Mexico's per capita gross domestic product was about $9,000 (CIA 2003); Oaxaca's was estimated to be about 40 percent of that figure, or about $3,600. Oaxaca's economy has consistently suffered from underemployment, high out-of-state migration, and an agricultural base close to subsistence level.

In 1980, approximately 60 percent of Oaxaca's total active labor force, or 474,793 people, were employed in agriculture and related activities (INEGI 1984, 750). By the year 2000, the percentage of the total active labor force employed in agriculture, cattle ranching, hunting, and fishing was 42.13 percent, or 438,312 people (INEGI 2001). This decrease coincided with the Mexican government's plan to move at least three million small farmer families out of the rural sector. This plan, instituted in conjunction with NAFTA, was a counterreform to Article 27 of the Mexican Constitution, ending land reform and making it possible to privatize the more than 50 percent of Mexican territory in nonprivate status. Most of Oaxaca's 3.5 million people live in small communities of fewer than 5,000. Most farm families work plots of less than five hectares (about twelve acres), barely large enough to meet their own subsistence needs.

A form of land tenure peculiar to Mexico is the *ejido*, communal property in which members have use rights, usually in an individual plot of land. Ejidos were created after the Mexican Revolution to satisfy the demands of landless peasants who had seen their communal village lands eaten up by large agricultural estates or had served as laborers on those estates. The term *ejido* refers to a specific area of land as well. The right to work ejido lands is either granted by the government to a group of petitioners or received through inheritance. In 1999 Oaxaca had 802 ejidos that benefited about 107,840 families or approximately 539,200 people, if we assume an average of five people per family. It was also home to 659 *comunidades agrarias*[2] that benefited about 240,723 families, or 1,203,615 people under the same assumption (Oaxaca 2002, 16). More than half the state's population (56.4 percent) lived in households that had access to nonprivate land in the 1990s, yet only about 42 percent of the economically active population in 2000 made a living from the land. The difference between those who may have access to land yet do not work on it represents a significant shift in what Oaxaca's rural population was doing to make a living in the 1990s. Those that did not emigrate moved away from agriculture into service industries, manufacturing, or some other sector. Census figures reveal that the number of people employed in manufacturing more than doubled between 1980 and 2000. This trend away from farming and related activities is expected to continue.

According to the 1980 census, 40,283 Oaxacans, about 4.7 percent of the state's economically active population, were employed in manufacturing concerns (INEGI 1984, 750). By 2000 that figure was 119,795 (11.23 percent) (INEGI 2000). Artisans working in craft production outside of construction continue to be an important part of this manufacturing base. Many are working in small factories and workshops of the sort referred to as microenterprises. In the mid-1980s it was estimated that there were close to 5,000 microenterprises employing fewer than five people each (Raisz 1986, 39). In 2000, 68 percent of persons employed in manufacturing were artisans and workers laboring outside of the construction industry, many of them doubtless in craft production (INEGI 2000). These microindustries are important sources of income for rural communities. Important rural industries include pottery, palm weaving, embroidery, weaving on treadle and backstrap looms, metate making, brickmaking, and mescal distilling (S. Cook 1982a). Oaxacan craft industries can be divided between those that produce for regional use and those that cater to the tourist and international markets.

MIGRATION

In most Oaxacan communities underemployment is high during the slack months of the agricultural year. The situation in many communities became quite dire in the 1990s as subsidies and credits for small farmers were significantly downsized. They had to compete with heavily subsidized imported corn and other products that hit the Mexican market as a result of NAFTA. In communities where there is no craft production, cash income is earned by wage labor, often in emigration.

Oaxacans began migrating as laborers to other parts of Mexico as early as the nineteenth century. Migration became more significant with the recruitment of Oaxacan men by the U.S. bracero program during World War II and after. Instituted supposedly to replace U.S. farm laborers who went either into the armed forces or into manufacturing for the war effort, this program allowed the importation of Mexican workers for annual harvests with the stipulation that they were to return to Mexico after their work was finished. Braceros were to work under contracts that specified their transportation, wages, health care, housing, and food and the number of hours to be worked. The contracts even stipulated that there should be no discrimination against braceros. The contracts were initially between the U.S. and Mexican governments; later they were switched to private contractors, most of whom ignored their terms, and braceros had no one to complain to. The bracero program ended in 1947, but it was renegotiated and started again in 1949. It finally ended in 1964.

After the bracero program was over, Oaxacans continued to migrate. From 1960 to 1984, 500,000 people from Oaxaca between the ages of 15 and 65 went to other areas to work. More than half of them left between 1975 and 1980 (S. Cook 1984b). Many went to the United States. It is estimated that by the mid-1990s, 60 percent of Oaxaca's 570 municipios had experienced significant emigration (Labra 1996). The 1990s appears to be a peak for Oaxacan migration to the north of Mexico and to various U.S. locations (see Reyes Morales and Gijón Cruz 2002). The numbers of migrants may have declined by the beginning of the twenty-first century, but the number of 83,172 given in the 2000 census seems extremely low (INEGI 2000).

Community-level surveys of migration trends, such as the one Rafael Reyes Morales and Alicia Silvia Gijón Cruz carried out in late 2001 and early 2002, provide a more accurate assessment of local migration than the census. They did a random sample survey of 217 households in seven communities in Oaxaca, including twenty-nine households in Teotitlán del Valle. Their sample included five communities from the Mixteca region and two from the Zapotec central valleys area. They found that the number of persons who had emigrated in Teotitlán averaged 0.55 persons per household. They calculated that there were approximately 953 households in Teotitlán, suggesting that at the time they carried out their survey, 524 Teotitecos were living outside of Teotitlán (Reyes Morales and Gijón Cruz 2002, 4, 20). This number is close to the 500 I calculated in 1990 for the Teotitecos living in Southern California and other areas near the U.S. border. Emigrants who have returned to the community have introduced significant changes in community life, including the formation of weaving cooperatives, a somewhat expanded role for women in the formal political system, more consumer goods, and increased capital used to invest in house construction and businesses.

THE ETHNOGRAPHY OF TEOTITLÁN

The Zapotecs have been one of the most heavily documented ethnic groups in the state of Oaxaca. Ethnographic work has covered the various regions in which they live as well as a range of topics.[3] The Zapotec community of Teotitlán del Valle has been researched by William Warner Wood (1995, 1996, 2000a, 2000b, 2003), Jeffrey Cohen (1999), Gilberto da Silva Ruiz (1980), Jaime Jesús Segura (1979), and Robert Taylor (1960, 1966). Taylor's 1960 dissertation is highly descriptive; he concludes that Teotitlán is a "typical" Mesoamerican community based on a list of characteristics generated from the work of Robert Redfield and Sol Tax (1952). In a later article (1966) he emphasizes cultural conservatism in Teotitlán and ties it to two factors: the reluctance of local innovators to push others to adopt their views and the reluctance of all Teotitecos overtly to imitate nontraditional customs accepted by others. Segura's work (1979, 1980) also focuses on the cultural conservatism of the community as manifested in the civil-religious cargo system.

Other ethnographic work focuses on the economics of weaving production. Da Silva Ruiz (1980, 5–27) documents class polarization in the community and attempts to fit a dichotomous class model of "bourgeoisie" and "exploited pieceworkers" onto the complexities of contemporary weaving production. Cohen (1999) offers many useful insights into how the political and economic dominance of Teotitlán is experienced by the citizens of the neighboring weaving community of Santa Ana. William Warner Wood (1997, 2000a, 2000b) emphasizes the flexibility and complexity of textile production and distribution in a global market, transnational relationships of importers and weavers, and ways in which the community has commoditized its ethnicity.

Many of these studies of Teotitlán emphasize two striking aspects of the community central to an analysis of gender roles: its successful expansion of weaving production for export and its retention of cultural institutions and events. These two foci have led ethnographers to one of two contrasting conclusions: either that Teotitlán is culturally conservative or that its socioeconomic structure has been completely altered by integration with international capitalism.

TABLE 1 Population of Teotitlán, 1890–2000

Year	1890	1910	1930	1940	1950	1960	1970	1980	1986	2000
Population	2,742	2,634	2,116	2,290	2,511	2,881	3,394	3,496	4,500	4,564

Sources: 1899, Archivo General del Estado de Oaxaca; 1900–1970, Dirección General de Estadística, censuses for 1900–1970; 1980, INEGI 1984; 1986, household survey by Lynn Stephen; 2000, Reyes-Morales and Gijón Cruz 2002.

POPULATION

In 2000 Teotitlán had a resident population of 4,564 (Reyes Morales and Gijón Cruz 2002, 4).[4] Until the 1900s, epidemics such as smallpox and ty-phoid kept the death rate higher than the birth rate, sometimes doubling it. During the colonial period, particularly between 1530 and 1650, the indigenous population in Teotitlán and throughout the state of Oaxaca was greatly reduced. Estimates put the valley's indigenous population at approximately 350,000 on the eve of the Conquest (Chance 1978, 69). The population declined steadily until the 1630s, when it reached a low of 40,000 to 45,000, a decline of 87 percent over 100 years. The total popu-lation of the valley had risen to nearly 70,000 by 1740 and to 110,000 by the 1790s (W. Taylor 1972, 17–18). The valley had 290,000 inhabitants in 1959 (Tamayo 1960, 13–31).

The chief cause of death during the colonial period was European dis-eases, for which indigenous Oaxacans had no immunity. Smallpox epi-demics, plague, measles, and other diseases swept through the valleys on many occasions during the colonial period and in later centuries. Until the 1950s, smallpox epidemics could kill three to four people a day in Teotitlán (Archivo Municipal de Teotitlán del Valle, 1863–1984).

Table 1 shows population figures collected from the community ar-chives and national censuses. They are only for the community of Teoti-tlán, exclusive of other communities under its jurisdiction. The popula-tion remained fairly stable from 1890 until 1960, when it began to grow. The first growth period came between 1960 and 1980. A larger period of growth between 1980 and 1986 coincides with the expansion of weaving production. The large number for 1986 may be traced to the fact that it comes from my census of the community rather than from a national cen-sus. Discussions with informants who administered government census questionnaires suggest that official population counts of Teotitlán are often low. The lack of population increase between 1986 and 2000 can be attributed to significant out-migration in the 1990s. It should be remembered that the residents counted in 2001 by Reyes Morales and Gijón Cruz were only those actually present; it is estimated that at least 524 more people live outside the community, in California, northern Mexico, and elsewhere.

GEOGRAPHY AND CLIMATE

Teotitlán is in the eastern Tlacolula arm of the Valley of Oaxaca, one of three arms that come together to form what are called the *valles centrales*. Other arms extend southward toward Ocotlán and northward toward the town of Etla. The Tlacolula arm of the valley is drained by the Río Salado, which flows westward to join the Río Atoyac near the city of Oaxaca (Kirkby 1973, 7–25). The town of Teotitlán is situated between two tributaries that flow into the Río Salado, the largest of which is called *ruʔor(n)* (oven mouth river).

The *ruʔor(n)* flows north to south from the Sierra Juárez. About one kilometer above Teotitlán it feeds into a large lake formed by the Presa Azul, a dam built by the Mexican government in 1968 as part of a large irrigation project. The lake is stocked with fish. The lake bed also serves as a source of sand and gravel for construction. The reservoir formed by the dam is the source of water for the main irrigation system of Teotitlán, used almost exclusively to augment sparse rainfall during the rainy season.

A second dam, constructed in 1975 along the tributary flowing on the eastern side of Teotitlán, has proved to be a failure. Built only of dirt and stones, it is dry throughout most of the year and has slowly eroded. It has been dry for much of the time it has been in operation.

The climate in the Tlacolula arm of the central valleys is semiarid. The average annual rainfall at the Tlacolula weather station between 1927 and 1975 was 542 millimeters. The heaviest months of rainfall are May through September; little rain falls between October and April (Secretaría de Programación y Presupuesto 1981). Rainfall tends to vary greatly from year to year. From 1981 to 1984 there was little rain. In 1984 it rained so excessively that farmers didn't have enough time to plant and harvest properly. Rain falls unevenly within the geographical bounds of the community, falling more heavily at higher altitudes and east or west of the primary tract of agricultural land. Several years in the 1990s it rained so little in August and September that some of the corn crop shriveled before it could be harvested.

The average elevation of the valleys of Oaxaca is between 1,000 and 2,000 meters (Tamayo 1982, 19). The altitude of Teotitlán is 1,590 meters, with much of the community's forest land falling at altitudes up to 2,200 meters. Until the 1950s, much greater use was made of the variety of altitudes found within the community's landholdings than currently. The land falls within areas that support both dry subtropical and coniferous vegetation (Tamayo 1982, 7–5).

LAND DISTRIBUTION

The community of Teotitlán has a total of 8,695 hectares or 21,477 acres of land.[5] Of the total land, 2,052 hectares is *temporal* (dry) farmland that is privately owned. As the area has no source of irrigation, *temporal* land is worked only during the rainy season. There are 6,643 hectares of communal dry land, which includes forests and about 600 hectares that are usable as farmland (Archivo Municipal de Teotitlán del Valle 1981). An additional 50 hectares of irrigated land are held privately. The land is fed by four main channels of the large dam built on the main river. In 1986, 153 households used these irrigation channels.

Teotitlán received no ejido land under the agrarian reform after the Mexican Revolution, so all its landholdings are communal or private. Interestingly, in the 2000 census, all of Teotitlán's land is registered as communal, with 136 beneficiaries—people who are registered as having access to the land. What appears to have happened is that although much of Teotitlán's land is officially registered with the government as communal, significant parts of it have become privatized through time. So far, communal lands cannot be privatized, but ejido lands can. However, changes to Article 27 made in 1992 do permit agrarian communities to change from a designation as comunidades agrarias with inalienable land to ejidos. If an agrarian community is converted to an ejido, then land can be parceled and privatized. The program that the Mexican government initiated to encourage and facilitate this process was called PROCECOM (Program for the Certification of Communal Lands). The goals of PROCECOM were to map and measure communal landholdings so that if a community desired, it could convert its communal holding to ejido holding and then privatize the land.

In the late 1990s, Teotitlán del Valle agreed to serve as one of the pilot cases for the implementation of PROCECOM in the state of Oaxaca. Its more than 8,600 hectares of fields and forests were measured and mapped. In a series of community meetings and through the establishment of special local commissions to accompany employees of the Procuraduría Agraria, all local boundaries for individually owned lands that bordered communal lands were documented and new maps were drawn that showed the boundaries of communal land with private lands, communal lands from other communities, and neighboring private lands and ejidos. While residents who were serving in local cargos at the time undertook the process to secure communal lands, others in the community took note of the underlying discourse promoting privatization. By 2002, the fencing of shared water resources, illegal occupation of communal land as private, and debates about proposals for privately exploiting the community's forest resources highlighted contrasting ideas of the rights community members held.

In 1986, roughly 55 percent of the households in Teotitlán had private holdings. The remaining 45 percent were landless. Whole new neighborhoods have been created on communal land, stretching out in four directions from the town center. By 2002 about 60 percent or more of the community was landless. For young couples who don't have access to private land through inheritance, the right to obtain a parcel of communal land for house construction is central to their ability to begin to establish themselves as an independent economic unit. Very few people currently petition for access to communal land for farming. As population pressures increase, communal land for house plots is edging farther and farther away from the central parts of the community. By the early twenty-first century many people noted that the community was achieving a kind of class segregation in housing. While the central streets of the community used to reflect a wide range of income levels in house construction, with older one-room adobe houses still standing next to newer two-story brick buildings constructed with remittances from emigrant family members, now the poor increasingly reside on the outskirts of the community, where they are claiming communal lands that used to be dedicated to farming. This emergent neighborhood segregation by class appears to have been accelerated in the 1990s.

TABLE 2 Percentage of full-time farmers, Teotitlán, 1930–2000

Year	No. of farmers/total pop. measured	Percent of total pop. measured
1930	160/267 households recorded	60
1950	387/901 economically active males in municipio	43
1960	660/1,227 economically active males in municipio	54
1970	462/1,088 economically active males in municipio	42
1980	309/1,201 economically active males in municipio who receive farming income	26
1986	17/154 households surveyed	11
2000	252/2245 economically active males in municipio	11.2

Source: 1910–1970, Dirección General de Estadística, censuses for 1900–1970; 1980, INEGI 1984; 1986, household survey by Lynn Stephen; 2000, INEGI 2000.

FARMING IN TEOTITLÁN: A DECLINING OCCUPATION

As farming decreased in importance in the local economy due to the blossoming of textile production, the number of full-time male farmers dropped dramatically. While 60 percent of the households in Teotitlán listed their primary occupation as farming in a local census in 1930, that number steadily declined as the twentieth century rolled on. The figures in table 2 are problematic because some include the population of Santiago Ixtaltepec (the agencia under Teotitlan's municipal jurisdiction) and others do not, but they do demonstrate the trend away from farming. Most of the censuses document only male farming activity.

As seen in table 2, a 1986 random sample survey of 154 households indicated that 11 percent included full-time farmers. The 2000 census gives the same number for the municipio of Teotitlán, which also includes the small nearby farming community of Santiaguito Ixtaltepec. If the numbers from Santiaguito were subtracted, the percentage of full-time farmers in Teotitlán alone would be smaller.

In 1986, up to 55 percent of the households in the survey farmed part-time. About 10 percent of those who farmed used irrigation. The non-

TABLE 3 Hectares of corn planted and harvested in Teotitlán, 1960–1983

1960	1961	1962	1963	1975	1976	1977	1978	1982	1983
768	710	710	372	92	111	114	244	232	534

Source: Secretaría de Agricultura y Recursos Hidráulicos, Oaxaca.

TABLE 4 Irrigated versus *temporal* corn yields for Teotitlán, 1960–1983

	1960	1961	1962	1963	1975	1976	1977	1978	1982	1983
Irrigated hectares										
Planted	60	60	60	34	0	20	29	140	90	149
Total tons yielded	52	54	54	30	0	32	21	116	211	447
Average tons yielded	0.9	0.9	0.9	0.9	0	1.6	0.7	0.8	2.3	3.0
Temporal hectares										
Planted	708	650	650	348	92	91	85	104	142	385
Total tons yielded	37	87	286	243	110	69	29	54	7	71
Average tons yielded	0.05	0.1	0.4	0.7	1.2	0.8	0.3	0.5	0.05	0.18

Source: Secretaría de Agricultura y Recursos Hidráulicos, Oaxaca, Datos Definitivos de Cultivos Cíclicos, 1977, 1978, 1982, 1983; Servicio Meterológico Nacional, Departamento de Archivo y Documentación Climatalógico.

farming population of Teotitlán (45 percent of the households) had access only to marginal communal lands, as recorded in local land records. The majority of farming households in Teotitlán cultivated plots of *temporal* of less than one hectare.

Local and state figures on the total number of hectares planted in corn on an annual basis also reveal a major drop in the number of hectares planted after the early 1960s. While the number of hectares planted increased again in the 1980s, it still did not reach the level of the 1960s.

In the 1980s, the average household of six people in Teotitlán consumed at least two kilos of corn per day. The use of corn for animal feed can boost daily consumption of corn to four kilos per day in many households, particularly where there are pigs. With a minimum of two kilos per day, families with one-hectare *temporal* plots would run out of corn

Figure 3. Once Teotitlán was a community of full-time subsistence farmers and part-time weavers. In 1986 only about 11 percent of the population engaged in full-time farming. By 2003 that percentage was probably less. Census figures for 2000 on farming include as part of the municipio of Teotitlán the neighboring community of Santiaguito, where farming continues to be important. Photo by the author.

about eight months after the harvest in a good year. In a year such as 1982, when yields were particularly low, the average *temporal* yield from one hectare would last only about twenty-five days. Most households purchase a majority of their corn with earnings from weaving production, whether or not they are farming.

THE AGRICULTURAL CYCLE AND
THE ORGANIZATION OF PRODUCTION

Most farming activities in Teotitlán take place between March and November. Planting is timed around the arrival of the rains, which may begin in April or May. Farmers plow the fields once before the rains to open the land up to the moisture and then again after the rains begin. The land must be plowed at least once before planting and preferably twice.

Planting for flat *temporal* land, the majority of land under cultivation, is done in late May or early June. The planting team consists of a farmer and his two oxen plus at least two seed planters. Increasingly tractors are used, although even in 2003, some ox teams continued to work because their owners preferred to work with animals. While the plow opens the furrows, two people walk behind it broadcasting seeds and covering them with dirt using their feet. One hectare can usually be plowed and planted by a team of three in one day.

About one month after planting, the plowman goes out again to clean out between the rows and push the dirt around the young plants. This process takes a team of two men about one day per hectare. Continued time investments before the harvest depend on whether or not the land is irrigated and how much weeding is necessary. If weeding is unnecessary, then the field may be left alone until harvesting time. If weeds are prevalent, the farm household makes several trips to the field to pull weeds during the growing season.

Harvesting takes place in late October or November. The largest agricultural work groups are formed for harvesting. A farmer can usually harvest one hectare of corn with four helpers in about one day. Harvesting also involves hiring a pickup truck and driver or an oxcart to transport the corn. Harvesting is done by hand with men, and often women and children as well, carrying large baskets on their backs that they fill with corn as they move down the rows.

The last step in the agricultural cycle is cutting down cornstalks, tying them together, and transporting them to the home. Cornstalks are used as animal feed and fuel. They are seen as a valuable part of the harvest, particularly by those who have oxen to feed. One hectare of cornstalks and leaves can be cut, tied, and transported in two days by a team of three men.

According to local farmers, the minimum number of adult labor days needed to farm one hectare of dry land is about twenty. Many weavers who are secondary farmers spend an average of three to four weeks per year in their fields. Full-time farmers go every day to their fields or to tend the animals. In the random sample survey of 154 households carried out in 1986, the average number of days spent in agricultural activities by adult male household heads was seventy-five.

THE GENDERED DIVISION OF LABOR
IN AGRICULTURE AND LABOR RECRUITMENT

While most agricultural activities associated with planting and harvesting are carried out directly by men, women also participate in agricultural production. In particular, female household workers help with weeding and harvesting. Seldom is a female seen planting or plowing. When no male labor is available, however, women also work in planting. The majority of female labor is directed toward supplying male workers with food during agricultural activities and providing supplemental labor during weeding and harvesting.

During the agricultural season, women begin their days especially early. They must prepare a meal to be served to their husbands, sons, and other laborers going to work in the field. Early-morning coffee is usually served at 6 A.M. Later they bring a lunch out to the field. In many cases they have to walk an hour or longer to reach the men. Once they arrive at the field they prepare a hot lunch and *tejate*, a corn drink that requires several hours of grinding. By 2003, many fewer women were making the labor-intensive tejate, preferring to bring soft drinks they could purchase. Women may provide another snack for workers when they return from the fields.

When weeding is done, an entire household usually goes to spend the day in a field. Food is carried by the family and prepared in the countryside. During harvesting season, women also work as supplementary harvesters, often scanning the field for ears of corn that have dropped to the ground or that have been missed by the male harvesters. They also use the time to collect plants and herbs used in cooking and herbal remedies.

Most agricultural activities involve recruitment of male laborers from outside the household. In rare cases where a household owns oxen and has many full-grown sons, no extra labor is needed. One of the chief complaints of farmers in Teotitlán during the 1980s and again in 2003 was the limited number of oxen available. Ox teams are needed for the majority of agricultural activities. Tractors can be substituted for some types of plowing. In 1986 there were three tractors in Teotitlán that worked on a limited basis. In 2003 there were at least six or seven. A random sample survey of 154 households in 1986 found that one in five owned at least one team of oxen. Informants estimated the ratio to be lower, with one team of oxen for every eight to ten households. Securing a team of oxen and additional laborers for planting and harvesting is the responsibility of male household heads. They usually try to rely first on guelaguetza exchanges. The demand for weaving laborers has had an effect on the availability of local labor for farming. Because weaving brings the most profitable return to labor, most able-bodied men far prefer to weave than to work as hired laborers in other people's fields. This fact caused agricultural labor and ox team rental to cost twice as much in Teotitlán as in neighboring communities. By 2002, a hired agricultural laborer charged 100 pesos (about U.S. $10) per day plus two meals. A day usually lasted about seven hours.

The high cost of local agricultural labor has discouraged women from wanting to plant even if they have land to work. Some widows have inherited land from their husbands if they have no sons or if all of their children have left. Some daughters inherit land as well. Working the land, however, usually requires women to hire agricultural laborers. Because traditionally women don't work on the land and because they have many other essential tasks occupying their time, they very seldom choose to carry out all aspects of planting, weeding, and harvesting themselves. As a result, some land has remained vacant. Ana, a 70-year-old widow who has about three hectares of land she could farm, explains: "We didn't plant this year. It's too expensive. It costs about six hundred pesos [U.S.$60] per hectare to plant, then we need to hire the oxen for the delicate tasks of plowing between the rows to take out the weeds. This costs another three hundred pesos. Then we have to pay a mozo about a thousand pesos a day plus his food. Then you have to do this several times . . . so I don't plant. I just buy the corn. It costs about twelve pesos for four kilos. That is much cheaper and easier."

Work guelaguetza has varying opportunity costs. If members of a household are concerned about cash flow, they may try to work out a guelaguetza exchange in which they trade their labor for someone else's rather than shoulder the high costs of hiring labor and oxen from Teotitlán. If a male household head is an exceptional weaver who earns a lot of money in one day, he may try to avoid guelaguetza labor exchanges so that he can invest his labor in weaving. Working one day at his loom gets him a higher return for his labor than receiving one day of farming labor through guelaguetza.

A male household head must also be flexible in his schedule in order to participate in work guelaguetza. Securing guelaguetza laborers is dependent on the schedule of others. Most men are usually not able to schedule such labor for all of their extra labor needs. Because of the necessity to plant and harvest within strict time frames, procuring agricultural labor is often difficult. Many men have to hire laborers to augment their guelaguetza labor. Because of the high wages in Teotitlán, about thirty men from neighboring communities also come to work during the agricultural season. They arrive each morning on the bus to stand in the market and go with the highest bidder. There is often bitter competition for their labor as farmers become desperate to plant and harvest on time. This situation continued in 2003, but was less severe as fewer people were still trying to plant their fields.

A second method for procuring labor for fields is to go *a medias*, which literally means going halves with another farmer in a sharecropping arrangement. Someone who owns land agrees to give half of the harvest to another person who in turn provides half of the labor. Households that have a shortage of male labor often engage in this practice as a way of cutting labor costs. But given the low yields of most dry farmland, their portion of the harvest is usually small.

ANIMAL PRODUCTION BY WOMEN

The yards of most households in Teotitlán are populated with five to ten turkeys, ten to fifteen chickens, and two or more pigs. Animal production by women provides household protein, an opportunity for savings, and a means of ritual investment for guelaguetza. However, animal production, like dry farming, appears to add little to household income. Analysis of women's animal raising done in the mid-1980s suggested, in fact, that when animals are raised in the home, the amount invested in them from birth is about double their worth as adults. While the economics of animal production is much less favorable to those who raise their own animals than to those who purchase them, the continued widespread occurrence of animal production in Teotitlán suggests that the motivation for production is not profit but the possibility of accumulating a significant amount of capital through slowly investing minimal amounts. In addition, having animals in their yards is also an important symbol of well-being to women. When they have chickens, turkeys, and pigs to feed, they feel that they have a little something to eat—even if it still walks!

Women who raise animals describe them as a *bancomer*, a pun on a former Mexican commercial bank that also means "a bank to eat." Women see animal production as one of the few ways available to them to "save money." Women in Teotitlán use pigs as a form of savings for rituals and to accumulate small amounts of capital to invest in goods for their households. The role of women's animal production in guelaguetza is discussed in greater detail in chapter 9. In many households money earned through pig and turkey production is used in the purchase of initial household looms. For young households, in the early stages of the developmental cycle, animal production is often their first source of capital. In some merchant households, animal production has been a significant source of initial income to purchase wool and yarn. In the 1980s and 1990s, migrant remittances also became important as initial sources of capital.

Women's investments in animal production also affect their other productive activities. Animals are fed twice a day, early in the morning and again in the afternoon. In five households where animal raising activity was monitored in the mid-1980s, women spent between one and a half and three hours daily in animal care. In addition, turkeys and chickens can require constant supervision, especially when they are young. Supervision of animals goes well with the weaving activities women perform between preparations for meals.

Activities that take women away from the home, however, are not compatible with animal production. When women work several days at a ritual event in another household, they all leave in midmorning and again in the afternoon to return home to check on their animals and feed them. Many women state that the reason they infrequently leave the community is concern for their animals. Because of the importance of animal production as a means of savings, women's control over animal production may give them leverage in dealing with male household members over financial matters. Often a household emergency is met by selling a pig. Because women have the capacity to sell their animals in order to take care of the household, they are able to push for more input into other types of household decisions. Through their role as supervisors of the household budget and of daily cash flow, women's roles as animal producers reinforce their control of the budget in weaving households.

Women's animal production also affects their relationship with male farming. Because animals consume fairly large amounts of corn, sometimes as much as the human members of the household, women are concerned with efficient household corn production. Farming can be expensive. If women are feeding their animals with corn from their own fields that have low yields despite the high cost of inputs, then the care of their animals will become cost-prohibitive. Thus, they may discourage their husbands from farming. When the government subsidizes corn prices, it is always cheaper to buy corn than to produce it in the household. The pleasure of having animals around and the security felt from their presence, however, seem to continue to be key factors in the large number of women who continued to raise animals in the twenty-first century.

OCCUPATIONAL DIVISIONS

In 1986 I counted 1,039 households in Teotitlán. A census I conducted revealed about 110 households (about 10.5 percent of the total population) were merchant households and a majority of the remaining 929 (about 68 percent) were weaving households. Updated numbers for the decreasing number of merchants in 2000 are given in chapter 5. Small farming sectors and service sectors also played an important role in the local economy in the 1980s and continue to do so in the twenty-first century. Most households and individuals had multiple occupational identities in the 1980s. The figures in table 5 represent the economic activity that was the greatest source of income (cash and in kind) in households from a random sample survey of 154 households conducted in 1986. Weaving is regarded as a primary household occupation. The other four occupations in table 5 are more often than not considered secondary occupations. They are usually carried out in conjunction with weaving activities. The expansion of the service sector in Teotitlán has been supported not only by growth in weaving production but by a high level of ritual consumption as well. This trend continued in the 1990s. Many of the occupations listed in table 5 receive primary support from the internal circulation of cash through purchase for rituals or through the reciprocal exchange system of guelaguetza.

A majority of merchants (about 95 percent) act as employers, either through piecework contracts with weavers, by hiring people to work in their workshops, or by commissioning complex pieces in advance in Teotitlán and from the surrounding communities of Santa Ana del Valle, Díaz Ordaz, and San Miguel del Valle. By the year 2003, a significant number of merchants, but not all, also acted as subcontractors for importers and entrepreneurs based in the United States (see Wood 1997, 2000a, 200b). Most of the work available in Teotitlán is through textile merchants either directly or indirectly, although by 2003 the cooperative sector described in detail in chapter 7 accounted for almost 15 percent of the weaving households. For many, however, even though they be-

TABLE 5 Percentage of household income yielded by five economic activities, Teotitlán, 1986

Weaving	69%
Merchant business	10
Farming (with weaving)	11
Service work (with weaving)	6
Work as musician (with weaving)	4

Source: Household survey conducted by Lynn Stephen, 1986.

longed to cooperatives, they still had to get some work through textile merchants.

Through the expansion of textile production and through remittances from migrants, Teotitecos have become avid consumers who support a wide range of other businesses. Building contractors, auto mechanics, beauticians, seamstresses, computer experts, restaurateurs, and others have found growing niches for their services and skills in Teotitlán. By 2003 a wide range of businesses existed in the community and many new kinds of products were offered in the indoor market and in a range of ever-expanding stores that are increasingly specialized.

HISTORIC MARKET LINKS TO OTHER COMMUNITIES

Like other indigenous areas in Mesoamerica, the Valley of Oaxaca is distinguished by its market organization. Jill Appel (1982) emphasizes that in pre-Hispanic times there was no mention of a major long-distance market in Oaxaca. She states (1982, 146) that the valley was not used for the production and distribution of goods to traders servicing the pan-Mesoamerican system, but instead specialized in the production of food as its major exchange item. While there is little ethnographic material on pre-Hispanic markets, both Fray Francisco de Burgoa (1934) and the *Relaciones geográficas* (Acuña 1984) mention early colonial markets. What is not known is how many of the colonial marketplaces recorded in ethnohistorical sources were already in operation before the arrival of Cortés. Documented colonial markets include Ayoquezco, Chichicapan, Chilateca, Cuilapan, Etla, Mitla, Ocotlán, and Santa Ana Zegache (Appel 1982, 147; Chance 1978).

Appel (1982, 147) notes that, while six of the eight markets are located in local administrative centers, the majority of administrative centers are not the sites of markets. This, she suggests, indicates a lack of isomorphism between commercial and administrative functions. Within this context, Teotitlán seems to have been one of the few administrative non-market towns that also had a strong emphasis on commerce.

In 1670 Francisco de Burgoa singled out Teotitlán and Coyotepec as being the most commercially oriented of the nonmarket towns in the Oaxaca Valley (Chance 1978, 110). Teotitlán had substantial numbers of traders who dealt in knives, machetes, scales, cloth, fish, and salt. These traders, known as *viajeros*, continued to operate from Teotitlán to the Isthmus and to the Sierra Juárez until the late 1950s.

According to John Chance (1978, 110), the largest indigenous markets in the late seventeenth century were located in San Juan Chilateca and the Villa de Etla. These markets and others mentioned above drew indigenous Oaxacans from many areas who came to trade cochineal, cotton mantles, and other products as well as Creole merchants from Oaxaca who sold Castilian goods. Many of the goods indigenous peoples produced for the markets were in response to Spanish demand. Undoubtedly, Teotitecos traded in most or all of these markets. Today they continue to go on a weekly basis to sell serapes, cacao, and occasionally other trade goods in Tlacolula, Ocotlán, Mitla, and occasionally in Etla. The history and operation of the cyclical markets of Oaxaca are best documented by Cook and Diskin (1976), who describe them as a basis for economic integration in the Oaxaca region.

Since the 1970s, Teotitlán has served as a primary conduit for weavings produced in several other nearby towns, Santa Ana del Valle, Díaz Ordaz, and San Miguel del Valle. Two of these towns were under its jurisdiction for much of the colonial era. Merchants in Teotitlán buy weavings from these communities on a regular basis and resell them throughout Mexico and the United States (see Cohen 1999, 43–54). U.S. importers and entrepreneurs have also created an international layer as they contract weavers through Teotitlán merchants and import the products to the United States.

THE HISTORICAL RELIGIOUS IMPORTANCE OF TEOTITLÁN IN OAXACA: X́IABETS, A SACRED PLACE

The geography around Teotitlán is still associated with gods and powers. The *Relación geográfica de Teutitlán* (Acuña 1984, 332–33) mentions a stark mountain that overshadows Teotitlán. This mountain, currently called *xiabets* (brother rock), is mentioned as a place where Teotitecos went to worship their idols and gods. The Zapotec name for Teotitlán, *xxía*, means "under the rock." According to local legend and several sources mentioned by Joseph Whitecotton (1977, 158, 312n), Teotitlán is associated with a sun god in the form of a bird that descended from the heavens to his temple. The location of the temple and the spot where he is supposed to have descended is on top of *xiabets*. Interestingly enough, on the map of Maquilxóchitl that accompanies the *Relación de Macuilsúchil y su partido* (Acuña 1984, map) there is a picture of a large sun located by Teotitlán, perhaps a reference to this sun god associated with *xiabets*.

The *Relación de Teutitlán* states that Teotitecos worshiped stone idols to which they offered their children in sacrifice. They "killed their children in rituals performed for the Devil" (Acuña 1984, 335). They also danced and drank in front of the gods. Teotitecos still return to the site of *xiabets* today. They make an annual pilgrimage on the third day of May to the site of the sun god, but instead celebrate a Catholic holiday, the Day of the Holy Cross. Many Catholic rituals celebrated in Teotitlán contain elements that seem to be tied to pre-Hispanic beliefs. For example, Holy Week is punctuated with small rites performed by household members to increase rainfall, provide more well water, and result in plentiful crops.

The sacred place of *xiabets* was probably visited by people not only from Teotitlán but from other communities as well. Burgoa (1934, 2:119) notes that Teotitlán had a shrine that attracted people from all parts of Oaxaca. In an article on Monte Albán's hinterland, Appel (1982, 144) states that the Oaxaca Valley kingdoms were interdependent religiously and economically as well as politically. She cites several communities with shrines that served regional rather than local functions. Teotitlán's regional importance was reinforced religiously as well as politically, by both indigenous and colonial institutions.

During the colonial era, Teotitlán served as an administrative center for the Dominicans. From the early 1600s until the mid-eighteenth century, it was a Dominican parish seat (Gerhard 1972, 191). During that time, the parish of Teotitlán included Tlacolula. Later, however, the parish seat was moved from Teotitlán to Tlacolula, where it was secularized after 1777 as a *distrito* or district. All parishes pertained to the bishopric of Antequera during the colonial period (Gerhard 1972, 191). Religious administration by parish missionaries and priests during the colonial era overlay local systems of ritual organization.

The largest rituals were mayordomías, organized in a hierarchy of importance. From the late nineteenth century until the 1960s, mayordomías were integrated with the civil cargo system of the community. This is described in detail in chapter 8. Today Teotitlán continues to be a major ritual center in the Oaxaca region, and its annual July festival of Nuestro Señor de la Preciosa Sangre (Our Lord of the Precious Blood) attracts people from many surrounding communities and brings back hundreds of Teotitecos who have migrated to the United States. The centrality of religious ceremonies in Teotitlán is described in further detail in chapters 8 and 9.

LANGUAGE, EDUCATION, AND LITERACY

Between 1980 and 2002 literacy and the ability to speak Spanish have increased significantly in the state of Oaxaca overall as well as in Teotitlán. In the 1980s, while certain sectors of the Teotitlán population (primarily men who migrated to the United States or textile merchants) had traveled and had had extensive contact with foreigners, not everyone had been able to participate in the wider world. Rates of monolingualism in Zapotec and illiteracy were significantly higher in the 1980s than in 2000, particularly for women. In 1980, 43.6 percent of women over the age of 15, or 517 individuals, were illiterate in the municipio of Teotitlán. About 25 percent of men over the age of 15, or 327 individuals, were illiterate in 1980. Overall, about 34 percent of the population over 15 were illiterate according to the 1980 national census (INEGI 1984, 1:523). According to the same census, about 21.3 percent of the population over 5 years of age were monolingual in Zapotec. No breakdown is given by gender, but these monolingual speakers were more likely to be women than men, as indicated in my survey of 1986 discussed in chapter 5 and as seen in the figures for monolingualism in 2000 broken down by gender. In the 1980 census, monolingualism in Zapotec was concentrated under the age of 10 and then more or less evenly distributed throughout the age continuum (INEGI 1984, 1:1319).

A very different picture emerges in the 2000 census with regard to illiteracy and monolingualism. All of the following figures are derived from the 2000 census (INEGI 2000). By the year 2000, the overall monolingualism rate had fallen to 6.19 percent or 290 individuals out of 4,726 over the age of 5. Most of these monolingual individuals, 243, were over the age of 50. One hundred ninety one of them were women over 50.

A reverse trend can be seen in the 2000 census: the youngest gen-

eration has practically no monolingual speakers of Zapotec and an increasing number of children who speak only Spanish. As recorded in the
2000 census, 516 individuals, or about 21 percent of the population over
5 years of age, did not speak Zapotec. Most of them were between the
ages of 5 and 14. A slight majority of children between 5 and 14 recorded
in the 2000 census are bilingual in Zapotec and Spanish, as is most of
the community. About 58 percent of boys between the ages of 5 and 14
speak Zapotec and Spanish (333 out of 579). About 56 percent of girls
speak both languages. Overall, almost 72 percent of the entire population over the age of 5 were bilingual in Zapotec and Spanish according
to the 2000 census. Almost 76 percent of men were bilingual and 67 percent of women. The difference in bilingual rates for men and women is
entirely due to a concentration of monolingual Zapotec speakers among
women over the age of 50.

Increasingly the population of Teotitlán has become bilingual in Zapotec and Spanish. Interviews carried out from 2001 to 2003 on the topic
of language use indicate that parents employ two strategies in teaching languages to their children. About half of the fifty or so parents I
interviewed stated that they were teaching their children both Zapotec
and Spanish. The other half said they were teaching their children only
Spanish at home and that the children learned Zapotec once they went
to school. This strategy will work if the parents who teach their children
both Zapotec and Spanish continue to do so. Discussions with young
people aged 6 through 18 indicated that more than half of them prefer to
speak Zapotec with their friends, with boys favoring Zapotec and girls
favoring Spanish when they move out of elementary school. It appears
that Zapotec is not fading in use, but is continuing to be learned in conjunction with Spanish. Ceremonial events, community assemblies, and
many conversations continue to be carried out in Zapotec. Persons who
have left the community and return more fluent in Spanish may resort to
it more often, but also continue to use Zapotec. Fluency in Zapotec is
still highly valued in the community among all age groups. Those who
don't speak Zapotec often express public regrets.

Like monolingualism rates, illiteracy rates have also declined significantly since 1980. By the year 2000, only 15.8 percent of the population
over the age of 14 in the municipio of Teotitlán were illiterate. Among
the 621 illiterate members of the community, a majority (72.6 percent,
or 451 individuals) were women. A majority of these women were over
the age of 44. When the population between 15 and 44 years of age is
analyzed, then the literacy rates for men and women are almost equal.

Ninety-eight percent of men between the ages of 19 and 44 are literate and 95 percent of women of the same ages are literate. This finding indicates a major change from significantly higher rates of illiteracy among women in the 1980s to almost equal rates for men and women by the year 2000. In addition, it suggests that almost everyone in the community who is under 45 years of age is literate.

As is to be expected, the significant increase in literacy rates and parity between men's and women's literacy is related to increased levels of education overall in the community, and particularly for girls. Teotitlán has two primary schools, a bilingual kindergarten and a secondary or junior high school. Children from seven other surrounding communities come daily to Teotitlán to attend the secondary school. According to the 1980 census, 55.5 percent of children between the ages of 5 and 14 attended elementary school, or 557 out of 1002. The highest percentage of children were attending school between the ages of 9 and 11 years (70.7 percent). Between the ages of 12 and 14, attendance had fallen to 42 percent (INEGI 1984, 2:61). Those under 12 years of age in 1986 were the first generation to attend school in significant numbers. Most were finishing the third and fourth grades, and more than 40 percent were completing their primary education. In the mid-1980s, almost equal numbers of boys and girls were attending school, although more boys were finishing the sixth grade (Secretaría de Programación y Presupuesto 1979–85).

In the 1980 census, 167 people, or 4.3 percent of the population, over the age of 10 were registered as having an education beyond primary school. Fourteen people had a high school–level or *preparatoria* education, fifteen had engaged in professional studies beyond the high school level, and six had attended a university (INEGI 1984, 2:254). There is no breakdown by gender given in the 1980 census in relation to education.

By the year 2000, almost 86 percent of children between the ages of 6 and 14 were attending elementary school (855 out of 997). It appears that many children are not entering school until they are 7 years of age. Between the ages of 8 and 14 almost all children—both boys and girls— were in school in the year 2000 (only ten children were not). Some had already moved on to middle school by ages 13 and 14. The figures from the 2000 census suggest that almost all boys and girls are attending primary school consistently and many are finishing.

Some are going beyond elementary school as well. In the year 2000, 27.8 percent of the population over the age of 12 had some kind of education beyond elementary school (1,191 out of 4,274 people) (INEGI 2000). Twenty-two percent of those with education beyond the primary level were women and 68 percent were men. Of those who had some kind of education beyond elementary school, 835 had completed or were completing secondary school, and 225 had completed instruction beyond this level. Of those 225 people who had completed something beyond a secondary-level education in the year 2000, 123 were men (55 percent of the total) and 102 were women (45 percent). Thus although only a small percentage of the population aged 15 and over (5.7 percent) were completing an education beyond the secondary level in the year 2000, women were not far behind men in that elite group.

Overall, the community experienced very significant changes in language use, literacy, and education from 1980 to 2000. Teotitlán has become predominantly bilingual in Zapotec and Spanish, almost everyone is attending and often finishing elementary school, and a small but significant group of people are engaging in professional studies at the high school level and beyond. During the summer of 2003 I counted at least eight people who were attending the university, and more were making plans to do so.

HEALTH SERVICES

Because of its status as a municipio center, Teotitlán has a government health clinic, and six or seven doctors are in practice there—more than in most indigenous communities in Oaxaca; several professional nurses provide health services as well. Women in Teotitlán also frequently go to a larger national health clinic in Tlacolula, particularly to give birth. A U.S.-supported clinic, Manos de Ayuda, also provides free health care and minor surgery in Tlacolula. Cataract removal is one of its specialties. Athough Teotitecos have better access to medical services than most people in rural Mexico, only about 7 percent of them have health insurance. The vast majority of people pay cash to doctors and nurses for each visit and to pharmacists for drugs. By 2003, there were four to five pharmacies in Teotitlán. Like people elsewhere in Mexico, Teotitecos often go directly to the pharmacy and ask the people who work there to supply them with medicine or to give them an injection. Medicinal herbs can also be purchased in the market and many of the older women and men in the community maintain knowledge of medicinal herbs and cures. They often treat illnesses with both a traditional cure and a drug from the pharmacy.

This abundance of Western medical assistance is a recent phenomenon. Before 1970, people in the community had to go to Oaxaca to receive medical treatment. Most treatment was given by local curers, who used a combination of divination and herbal remedies to cure diseases. Several midwives continue to practice in the community. In the 1990s, the largest emerging health problem was diabetes. Almost every extended family had a member diagnosed with diabetes, and awareness of the disease and how to control it was just beginning. Decreasing deaths and illness from diabetes was a top priority of the community's health committee in 2002. By 2003 the local health committee was also targeting the reproductive health of women as a priority.

POLITICAL TIES

Politically, Teotitlán served as a district seat for the colonial government of Oaxaca and as a municipio since Mexican independence. This important position has made the community a political as well as economic center for a long time. While Teotitecos have learned to wheel and deal with state and federal officials in order to get funds for local projects such as road construction, schools, and running water, they have also achieved a significant degree of political autonomy through their ability to fund a lot of their own public works projects. The community's economic prosperity since the early 1980s has enabled it to fund many public works projects without going to outside sources for assistance or using state funds in conjunction with local contributions. In addition, political parties have never run the local government. Community assemblies, structured by what are now called *usos y costumbres* (uses and customs), have become the venue for selecting community authorities. This is described in detail in chapter 10.

People in Teotitlán are proud of the face-lift they have given their community since the 1980s: they have renovated their church; constructed a new market, numerous basketball courts, and a community museum; installed drainage and water systems that deliver potable water to many houses; and paved the main streets. They are also aware of the benefits of using local funds to pay for part of these projects. Receiving funds from the government for public works projects is often seen as a payback for community loyalty to the political party in power. Until the year 2000, the PRI controlled much of Mexican politics, although opposition parties made significant inroads in Oaxaca beginning in the 1980s. While Teotitlán did not actively oppose the PRI until the 1988 presidential elections, when the PRD (Party of the Democratic Revolution) won a majority of votes there, community members are reluctant to do anything but cooperate with officials from any party when they come to monitor state and federal elections. As explained above, municipal elections do not involve the participation of political parties. In the presidential elections of 1988, the community voted overwhelmingly (80 percent) for Cuauhtémoc Cárdenas, identifying him as an alternative to the PRI and someone who understood "people like us" because he is part indigenous. In 1994 the PRD won by a slim margin in Teotitlán, but in the 2000 elections a majority voted for Vicente Fox of the PAN (National Action Party), as elsewhere in Mexico. The PAN has not taken root in Teotitlán, and most people view the 2000 vote as a rejection of the PRI, not a strong endorsement for the ideology and platform of the PAN.

Since the 1980s, people in Teotitlán have participated in a variety of political parties. While some individuals have become activists in political parties, the community still cherishes its political independence. Political parties have been discouraged from participating in municipal elections as well as from trying to take over local organizations (see chapter 7). The community's historical relation to Mexican political parties is described at length in chapters 8 and 10.

When state or federal government officials want to monitor community activities, Teotitecos react with strong indignation. They feel they have the right and ability to run all of their community affairs and greatly resent outside interference. Suggestions of state taxation of looms have been met with strong local protests, a continuation of a historical trend. While Teotitecos welcome tourists and foreign importers who come to purchase their wares, they do not tolerate behavior that they deem to be inappropriate and restrictive of the freedom of people in the community. Several North Americans have been forcibly expelled from the community, and outside merchants have frequently been reminded at town meetings that they need to behave themselves if they want to continue working in the community. The community has denied outsiders access to community assemblies and even threw out officials from the Oaxaca State Commission on Human Rights in 2000, when they were deemed to be interfering in community political processes (see Stephen 2005).

CONCLUSIONS

Through their exporting and migration experience, Teotitecos have
come to picture their world as reaching far beyond the borders of their
community. They know the daily exchange rate for the dollar and current political issues in the United States. They have a high awareness of
their community's relation to Mexican national politics, of international
trade agreements such as NAFTA, and of movements for indigenous autonomy both inside and outside of Mexico. Teotitecos are also informed
about immigration policy in the United States, the state of militarization on the U.S. border, the ever-increasing rates for crossing the U.S.-
Mexican line secretly with a coyote or human smuggler ($2,500 to $5,000
in 2003), and the minimum wage in California.

At the same time, the internal life of the community expressed in
weaving production, the aesthetic pleasure of producing textiles, the
rhythms of family life, ritual, farming, and cash-based and reciprocal
systems of exchange is also part of daily existence. Through their ongoing interactions, the women of Teotitlán navigate the intricate realities
of the theoretical abstractions we call neoliberalism, transnationalism,
gender, class, culture, ethnicity, and kinship.

CHAPTER 5

Contested Histories

Women, Men, and the Relations of

Production in Teotitlán, 1920–1950s

> In 1945 my son went away to the United States on a contract.
> More than two hundred men went away. When the men were gone,
> some women began to weave. They wove blankets with stripes. . . .
> Those who didn't weave had to make tortillas and sell them or else spin
> wool into yarn and sell it. It was very hard on the women. We had to
> do all the work, sometimes work in the fields, get firewood, haul the
> water in addition to doing all our other chores. —Amelia, age 85

Economic factors that influenced the weaving system of Teotitlán, particularly since the 1940s, include the initiation of the second United States bracero program in 1942; the completion of the Pan American Highway through Mexico in 1948; the loss of a regional market for handmade wool blankets to mechanized synthetic textiles made in Tlaxcala; and increasing tourism beginning in the 1950s. The first factor is examined here and the last three in chapter 6.

These economic changes were accompanied by political changes, beginning with the administration of Plutarco Elías Calles (1924–28), which resulted in the consolidation of the Mexican state and increased state intervention in local economies and political institutions. The Calles administration was marked by anticlericalism and the creation of national commissions such as those of agriculture, roads, and irrigation (Hamilton 1982, 79–80). Continued state intervention under Lázaro Cárdenas in the 1930s to support land reform, federal education programs, the establishment of ejido committees, detailed census and record keeping of agricultural and small industrial production, and the incorporation of labor unions and peasant groups into the government party all affected economic development in communities such as Teotitlán. In the 1940s, national policy aimed at integrating Mexico's indigenous population (at the time meaning those who spoke indigenous languages and lived in poverty in so-called Indian villages) with the larger society further influenced local economic and political relations, as did government development programs promoting craft production that began in the 1950s.

The programs aimed at increasing the state's presence in indigenous communities and in turn integrating such communities into the national polity can also be considered in respect to gender and ideology. Post-revolutionary state policy, documents, and programs promoted gender roles, including proper behavior and dress for boys and girls in school, appropriate categories of work for women (the most prominent being *quehaceres de la casa*, or housework), and a bureaucratization of munici-pios that effectively put all local government positions into male hands.[1] Women were eliminated from most formal occupational categories and were represented in few official organizations.

In general, the postrevolutionary Mexican state's programs for the development of indigenous populations provided an externally defined notion of "Indian" against which communities like Teotitlán constructed their own economic history and ethnic identity. Such histories and iden-tities were locally based and, like that of Teotitecos, involved staking a claim to a particular economic or political resource. Teotitecos focused primarily on laying claim to their textiles and to a secondary degree to other institutions locally associated with social reproduction, such as kin and compadrazgo networks, certain forms of ritual celebrations, the local language, and the idea of *respet*.

An analysis of oral histories and local correspondence suggests that Teotitecos most likely manipulated official occupational categories, in-cluding those that were gendered, in order to obscure the nature of their economy. Such efforts also worked to obscure merchants' activity as the community sought to escape taxation on weaving production and marketing. Most important, efforts to downplay the dynamics of local textile production are indicative of a desire on the part of Teotitecos, particularly those holding political power, to retain both real and sym-bolic ownership of the textiles they produced. Local officials indicated an awareness of the commercial potential of their product as early as the 1930s and were quite interested in protecting it from outside interfer-ence.

THE POSTREVOLUTIONARY MEXICAN STATE
AND THE DEVELOPMENT OF INDIGENOUS PEASANT
COMMUNITIES

Like many communities, Teotitlán had few collective or individual resources left by 1920. From 1915 until 1920, Teotitlán was caught between
the federal troops of Venustiano Carranza, stationed in Tlacolula, and
the rebel *serrano* mountain troops of General Isaac M. Ibarra. The serranos operated out of the Sierra Juárez, directly behind Teotitlán. For five
years, Teotitecos regularly provided cattle, pigs, corn, beans, tortillas,
and firewood to both sides. Transcripts of correspondence between Ca-
rrancista troops and the president of the municipio of Teotitlán show
increasing pressure on the community. In an October 18, 1918, memo the
municipio president apologizes to a captain in Tlacolula for his inability
to send more food: "I am sending you three head of cattle given volun-
tarily by the people of this town to help sustain the troops in this garri-
son. I hope you can forgive us for things that have occurred in this population during the last few years that do not make it possible for us to send
more things to help. The people in this town remain disposed to help
you as much as we can" (Archivo Municipal de Teotitlán del Valle 1918).

The people of Teotitlán also gave food to rebel troops based in Villa
Alta. Teotitlán provided a temporary market site about one mile outside
of town for serranos who could not market their goods in Tlacolula because they would be captured by government troops.

Supplying food for both sides during the Revolution may have saved
Teotitlán from armed confrontations, but the price of peace was tremendous pressure on the local economy and continued poverty into the 1920s.

While it is difficult to find documentation of occupational breakdowns
from 1910 until almost 1930, voting lists and the district censuses suggest that Teotiteco households engaged in both weaving and subsistence
farming. Because of the economic hardship felt in the community during
the Revolution and after, most elderly informants recalled that almost
everyone was impoverished and trade in woven blankets diminished significantly due to the danger of continued fighting at least until 1920.
Oral histories and census records do confirm, however, the existence of
a small group of merchant/traders who had more land than other households and who dominated economic relations through their indirect
control on labor through obligatory mayordomías (Dirección General

de Estadística 1906, 44–45; 1936, 275). These families were the primary source of employment and cash in the community, and few Teotitecos left to seek wage labor elsewhere until the 1930s. This small group of merchant/traders seems to have grown somewhat during the late 1920s as regional trade routes began to function again after the Revolution.

When Elías Plutarco Calles took office in 1926, the treadle loom weaving industry centered in Teotitlán appeared to be stabilizing. The number of merchants was on the upswing and trade was expanding into the Sierra Juárez and down to Chiapas by mule. This progress was occurring quietly in the south of Mexico without much discussion at the national level. The government had not made a detailed census count of people or production in Oaxaca since 1910. The period of the Mexican Revolution had left national information agencies in a shambles.

The decade of the 1920s in Mexico was marked by the centralization of the state and by the creation of institutional machinery set up for government intervention in the economy (Hamilton 1982, 79). By the time Calles took office, institutions such as the National Roads Commission, the National Agrarian Commission, the National Irrigation Commission, and the Agricultural Credit Bank had already been established. Calles's tenure is remembered most clearly for its rabid anticlericalism, the Cristero Rebellion, and his interpretation of the 1917 constitution, which gave legitimacy to the concept of an interventionist, centralized state (Hamilton 1982, 109).

While building its political power from a fundamentally different constituency, particularly the working class and peasants, the administration of Lázaro Cárdenas upheld the notion of an active interventionist state, controlling and directing the economy down to the local level. The agrarian reform program, in which Cárdenas redistributed more land than all of his predecessors combined, inserted the state into all areas of the local economy, including agricultural credit and ejido decision-making groups. The theme of the six-year plan outlined in 1933, which was the blueprint for Cárdenas's time in office, emphasized integration. It gave the state wide leeway in directing and redirecting society, focusing on physical integration through the construction of roads and communication links as well as ideological and cultural integration through the dissemination of so-called socialist education. Building on the school program begun by Calles, Cárdenas's vision of socialist education was oriented toward collective work and achievement, replacing the fanaticism and superstition generated by clerical influence (Hamilton 1982,

136). Under Cárdenas the number of schools and teachers multiplied. His administration also consolidated the state's indirect hold on productive land.

By the end of 1940, 47.4 percent of the total cultivated land in Mexico was held in ejidos linked to the state (Hamilton 1982, 175). Many peasants were also tied into the official party through loans and membership in the Coordinadora Nacional de Campesinos, or CNC (National Peasant Confederation). Communities such as Teotitlán that did not receive ejido land remained at more distance from institutions such as the CNC that tied peasants directly to the state. The biggest influence on the community was probably the establishment of a more extensive education program with emphasis on national identity. This education in national identity was to continue as the community became one of thousands targeted by promoters of indigenous integration in the 1940s. Because of the particular nature of the weavings produced in Teotitlán and surrounding communities, the integrationist policies of the National Indian Institute and later programs to promote so-called Indian crafts had a greater impact on Teotitlán than the agrarian reform policies of the Cárdenas administration.

INDIGENISMO AND THE CREATION OF THE OFFICIAL MEXICAN INDIAN

While the Inter-American Indianist Congress held in Pátzcuaro, Michoacán, in 1940 is often viewed as the initiation of indigenist policy in Latin America, Mexico had special programs aimed at educating its indigenous population before the 1940 congress. In the early 1920s, a Department of Education and Culture for the Indian Race was set up in the Secretariat of Public Education. In 1927, the Casa del Estudiante Indígena announced its objective: to "eliminate the evolutionary distance that separates the Indians from the present epoch, transforming their mentality, tendencies and customs . . . to incorporate them within the Mexican community" (Adams 1967, 477). In 1936 the Autonomous Department of Indian Affairs was established, followed the next year by the Department of Indian Education. These programs were to provide all students with agricultural and technical training that would lead to success in their communities. While these educational programs operated in some areas of Mexico, it was not until the 1940s, after the first Inter-American Indianist meeting, that a systematic political, economic, and social policy was created for Mexico's more than fifty ethnic groups. The creation of the Instituto Nacional Indígena, or INI (National Indian Institute), marked the beginning of extensive programs carried out through local centers with the general purpose of nationalizing the Indian.

As Cárdenas was winding up his six-year term, the Inter-American Indianist Congress held in Pátzcuaro in 1940 articulated the goal of "the integration of the Indian into national society, with all of his cultural trappings, giving him the instruments of civilization necessary for his articulation within modern society" (Aguirre Beltrán 1975, 27). One of the questions that preoccupied those who attended the congress was how to identify Indians clearly so that social and economic programs could be created to integrate them into national society. To aid in this identification process, material indicators were chosen to distinguish Indians from non-Indians in the Mexican population. While anthropologists who attended the Pátzcuaro congress felt that cultural characteristics needed to be considered as well, material characteristics were the initial focus of the government in identifying just who Mexico's Indians were.

The 1940 census reflected a contradictory state policy of development that was supposed simultaneously to allow for the continuation of indigenous culture and yet integrate indigenous communities into modern society, materially and ideologically.

Beginning with the program plan of the 1940 First Inter-American Indianist Congress, the government also took an interest in *artes populares indígenas* (indigenous folk arts). The first program plan, later adopted by the INI, called for the protection of indigenous arts, the organization of expositions, and national competitions (Marroquín 1977, 39–40). The government's interest in promoting indigenous arts became an important part of its contradictory program of protecting and integrating indigenous peoples into the wider society. Such programs not only attempted to create new markets for crafts but also helped the state create ethnic identities for its Indians. Since the 1950s, when the Mexican government sought to encourage tourism as a way of generating foreign exchange, indigenous ethnic groups have been encouraged to maintain and reproduce certain outwardly picturesque characteristics — in particular, dress, ritual, and crafts — which make them identifiable as Indians to tourists (see S. Cook 1984a; García Canclini 1982; Graburn 1982). Ultimately, state creation of Indian identities also influenced the construction of local ethnic identities and served as a foil against which communities such as Teotitlán created a self-determined identity not controlled by the state. An important part of creating such an identity as a subtle form of resistance involves obscuring and limiting outside access to some areas of social, economic, and political organization. In looking at this process we shall see that gender was an important element and is one of the areas in which the state had little understanding of cultural and economic relations.

THE CREATION OF GENDERED INDIGENOUS ECONOMIC HISTORY BY THE STATE

The first six official population censuses of Mexico, beginning in 1895, provide evidence of how ethnic and gendered occupational categories were constructed over a fifty-year period by the Department of General Statistics. The discussion here focuses on the census categories and the number of men and women reported in each. Not all categories are given, and the statistical significance of the numbers is not considered because the accuracy of census figures cannot be assumed.

The census of 1895, which was reported at the level of the district, put all women in the district of Tlacolula (to which Teotitlán belongs) into occupational categories, reporting 1,129 female weavers and 1,179 male weavers. We can assume that most of these people were located in Teotitlán del Valle and Díaz Ordaz, with a few in Santa Ana and Mitla. According to the administrative memoranda of the governor of Oaxaca in 1900, Teotitlán reported 150 weaving households, which produced 10,000 pieces per year; Díaz Ordaz reported 100 weaving households producing 8,000 pieces; Mitla reported 50 households producing 4,000 pieces; and Santa Ana reported 40 households producing 2,000 pieces (Clements 1988b). Table 6 shows highest economic participation by men and women based on the 1895 occupational census for the district of Tlacolula. The majority of women were registered within specific occupational categories, the greatest numbers as *molenderas* (corn grinders) and then as *tejedoras* (weavers). The census does not distinguish between backstrap loom weaving, done almost exclusively by women, and treadle loom weaving, dominated by men. The classification of women as corn grinders under the subheading of *industria de alimentación* (food industry) similarly provides them with an occupational identity.

In 1900, when occupational breakdowns were given by municipio in the population census, women almost dropped out as weavers. For the district of Tlacolula, only 132 women were reported as weavers compared

TABLE 6 Number of male and female workers in eight occupational categories, District of Tlacolula, census of 1895

	Male	Female	Total
Agriculturalists	14,177	—	14,177
Merchants	52	21	73
Weavers	1,179	1,129	2,308
Seamstresses	—	276	276
Domestic workers	43	72	115
Washers	—	82	82
Lard producers	93	—	93
Corn grinders	—	7,569	7,569

Source: Dirección General de Estadística 1897–99, 44.

with 1,824 men. In Teotitlán only 4 women were classified as weavers in the 1900 census.

Reporting at the level of the municipio in the 1900 census was correlated with the disappearance of significant numbers of women weavers, but most men in the community were reported as weavers rather than farmers. There is nothing in the historical record to indicate that women stopped weaving on backstrap and treadle looms at this time. Most likely the four women who were reported as weavers were single heads of household who wove on treadle looms. Women weavers who were not single heads of households do not appear to have been reported to census officials. It is unclear why so many men would have reported themselves as weavers. The number is unusually high for the period.

The 1910 census was aggregated by district only and, like the 1920 census, may indicate the general bureaucratic disarray of Mexico between 1910 and the early 1920s. In the 1910 census for Tlacolula, the number of women reported as weavers rose to 902. Women do not appear as agriculturists and begin to appear in larger numbers in the category *quehaceres domésticos* (domestic chores). However, the majority are still registered with particular occupations.

The national census of 1921 reports occupations only for the country as a whole, indicating that the data were probably in serious disarray after the Mexican Revolution. What is significant about this census, however, is that the majority of women appear in the category of *queha-*

TABLE 7 Most significant gendered occupational categories
in 1900 census, Teotitlán del Valle

	Men	Women	Total
Independent agriculturalists	9		9
Landless laborers	43		43
Muleteers/traders	18		18
Seamstresses		2	2
Corn grinders		842	842
Domestic laborers		60	60
Firewood gatherers	96		96
Weavers	565	4	569

Source: Dirección General de Estadística 1906, 42–67.

TABLE 8 Gendered occupational categories for 1910 census,
district of Tlacolula

	Men	Women	Total
Independent agriculturalists	9,116	27	9,143
Landless laborers	2,309	55	2,364
Weavers	1,210	902	2,112
Washerwomen		135	135
Seamstresses		530	530
Merchants	80	39	119
Door-to-door salespeople	140	18	158
Domestic workers		3,228	3,228
Maids and servants	104	165	269
Corn grinders		9,754	9,754

Source: Dirección General de Estadística 1918, 925–929.

TABLE 9 Gendered occupational categories in 1921 national census

	Men	Women	Total
Agriculturalists	623,642	6,819	630,461
Gañanes[a] (migrant labor)	2,750,075	21,463	2,771,538
Cotton and wool weavers	10,959	2,256	13,215
Palm weavers	4,634	2,415	7,049
Clothing makers/designers		70,563	70,563
Muleteers	20,046	43	20,089
Merchants	202,351	42,398	244,749
Door-to-door salespeople	7,050	2,862	9,912
Domestic workers		4,495,959	4,495,959
Maids, cooks, servants	35,803	153,889	189,692

Source: Departamento de la Estadística Nacional 1925–28,82–98.
[a] The census did not include the category of *peones* or *jornaleros*.

ceres de la casa (housework), subheaded as *señoras y señoritas ocupadas en su casa* (married and unmarried women occupied in their homes).

While it is not known how many women in the district of Tlacolula were included in this category, it is apparent that women dropped out of most occupations under which they were previously listed, including molenderas and tejedoras.

As seen in tables 8 and 9, the total number of women weavers in Mexico in 1921 was only double that reported for the single district of Tlacolula in 1895. Comparative data aggregated nationally by gender and occupation are not available for 1910 or 1930. While weaving technology was beginning to change in this period and backstrap loom weaving of cotton for commercial exchange was decreasing due to mechanization of textile production (Young 1978), local records and oral histories indicate that women continued to weave in many areas for self-consumption and for exchange. They did not simply stop weaving, but were no longer counted as weavers. The overall trend indicated by the 1921 national census was reinforced in local occupational censuses in 1930 and 1940: women were eliminated from many occupational categories, and their labor was subsumed in the categories of housework and nonproductive occupations.

TABLE 10 Gendered occupational categories for Teotitlán del Valle, 1930 and 1940 censuses

	1930			1940		
	Men	Women	Total	Men	Women	Total
Agriculturalists (may employ others)	578		578	175		175
Workers, day laborers				50		50
Work alone, don't employ other laborers				119		119
Small industry weavers	214	2	216	567	19	586
Merchants	6		6	26	2	28
Domestic workers	1	825	826	5	870	875
Servants				5	5	10

Source: Dirección General de Estadística 1946, 567.

The 1940 census for Teotitlán also indicates that large numbers of men moved from agriculture into weaving. The number seems disproportionately high, compared to earlier figures for the 1920s and later ones for 1950 and 1960. The census also records the emergence of twenty-two new merchant households in 1940 as well, a figure that seems more consistent with the gradually increasing number of merchant households. Overall, it appears that there may have been some motivation in 1940 for people to appear as weavers and merchants instead of as farmers.

THE INDIGENOUS WOMAN AS REFLECTED IN THE 1920 AND 1940 CENSUSES

National census documents from 1920, 1930, 1940, and after used gender and ethnicity as important categories of analysis, projecting statistical portraits of indigenous women that became the object of policies aimed at integrating the many ethnic groups of Mexico into national society by eliminating their basis for autonomy. After the Revolution, the Department of National Statistics demonstrated a strong concern

TABLE 11 Literacy rates by gender and "race," State of Oaxaca, 1920

	Women			Men		
	"Indige-nous"	"Mixed race"	"White"	"Indige-nous"	"Mixed race"	"White"
Can read or write	7%	15%	42%	18%	32%	53%

Source: Departamento de la Estadística Nacional 1925–28, 46.

with distinguishing Indians from the rest of the population. In the 1920 census, for example, ethnic categories were used to discriminate literacy rates among the population. Table 11 shows figures for the state of Oaxaca. Indigenous women have the lowest literacy rate among the gendered ethnic groups included in the 1920 census. In 1940, in accordance with the government's endorsement of the 1940 Inter-American Indianist Congress, census officials removed overt references to ethnicity. Instead, ethnic categories were reconstituted as cultural categories. In the 1940 census being "Indian" was correlated with speaking an Indian language; sleeping on the floor or using a *petate* (mat) or hammock; not wearing shoes of "Spanish" type; and eating tortillas rather than bread.

When the data aggregated in these categories are looked at in terms of gender, a clear picture of the Indian woman emerges. For example, women from Teotitlán del Valle, Oaxaca, were pictured in the 1940 census as primarily monolingual in Zapotec (74 percent) with a low literacy rate (6.57 percent could read and write); 98 percent of those who spoke Zapotec were noted to have gone barefoot. Despite the absurdity of the cultural categories used to measure Indian identity among Mexico's indigenous population in 1940, such categories did create a national picture of indigenous women as existing on the margins of civilization — poor, barefoot, monolingual, illiterate, sleeping on the floor, and eating tortillas. While this characterization was originally the baseline from which the indigenous population was to be pushed toward modernity, in the packaging of Indian identity for sale to tourists, such marginality was converted into tradition and exoticism.

COMMUNITY REACTION TO THE BUREAUCRATIZATION
OF THE MEXICAN STATE

In Teotitlán, detailed questionnaires began to come to the municipio during the Calles administration as the state moved to document agricultural and industrial production with an eye toward increasing production. They continued during the Cárdenas administration in the 1930s. An examination of Teotitlán community correspondence with various state offices during the 1930s reveals that municipio officials reluctantly responded to inquiries regarding the doings of local government and the specifics of economic production (Archivo Municipal de Teotitlán del Valle 1930–39). The town is probably not atypical. After the Revolution, many indigenous communities tried to defend what little autonomy they might have gained as a result of land redistribution and broken bureaucratic links to the federal government, which fell apart during the Revolution.

Instead of responding straightforwardly to official inquiries regarding their economy, Teotiteco officials avoided reporting the exact nature of weaving production. In this process they continued to report themselves as both agriculturists and weavers and not to include specific information on the economic activities of women and children or the quantity of textiles produced in the community. By evading official inquiries about weaving production in the 1930s and 1940s and later efforts by the state to organize craft cooperatives in their community, Teotitecos avoided having the state serve as an intermediary for their weaving products. This historical precedent became even more important in the late 1970s and 1980s as merchants from Teotitlán began to negotiate directly with United States importers, cutting out both Mexican middlemen and state officials from agencies such as the Fondo Nacional de Artesanía (FONART) from their export transactions. At a time when state bureaucrats and Mexican handicraft entrepreneurs began to claim popular folk arts as the common heritage of Mexico, people in Teotitlán asserted their claim as a long-standing community of Zapotec weavers.

In their correspondence with state officials during the 1930s, municipio authorities carefully reproduced dominant ideas regarding poor, humble Indians struggling to survive, engaging in what might be called counter-hegemonic activity to protect their own interests. Merchant activities were deemphasized and poverty was projected as the norm. While most of the community was poor, there were at least six to eight wealthy mer-

chant/landowner households whose activities were not recognized—
nor was the business potential of weaving production. A response from
the mayor of Teotitlán to the head of national statistics in 1932 is representative of such letters:[2]

> 1. The majority of the people in this town have looms that they use to
> make the beautiful blankets that have brought significant fame to our state
> of Oaxaca, but they do not have enough resources to work daily. They must
> also work as wage laborers and during the agricultural seasons they work
> as subsistence agriculturists in order to grow grain for their own consump-
> tion.
> 2. Commerce is very dead in our community because of a lack of money.
> Many have stopped working and although names can't be provided, I can
> say that there are no houses here that could be considered factories.[3]
> 3. The only people who have a regular income are those *regatones* [mer-
> chants] who resell their product in Oaxaca.
> 4. We estimate the total income generated from production to be about
> 50 pesos per month from different-sized products. (Archivo Municipal de
> Teotitlán del Valle 1932)

This answer to an official inquiry regarding the number of weavers and
merchants, presence of factories, and income from farming and weaving suggests a muted version of the reality of weaving production at the
time—certainly of merchant activities. While this response guarded the
exact nature of their production and referred only vaguely to a few merchants operating in Oaxaca, other correspondence from the same decade
indicates that the community had an avid interest in merchant activity
and in improving local infrastructure.

For example, a letter written by Teotiteco authorities in 1931 in response to an inquiry from the undersecretary of industry, commerce,
and labor highlights the lack of capital resources and infrastructure in
conjunction with the beauty of Zapotec textiles. The letter ends by turning a request for production information into a petition for a post office:

> Let me inform you that the merchants, agriculturists, and producers here
> all work with very scarce capital as you will see below: the merchant here
> who has the largest general store would make no more than 100 pesos, the
> agriculturist with the largest piece of land plants 3 hectares. In the notable
> industry of wool blankets, which is undertaken here in this town, all of
> the inhabitants know how to weave blankets of distinct designs such as the
> Aztec calendar, idols, and different animals, in fast colors. All the people

work for themselves, having in their house up to two simple looms and up to one arroba [25 pounds] of wool with a current value of 10 pesos. Nevertheless, despite the fact that this town is very old and large with four thousand industrious inhabitants, the government has not yet established a post office here, something that would help this town prosper. Because we have no post office here, our industry cannot be spread to other areas of the Mexican Republic.

If you could help us with the creation of the post office that we are so-liciting, we shall remain very grateful. (Archivo Municipal de Teotitlán del Valle 1931a)

On August 31, the undersecretary of industry, commerce, and labor wrote back with his recommendation for the establishment of a post office in Teotitlán (Archivo Municipal de Teotitlán del Valle 1931b).

The community's effort to defend its economic interests is perhaps best reflected in a letter sent to President Cárdenas in 1938 in which the signatories asked the president to intervene to prevent the Japanese from fabricating imitations of their blankets. The very fact that Teotitecos were aware of the dynamics of international trade and marketing indi-cates the foresight with which they protected their interests. The adop-tion and use by Teotiteco authorities of phrases such as "designs and idols that signify the history of Mitla and Monte Albán" suggests that the categories used to promote both Indianness and Indian crafts could be adopted and used to defend local economic interest.[4] The words *arte-sanía, cultura, historia, costumbre*, and others that are now a part of the every-day Teotiteco Zapotec vocabulary were used in municipio documents as early as the 1930s and perhaps before, again indicating an awareness on the part of officials about what these terms mean and how to use them. The community's repeated encounters with the state in the 1930s and be-fore are firmly entrenched in contemporary spoken Zapotec. The letter regarding the threat of the Japanese reads as follows:

The native citizens of Teotitlán del Valle, Tlacolula, State of Oaxaca, state for you that we have become aware of the fact that in the country of Japan they are producing Mexican articles with the intent of passing them off as coming from Mexico. Among these articles . . . are found those from the small industry of Oaxaca blankets, adorned with designs and idols that sig-nify the history of Mitla and Monte Albán and Zapotec and Toltec figures. We understand for certain that, among other things, Japan is producing imitations of the Oaxacan blanket, an article to which we dedicate ourselves as humble people working on simple home looms. This news has caused us

great alarm because, at the moment, we are in a precarious economic situation. It has therefore occurred to us to request that you dictate measures
that will protect our small weaving industry here in Oaxaca, also international measures that will take care of this phenomenon that has come to
our notice. . . . (Archivo Municipal de Teotitlán del Valle 1938)

Teotitecos clearly saw the state as necessary for protecting their interests at the national and international levels, yet also resisted providing
the specific information on production requested by the Office of National Statistics. While the state was busy measuring and categorizing
the indigenous population of the country, indigenous people such as the
Teotitlán Zapotecs were also busy building their own locally based ethnic identities and staking specific claims in terms of these identities. The
voices reflected in the Teotitlán archives that make continued claims on
Zapotec weavings as cultural symbols are reworking the state's strategy
of adopting the Indian as part of national culture (García Canclini 1982;
Marroquín 1977; Novelo 1976, 1988). The officials who penned the community's responses to government inquiries appear to have understood
the emerging construction of the Indian and the way it was being integrated with government policy. The voices of Teotitecos who spoke of
conditions in the 1930s and 1940s present a more complicated picture of
Teotiteco identity, one that is riddled with contradictions and questions.

UNOFFICIAL VOICES: GENDER AND
CLASS RELATIONS, 1930–1940

When elderly people in Teotitlán recall the past, they often begin with a
description of what it used to be like to farm in the mountains surrounding the community. They point north to the Sierra Juárez stretching behind the town and recall large beans and squash carefully cultivated with
hoes in fields where oxen could not plow. These are communal lands.

Today communal land is characterized by faint terraces that extend up
into the mountains. These communal terraces remain barren, no longer
used by local farmers. Most farming is done on privately held land located on the flattest parts of the landscape. Farmers recall that all of the
hillside terraces were planted until the 1940s:

Before people started going to the United States, a lot of people would go
up to the mountain and plant together. About ten to fifteen people would
get together and build a big corral to protect the land from cows. Each of

them would farm a little piece inside the corral, an eighth or a quarter of a hectare. We would work together planting and maintaining the corrals without pay. For example, if the fence was broken in one place, everyone would get together and fix it. The problem after the *bracería* [migration program] was that no one was around to help, so people just stopped planting in the mountains. (Antonio, age 80)

As is the case today, everyone in the community had a right to use communal land. Because there were few sources of income until migration began and the export market opened up, most households devoted significant amounts of time to farming, weaving very little during the spring planting and fall harvesting seasons.

The reciprocal labor institution of guelaguetza also played an important part in the farming of communal land. When elderly people are questioned about the concept, both men and women recall not only ceremonially based guelaguetza, but also agricultural guelaguetza associated primarily with the working of communal land. In contrast to communal lands, small private holdings were worked by household labor pools, including men, women, and children as well as guelaguetza labor. Larger plots owned by merchants in Teotitlán were worked by local farmers paying off loans they had taken out in order to pay their mayordomía expenses. This arrangement came to an end in 1930, when obligatory mayordomías ended. Later larger merchant-owned plots were worked by a combination of wage labor and agricultural guelaguetza labor.

Teotitecos identified three kinds of guelaguetza connected to agriculture: *xɛlgɛz daχn*—labor exchange for corral construction, planting, weeding, and harvesting on communal land in the mountains; *xɛlgɛz (h)lats(v)*—labor exchange for planting, weeding, and harvesting on flat land, mostly privately held; and *xɛlgɛz xedjaχ*—labor exchange to gather firewood and cook communal meals for wood gatherers (usually for ceremonial purposes).

Guelaguetza labor was an institution that allowed the poor to help each other outside of the exploitative framework of debt peonage. In the minds of Teotitecos, this labor was of primary importance in subsistence-level production and ceremonial events, not to mention weaving production, which later became the mainstay of the local economy. The integration of guelaguetza labor with wage labor under commercial capitalism became an important factor in the successful transition of production for a regional use market to an export market in the 1970s.

The division of guelaguetza labor for farming and wood gathering was gendered, but male and female informants differed in their descriptions of what men and women actually did. Elderly men stated that women participated in guelaguetza only for ceremonial purposes, where their roles were to prepare large communal meals. Women stated that in addition to preparing meals they participated in reciprocal labor exchanges for planting, weeding, and harvesting, working in the field alongside men.[5] Today women continue to be active during weeding and harvesting seasons, pitching in alongside men as needed. Helen Clements (1988a, 256) notes that 29 percent of the women surveyed in the neighboring community of San Miguel participated in planting and 31 percent in weeding.

In the 1920s, after the Mexican Revolution, privately owned land in Teotitlán was held in greater concentration than it is now. At this time, working as a *jornalero* (day laborer) for others was the primary source of cash income for many households (Archivo Municipal de Teotitlán del Valle 1868, 1890, 1900, 1920). In addition, many people ended up working as indentured laborers for local merchants after going completely broke from serving as mayordomos. Elderly informants vividly recalled the differences between the few rich and the majority poor. "The poor people who were appointed to be mayordomos would sell themselves to the rich people to work in their fields and in their houses," recalled María, age 80. "And even without being a mayordomo, it was the only way to earn money. I earned fifty centavos a month when I was young working in people's houses making tortillas and carding and spinning their wool. I kept doing this work even after I got married. There was no other way to pay for things."

> My parents were very poor, like a lot of people's. When I was a child I worked for other people taking care of their animals. I remember I had only one set of clothing. Those of us who worked as children herding other people's cows and goats would wash our clothes by the river. We had only one pair of pants and one shirt so we would wait for them to dry by the river. The women had only one complete outfit as well. . . . You know there were a lot more poor people when things were cheap, and now when things are expensive there are a lot more rich people. Before the rich people had land and oxen, and sometimes a little bit of money, but not like the money people have now. You could tell the rich by what they wore. The merchants, four or five of them, had a lot of land. The men wore leather shoes and the rich women wore *biuχ* [hand-loomed fine wool cloth dyed with cochineal]. (Pedro, age 84)

Elderly informants concurred that a small group of merchant/traders had a corner on the land market in the 1920s and, particularly with the help of forced ceremonial sponsorships, succeeded in buying up land quite cheaply as people sold it in desperation to meet the heavy financial demands of mayordomía sponsorship. "There were about six families who were merchants and owned oxen. They sold blankets in Oaxaca and were acquiring land for very little money. As I remember there were three sets of brothers from three families who did most of the commercial selling and were absorbing a lot of land. Everyone else worked communal lands," recalled Tomás, age 74.

It is unclear what percentage of the population engaged in indentured servitude in the houses and fields of the community elite. What remains strongly etched in the minds of elderly Teotitecos is the contrast between the majority poor and the few rich families. Wealth differences were clear, but class differences in the community were less obvious than they are today; the appropriation of surplus labor occurred not through the buying and selling of labor but through merchant/landholding households' controlling its product by receiving labor in return for loans made to poor mayordomos and their families. Because the small group of merchant/traders in Teotitlán supported the political authority of ritual elders who appointed people to be mayordomos, their hold on labor was effectively sanctioned by local authorities. As Gerald Sider has noted (1986, 34–35), merchant capital does not exploit labor directly at the point of production, but exploits it indirectly through exchange and often through community-controlled and locally sanctioned institutions—in this case obligatory mayordomía. It was not until the state intervened to discourage mayordomías and other sources of cash became available to people in Teotitlán that the hold of local merchants over the majority of the population was loosened. Later, under conditions of commercial capitalism, the rich directly appropriated labor by purchasing it, but the class system also became more complex, with more middle levels between the majority poor and the few rich.

This change is somewhat consistent with the distinction Marx made between the formal and the real subsumption of labor to capital. Under formal subsumption of labor, as under the conditions of merchant capitalism in Teotitlán, existing labor and production processes end up under the control of capital, but the production process itself is not changed (Bennholdt-Thomsen 1980, 108). The real and more direct subsumption of labor to capital involves the production of relative surplus value through direct relations between wage-laboring producers and petty capitalists, as in the case of pieceworkers working for large merchants. However, because of the ever-present mediating factors of kinship, compadrazgo, and the types of reciprocal exchanges attached to their relationships, labor-capital relationships in Teotitlán never become completely visible as the "real subsumption" described by Marx (1881/1967) in "Results of the Direct Processes of Production." Instead, the language of kinship and patterns of family cooperation/exploitation remain important in the formation of petty capital. And the heavy ceremonial obligations undertaken by all Teotitecos, although seemingly less by merchant households, also can act as a brake on capital formation in some instances.

PRODUCTION AND DISTRIBUTION FOR REGIONAL MARKETS UNTIL 1960

To understand the international, national, and local dynamics of commercialized Zapotec weaving production, we must first trace the history of weaving production through the centuries to the 1960s. The weaving complex centered on Teotitlán del Valle historically included the neighboring communities of Díaz Ordaz (Santo Domingo), Santa Ana del Valle, and to a limited degree Maquilxóchitl. These communities wove cotton for local consumption as well as for tribute payments before the arrival of the Spaniards. The first documented evidence of weaving in Teotitlán is found in the *Relaciones geográficas*, which states that Teotitlán paid tribute in cotton mantles to Zaachila (Acuña 1984, 335). This cotton cloth was woven on backstrap looms. It is also probable that Teotitecos were paying tribute to the Aztecs, directly or indirectly, after Teotitlán was incorporated into the Aztec province of Coyolapan (Barlow 1949, map).

According to Oaxaca oral history, wool was introduced to Teotitlán by the first bishop of Oaxaca sometime between 1535 and 1555. In a move that changed the community's future, Bishop López de Zarate not only gave the Teotitecos sheep but provided them with their first stand-up treadle looms as well. He taught them how to card and spin the wool and to work the large treadle looms. By the mid–seventeenth century, the woolen blanket industry inspired by López de Zarate was probably well under way. Fray Francisco de Burgoa mentions the weaving of woolen blankets and serapes as an important economic activity in Teotitlán as well as in Santo Domingo del Valle (now Díaz Ordaz), Mitla, Tlacolula, and Maquilxóchitl (Chance 1978, 110).

Throughout the colonial period and beyond, Teotitlán, Santa Ana, Díaz Ordaz, and Maquilxóchitl continued to weave in conjunction with subsistence farming. Censuses of Teotitlán and Santa Ana from the 1850s through the 1890s indicate the steady presence of both male and female weavers (Clements 1988b; Stephen 1987a). At the turn of the twentieth century and through the Mexican Revolution, the communities of Teotitlán, Santa Ana, and Díaz Ordaz continued to weave, each specializing in a particular type of blanket.[6]

Díaz Ordaz artisans produced a third-class blanket called a *pelusa*, which is a mixture of animal hair and cotton (Vargas-Barón 1968, 46). This cheaper product occupied an important niche in local markets until the 1930s. Santa Ana artisans specialized in production of second-class wool blankets with little or no design, while Teotitecos wove first-class woolen blankets with complex designs.

Tracing changes in the development of the Oaxaca Valley weaving complex of Díaz Ordaz, Santa Ana, and Teotitlán, Emily Vargas-Barón (1968) describes how the regional market for weavings expanded during the 1940s and was then replaced by a national and international market for high-quality weavings in the 1950s. As a result of this change, weaving activities have greatly declined in Díaz Ordaz while they have increased in Santa Ana and Teotitlán. As people in Díaz Ordaz abandoned weaving, they began to make improvements in cultivation techniques. The opposite happened in Teotitlán and Santa Ana, where increased weaving activity displaced subsistence agriculture. Vargas-Barón also points out that high-quality land in Díaz Ordaz and a superior irrigation system make farming more attractive there than in Teotitlán or Santa Ana.

Until 1890, the network for sales distribution of blankets from Díaz Ordaz, Santa Ana, and Teotitlán extended only to the markets of Oaxaca and Tlacolula. From 1890 to 1920, this network expanded locally to include other valley markets in the area such as Ocotlán, Etla, and Miahuatlán. The years 1920 to 1950 were a period of significant growth in the industry, particularly in relation to the production of first-class blankets (Vargas-Barón 1968, 186). The peak in demand for pelusa blankets was from 1910 to 1930, according to Vargas-Barón. In the 1930s, a steady decline occurred in the number of weavers from Díaz Ordaz; pelusa production was extinguished in the late 1940s as factory-produced blankets from Puebla and Tlaxcala arrived in Oaxaca via the Pan American Highway.

Teotitlán and Santa Ana marketed first- and second-class woolen blankets to the Sierra Juárez and to Chiapas from 1920 until 1950. The booming market of Tlacolula was a center for salesmen and merchants who traveled by mule. About twelve to fifteen viajeros from Teotitlán continued to sell in Chiapas, the Isthmus of Tehuantepec, and the Sierra Juárez until the 1950s. Teotitecos also became part of the market for folk art beginning in the 1920s. It seems that weavers in the community were probably engaged in several kinds of markets at the same time during the years from 1920 to 1950. They wove for regional markets but also began producing for artists, intellectuals, travelers, and eventually tourists, who began to collect folk art in the late 1920s and 1930s. There is evidence that they were selling to tourists as early as 1921, as we shall see.

One way to trace the development of the weaving industry from the turn of the century is to look at the growth of the merchant sector. Census material provides sufficient evidence to show that the merchant sector grew slowly but steadily through the 1930s, and at a faster pace after 1940. Between 1930 and 1960, the number of merchants steadily increased, with the exception of viajeros or muleteers, who had stopped selling their wares by the early 1960s. Some of them later moved into other forms of commercial activity.

Table 12 shows the number of merchants registered in Teotitlán according to censuses and other local documents from 1868 through 1986. The table also includes the number of merchants and viajeros recalled by elderly people in Teotitlán. Both types of data are included to provide as accurate a picture as possible. The census data may be just as problematic as oral histories or more so, given the way occupational categories were changed by the state and manipulated by local officials in their eagerness to underreport the number of weavers and merchants.[7] In addition, the great increase in the number of merchants noted from 1980 to 1986 is in part a reflection of the greater accuracy of my household occupational census than the official Mexican census. My count of merchant households was revised several times and the list of merchant households checked with more than twenty informants in the community to verify its accuracy.

As table 12 indicates, the number of merchants remained low until the 1940s, when the local market for the first-class blankets produced in Teotitlán opened up. With the advent of the tourist and international markets, the number of merchants more than quintupled between 1950 and

TABLE 12 Numbers of merchants in Teotitlán del Valle, 1868–1986

Year	Population	No. of merchants	Census source	No. of merchants cited by informants	No. of viajeros cited by informants
1868	1,899	3	Archivo Municipal de Teotitlán del Valle, 1868		
1890	2,742	3	Archivo General del Estado de Oaxaca 1890		
1900	2,540	16	Dir. General de Estadística 1906, 4, 44–45		18
1910	2,634	n/a	Dir. General de Estadística 1918–20, 54		
1920	1,891	n/a	Dept. de la Estadística Nacional 1925–28, 166–167	5–6	8–10
1927				8	16
1930	2,116	6	Dir. General de Estadística 1936, 275	10	
1932				9	
1940	2,290	28	Dir. General de Estadística 1946, 566	6–7	
1945				15	
1948				20	
1950	2,511	19	Dir. General de Estadística 1954, 445	22	
1960	2,881	27	Dir. General de Estadística 1963, 1898	25	
1970	3,394	22	Dir. General de Estadística 1973, 406	52	
1980	3,496	53	Instituto Nacional de Estadística, Geografía e Informática 1984, 1:398	80	
1986	4,500	110	Stephen 1986 household survey, Teotitlán		

1985. Teotitecos say that since 1972 they have seen the biggest increase in demand for serapes. This growth can be linked to Teotiteco migration to the United States.

MEN MIGRATING TO THE UNITED STATES AND WOMEN LABORING AT HOME

In the 1940s, after Cárdenas's tenure in office, the initiation of the second bracero program had a major impact on Teotitlán's textile industry. Without exception, elderly people remember the bracero program as a major factor in decreasing subsistence production, pushing women into a wider range of jobs with heavier workloads, and launching a real money economy. The labor of women maintained the local economy while men were away accumulating cash in the United States.

The bracero program was the first opportunity most Teotitecos had to earn a substantial cash income, and significant numbers of men began to migrate to the United States in the 1940s. Estimates by elderly informants are that at least 25 percent or about 200 out of 800 male members of the municipio's population over age 15 migrated to the United States in the late 1940s (Dirección General de Estadística 1954, 94, 118). Many estimates are higher. Of households included in a stratified random sample in 1986, 63 percent indicated that they had at least one person who had migrated to the United States. The migrants included people of two generations, those over 40 as well as those younger. About half of the 154 households surveyed had at least one member who temporarily migrated to another part of Mexico.

The 1940s mark the full-fledged entrance of commercial capital into the community as well as into the region as a whole (Young 1978). As male migrants returned with cash, it was used to purchase goods that had previously not been used or had been locally produced. In time, cash was also used to purchase agricultural labor to take the place of male laborers who were in the United States, changing the nature of local class relations. Labor became a commodity that was directly bought and sold on the market. In Teotitlán, paying cash for agricultural labor preceded the widespread piecework relations of production found today. Ironically, the bracero program placed many Teotitecos in agricultural labor jobs but kept them from cultivating their own fields. Women were pushed into a double work shift as they pitched in to do men's jobs along with their own.

After the United States entered World War II in 1941, many growers claimed that they were suffering a severe labor shortage. Their strategy for persuading the U.S. government to establish a second bracero program was based on a claim that their workers had abandoned them for higher-paying jobs in the defense industry and that uninterrupted farm production was crucial to military success (Kiser and Kiser 1979, 67). The second bracero program was carefully negotiated between Mexico and the United States. Seeking to protect workers, Mexico demanded that the U.S. government run the program. From 1942 until 1947, with the United States serving as the formal employer, laborers were guaranteed round-trip transportation between the work site in the United States and their home village, a minimum number of working days, minimum or prevailing wages, and adequate housing (Kiser and Kiser 1979, 68). The

Mexican government seemed to maintain active control over the program during this period and kept the upper hand in protecting workers' rights, even excluding Texas from the contract process because of a history of discrimination against Mexicans.

In Mexico the program involved three state agencies,[8] the offices of state governors, and the mayors of the municipios where migrant workers resided. Notices went out through the mayors that work was available. Officials from the Mexican Secretariat of Labor and Social Provisions screened bracero candidates and turned them over to the U.S. Department of Labor, which acted as an agent for U.S. employers (García y Griego 1981, 19–20).

Teotitecos say that word of the program did not reach Teotitlán until 1944, two years after it began. That year fifteen to twenty Teotitecos signed up for eight-week contracts for the months of May, June, and July. They were transported to the recruiting center in Mexico City, where they were inspected by Mexican officials and turned over to representatives of the U.S. Department of Labor. "The first year we went to Mexico City they took us up there, cut our hair, gave us new clothes, and got us ready. Some people in Mexico City threw rocks at us because they were angry that now the recruiters were going south for workers. There were a lot of people who needed work," recalled Manuel, age 70. Former braceros recalled that many men from Teotitlán did not go in 1944 because of rumors that they were not going to work on farms, but would be sent off to fight the North Americans' war. But in July 1944, the first Teotitecos to go to the United States returned safely with shoes, blue jeans, other items of clothing, and, most important, cash. When the recruiters returned in 1945, between 150 and 300 men left the community to be braceros. As one man recalled, wages in the United States were extraordinarily high in comparison with wages in Teotitlán. "The next year a lot of people went—maybe three hundred or up to a thousand. The whole town went to the United States. In 1944 and 1945 I got paid twenty cents a box for my work picking tomatoes in the United States. I could pick thirty to thirty-five boxes a day and earn up to eight dollars a day. At that time in Mexico if I worked as a jornalero here I could earn about the equivalent of twenty-five cents. You couldn't compare it," said Juan, age 68.

In recalling their time in the United States, many braceros commented on how easy it was to get there. They did not have to worry about obtaining official papers, and transportation was taken care of. When the first groups came back safely with some money, many more were encouraged to go, seeing the bracería as the only available opportunity to emerge from the poverty of Teotitlán.

Many Teotitecos recall 1945, 1946, and 1947 as the years when only women were left in the community. While memories of the numbers of men who left varied, everyone had a clear mental image of the results in the community. Most people recalled that the communal lands were largely unworked. Some people left behind sons to work their land or left it *a medias* (sharecropped with another farmer), but significant amounts of land remained unplowed. The critical timing of the contracts, which fell during the planting season, also contributed to the abandonment of community lands. In addition, as contracts became longer and men began to be away for longer periods, weaving production was affected. There was a shortage of weaving labor because weaving was done primarily, although not exclusively, by men. Because weaving production had yet to be expanded for export production, however, the absence of men through migration did not result in a strong demand for female weaving labor such as occurred during the 1970s, when greatly expanded production for export pushed large numbers of women and girls into the labor force. Continued male migration in the 1970s exacerbated the need for female weaving labor during that period.

Women in Teotitlán recall the bracería of the 1940s and the continued absence of men in the 1950s as a time of great hardship. They had no sources of income while men were gone and they were saddled with additional chores. Many women reported that their husbands sent them little or nothing, leaving them as the sole income earners for their families. While some men later returned with savings, others did not. Some women wove during this time, but also had to maintain their food processing, child care, and animal care in addition to taking care of agricultural work. Many tried to earn extra cash by selling the yarn they spun, not having time to weave it themselves or not knowing how.

Until 1947, the ease with which people got to the United States was part of the structure of the formal bracero contract program. After 1947, the Mexican bargaining position in the bracero program began to deteriorate and it became clear that Mexico could not control emigration to the United States (García y Griego 1981, 22–29). After 1947, Mexico lost its ability to defend workers' rights and to prevent the deployment of braceros in areas that had a history of abusing them.

After 1947, the United States refused to continue in its role as formal employer and U.S. growers contracted directly with braceros. Unlike the U.S. government, the growers did not come all the way to Oaxaca to recruit. They recruited primarily in the northern states of Sonora and Chihuahua. Oaxaqueños had to get themselves up to the northern border in order to be contracted. This made it more difficult for poorer households to send braceros. They had to be able to afford transportation to the border and back. Teotitecos who had already been to the United States had enough cash to finance trips to the border. Continued migration was funded by previous migration. About 25 percent of the households in Teotitlán continued to send one or more workers to the United States every year until 1964, when the bracero program ended. After that, even more went as undocumented workers. Some have received legal permission to work under the Immigration Reform and Control Act of 1986.

Beginning in the 1940s, a significant percentage of the women in Teotitlán had to spend long periods being the sole supporters of their families. Their continuous labor in the community since the 1940s is an important but invisible part of the process that pushed the community into conditions of commercial capitalism. It also supported many men's initial capital accumulation. Some men were able to use money earned in the United States along with unpaid family labor to move their households into merchant activities in the 1970s and 1980s.

Josefina's story captures the experiences of many women who, married at the age of 14 or 15, had never been alone, and then suddenly, when their husbands migrated, found themselves in charge of a small farming and weaving enterprise as well as having to feed and clothe their children. Josefina supported her family alone from 1952 to 1964 while her husband worked for extended periods in the United States. After 1964, she had to support the family again when he returned for short trips to the United States:

> I first got to be independent when my husband went to work in the United States in 1952. I had to be. He was gone most of the time from 1952 until 1964, from two to twelve months a year. The whole time he was away he sent money only twice, about twenty dollars. I didn't spend this money; I saved it until he returned. I had six children born during that period. When he left the first time, I already had two little ones.
>
> When he was gone I carded the spun wool so that my father would make my serapes. He used to come to my house and work here. I couldn't weave because I had to take care of my children and my animals. I also used to make yarn to sell while the men were gone. This gave me money so I could go to the market and buy things. I would also sell the blankets my father made. My children were too little to weave.

You know, this whole time I worked like a mule. I would make three kilos of yarn in two days for making blankets. First I would get up and make tortillas for two other women in order to earn money. I also made tejate for another woman. Her husband had a lot of money so she paid me to work for her. I got paid two centavos for making those tortillas. It was a hard life.

Josefina later recalled that while her husband was gone he sent money to another woman he was involved with, but not to her. The fact that men were sometimes involved in multiple relationships with children in other households could further reduce the financial resources sent to their wives. In the end, most women said they learned how to survive. They also noted that after their husbands returned, they no longer accepted their dominance in decision making. As one aptly stated, "If I could get along all those years and raise eight children, why should I suddenly stop being able to decide what's best for them?"

When the men returned, their small savings were quickly spent or invested, primarily in oxen, looms, or raw wool. During the late 1950s several men who are now the largest merchants in Teotitlán began investing savings earned in the United States in wool for yarn. Some households used their money to buy land and others to pay off ceremonial debts. Most Teotitecos recalled that the influx of cash raised local prices and the price of wage labor. Many braceros used their savings to begin paying other people to work for them in their fields while they went to the United States to earn more money.

CONCLUSIONS

A pattern of male out-migration while women's labor maintains households and communities is not unusual in Mexico or elsewhere. As opportunities for wage labor open up for men in commercial agriculture, mining, urban construction, and assembly work, women may remain behind to engage in subsistence labor and craft production. Maria Mies (1982) has documented this pattern in relation to women lacemakers in Narsapur, India; Jette Bukh (1979) for women agriculturists in Ghana; and Carmen Diana Deere (1979) comparatively in the Third World. Maria de los Angeles Crummet (1987, 252–54) suggests that when women remain behind, a common result is a new gender division of labor within the household: women are relegated to the subsistence sector in agriculture. She states that the work burden of women and children can increase in rural areas where male out-migration prevails. Most research shows, however, that the extent to which women are affected by migration relates to the household's economic standing within the rural community (Crummet 1987, 252; Margolis 1979; United Nations Secretariat 1984; Weist 1973; Young 1978). Summarizing several cases from Mexico, Crummet (1987, 254) concludes: "Among landless and poor peasant households, in particular, male migration had important consequences for the household division of labor: Women increased their participation in agricultural production and wage work while retaining their traditional responsibilities for child care and family welfare. Thus the intensification of women's labor in paid and unpaid work and productive and reproductive activities sharpens not only the analysis of migration, but also of class and household relations."

The women of Teotitlán appear to have taken on an increased domestic work load during the 1950s and 1960s, years of significant male out-migration. The burden was probably greatest for women of landless weaver households. Because only a handful of women were part of large landholding merchant households in the 1940s and 1950s, however, the burden of male migration probably fell hard on most Teotitecas. Ironically, it was the labor of women that sustained many families in the community while significant numbers of men were off laboring in the United States, earning cash that enabled some to begin a business. Male migrants in the United States suffered from exploitative labor conditions, but women who remained home seem to have derived fewer ultimate benefits from their sacrifices than migrant men. Men's experience in the United States, as we shall see, gave them an advantage over women in running the increasing number of merchant businesses that began to appear in the 1970s.

The pattern of male migration in Teotitlán during the 1940s and 1950s may be different from that found in other parts of Mexico. Lourdes Arizpe (1985) found in the Mazahua region of Morelos that both male and female migrants left in alternation with their parents, depending on the point in the domestic cycle. Thus only one generation of men left the household at one time. Other investigations of migration in Mexico (Nutini and Murphy 1970; Rothstein 1982) found that when some rural men migrate, their extended families gather in one household, so that women are not left alone as the sole wage earners.

I did not gather data that would permit a comparison of migration patterns from Teotitlán in the 1940s and 1950s with those of the 1960s and 1970s. The primary change in migration patterns noted was that significant numbers of young women began to migrate along with young men in the 1970s, going primarily to urban locations in Mexico. They did not begin to reach the United States until the 1980s. This was the period when some Teotiteco households began to establish themselves in the border areas of Tijuana and Ensenada, and through their presence formed a staging area for attempts to cross the border into San Diego County. Research on undocumented Mexican migrants in San Diego County (Chávez, Flores, and López Garza 1989) shows the presence of women in the population and suggests that they come for economic as well as familial reasons.

Both during the initial period of male migration and later with the expansion in weaving production, women's labor has been critical in the reproduction of the labor force as well as in maintaining household ceremonial economies. While comparative data on rates of household fiesta sponsorship and participation were not gathered for the years 1940–60 and thereafter, oral histories make it clear that the ceremonial life of the community continued in the 1950s and 1960s. The labor of women was important not only in maintaining household economic production but also in generating surpluses that could be invested in guelaguetza, mayordomías, and other ceremonial institutions. Women also continued to engage in reciprocal labor exchanges in relation to ceremonial activities. Male out-migration during the 1940s and 1950s was significant not only in shifting the gendered household division of labor but in solidifying the importance of women's labor in the ceremonial activities that are as much a part of social reproduction as feeding and caring for the future labor force.

CHAPTER 6

Weaving as Heritage

Folk Art, Aesthetics, and

the Commercialization of

Zapotec Textiles

I do a lot of the work here for my husband. I dye all the yarn
for the people who work for us. I also cook and make tortillas. If I
need money to buy something for the house or to pay people,
I have to ask him for it. The business belongs to both of us,
but he keeps the money. —Godelia, age 55

We are weavers. Merchants don't make serapes, they have
businesses and buy them. They don't work like we do . . . their
money works for them. —Lucia, age 50

I really like creating my own designs, particularly landscapes.
These often sell, but just as often people want to buy designs and
colors I don't find attractive. That's why it's important to have space
to develop my own designs. —Marcela, age 48

The commercialization of weaving production in Teotitlán that
began during the 1920s had a major impact on both class and gender relations. More than any other factor, the integration of weaving
production into national and international capitalist consumer markets
through commercialization has heightened some of the incipient contradictions in the community. Class stratification based on mercantile
capitalism changed as first migration and then the U.S. export market
provided increased opportunities for merchant activity based on international commercial capital. Under these changing conditions of capitalist development, a new and bigger merchant class began to emerge
in Teotitlán during the 1970s.

These merchants purchased labor directly, by employing weavers in
workshops and by the piecework production system. Yet, in spite of current class differentiation, the community has also maintained a strong
sense of local ethnic solidarity, reflected most strongly in claims to Zapotec weaving production. It is also seen in an intensification of ritual

activity specifically identified with community solidarity in Teotitlán. While authors such as James Greenberg (1989, 199–203) have identified conflicts between class- and kin-based ideologies as pitting the mestizo moral order against the Indian—capitalistic institutional Catholicism against indigenous folk religion promoting reciprocity, equality, and co-operation—in Teotitlán this conflict does not correlate with ethnic differences, but is played out along gender and class lines.

THE MEXICAN TEXTILE INDUSTRY AND MARKETS FOR INDIGENOUSLY PRODUCED WOOL PRODUCTS, 1920–1970

The transformation of the Teotitlán-centered weaving system from production for regional use to production for tourist and export markets was tied to national and international economic factors that affected the Mexican textile industry. The textile industry has been an important part of the Mexican economy since the beginning of the colonial period. Organized first as colonial *obrajes* (textile manufactories) run largely with indigenous labor,[1] the cotton and wool textile industry in Mexico City, Puebla, and Tlaxcala remained organized around the same basic technology until the early 1900s, when the entire industry began to mechanize (Heath Constable 1982, 54). Whereas obrajes were built around a resident labor force that lived on the production site, later production in Tlaxcala and Puebla involved factories with a wage labor force that lived in the neighborhood. Some of these factories became large-scale enterprises; few retained the status of household workshops and they did not evolve into piecework operations, as in Teotitlán.

The first automatic looms were built at the turn of the twentieth century and imported from the United States. In many factories, the technology imported in the first decades of the century remained in use until the early 1960s, when some factories retooled to be able to include the production of synthetic fabrics (Mercado García 1980, 661). Once mechanized, many factories in Tlaxcala and elsewhere diversified their production in an effort to reach a larger consumer market. Enterprises such as La Providencia in Tlaxcala diversified and produced over 140,000 blankets, serapes, ponchos, and shawls per year for sale in Mexico City, Puebla, and Veracruz (Heath Constable 1982, 19).

From the 1920s through the 1940s, cotton and wool factories spun thread and yarn and produced cloth for the Mexican consumer market. During World War II the textile industry grew significantly as produc-

TABLE 13 Mexican national production of bland textile
fibers, 1960–1976 (thousands of metric tons)

Year	Cotton	Wool	Synthetic fibers
1960	457	3.0	20.2
1961	443	3.1	19.2
1962	477	3.2	21.2
1963	490	3.2	23.7
1964	488	ND	28.6
1965	515	ND	38.6
1966	560	ND	41.1
1967	447	ND	46.0
1968	525	2.8	50.6
1969	418	2.7	60.0
1970	324	1.4	73.9
1971	352	1.3	92.4
1972	396	1.7	112.4
1973	363	1.1	144.0
1974	502	1.0	153.7
1975	228	1.0	172.3
1976	204	1.0	187.6

Source: Adapted from Mercado García 1980, 138, fig. II.

tion was interrupted elsewhere and Mexico began to export cotton and wool products in significant quantities, particularly to other parts of Latin America (Heath Constable 1982, 84). In addition, the internal market grew because of a reduction in imported textiles. The industry was able to grow without any technical innovation or significant investment in new technology (Martínez del Campo 1985, 73).

This short-term advantage, however, quickly became a disadvantage as international production of synthetic fibers began in earnest in the late 1950s and Mexico's textile factories were not equipped to begin production of polyester (Heath Constable 1982, 84; Mercado García 1980). The growth spurt that the cotton and wool textile industry experienced during the 1940s was cut short by 1960 as the production of polyester and other synthetics began to take hold in Mexico. Between 1960 and 1976, the growth of synthetic fiber production was greater than that of

TABLE 14 Evolution of the Mexican market for polyester, 1969–1976 (thousands of tons)

Year	National production	Imports	Exports	National consumption	Percentage growth of consumption
1969	3,026	56.9		3,082.9	
1970	7,584	150.5		7,734.5	150.9
1971	17,224.8	133.2	592.3	16,788.9	117.1
1972	32,508	188.3	0.4	32,695	94.8
1973	50,000	2,967	5.0	52,692.3	62.0
1974	56,294	8,512		64,806	22.4
1975	70,577	1,254		71,831	10.8
1976	68,977	652		69,627	−3.2

Source: Adopted from Mercado García 1980, 149, fig. 23.

all other textiles (Mercado García 1980, 137–38). In 1960, synthetic fibers accounted for 4 percent of the production of soft-textured fibers, and by 1976 they were a full 48 percent. Between 1966 and 1973, the national market for polyester grew by leaps and bounds each year, finally leveling off in 1974 (Mercado García 1980, 35–38).

As table 15 indicates, a high level of polyester consumption in Mexico continued from 1976 to 1985; cotton and wool consumption remained steady, but low in comparison with synthetic fibers. With the development of a strong internal market for synthetic fibers by the early 1970s, producers of wool products could no longer sell goods to the national population. While Mexicans continued to import wool in the 1970s, they had to find other outlets for their production. This is illustrative of a larger relation between increasing local consumption of mass-produced goods in Mexico and the growth of a market in urban areas of Mexico and outside of Mexico for hand-produced goods that came to be seen as "folk art."

The Pan American Highway connected Oaxaca City and smaller towns with the larger Mexican economy in the late 1940s. The booming textile industry of Tlaxcala and Puebla then began to reach the regional Oaxacan consumer markets, which previously had been supplied with blankets and ponchos produced by the Zapotecs and other indigenous

TABLE 15 Mexican national consumption of bland fibers, 1976–1985 (thousands of metric tons)

Year	Cotton	Wool	Synthetics	Total
1976	84,870	4,885	179,858	269,613
1977	111,550	4,201	200,730	316,481
1978	129,825	5,700	212,989	348,514
1979	157,950	6,500	246,437	410,887
1980	176,400	6,900	256,610	439,910
1981	147,675	7,600	249,767	405,042
1982	82,125	5,046	213,125	300,296
1983	126,730	4,261	246,553	377,544
1984	120,750	4,615	237,664	363,029
1985	138,000	5,534	276,446	419,980

Source: Adapted from Instituto Nacional de Estadística, Geografía e Informática 1986, 55, fig. 11.9.

groups. The growth of the polyester industry caused a decline in indigenous consumption of handmade blankets produced in weaving communities such as Teotitlán del Valle. The completion of a national highway in 1948 reaching Oaxaca also accelerated the commoditization of the Oaxacan economy, spurred on by the cash earnings that returning migrants began to spend on products produced in Mexico and the United States. By the early 1950s, local class relations were becoming firmly entrenched in commercial capital, with increased demand for new commercial goods providing new opportunities for local and regional entrepreneurs.

If the only factor involved in the creation of markets for Zapotec weavings had been internal consumption among indigenous populations, the weaving system centered in Teotitlán del Valle probably would have died by the mid-1960s. Unlike items such as metates, which continue to be locally produced and used, Teotiteco blankets and ponchos became quite expensive in comparison with machine-woven polyester-blend textiles. Because metates and certain other indigenous implements were still cheaper and more efficiently produced by hand (S. Cook 1982a), they continued to have a local niche in the periodic markets of Oaxaca.[2] The current market for Teotiteco textiles had to come from elsewhere.

As the Mexican state began to promote indigenous crafts, Zapotec weavings were transformed from objects for use to art objects and folk art. Several factors were important in the creation of a market niche for them in urban Mexico and in the United States. Always high-quality products, they are light and easily transportable, can be used as household objects abroad, and can also be art objects because of their designs. The same claims cannot be made for metates and some other indigenous crafts that have not found a market abroad. However, pottery items, especially from Coyotepec and Atzompa, have also found a market in the United States as art objects that can be used.

NATIONALISM AND FOLK ART IN MEXICO

The struggle over who lays claim to Mexico's indigenous artisans and to the aesthetic value and cultural meanings of their creative work in relation to nationalism can be traced back to the period of Mexican independence. Initially efforts to define Mexican "arts" came from abroad as well as internally. After Mexican independence in 1821, heightened interest in Mexican popular arts among scholars, travelers, and collectors helped to construct both independent and neocolonial visions of the newly independent nation. Baron Alexander von Humboldt, Henry George Ward, John Lloyd Stephens, William Bullock, and others were involved in publicizing the history and culture of Mexico. According to James Oles (2002), a famous showman of nineteenth-century England, William Bullock, was the first to present Mexican arts to the public in the postindependence period. Visiting Mexico in 1823, Bullock spent six months collecting "scientific information" that amounted to a vast array of flora, fauna, pre-Columbian manuscripts, sculptures, and other artifacts. In 1824 he opened two shows, Ancient Mexico and Modern Mexico, at Egyptian Hall, his museum in London. The exhibit recreated a simple rural dwelling complete with a "'native Mexican Indian' from a village near Texcoco to live in the exhibition" (Oles 2002, 13). The installation included baskets, ceramics, and other objects that were supposed to document rural life in Mexico. In his catalogue describing the Modern Mexico exhibition, Bullock praised the creators of the folk art he exhibited: "The mode of working in leather; the cloths of many colours which are manufactured by the natives; their embroideries, sometimes fantastic, but generally very tasteful, and always very rich, their dyed goods, and a multitude of things prepared by artificial means and human labour, throw a light over these branches of productive industry" (Bullock 1825, 3–5).

Oles documents the second major presentation of Mexican folk art as also being held in London, by Frederick Starr, a leading physical anthropologist who helped to found the Department of Anthropology at the University of Chicago in 1892 (2002, 15). In 1897 he assembled a collection of Mexican "folklore" for the London Folklore Society that included a broad array of Mexican material culture. Starr's collection did not include indigenous folk art. His *Catalogue of a Collection of Objects Illustrating the Folk-Lore of Mexico* states:

> The pure-blood Indians, who form the population of Southern Mexico, are not represented in it. Objects illustrating their life and customs are hardly folklore objects. The six hundred and thirty or more objects gathered together represent the Mestizos, or mixed bloods of Northern and Central Mexico. Their blood is a mixture of Spanish and Indian: their life is a mixture of that of South Europe in the fifteenth and of America at the end of the nineteenth centuries: their religion is a mixture of native paganism and Christianity. (Starr 1899, xi)

While the exhibit and catalogue noted the importance of local traditions, paid some attention to individual artists, and acknowledged the growing influence of tourism, the arts of Mexico's indigenous peoples were seen not as objects of folklore but as "ethnographic objects" (Starr 1899–1900, xi).

After the Mexican Revolution, the place of indigenous cultures and arts as well as the definition of mestizaje itself underwent a refitting for the purposes of creating a unitary nationalism that would attempt to heal the divisions of the civil war. After the Mexican Revolution, indigenous identities were claimed as part of the Mexican national heritage. In 1921 indigenous arts were officially recognized within Mexico as *arte popular* when the tenth anniversary of the Mexican Revolution was celebrated with a national artisans' exhibit inaugurated by Alvaro Obregón in Mexico City (García Canclini 1982, 102). Before the exhibit, some painters such as Saturnino Herrán and Germán Gedovius had used glazed ceramics and wool serapes as props in their paintings to symbolize national identities (Oles 2002, 19). This trend was followed later by Diego Rivera, Frida Kahlo, Miguel Covarrubias, and others.

The 1921 Exposición de Arte Popular was organized by the artists Roberto Montenegro and Jorge Enciso. The exhibit was the first in Mexico to emphasize the aesthetic value of the objects produced by Mexico's artisans. In his catalogue of the exhibit, the artist Gerardo Murillo, writing as "Dr. Atl," defined *artes populares* as "all manifestations of the ingenuity and talent of the Mexican people" (Oles 2002, 19). The exhibit contained a wide range of objects, including many types of textiles. Photographs indicate that textiles from Teotitlán were included. Atl recognized them in his 1922 publication *Las Artes Populares en México*, stating that the weavers of Teotitlán were selling their weavings to tourists at "elevated prices" (Atl 1922, 10).

In the 1920s, Mexico's indigenous and rural traditions became the focus of debates on national art and aesthetics. Indigenous arts were proclaimed to represent "*lo más mexicano de México*" (the most Mexican of Mexico) (R. López 2002, 52). A more positive attitude toward Mexico's indigenous cultures was promoted by the Ministry of Public Education after the departure of José Vasconcelos, whose vision was to "mestizoize" the nation: Mexico's indigenous cultures would assimilate Western art, philosophy, and ways of living. Essentially Vasconcelos wished to whiten Mexico. In his essay "The Cosmic Race," Vasconcelos wrote: "In regard to the Whites and their culture, the fifth race (the cosmic race) already relies on them, and still expects benefits from their genius. Latin America owes what it is to the white European, and is not going to deny him. . . . By the same token it needs all of the other races. However, we accept the superior ideals of the Whites but not their arrogance" (1979, 25). After Vasconcelos left, pro-Indian nationalists (*indigenistas*) such as Manuel Gamio and Moisés Saenz rose to prominence in the ministry and were part of a broad group of writers, artists, researchers, and aficionados who promoted indigenous arts. Their efforts were part of the discourse that became known as *indigenismo*. The meaning of *indigenismo* has changed through time, in accordance with views on Mexican nationalism and efforts aimed at encouraging assimilation of indigenous peoples.

One of the issues raised by the 1921 exhibit of arte popular in Mexico City relates to the definition and meaning of work described as folk art. Eli Bartra sees three distinct fields: folk art, handicrafts, and folklore. Even for her, folk art as a distinct category proves to be somewhat slippery to define. In an essay on folk art and Mexican identity, Bartra defines folk art in opposition to handicrafts and folklore.

> All folk art is made by artisans, but not all that artisans make is folk art. For example, chairs of palm fronds or clay pots, while handmade and often

decorated, are not what I consider folk art. Although the distinction does not always hold true, . . . handicrafts are generally produced in series and often collectively; they tend to be utilitarian and repetitive, the result more of manual dexterity than of creative imagination. Folk art seems unique, more personal, more imaginative, more . . . art. Folklore, on the other hand, is something apart, made up mostly of oral and musical expressions: stories, songs, legends, dances. It is another kind of artistic production entirely. (2000, 53)

Bartra also describes folk art as the art of the poor because they often have little or no formal education: for her folk art is in constant transformation, always appears in new forms, and is as distinct from elite art as walking is from driving (2000, 54–56). However, the particular meaning of "folk art" is easier to define in a concrete national and historical context. In Mexico, this context is nationalism as constructed from the 1920s to the present. Bartra rightly argues that folk art has been a central ingredient in the postrevolutionary government's quest to concoct a national culture in Mexico. She notes that folk art and handicrafts are often held out as symbols of the "pre-Hispanic roots of the modern Mexican nation. . . . In fact, a substantial part of those popular expressions have their origin in Spain including votive paintings, Judas figures, foot-driven textile looms, several kinds of pottery" (2000, 57).

Textile production in Teotitlán provides an apt example of what Bartra is pointing to. While it is rooted in pre-Hispanic techniques of producing cotton textiles on backstrap looms, it is not a "pure form" but is melded with the use of Spanish foot-driven looms. In the realm of folk art, Teotiteco textile production is considered representative of an authentic expression of indigenous Mexicanness. It is, but it is also representative of the conditions of colonialism under which Zapotec weavers lived after 1519. Under some definitions of folk art, Teotiteco weaving would be classified as what Raymond Williams calls a selective tradition —an intentionally preshaped present, which is often powerfully operative in the process of social and cultural definition and identification (1994, 601). A realistic definition of Mexican folk art would acknowledge its link to colonization and Spanish inheritance. This is the way Teotitecos themselves portray weaving. A more realistic definition of folk art will acknowledge its changing meanings, techniques, and purposes. Bartra writes:

"Authentic" pieces of folk art are converted into cheap merchandise and placed in stores, galleries, exhibition halls, and even museums; there they lose the meanings they had when and where, for what and for whom, they were produced. This has been a common fate for many forms of Mexican folk art, resulting in much of it now being produced as merchandise. Thus, the meaning of a work, as derived from satisfying the needs of its original producers-consumers, is constantly modified by the demands of extra-community consumption. . . . For a long time, capitalism has imposed its laws on the production of folk art; contents and forms are in constant transformation in response to an external market. (2000, 58–59)

The quest for "authenticity" that can result in a blindness to the changing meaning of folk art also drove artists and intellectuals who first promoted folk art.

Perhaps the heyday of arte popular was in the late 1920s and 1930s, when a wide range of artists and intellectuals considered it the most authentic form of representation. In the 1930s, intellectuals and artists declared arte popular to be an important part of the Mexican heritage, suggesting that articles such as straw dolls, clay toys, and multicolored serapes were giving Mexicans "an elevated sense of race and a national conscience that was previously missing" (Novo 1932, 56, cited in Novelo 1976). Circles of Mexican academic artists and intellectuals as well as U.S. dealers, patrons, tourists, diplomatic personnel, and anthropologists all had roles in promoting arte popular in the United States as well as in Mexico.

After the tremendous success of the 1921 exhibition, the first exhibition of Mexican folk art held in the United States opened in Los Angeles in 1922. This project was led by the artist Jorge Enciso in conjunction with Miguel Covarrubias, Xavier Guerrero, Adolfo Best Maguard, and the writer Katherine Anne Porter, who was then living in Mexico. It seems likely that some textiles from Teotitlán were included.

Some of these same individuals as well as the artist Diego Rivera, U.S. Ambassador Dwight Morrow and his wife, Elizabeth Morrow, the art historian and anthropologist Anita Brenner (a student of Franz Boas), and others were part of a circle of friends who from the late 1920s through the 1930s and into the 1940s were fundamental in bringing folk art to a wider market as well as promoting it as a part of Mexican national identity. They did so through personal collecting, helping to mount exhibitions in the United States and Mexico, hosting parties that featured folk art, traveling to rural Mexico to meet with folk artists, and writing about places to visit that encouraged the development of tourism. Oaxaca was a prominent focus of these efforts.

William and Elizabeth Morrow visited Oaxaca in 1928 and 1929, stopping in Oaxaca City, Monte Albán, Santa María del Tule, Mitla, San Bartolo Coyotepec, and probably other sites as well (R. López 2002, 54–58). In their Cuernavaca home, called Casa Mañana, the Morrows developed an extensive collection of folk art that included Oaxacan pottery, Saltillo serapes, and probably a few pieces from Teotitlán. It appears that well before this time, weavers in Teotitlán were adept at imitating the Saltillo style and often did so (see Fischgrund Stanton 2000, 44–47, plates 11–13). Their home was visited by Frida Kahlo and Diego Rivera, who developed extensive personal collections of folk art, including many objects from Oaxaca. Several Oaxacan art dealers connected to the intellectual and artistic circles of Kahlo, Rivera, and the Morrows began to sell Oaxacan folk art in the capital city in the 1930s and 1940s. The items sold to these artists and intellectuals included textiles from Teotitlán. As Eli Bartra notes, Diego Rivera "was one of the greatest defenders of folk art, although populism often lurked behind his stance—suggesting that what he was promoting was more populist art than folk art in his murals" (2000, 59).

Anita Brenner popularized folk art through her *Idols behind the Altars* (1929), which emphasized artists who drew inspiration "from the experiences and aesthetics of Mexico's popular classes" (R. López 2002, 55). In 1930 Frances Flynn Paine (who had organized a show of Mexican folk art in New York in 1928), Abby Aldrich Rockefeller, Elizabeth Morrow, and others founded the Mexican Arts Association "to promote friendship between the people of Mexico and the United States by encouraging cultural relations and the interchange of Fine and Applied Arts" (Oles 2002, 24). From 1930 to 1932, an exhibit titled Mexican Arts circulated in the United States and opened at the Metropolitan Museum of Art in New York. It included over 1,200 works and was supported by Mexico's Ministry of Education. The Mexican Arts show was widely covered in the press and was credited with creating a boom market for Mexican folk art in the United States. The objects included in the exhibit were treated as art (Oles 2002, 24). In 1940 the Museum of Modern Art in New York opened a huge exhibition titled Twenty Centuries of Mexican Art. This exhibit included a broad selection of folk art and generated widespread public interest.

These and other exhibits—for example, those appearing at the world's fairs—along with a complex circle of political, artistic, business, and literary friends and colleagues were among the key elements in moving Mexican folk art into mainstream recognition and demand. Elizabeth

Morrow continued to collect and promote Oaxacan folk art until her death in 1955. She visited Oaxaca in 1948 and encouraged her friends to do the same.

Where Teotitlán artisans and their work were featured, however, they were characterized overwhelmingly as male—a trend that often continues today despite the fact that most women now know how to weave. National and international contests for folk art were not without their gendered aspects as well. The practice of bringing winning artisans to Mexico City and as far as London, for example, summarily excluded women, who usually had children to take care of and could not leave their communities. These first presentations of Mexican *artesanos* to the Mexican upper classes and to foreigners gave the impression that an artisan was necessarily male. Contests that recognized the weaver as the sole creator of a textile also went against community perceptions of who participates in production. Textiles are seen as belonging not just to the weaver but to all who participate in producing them, including carders, spinners, and dyers. While the majority of weavers probably were men when such contests took place (before the 1970s), the labor of women as spinners, dyers, and carders went unrecognized in these contests.

Because of the interest generated by exhibits and publications about Mexican folk art, people from all over Mexico, the United States, and Europe began to visit Oaxaca as tourists. They were drawn to explore the indigenous communities that produced the now renowned Mexican folk art. The 1948 new Pan American Highway passed within six kilometers of Teotitlán. This highway made the state capital of Oaxaca infinitely more accessible to Teotitecos and Teotitlán more accessible to tourists. While tourists did arrive in Oaxaca before the completion of the Pan American Highway and Teotitecos are recorded as selling their weavings to tourists as early as 1922, the tourist market did not begin to develop in earnest until the late 1950s. Bus service from Teotitlán to Oaxaca began in 1935 and operated on Fridays and Saturdays. With the inauguration of the Pan American Highway, however, it became possible to go to Oaxaca and back in half a day, encouraging Teotitecos to hawk their wares there more regularly. Teotitecos were also actively involved in bringing tourists to their community in the 1950s, according to interviews. Thus they also acted to promote their textiles as infrastructure was improving.

The road also began to draw more and more tourists directly to Teotitlán. These tourists visited the town to see for themselves how Zapotec weavings were produced. A 1962 book titled *Folk Art of Mexico* says, "The finest serapes are made in the state of Oaxaca (in particular in Teotitlán del Valle. . . .)" (Dörner 1962, 16). A later book on Mexican folk crafts states: "The serape weavers in Teotitlán del Valle can copy any design with extraordinary fidelity, which shows the excellent skill with which they operate their looms" (Espejel 1978, 135). Thus as early as the 1920s Teotitlán was put on the map of folk art. By the 1960s it had become a mainstay of the Oaxaca tourist market and was a featured stop in guidebooks along with archaeological sites, periodic markets, and other artisan communities.

Tourism became one of Mexico's biggest income generators. Between 1976 and 1980, tourism grew by an annual average of 11 percent. Foreign tourism grew by an annual average of 18 percent (Lozano and Vargas 1982, 30). By the year 2000, tourism was second only to oil as a source of foreign revenue in Mexico. To capture the interest of tourists, particular features of cultural and material production were commoditized and packaged for sale by the federal government. The ideological package that was and is sold to tourists who came to states with large indigenous populations is based on a homogenized image of "Indian culture" and the material remains of that culture that can be visited or purchased and taken home. Of primary import in this cultural package is the Mexican Indian. Since completion of the Pan American Highway, tourism has continued to grow at a steady pace in Oaxaca, with the encouragement of the Mexican government.

FOLLOWING UP ON THE SUCCESS OF FOLK ART: STATE
DEVELOPMENT PROGRAMS IN TEOTITLÁN, 1960–1990

One of the first efforts of the federal government to promote Teotiteco weaving came through BANFOCO (Banco de Fomento Cooperativo), a national agency with state offices in Oaxaca and elsewhere. In the early 1960s, BANFOCO attempted to run a cooperative for weavers in Teotitlán. The effort was part of a broader one to sponsor cooperatives for the weaving, pottery, basketry, jewelry, and clothing industries throughout the Oaxaca Valley. The primary activity of the bank was to extend credit to artisans for the purchase of materials.

Launched in 1963, the cooperative had a short life and ended with only eight members in 1965 (Vargas-Barón 1968, 198). Throughout its shaky life, the cooperative had problems, the most important being that the community did not decide it needed a cooperative; rather, BANFOCO officials identified Teotitlán as a good site for the program and proceeded to begin it with a few local men. Because Oaxaca BANFOCO officials did not take into account the real relations of production and distribution, the cooperative was probably doomed from the start. In particular, they did not pay attention to the structure of production in which weavers and merchants were tied together through kin and compadrazgo relationships. As one person explained, "Why would I sell to BANFOCO when I've been weaving for my uncle since I was fourteen years old?" Most merchants in the community opposed the cooperative because it competed with them in marketing weavings and obtaining workers. In addition, weavers in the project who received credit had no marketing skills and were unsuccessful in attracting clients to purchase the weavings owned by the cooperative. And differences in the weavers' abilities and talents caused disputes about how much individuals should be paid.

Soon after the cooperative began, some weavers left it and began to work independently (Vargas-Barón 1968, 199). They made contacts with Oaxaca merchants, who paid much more than they were making by selling their work to the cooperative. They thus began to deal directly with these merchants and circumvented the state-sponsored cooperative, a pattern that both independent producers and merchants have demonstrated since the 1960s. In general, Teotitecos claim that the cooperative was always controlled by a few men and never worked to benefit most of its members.

As far as most people recall, all of the formal members of the cooperative were men. While some women indirectly sold their weavings to the cooperative through a male household member, they were never structurally included. BANFOCO officials approached only men, probably on the assumption that all weavers were men and that as heads of households they were in charge of decision making. This was not the case, however. At this time, women were weaving in increasing numbers and were taking an active part in production decision making in weaving households.

After BANFOCO's unsuccessful attempt to create a widely supported cooperative, FONART (Fondo Nacional de Artesanía), an offspring of BANFOCO, began to work in Teotitlán. According to a Oaxaca FONART official, FONART's mission is to "conserve, rescue, and promote popular and traditional art with commercial support, with credit, and through supplying primary materials" (October 1985 interview). A major part of the FONART program revolves around a series of national stores that have huge inventories of crafts from all over Mexico. Thus FONART acts as a national intermediary for craft producers, supposedly redistributing profits to producing communities. It does so, however, only after it has deducted the cost of maintaining the bureaucracy. Rather than help to support FONART's bureaucracy and add an extra layer to the marketing process, most Teotitecos, particularly in the emerging merchant class, have limited their involvement with FONART.

The marketing methods of FONART have an important cultural dimension as well. FONART stores dissolve ethnic differences in favor of a nationalistic and homogeneous vision of Mexican Indianness, displaying crafts from Michoacán, Guerrero, Oaxaca, and Yucatán side by side as genuine Mexican folk art. Ultimately, as Néstor García Canclini (1982, 128) points out, the dissolution of ethnicity into nationalism also reduces particular ethnic creations to "typical" crafts, *lo típico*. Since Teotitecos' claim to their textiles rests on the fact that they are Zapotec weavers producing Zapotec textiles, their products lose prestige and distinctiveness in state FONART stores, which simply market hundreds of products from thirty or forty ethnic groups as "Mexican crafts."

FONART first worked in Teotitlán from 1971 until 1983 with a program for the community. The original FONART program provided credit to weavers who were producing what were identified as traditional designs. FONART supplied loans for the purchase of primary materials such as wool and yarn. According to a Oaxaca official involved in the Teotitlán project, one of the major problems was that FONART did not have enough capital to keep the project going.

From 1972 through 1978, a group of twenty or more Teotiteco weavers were involved in a Oaxaca state FONART program at a time when probably more than a thousand weavers, both men and women, were active in the community. In 1979, when this group was reorganized through a federal FONART program, its official membership went from 20 to 200. Through the federal government, the members received a large sum of money to buy primary material such as wool and yarn directly from factories in Tlaxcala and Puebla. Apparently the FONART cooperative purchased four tons of wool. The official interviewed did not specify how the program ended. According to those involved, however, the large wool purchase caused jealousy among those who were not in on the deal, and the program fell apart. Adding to the conflict, significant portions of the wool remained unaccounted for as the project disintegrated.

According to many people in Teotitlán, the FONART program never really had 200 members. For many years, the Oaxaca FONART office purchased large numbers of weavings from several of the wealthiest merchants who had large piecework operations. Some independent artisans were aided with credit, but most pieceworkers continued to work as contract labor.

During the 1980s, FONART was consistently unable to pay artisans for their products at the time of delivery. In some cases, entire communities worked diligently to fill a FONART contract only to find that when they finished, FONART did not have enough cash to pay them for the work they had completed. In 1985 FONART sold a large lot of merchandise to commercial stores such as Sanborn's and Sears in order to raise money owed to artisans. This cash-flow problem probably further encouraged producers in many communities to circumvent FONART programs and deal with commercial Mexican intermediaries. Some producers in Teotitlán followed this strategy, but the enterprising merchant class of the 1970s also began to forge direct links to U.S. importers.

In the mid-1980s, Teotitecos agreed that they did not need FONART. They commented that FONART always wanted to pay below the market price for their goods, lower than what they could get from U.S. importers. As a result, FONART bought primarily from large merchants who would give them a price break because they bought in bulk. These merchants treated FONART as they would any other client. Thus the majority of merchants and producers were not involved in the FONART project, but were busy building direct links with U.S. importers, sometimes with people they met while working in the United States.

When discussing FONART, most Teotitecos state that they prefer to make their own contacts with foreign clients or simply to produce for those in their community. The dream of every weaving household is to find a *cliente*, a foreign buyer to whom they can sell directly. If they fail to find one, they would rather deal with local merchants than with officials of state craft development programs. Weavers emphasize that, unlike the government, local merchants, who are often kin or compadres, will give them credit and a good price for their weavings. They can also be counted on to provide help for children's education and to sponsor them at school graduations and Catholic rites of passage. They find this arrangement preferable to the government program, where they were paid less and often had to wait to obtain credit to use in purchasing yarn.

In 1985 FONART began a cooperative in neighboring Santa Ana. Apparently seventy weavers were registered with the cooperative; but, according to the FONART official in charge of the program at the time, only twenty of them actually worked in the program. The other fifty preferred to produce for merchants in Teotitlán. Many Santa Ana weavers received their primary materials from their employers in Teotitlán and got paid for their work, rather than working in the FONART cooperative. Although they can purchase wool below market price when they work in the FONART cooperative, because social and economic ties between Teotitlán and Santa Ana are so strong, many Santa Ana weavers continue to work with Teotitlán merchants instead of the government. Many of them are in compadrazgo relationships with people in Teotitlán and can count on them for a lot more than the government can offer. However, these relationships can be fraught with tension as weavers in Santa Ana continually struggle to establish an independent reputation for quality goods and to gain access to a market long dominated by Teotitlán.

When the peso was devalued dramatically in 1982 and 1983, many U.S. merchants who had previously bought from Mexican wholesalers as well as from FONART began to go directly to craft-producing communities. Cheaper airfares, hotel, restaurant, and car rental rates, and guide fees made it attractive to do so. Textile importers no longer went through middlemen in Mexico City and Oaxaca, but went directly to Teotitlán instead. According to a FONART official interviewed in 1985 who worked in Teotitlán, "Since the devaluation of the peso, production has steadily increased in Teotitlán. Since that moment they have no longer needed FONART. They are maintaining themselves and several other towns as well. The influx of U.S. merchants to the community was tremendous."

The emerging merchant class in Teotitlán seems to have anticipated this change before 1982. In 1980, a local group of men, among them several prominent merchants, organized to build a paved road running directly from Teotitlán to the Pan American Highway. Previously, the community was linked to the highway by a dirt road that ran through the neighboring town of Maquilxóchitl. Apparently jealous of the success and long-standing dominance of Teotitlán, residents of Maquilxóchitl frequently steered visitors away from Teotitlán, telling them that the town was in the opposite direction. There were also several confrontations in which buses from Teotitlán were stopped in the road and vandalized.

The move to build the road from Teotitlán was widely supported in the community, and about 75 percent of the cost of construction was raised there. The remaining 25 percent was obtained from the Oaxaca governor's office. Each household provided at least one male laborer to work on the road. Several merchants who became active in the project spent almost two years overseeing the road construction. The project was supported by municipio authorities, but in the minds of community members it remains the project of those merchants who organized it.

The road also marks the beginning of tension in the structure of political authority in the community. Merchants negotiating outside of the formal political system subtly began to challenge traditional political authority based on ritual experience, traditional knowledge, and custodianship of communal resources and rights. While some of these merchants proposed selling the communal resources of the community, others defended the importance of community control over collective goods.

According to people interviewed in 2001, one of the merchants who coordinated the building of the road in 1980 also invited an official of the Ministry of Agriculture and Water Resources (SARH) to a community assembly. There the official, named Chaga González, explained how the community could sell off its forest at a tidy profit. He offered to help the community set up a business. He brought detailed maps and specified the number of metric feet of wood available to sell. While some of the people on the road construction committee were enthusiastic about this prospect, one merchant in particular, the idea did not go over well in the community assembly. According to the granddaughter of one of the elders present, "My grandfather was there. He said, 'No one has ever come here to cut down and sell our trees! Why would we want to start doing that now?' With that said, the whole discussion ended."

The community undertook to sell textiles and to bring more tourists into town. In 1985 a local food market was converted to an artisan market for tourists. Later one of the buildings was used for a community museum. Rather than go to the state for resources, the community paid the bill for construction and used local labor. A new food market was built with government assistance, and the new artisan market in front of the town hall now houses stalls for local merchants and independent weavers. For the women who staffed the market up to eight hours a day in the 1980s, their low-level involvement in its creation and their exclusion from the committee that oversaw it were points of contention. These women's feelings about wanting to have control over an institution they helped build and maintain surfaced strongly in the 1990s. At that point, women were more successful at getting elected to offices of the marketing committee and attending meetings as members. The ongoing importance of community control over their textile industry was illustrated again in relation to another government development project.

LA LANERA DE OAXACA:
A CONTROVERSIAL DEVELOPMENT PROJECT

One of the most controversial government-supported projects to have taken place in Teotitlán is La Lanera de Oaxaca (The Oaxaca Yarn Factory). The yarn factory opened its doors in 1984 on land supposedly donated by the community. In addition to what turned out to be a dubious community land grant, the factory was funded jointly by federal and state agencies.[3] Its initial purpose was to provide weavers with locally produced high-quality yarn at low prices. Specifically, the project was supposed to result in lower prices than those charged by Teotiteco merchants who imported yarn from Tlaxcala.

Before 1984, the demand for machine-spun yarn had been met solely by a group of local merchants who purchased industrial yarn from large factories in Tlaxcala and Toluca. They shipped it by rail or truck to Teotitlán as often as every two weeks. Because of the difficulties that have plagued La Lanera de Oaxaca since it opened, yarn merchants who were supposed to be put out of business have been able to continue to sell yarn. In the 1980s, many Teotitecos commented that the yarn factory was never approved by the community. Some observed that even the name, which identifies it as Oaxacan, demonstrates that the project does not belong to the community. "The factory hasn't helped the town," complained Luis, age 55. "We don't really know who it belongs to. It seems like a private business. Didn't you see the name? The Lanera of Oaxaca? Why isn't it called the Lanera of Teotitlán?"

Many of the problems associated with the factory can be traced to a pattern of top-down administration, in which state officials negotiated with a few local men. When officials from the Secretariat of Oaxaca State Programs approached the mayor and his adviser in 1983 about the availability of land for a local factory, these two individuals began to negotiate on their own. A site was designated that supposedly involved only communal land, but also included some privately owned farmland. The families that owned the land were to have been compensated with other land of comparable quality, but many say they never received any. Members of these families continue to battle with the municipio over the loss of their land. Most people in the community complain that they were never consulted about the establishment of the factory, although it does appear to have been supported by an initial faction that backed the mayor. Most of the population was not included in the decision-making process, and many people, particularly women, have protested the actions of the factory and blamed it for escalating yarn prices in the community.

When the factory was completed, its administrators offered both men and women jobs as apprentices. The low daily wages, about one-third of what a skilled weaver could make, discouraged most Teotitecos from applying. In addition, weavers said that they did not want to work in a factory with set hours. They felt strongly about working in their own homes on their own schedules. In addition, working at home let them take time off for family affairs, ritual celebrations, farming, and domestic chores. No one wanted to work in the factory. After trying to recruit local workers for a few months, the first director of the factory imported male workers from Tlaxcala. In the mid-1980s, the only person from Teotitlán who was employed at the factory was a young woman who sold yarn. The workers from Tlaxcala led an isolated life, living in housing on the factory grounds. They were socially marginalized in the community.

In addition to severe political problems, the economics of factory yarn production were dismal, offering a lesson in bureaucratic inefficiency. The director attempted to run the factory efficiently during 1985 and 1986, but he was hampered by several factors. First, because the factory was closely monitored by the government, a legitimate 15 percent sales tax was charged. In contrast, yarn wholesalers in Tlaxcala do not write receipts or keep records, so no tax is charged to Teotiteco merchants for their purchases. Essentially, the factory had to produce yarn 15 percent cheaper than Tlaxcala yarn in order to sell it competitively in Teotitlán. A second problem centered on the logistics of production. Since the factory was built with very little capital, it had no wool-washing facility. Wool was purchased in local markets in the Valley of Oaxaca and then shipped to Mexico City, where it was washed. It was then shipped back to Teotitlán, where it was spun. About 13 percent of the final price of the yarn sold in the factory was accounted for by the cost of transporting the raw wool to Mexico City to be washed and returned. Finally, the factory had virtually no working capital. During local wool shortages, factory administrators had no sources of credit to import wool. From November 1984 through January 1986, the director of the factory tried in vain to get government credit to import wool from Argentina. Because the wool had to be purchased with dollars and the price changed daily, he was never granted permission to buy the wool.

Many people in the community continued to be dissatisfied with the fact that the factory was not run by the community. Renaldo Soza recalled the strong feelings that ran through the community in the 1980s and the process he and a group of men went through to recover administrative control for the community.

> We were very unhappy that the factory was named after the state and not after the town. A lot of people thought that Teotitlán had donated the land and was a minority partner. We went into the town hall to look up the records, to see how the factory was set up. At that time the community didn't even administer the factory. Our group was made up of five of us who played basketball together. We formed a nonprofit organization to administer the factory. At the beginning the factory sold the wool at a very high price. They were selling it at eighteen-fifty [pesos] per kilo when in town it was selling at fifteen. When we started running the factory as a group, the price went down.

Throughout the 1990s, the factory came increasingly under community control. A factory committee monitors its production and in 2004 the factory was peacefully coexisting with local yarn merchants. A new niche in yarn production emerged in the late 1990s: small local merchants purchased undyed yarn, dyed it, and then sold it at a small profit. The factory was sometimes the source of this yarn, depending on availability and prices elsewhere.

KINSHIP, CLASS RELATIONS, AND GENDER
UNDER COMMERCIAL CAPITALISM

By the mid-1980s, significant capital had been accumulated in Teotitlán and on a smaller scale in Santa Ana del Valle and San Miguel. All three communities experienced growth in their merchant sectors, with Teotitlán dominating the others. The majority of merchants in Teotitlán contract weavers in local households as well as in other communities, often through kin and compadrazgo ties, for a certain number of pieces, determining the design, color, and shape to be produced.

Teotitlán merchant households significantly expanded their scope of activity in the 1980s, far outstripping the development of merchant households in nearby Santa Ana del Valle. Jeffrey Cohen notes that whereas the 1990 Mexican census identified only one resident of Santa Ana as a patron or buyer (what I call here a merchant), by 1995 there were at least two more (1999, 48). Cohen's study and another by Scott

Cook and Leigh Binford (1990) note that apart from these few individuals, most weavings produced in Santa Ana are controlled by buyers and exporters from Teotitlán. Cook and Binford's survey of the 1980s indicates that at least 40 percent of Santa Ana's weavings were controlled by Teotitlán merchants (1990, 89), while a survey conducted by Cohen in 1990 indicates that over 60 percent of the textiles produced in Santa Ana were sold through merchants in Teotitlán.

Relations of production between merchants and weavers are simultaneously class relations and ties of kin and compadrazgo—the same relationships that form the basis of reciprocal labor networks at fiestas. Merchants tend to have more godchildren than weavers. Many Teotitecos assume it is easier for them to shoulder the heavy costs of godchild sponsorship. Many merchants have their godchildren working for them as pieceworkers: they provide the materials and the godchildren produce weavings in their homes.

In the relations of production, respect is so inculcated into the godparent-godchild relationship that a godchild may be in too weak a position to refuse a godparent's request for labor. Yet from the perspective of the godchild, having a godparent with significant financial resources also makes it possible to ask for a loan (often without interest) in a time of financial need. Heads of weaving households often seek out merchants as godparents for their children in the hope that the merchants will be able to help their children economically.

Weavers often receive interest-free loans and primary materials from merchants. When demand for weavers causes a shortage of labor, weavers may have more work than they can handle. In deciding which work to do, they give priority to requests from relatives or compadres. If a compadre is unwilling to pay the wage a weaver wants, however, he or she will quietly go elsewhere to work. As long as labor is in short supply, merchants cannot take too much advantage of their position as compadres. Conversely, during periods of low market demand, weavers lose their negotiating power.

A census conducted in 1985 revealed that there were approximately 110 self-identified merchant households out of a total of 1,039 households in Teotitlán. In 1985, Teotitecos conceptually divided merchants into three types, depending on the volume of their inventory. Approximately ten households were classified as "large" merchants, handling the largest share of distribution within Teotitlán and working in Santa Ana and San Miguel as well. About thirty households fell into the category of "medium" merchants, with the remainder labeled as "small." Small merchants purchased limited numbers of weavings or sold their own products in the local artisan market.

As the peso crisis of 1995 set in, the number of merchant households in Teotitlán declined. After the stock market dive at the turn of the twenty-first century, the number of merchant households appears to have declined even further. The 2000 Mexican census identifies twenty-one employers within the textile manufacturing sector of the municipio of Teotitlán (INEGI 2000, empleado 6A). Census data include the nearby affiliated town of Santiaguito. The town does not produce textiles, however, so the census numbers for the weaving sector are not affected. While the number of merchants in Teotitlán has decreased since I conducted my own survey in 1985, I am skeptical about the accuracy of the 2000 census figures. The number of actual merchant households is probably at least double that reported by the census and most likely also includes another fifteen to twenty-five households that may move in and out of functioning as small merchants, depending on their household finances. Cohen (1999, 48) suggests this same problem in interpreting census data on merchants in Santa Ana as well.

While the overall number of merchant households appears to have declined somewhat since 1985, at least seven of the ten "large" merchant households of the 1980s survived and businesses were handed down to sons and daughters. At the end of the 1990s it became increasingly difficult for entrepreneurs who did not come from established weaver households to become merchants. Some young couples were able to become part-time merchants with the help of their savings from work in the United States, but if they remained in Teotitlán for several years, they would most likely support themselves as independent weavers who sometimes had to sell their textiles to local buyers when they were pressed for cash.

The occupational classes of merchants and weavers described in chapter 1 participate in four basic types of production units that do not necessarily coincide with households (see S. Cook 1988, 5).

1. Independent weaver household workshops. All weavers in this production unit are household members. They are not paid for their labor. Such households own the means of production and provide their own wool, yarn, and dyes. Weavers produce textiles in their own homes that are sold to tourists, importers, or local merchants. Men, women, and children working in this type of production unit belong to the weaver class. Both men and women weave in this type of production unit.

2. Merchant workshops with on-site contract laborers. Labor in this type of production unit includes both unpaid merchant household members and hired weavers from weaver households. Contract weavers who work at merchant workshops do not own the means of production, nor are they responsible for providing yarn or dyes. They are paid by the piece by the merchant who owns the workshop. This production unit includes people from the merchant class and paid weavers from the weaver class. Paid laborers are usually male, although they may be single women as well. Unpaid household laborers from the merchant class often include women and children. They may be weavers or supervisors of paid weavers. The contract weavers here are in a strict labor/capital relationship with merchants.

3. Merchant workshops with contracted pieceworkers. Labor in this type of production unit can include both unpaid merchant household members and contracted weavers in pieceworker households who are working in their own homes. Pieceworker weavers usually own their own means of production, but often are not responsible for providing inputs. Usually they are given materials and weave finished products that are purchased by the piece by contracting merchants. This production unit includes petty capitalists from the merchant class, paid laborers from the weaver class, and unpaid laborers from merchant households, usually women and children who may be weaving or doing other preparatory work to supply pieceworkers.

4. Pieceworker households. Weavers work in their own households and use their own means of production. A merchant usually supplies yarn and dyes. Merchant households pay weavers by the piece. This production unit includes only people of the weaver class and may involve men, women, and children who weave at home. Women are much more likely to weave as pieceworkers at home than in a merchant's household because they can combine weaving with other domestic duties.

While these are the four basic types of production units found in Teotitlán, other variations are possible. An important distinction among the four types is that types 2 and 3 are based in households that belong to the merchant class while types 1 and 4 are based in weaver households.

While most households are related primarily to one type of production unit, laborers of a particular household may be involved in two or more types of production units simultaneously. They may, for example, work some of the time at home as part of an independent household workshop and some of the time at a merchant's house as part of a workshop with hired laborers. In the 1980s, a greater number of households could function consistently as independent weaver household workshops, but with the decline of the peso in the mid-1990s and then a decrease in tourism and sales in the twenty-first century, fewer weavers have been able to support themselves as part of independent production units. Often they have to do piecework for merchants part of the year. Almost all weavers aspire to be independent artisans. This was a major motive for the dozens of women who formed cooperatives in the late 1980s and 1990s. In reality, however, such groups are not able to support their members as independent artisans throughout the year. As we shall see, women's cooperatives may offer their members the possibility of producing and selling directly to tourists during certain times of the year, such as the Christmas holidays and the Guelaguetza celebration, held in July in Oaxaca City. During other parts of the year, however, women have had to continue to sell their labor to merchants in order to make ends meet.

One of the key issues to be explained here is how households move from weaver to merchant status under the present conditions of commercial capitalism. As we shall see, the role of gender is important in this process. Most households that have achieved merchant status used a combination of unpaid household labor and accumulation of initial capital through migration to the United States to do so, according to in-depth interviews with members of twenty merchant households.

An important question is how weaver households become small capitalist enterprises. My research concurs with the survey research of Cook and Binford (1988, 7–8), who write that "the movement of peasant-artisan household enterprises from conditions of petty commodity production to those of petty capitalism is significantly affected by household demographics through their impact on productive capacity, capital accumulation and material wealth. . . . Family labor contributes critically to the accumulation of capital and material assets in most household units which experience this movement." Cook and Binford emphasize that most households that experience an accumulation of capital through family labor do not cross the threshold to petty capitalist production. Those that do represent an exception to Chayanov's emphasis on simple reproduction of the household unit and "illustrate Lenin's thesis that 'family cooperation' is the 'foundation of capitalist cooperation'" (Cook and Binford 1988, 8). The labor obligations entailed by family and household membership have allowed some households to benefit from unpaid household labor as well as to take advantage of the reciprocal obligations implied by kinship and compadrazgo with those outside of their immediate household.[4] In Teotitlán, the gendered dynamics of migration to the United States were critical in this process as well.

Under emerging conditions of circulation capital from the late 1940s until the early 1960s the labor of women sustained a significant proportion of the population of Teotitlán while men were laboring in the United States. Most men did not send money home; if they did return with savings, they invested it in land, animals, or the means of production for weaving. Later women's labor was also important in helping households to build up capital for paying pieceworkers. As tourist and export markets for Zapotec textiles steadily grew, the availability of weaving labor became a critical variable in the expansion of production. In the early 1970s, young women began to weave along with their brothers, so that the pool of family weaving labor was expanded.

By the 1980s, the additional labor of women and girls was critical in helping households to begin functioning as employers. The factors of migration and unpaid female and child labor seem to have been important in allowing some weavers to move ahead in the 1970s and 1980s and begin to act as employers by paying nonhousehold workers. As demonstrated by Cook (1982a, 20; 1984a) and supported by my work in Teotitlán, most merchant households in the 1980s began as pieceworkers or independent producers. This situation began to change as the merchant class of the 1980s consolidated and passed on capital to offspring to be used in starting new businesses.

ZAPOTEC AESTHETICS AND THE ARTISTIC MEANING
OF TEXTILES TO THEIR CREATORS

The textiles created by Teotitecos are not only commodities with a use or exchange value but also representations of human creativity. Some artisans have begun to experiment with weaving techniques, establishing new textures and forms for their pieces. Weavers frequently discuss their designs and color combinations with one another and will express admiration for designs that they find particularly compelling. Debates about color, design, size, and texture are part of what women in weaving cooperatives discuss in their meetings and workshops.

Of greatest interest to weavers are innovations and changes in design and color combinations. Many women become animated when describing new ideas they have for textiles. This comment by María Gutiérrez, a founding member of the first women's cooperative and president of one of the current cooperatives, illustrates such discussions about innovation. "I am very interested in elaborating new designs. . . . I became interested in working in wool, but in thinking about new forms to work in and new ways of working in and out of the weave itself—incorporating other materials, other textures. . . . Now we make a wide range of things, tablecloths, place mats, rugs, and other objects but also with a new feel to them."

Many weavers have a catalogue of personal designs or those that have been conserved in their families for several generations. Recipes for dyes and color combinations are acknowledged as an important part of the asethetic impact of a particular textile.

Many people are tempted to romanticize Teotiteco weavers as "conservers of tradition" in their textiles, but I have found that the artistic curiosity and style of many weavers are focused on experimentation and innovation, something also noted by Eli Bartra in relation to Mexican folk art. She writes: "An eminently traditional form of expression, folk art is often conceived of as unchanging and static. Nothing is farther from the truth. Though it changes in ways distinct from those of elite art, it is in constant transformation, a result both of artists perfecting their techniques and of adaptation to market demands" (2000, 53).

Most weavers in Teotitlán who have been celebrated as original artists—of elite art or high art—are male. Their sense of aesthetics as well as innovations in design and style is applauded, as in the description of the work of the artist Arnulfo Mendoza in *Great Masters of Mexican Folk Art* (Fomento Cultural Banamex 2001, 385–87):

> Mendoza is able to interpret the timeless artistic forms as well as carefully observe and absorb modern ideas. He has made the transition from one culture to the other, tracing the path of Mexico's metaphorphosis over the centuries. . . . His early works were decorated with the traditional designs native to Teotitlán such as frets found in the ruins at Mitla or Monte Albán, the flor de Oaxaca, dancers, celestial motifs and patriotic symbols designed by Jorge Enciso. Today, he creates his own designs including highly stylized geometric motifs for his special rugs . . . colored with natural dyes, woven on a pedal loom with silk, cotton, gold and silver threads.

This description of Mendoza's highly original work in part describes the type of innovations that many weavers in Teotitlán are experimenting with—if they have the time. However, the majority of women and men

Figure 4. Arnulfo
Mendoza, weaver.
Photo by Mary Jane
Gagnier.

who weave are doing so as contract laborers for merchants and thus have
little time for artistic innovation. The kind of excitement María displayed
when she talked about new weaving techniques, designs, ways of establishing texture, and new ways of using color is typical. Thus while coffee
table books such as *Great Masters of Mexican Folk Art* and *Zapotec Weavers
of Teotitlán* (Fischgrund Stanton 2000) feature only a few male weavers as
exemplary of folk artists, the kinds of innovations, originality, and creativity discussed in relation to their work are potentially shared by all. In
general, many books on folk art have featured men; a new volume edited
by Eli Bartra, *Crafting Gender: Women and Folk Art in Latin America and the
Caribbean*, is a happy exception, as are some of the recent works she discusses (Bartra 2003a). The weaving cooperatives described in chapter 7
provide an important arena for women and men to discuss their sense
of aesthetics and to experiment with innovations.

THE WEAVING PROCESS

When hand-spun yarn is used, the most labor-intensive part of weaving production begins long before a weaver begins to throw the shuttle across the loom. Since wool is usually not available locally, Teotitecos often purchase it at the markets in Oaxaca, Tlacolula, and Ocotlán. Weavers may try to purchase in bulk, storing as much as they can for use in periods when wool is unavailable, as during the last few months of the rainy season. Once the wool is bought, it is sorted by color before being stored. More and more, however, local weavers are being supplied with wool and yarn by local merchants.

When a completely handmade textile is being produced, wool of the proper color and grade is first selected. The wool is then separated and taken down to the river for a thorough washing. Both men and women can be seen washing large lots of wool in harvest baskets. Once it has been washed, it is spread out in the sun to dry.

Once dry, the yarn is carded. The cards used are manufactured in the neighboring community of Díaz Ordaz. Carding is usually done by women and children in spare moments or continuously if a large lot of yarn is needed. The wool is brushed back and forth between the metal-toothed cards until it reaches a smooth consistency. It is then deposited in a basket for the spinner.

A spinning wheel is mounted on a low wooden bench. The wooden wheel is connected to the front spindle by a heavy woolen drive cord. The spindle is about fifteen inches long. The spinner cranks the wheel with the right hand and manipulates the wool with the left hand. A layer of carded wool is folded and split in half. The wool is attached to the spindle, and the spinner pulls the yarn outward so that a long, thin strand of yarn is created.

Spinning is a respected art. Teotitecos especially value well-spun yarn. Hand-spun yarn from Teotitlán fetches a higher price than that produced in other places. Yet because the demand for hand-spun yarn is often greater than the amount available, it is frequently purchased from other areas. One producing community, Chichicapan, has a long-standing relationship with Teotitlán as a supplier of hand-spun yarn. People in Chichicapan no longer weave, but they continue to produce yarn. Several yarn vendors come to Teotitlán to sell the yarn each week. The price of Chichicapan yarn is always about 25 percent lower than the price of hand-spun yarn from Teotitlán.

The best spinners in Teotitlán are elderly women and men. Many widows, unable to oversee agricultural production or engage in other types of labor, work as spinners. Most work for their own families, but some are hired by merchants to produce fine yarn. A good spinner working in conjunction with a carder can produce between one-fourth and one-half kilo of yarn a day. A kilo of hand-spun wool completed in two to three days brings about half the wages a weaver could earn in the same period. After wool is spun into yarn or yarn is purchased, it is wound into skeins and washed before dyeing. This is often the work of children. The four natural colors of wool used in weaving—white, black, brown, and gray—are separated to be wound onto bobbins.

Dyeing, like spinning, is a time-consuming process. Most households reserve at least one or two days a week for it. In pieceworker households and independent household workshops the process is carried out by husband-and-wife teams. In merchant households, where men are often out of town or busy with clients, dyeing is often the responsibility of women. It is the hardest and most uncomfortable work involved in the weaving process. Large vats of water, one for each color, are set to boil over large wood fires. Dye substances, natural or chemical, are then stirred into the vats. Skeins of yarn are left in the dye for various periods of time, depending on the desired shade and intensity of color. When the right hue is reached, the skeins are pulled out of the vats, washed in cold water, wrung out, and hung in the sun to dry on wooden poles. Stones are often used to weigh down the drying skeins so that the yarn does not shrink. Once dry, the skeins are removed from the dyeing poles to be spun onto bobbins with the spinning wheel. This task, which is often carried out by children, must be done steadily so that weavers can keep working. Often children work before and after school to create a supply of full bobbins for their parents.

The weaver's task begins with the preparation of the warp yarn for the loom. Warp yarn is usually factory made. It is of a lighter grade than weft yarn and is usually 80 percent wool and 20 percent cotton. Few weavers use hand-spun warp yarn unless it is for a special order. The warp yarn is measured between poles inserted in the ground. When the proper number of strands have been counted, the weaver winds the yarn into a skein. If he or she is going to begin weaving immediately, the warp is attached to the fibers of the loom.

The foot-powered treadle looms used today in Teotitlán differ little from the basic model introduced by the Spaniards in the sixteenth century. The only difference between current and earlier models is that looms have gotten progressively bigger. The largest loom in Teotitlán is between two and three meters long. It has eight pedals and is used for producing carpets. Most looms are mounted on four posts and sit in a table-like construction. The batten (or beater) and the heddles are suspended from crossbars at the top of the loom. The warp threads of the loom are on two rollers, one acting as a take-up roller as the weaving progresses and the other as a warp roller. The heddles are controlled by two foot pedals that are connected to them by cord.

The weaver stands in the loom, often on a box to have better access to the entire loom. The size of a loom can be a problem, particularly for children. To weave, the shuttle is thrown across the loom while the warp threads are held open by the heddle attached to one foot pedal. When one trip of the shuttle across the loom is completed, the other pedal is depressed, closing the warp threads around the weft. When the weaver is weaving one color or a stripe design, the shuttle moves rapidly across the loom. Most designs, however, are more complex. In this case, the weaver must change bobbins every time there is a color change in the design. In order to do this correctly, the weaver counts the appropriate number of warp threads, lifts them up, and pulls the bobbin under. The batten suspended from overhead is then used to tighten up the weave.

Once a textile is finished, it is rolled onto the take-up wheel of the loom. Usually four to five pieces are produced at once and cut loose from the loom. They are then scraped with a metal scraper to remove loose wool and picked clean of any burrs or other material found in the wool. The final job is tying up the warp ends. When a weaver has completed several pieces, the head of the household (male or female) either delivers them to the merchant who commissioned them if they are piecework or goes from door to door trying to sell them to local merchants. After the weavings are sold, a weaver household usually invests immediately in more wool or yarn in order to keep on working. If weavers have no cash for yarn, they may then decide to do more piecework for a local merchant. The merchant will most likely supply the materials. The production cycle thus repeats itself.

In general, older people in Teotitlán have a much wider knowledge of weaving processes than people under 40. For example, older people have greater knowledge of dyeing processes and designs. While most serapes in Teotitlán are made with "vegetable colors" (i.e., the colors of vegetables, not vegetable dyes), most yarn is dyed with chemical dyes. Many young people do not know how to use natural dyes or how to find the plants that yield them. An exception to the use of chemical dyes is

Figure 5. This man is weaving a small textile commissioned by a local merchant on a piece-work basis. Photo by the author.

Figure 6. Many women under 30 now spend a significant portion of each day weaving. Photo by the author.

Figure 7. Weaving itself is only one part of creating a textile. Here a weaver prepares dyed yarn for winding onto bobbins as his wife ties up the end of her completed textile. Photo by the author.

found in the workshops of several high-quality weavers. In the 1970s, a local weaver studied ancient dye processes and encouraged Teotitecos to use natural dyes. The materials often used include cochineal (producing reds, pinks, and oranges), indigo (blues and greens), rock lichen (yellow), acacia beans (black), pecan shells (tan), and the dodder vine (yellow). Unfortunately, the cost of dyes such as cochineal, which is about U.S.$90 per pound, is prohibitive to most weavers. The older generation of Teotitecos still has the knowledge of how to obtain and use a wide variety of dyes.

Increasingly, however, younger weavers have shown interest in this local intellectual property as well. In the 1990s and in 2001 and 2002, workshops offered by a variety of government institutions focused on educating people in natural dye techniques and encouraged them to use this knowledge as part of their marketing strategies. Weaving cooperatives formed in the 1990s emphasized this aspect of their production techniques in brochures and information. The current emphasis on the use of "indigenous local knowledge" of plants, herbs, and dyeing techniques is part of a long-standing strategy of marketing Zapotec ethnicity along with the textiles. For example, tags to be attached to textiles produced by the women's cooperative Dgunna Gulal Ni Ruin Laadti/Mujeres Antiguas Que Hacen Tapetes (Traditional Women Weavers) feature the words "100 percent pure wool, dyed with all-natural colors." Another tag states, "Hand woven on treadle loom by Zapotec craftsmen." The front of the tag identifies the articles as being from Teotitlán and features two Zapotec traditional designs carved in the walls of local pyramids. The Zapotec geometrics that weavers prefer are taken from the friezes in archaeological sites in Teotitlán, Mitla, and other surrounding communities.

THE POLITICAL ECONOMY OF FOLK ART AND
HIGH ART FROM TEOTITLÁN

Interest in handicrafts probably began at a certain stage of our industrial revolution. Until the mechanization of carpet weaving in the West in the mid–nineteenth century, Oriental carpets seem to have been important more as an exotic textile for which (until Axminster) there was no Western equivalent, and (once they were culturally assimilated and recognized as exotic) valued for their design rather than for their utility. From that time on, however, the fact of their being handmade became a significant characteristic, and as the craft was gradually drawn into the world economy, the survival of traditional relations of production became an additional factor—the rug was an exotic product made in its own exotic process for its own exotic purpose (Spooner 1986, 222).

The mechanization of textile production around the world has resulted in a desire for handmade shawls, blankets, rugs, wall hangings, and more on the part of middle-class and elite Western consumers. A desire for the traditional is met with hand-produced commodities that usually originate outside of the Western world or come from marginalized groups within Western societies that have been relegated to the "exotic," such as Native Americans in the United States. In Mexico, middle- and upper-class consumers' desire for "the traditional" coincided with the fetishism of "the indigenous" through a turnaround in the symbols of Mexican nationalism in the 1930s, which reclaimed Mexico's indigenous past as part of its historical uniqueness.

The mechanization that makes industrial consumers long for "genuine" crafts and folk art also eliminates peasant consumer markets for hand-produced objects as they are replaced by polyester blankets, nylon jackets, and plastic water jugs—industrial articles that are more attractive because they are cheaper or are associated with modernization (García Canclini 1982, 96). In Mexico, craft production faced a doomed future in regional consumer markets but was revitalized because of a market for the exotic and the authentic, now as folk art. A key dimension in the value of crafts and folk art is their authenticity, particularly in higher-priced items such as the weavings produced in Teotitlán and Santa Ana. An important part of perceived authenticity has to do with the survival of what are viewed as traditional relations of production.

For consumers, Zapotec weavings are authentic handicrafts made with exotic production processes—even though wool and foot-powered looms were brought by the Spanish and the historically "authentic" looms were backstrap looms used to produce cotton textiles. As seen in a California importer's description of Zapotec culture and weaving in 1986, the survival of seemingly exotic relations of production is the key to the "authenticity" of the product.

> Their 2000 year old heritage is as deep and fertile as the Oaxacan Valley of southern Mexico where the Zapotec Indians have woven a culture from the fibers of their own strong roots dyed with influences from the Mayans, Aztecs, the colonial Spanish and more recently the "modern World" as it spins towards the 21st century.
>
> The weavers of Teotitlán del Valle, while maintaining a traditional standard of design, which distinguishes them as time-honored artisans, have evolved their wool-weaving art, adapting and absorbing ideas from other cultures through history. The Zapotec today, in weaving each piece, still use 100 percent sheep's wool and natural dyes derived from the plants and insects of this rich region. The Spanish colonial floor loom was introduced during the conquest of Mexico and has been adapted and maintained as the machine of the predominantly male craftsmen. . . .

Until the 1970s, a majority of sales of Teotiteco textiles were to Mexican nationals and foreign tourists in Mexico. As the spiraling devaluation of the peso began in 1982, the market for Zapotec textiles shifted dramatically to an export market centered in the United States and somewhat in Europe as Mexican nationals could not afford to buy the textiles. Another important ingredient in this change was the more active role taken by importers beginning in the 1980s as they began to exert a greater degree of control over the product to get the right look. "By the early 1980s," writes Wood, "middlemen from Teotitlán and the United States were doing much more than simply letting artisans know of their interests in purchasing particular designs. Businessmen from the United States had also begun to work directly with middlemen and weavers in their workshops, initially creating new designs and overseeing the dyeing of wool into colors they knew would sell in the U.S." (2000a, 139).

As the purchasing power of U.S. dollars rose dramatically in Mexico in the 1980s, more North American businesspeople began to import Mexican crafts. Many Mexican middlemen interviewed stated that their profit margins were drastically reduced since 1982, as they cannot compete with North Americans who come to buy crafts with dollars. Thus the combination of greater purchasing power after the peso devaluation and a move by U.S. importers to exert greater control over Teotiteco textiles results in much tighter links by the mid- to late 1980s between merchants in Teotitlán and U.S. importers. This period also coincides with the craze for the Santa Fe style, in which particular "cultural, social, and geographic features of the American Southwest" were highly commercialized (Wood 2000a, 139). Some of the design elements that were consolidated as a staple of the Santa Fe style were from Navajo textiles. As Wood comments, in Santa Fe, Zapotec textiles were "no longer being sold as Zapotec textiles, but as Southwestern U.S. textiles (or more accurately as inexpensive, vaguely ethnic or Native American textiles)."

In 1985, North American merchants interviewed reported selling Zapotec weavings in the United States at 250 percent to 600 percent of their purchase price. However, an examination of wholesale prices in Teotitlán and retail prices in U.S. stores suggests that U.S. retail prices are often as high as 1,000 percent of wholesale prices. Profits for U.S. importers are quite high, in view of the fact that most do not spend more than about 38 percent of the purchase price for taxes, shipping, broker's fees, and their traveling expenses to get the weavings to the retail market. In 1987 the United States imposed an 11 percent tax on woolen goods imported from Mexico. The Mexican government had a 2 to 3 percent export tax. By the year 2000, most wool textiles produced in the treadle loom weaving communities of the Oaxaca Valley were funneled through the dominant marketing structure of Teotitlán to an ever-expanding group of U.S. importers who distributed them through trade shows, privately owned and chain stores, and interior decorators. This pattern, however, was increasingly challenged by the growing cooperative movement in the community that began in the mid-1980s and blossomed in the late 1990s.

Today production includes high-priced original pieces, limited editions of codices and other reproductions, high-quality geometric designs, and mass-produced simple pieces produced primarily in the subordinate towns of San Miguel and Santa Ana. At the high end of the market for Teotiteco textiles are those pieces sold as high art, not as folk art. These textiles can cost more than U.S.$10,000 and are made by about a dozen artists with international reputations. Artists such as Arnulfo Mendoza and Isaac Vásquez García regularly exhibit their work in U.S. galleries and have their own galleries and shops in Teotitlán and Oaxaca. Mendoza combines traditional dyeing and weaving techniques with tapestry techniques learned in France and also incorporates silk in his weavings. Vásquez concentrates on images from pre-Hispanic codices from a variety of Mexico's indigenous ethnic groups and emphasizes traditional dyeing techniques and color combinations. These men and others who sell their work directly to galleries do so as artists and have been honored in Mexico and abroad for their masterful work.

Interviews in 1985 and 1986 revealed that importers who purchased weavings around the Third World were cross-fertilizing designs and materials between ethnic groups in an effort to reach new market niches in the United States. This trend accelerated in the 1990s. Several importers commented that, while Mexican rugs are cheaper than Navajo, Pakistani, and Afghan rugs in the U.S. market, Dhuri rugs produced of cotton-wool blends in India are cheaper and compete with Zapotec rugs at the lower end of the U.S. carpet market. These importers have contracted weavers in India to produce "Zapotec" rugs made of cotton and cotton-wool blends. Such rugs can be found in chains such as Pier I Imports across the United States. These same importers stated that they tried in vain to get Teotitecos to produce Eastern designs so that more Zapotec rugs could compete in the high-end Oriental rug market. Teotitlán weavers would not produce many of the designs, stating their preference for Zapotec geometrics. While Zapotec weavers did not take to Middle Eastern and South Asian designs, they did become major producers of Navajo designs, something that Cohen (1999) notes in Santa Ana del Valle as well.

ZAPOTEC AND NAVAJO DESIGNS IN
THE POLITICAL ECONOMY OF GLOBALIZATION

> LYNN: How do you respond to the criticism that some weavers from Teo-
> titlán who began to produce Navajo designs for export to the United States
> that now compete with Navajo products committed a form of robbery?
> ARNULFO: This is a criticism that comes from outside of Mexico?
> LYNN: Yes. From the United States to Mexico.
> ARNULFO: On the one hand we could say that there is merit to this criti-
> cism because all criticisms are important. But nevertheless, there is room
> for everything. I would say that this includes this repetition or reinterpreta-
> tion of the foreign images that have been interpreted in Teotitlán, not just
> from the Navajos. . . . I am sure that Picasso never dreamed that one day
> his work would be interpreted by people in Teotitlán del Valle. He prob-
> ably might even have liked the idea of that. But maybe the real heart of
> the artist, the real artistic will to produce art is something that shouldn't
> be discussed. . . . You could say that if someone is inspired by or following
> someone else's work that it is like a school. That's how I see it, like a school.
> But nevertheless, as in this case, Teotitlán can't be made directly guilty for
> what happens. I think it is more an example of a people who don't aban-
> don their craft that is more than a thousand years old when sales decrease.
> There is always something that the people can do to maintain themselves
> as weavers. . . . In other communities, people have lost their craft because
> there is no market for it. . . . So I couldn't criticize Teotitlán in this way.

The people of Teotitlán have been documented as weavers at least
since the fifteenth century. Throughout their history, they have employed a wide range of design elements, some corresponding to local
ritual and architectural elements and others coming from farther afield.
In fact, what have often become identified as "traditional" design elements in many cultures often originate elsewhere. This pattern in cultural histories raises a series of important questions. Can indigenous artists maintain intellectual property rights over their designs, techniques,
and forms of production through time? Who owns pre-Hispanic designs? How does the idea of intellectual property rights function in relation to collectively held property that is the inheritance of many communities and possibly many indigenous ethnic groups? These questions are
increasingly discussed by Zapotec weavers. The most frequently asked
question is, Who has the rights to these designs?

The "Zapotec" contents of many textiles come from a wide range of sources. Teotitecos have incorporated elements from Mayan, Mexica, Mixtec, and other indigenous groups in their textiles. Decorative elements used in Teotiteco textiles that are found in archaeological sites in Oaxaca can also be found in other places and vice versa. How do we determine "legitimate" ethnic owners of textile designs when the elements of those designs have been circulated throughout Mexico through many centuries of political, religious, and cultural history? And before the current U.S.-Mexican border was established in 1848, Mexican indigenous designs were circulated within what is now the southwestern United States as well. James Jeter and Paula Marie Juelke (1978, 26) suggest that by 1885, Saltillo designs had become dominant in Navajo blankets.

The fact that Zapotec weavers have incorporated in their textiles elements that are labeled "Navajo" is no secret. It is important to note, however, as Wood does (1997, 2001), that one of the major impetuses to produce Navajo rugs came from U.S. businesses that in the 1980s went from showing a few books on Navajo textiles as examples to placing mass orders for Navajo designs and using skilled Zapotec labor to produce them. He quotes one longtime buyer:

> "Before 1980 it was just a real casual thing and I didn't really do any designing. I may have brought down a few Navajo books, but not much. . . . And I left for a year . . . and when I returned . . . there was a notable shift in the style of production, that they were doing more volume, more repeat orders. There wasn't a man in his house sort of feeling—[deciding] what type of color he wanted to work with and the design that [he would be weaving] in the next few weeks on the loom but . . . having someone in his family let him know that that if he wove ten of those, he would sell them to that man. So there was a lot more mass production at that time." (Wood 1997, 201)

At that time many women were involved in weaving. And while many of them began to feel as though they were contract workers who had no choice in what they produced, others who continued to produce independent designs and even contract workers who did creative work on their own time saw the Navajo elements introduced by U.S. merchants as part of the wider panorama of design elements. While it seems clearly established that U.S. merchants were responsible for the mass production of Navajo designs in the 1980s, it is important to avoid viewing Zapotec weavers as passive recipients of orders for "Navajo" textiles and for designs from a wide range of inspirations.

Artists from Teotitlán such as Arnulfo Mendoza openly discuss the many sources of designs that have influenced Zapotec weavers, including the work of such modern painters as Miró, Picasso, and Rivera. The writer Kathy M'Closkey has viewed work that documents Zapotec production of textiles that reproduce "Navajo" designs, as my own does, as "sanctioning an activity that threatens Navajo lifeways" and providing "an intellectual rationale for equating the symbols of consumerism with emergent types of communal identity" (2002, 14).

My earlier writing on American importers' encouragement of Zapotec weavers to produce Navajo designs was intended to demonstrate the ways in which U.S. importers were instrumental in the definition of specific markets for Zapotec and other indigenous craft products. Wood (1997, 2000a, 2000b, 2001, 2003) has demonstrated the very specific role of markets in Santa Fe and Taos, New Mexico, in encouraging particular kinds of design and color innovations to support the "Southwest" look. As Arnulfo Mendoza and other indigenous intellectuals from Teotitlán have observed, the ability of Teotiteco weavers to interpret, experiment with, and incorporate elements from a wide range of sources in their textiles has had the positive effect of keeping alive a craft that might have died out. The same could probably be said of Navajo weavers, who also have incorporated a range of elements in their work, including some that originated outside their traditional territory. A more important question to be asked about both Navajo and Zapotec weavers might be, How is each group positioned in the global economy in order to be able to defend their craft as importers and entrepreneurs continue to seek cheaper and cheaper sources of labor to produce "hand-crafted" textiles?

Acceleration of global markets and of the race to the bottom for the cheapest labor have combined to produce a situation that is detrimental to both Zapotec and Navajo weavers as their designs are brokered by traders to weavers elsewhere in the world who can produce them for much lower prices. M'Closkey documents Navajo designs woven in India that sell for less than $1,000, whereas a Navajo-produced rug would retail for $6,000 to $8,000 (2002, 198). Such products are now sold at a trading post within the boundaries of the Navajo reservation and on elaborate Web sites. Petrona López, a community leader and longtime participant and leader in several women's cooperatives, commented, "I have gone to craft fairs and seen textiles made in China with designs from Teotitlán. They are not made of wool, but of other materials. But the designs are the same. Now they are making them in Guatemala, Peru, and Colombia as well." These developments have lowered the prices for both Zapotec and Navajo textiles and have generated efforts such as that of the textile cooperatives in Teotitlán to market their products directly to consumers either in person or through their own Web sites. Prices of Zapotec textiles declined significantly in the 1990s in real dollars.

The decrease in prices paid to Navajo and Zapotec producers has brought some Zapotec and Navajo weavers into contact with one another to discuss their mutual interests and ways of protecting one another's products. Discussions and organizing around indigenous intellectual property rights have advanced, primarily in the area of genetic codes and plant species, but discussions about designs and techniques have entered the conversation as well. Weavers in Teotitlán are well aware of their vulnerabilities as well as those of the Navajos and other indigenous groups. Many Teotitecos feel that it is problematic to stake individual or group claims for all the design elements used in textiles. Instead, they focus on what they will have to do to stay ahead in the market. I asked Marisa, founder of one of only two mixed male-female cooperatives in Teotitlán, about issues of design copying in 2001.

> LYNN: Do you worry about copying other people's designs or having other people copy yours?
>
> MARISA: Well, some people copy Navajos. Some people copy Mayan and Aztec designs. We are all copiers—we copy Navajos, we copy Diego Rivera, and now people in Guatemala copy us and we copy them. In India they copy us. How are we going to complain when other people copy us if we have always been copying as well? What we all have to think about is what we are going to do when the market is saturated with our products.

I had a related discussion with Imelda, who has also participated in cooperatives, regarding her concern with falling prices for Teotiteco textiles in the late 1990s.

> IMELDA: I have talked with my sister and others about how there is going to be a time when our tapetes won't sell because people in other countries are going to be making the same kind of textiles, but of another quality. They will make them with cotton and another type of material that looks like wool, but isn't. They will be cheaper. In fact, in the United States they are already buying these kinds of textiles. Then they come here and say, "How come these other textiles are cheaper and here they are more expensive?" I say, "It's because we use wool, another kind of material." Then they say, "Well, they have the same designs as here. They have the frets from

Mitla, the rain and fire gods." They are copying all this. In Chile they make these textiles, and in Africa.

LYNN: Have you even seen them?

IMELDA: I haven't, but my sister has. She says they're made of cotton but they have the same pre-Hispanic designs on them from Oaxaca that we produce. I'm telling you this because we are going to have to think about other things to sell because the day will come when we can no longer sell our textiles. But what will we do? If we don't study, we won't have work.

While Zapotec weavers readily acknowledge the use of Navajo and other non-Zapotec designs, they also show concern for themselves and other artisans who are suffering under competition from cheaper imitations from India, Africa, and Chile. M'Closkey is certainly correct in implicating primarily U.S. importers and entrepreneurs in appropriating Navajo designs and their Zapotec counterparts and having rugs of all sizes woven in India and then sold as "Navajo" or other types of rugs (2002, 197–98). In addition, U.S. and European textile designers continue to appropriate design elements from a wide range of indigenous groups. Andra Fischgrund Stanton's *Zapotec Weavers of Teotitlán* documents the influence of specific textile designers and importers such as Richard Enzer on textile production in Teotitlán (2000, 56–57). Fischgrund Stanton maintains that Enzer's ideas are still reflected in many weavings made in Teotitlán, even though Enzer himself has moved on to teach his designs to weavers in Eastern Europe. While Enzer says his move is related to "finding his own tribe," it is notable that he was asked to leave Teotitlán by community authorities and his move to Eastern Europe coincided with the opening of those markets and access to fairly cheap labor there after the Berlin Wall came down.

To understand the relationship between Zapotec and Navajo (and other indigenous) weavers we have to look at the production networks between Oaxaca and Santa Fe, but we also need to place the production dynamics in the larger historical context of globalization. The accelerated integration of global consumer and labor markets in the 1980s and 1990s has placed both the Zapotec and the Navajo at a disadvantage in relation to other weavers around the world who are willing to weave any designs introduced by designers and importers for very low prices using cheap materials (see Nash 2000, 179). Ironically, one response to this situation is that many weavers in Teotitlán, particularly those in cooperatives, are returning to local designs as sources of inspiration. Some of these pieces are displayed in the community museum.

While it is very difficult to patent as "uniquely Teotiteco Zapotec" the design elements found in codices, local archaeological sites, and other regional sources, weavers are increasingly interested in claiming these design elements as part of their heritage and ethnicity and promoting them as such. Efforts such as those reflected in the creation of local museums and in the work of cooperatives to create and market their own products directly to consumers represent strategies for at least short-circuiting some of the effects of the globalization of textile production that threaten Zapotec and Navajo producers.

A COMMUNITY MUSEUM THAT CHALLENGES IMPOSED REPRESENTATIONS OF INDIGENOUS ARTISANS

The ways in which Mexico's indigenous peoples were represented as folk artists in the early and mid–twentieth century are in sharp contrast to developments in indigenous organizing and identity claims since the 1970s. A wave of indigenous organizing beginning with events such as the First Indigenous Congress, held in San Cristóbal de Las Casas in 1974, which included 1,230 delegates from four ethnic groups, culminated in the 1990s with the creation of the National Indigenous Congress (CNI) in 1996. The CNI is a network of hundreds of indigenous organizations, communities, and coalitions that focuses on coordinated organizing for indigenous rights and culture (see Stephen 2002, 328–34; 1997b; 1997c; Fox, Rivera-Salgado, and Stephen 1999). The Zapatista rebellion of 1994 and the establishment of dozens of autonomous indigenous communities in rebellion in Chiapas provided a major political opening in Mexico that propelled the already developing national movement for indigenous rights.

Key in the discourse for indigenous rights and culture is the concept of autonomy. Self-determination demands respect for the internal governing and cultural practices and decision-making modes of indigenous peoples, empowerment of indigenous peoples in national and state-level decision-making bodies, and acknowledgment of the current as well as past contributions of indigenous peoples to Mexico's history and culture. The community museum movement of the 1980s and 1990s was a part of this process. In Oaxaca, eleven community museums were formed with the support of the National Institute of Anthropology and History (INAH), in which indigenous peoples decided how to tell their own histories. In Teotitlán del Valle, the community museum emerged simultaneously with the consolidation of the national indigenous movement and provided a local site for Zapotec cultural activists to frame their own history in articulation with increasing national claims for the right to self-determination. The gendered Zapotec history in the museum provides a direct challenge to exhibits that ignored women's presence in descriptions and acknowledgments of Teotiteco textile production.

EL MUSEO DEL TEOTITLÁN DE VALLE
BALAA XTEE GUEDCHI GULAL

Española: Díos está con ustedes, hombre, Díos está con usted mujer donde estan y estan tan lejos que Díos les dio un lugar de nuestro continente Europeo. Por eso queremos a ustedes todos, que llegan con nosotros en nuestro pueblo donde está nuestro Museo donde estan guardados las reliquias sagradas de ñuestro antepasando. Por eso queremos con el respeto que merecen cada uno de ustedes señores que nos visitan el lugar de nuestro museo de Teotitlán del Valle.

Zapoteco: llchan dad llchan naán ysaate yubtu ni révesne llchan yubtu cudd vanilli llain cudrives yubtu steecaa guelliliu cud rives isaatee yubtu dononm ricason gasuiñ ne llan yubtu lo guelli dullteñon tee yubtu gumbetu veni gulas ni basaan dullpengulun ni rivisneaun donon raves lo galvany lletee yubtu donon cabesun dunuañ lo galbain lleetu yubtu lis du dullpeni gulason

God is with you, man. God is with you, woman. Wherever you are, and you are so far away, European, that God gave you a place on our continent. That is why we want all of you to come and visit our town where our museum is that houses the sacred relics of our past. That is why we are inviting you—each one of you with all due respect—to come and visit us. The place is our museum of Teotitlán del Valle.

The dedication above appears in Zapotec and Spanish on the home page of the Web site of Teotitlan's community museum (Casa del Pueblo Antiguo). I have added an English translation for readers. The Spanish inscription is clearly directed to the nonindigenous Web browser and is written to invite potential tourists to come and visit the museum in the flesh, and the Zapotec inscription uses ceremonial language to invite local men and women to visit.

Opened in 1995, the museum involved the active participation of a wide range of community members as well as staff from the INAH. Its primary purpose, according to the authors of the Web page (a group of elderly volunteers and the museum's 1999–2001 committee, named in a community assembly) was "to create a place to familiarize and safeguard the great richness of our cultural patrimony." The museum committee is charged with maintaining, promoting, and improving the museum. The committee's president, interviewed in 2003, commented, "The purpose of the museum is to defend what is ours, our heritage, and to attend to the people who come to visit. . . . What we want is for the people to not forget their Zapotec language and their cultural inheritance. We bring all the children from our schools here. We want people to value what is ours, our inheritance." Another member of the committee added, "Do you see that sign there in Zapotec? It doesn't say 'museum' in our language, it says 'our house.' What we are trying to do is to conserve our history for our children and our grandchildren. We are also trying to prevent things from being taken out of our town, away from a people who want to fight for their culture." The process of conserving local history through the creation of a museum involved the collaboration of a wide range of people both inside and outside the community.

In 1992 the community solicited the INAH's support of the local population's efforts to put the museum together. A community assembly named three volunteer committees, one for construction and two for research, to carry out the work necessary to get the museum off the ground. The research committees organized a workshop on oral history, interviewing community members and reviewing documents in the community archive, some of them dating back to the sixteenth century. People in the community donated archaeological pieces, offered historical and cultural information, helped with construction, and produced murals. Community members helped to restore archaeological objects and organized a donation campaign and a historical photograph contest. In 1992 the community joined the Union of Community Museums of Oaxaca. The museum's organization appears to be similar to that of the museum in neighboring Santa Ana del Valle, opened in the 1980s (Cohen 1999, 146–52).

In 1993, community members in conjunction with archaeologists from INAH identified a major archaeological ruin underneath the Catholic church in the center of the community. Many people in the community already knew of the pyramid below the church. The church walls contain stones with geometric designs that most people told me in the 1980s were from ancient structures under the main plaza. The "discovery" of this ruin no doubt pushed forward the community museum project but also redoubled local efforts to ensure that the cultural patrimony of the community remained there. The ruin has been partially excavated but the parts directly under the present-day church have been left undisturbed. Locals now identify this site as the most important ceremonial center of their ancestors.

The museum itself is a blend of local oral history, culture, and tradition with the discourse of archaeology. One of the museum's three rooms, the Archaeology Room, features maps and documents from 1564, 1596, and 1787 as well as clay, stone, and other artifacts that place the foundation of Teotitlán as contemporary with the period known as Monte Albán I, 500–200 B.C. The archaeological discussion works to distinguish Teotitlán as an early and important population site in the Oaxaca central valley. It also provides scientific evidence to buttress local claims that weaving was carried on there long before the Spanish arrived. Labeled "Laachi benni ni ruinchi laadi guichi"[5] or "Community of people who make blankets of wool," the exhibit in the next room locates Teotiteco weaving in the 2,000-odd years of the community's existence and ties it to Teotiteco ethnic identity through time. Here weaving is divorced from the "arte popular" framework, which views Teotiteco textiles as part of Mexico's national heritage, and is reclaimed from below as a key component of one of Mexico's original important population and culture sites.

The exhibit specifically documents the role of women as weavers of cotton cloth before the Conquest, the introduction of sheep, wool, and treadle looms by the Spanish, and the commercialization of textiles. The museum recognizes the continuity between women's precolonial and current roles as weavers. Museum visitors are told: "In the pre-Hispanic period, only women were obliged to weave in order to produce clothing for their families. . . . Codices show us that women were weaving and spinning. . . . Women helped to card wool, spin it, dye it, clean it, and prepare it for sale. Later it was not normal for women to weave, but beginning in the 1950s and 1960s, women returned to their role as weavers. And now women are seen as equally good weavers with men and this is seen as normal.".

The last room in the museum focuses on a traditional form of local wedding known as *gal ruuchi nia za guili*, or wedding with music. The exhibit goes into great detail about all of the ceremonial elements, events, and objects that are involved in this multiday ceremony and contrasts it with photographs and discussions of more contemporary weddings. Many people in the community view this form of wedding as representing the most concentrated form of significant cultural elements in the ceremonial life of the community, perhaps rivaled only by the mayordo-mías. The exhibit focuses on the metate and the hope chest as symbols of continuity between past and present weddings.

Overall, the museum functions as an autonomous space where a wide range of community members have participated in telling their history in a way that reinforces their cultural, economic, and political claims not only to Zapotec textiles but also to political and cultural autonomy. I was not present when the museum was developed, and the understand-ing of the museum has no doubt changed from the way it was under-stood while it was being created. According to William Warner Wood, who was living in the community at that time, "there was some tension between INAH staff and the young men they instructed about how to do the research and organize the exhibit" (personal communication, 2004). At least one young man quit the museum committee in 1992 because of the tension. What I found interesting in 2002 and 2003 was that the story told in the museum was being adopted by sectors of the community that often are in competition for access to and hegemony in the regional, na-tional, and international markets for their textiles. Merchants, weavers, and members of cooperatives praised the museum in conversations with me and suggested at least some common interest in the unified history of the community captured in it. It functions as a legitimating source for all of them and captures the multiple meanings of textiles in their lives as culturally significant, sources of aesthetic pleasure and pride, and com-modities in an exchange system where they have both a use value and an exchange value. Almost everyone in Teotitlán I have spoken with likes the museum and agrees that it is a valuable community asset for many reasons. Disagreements come not over the ethnic history presented in the museum but about who truly has the right to claim this history as a part of their daily life in the present. Weavers and members of coopera-tives often point out that merchants are no longer directly connected to that history because they don't weave themselves, they only sell the weav-ings and the labor of others.

CONCLUSIONS

As use commodities were transformed into folk art, the relations of pro-duction, the gendered division of labor, and local ethnic identity were all affected. A new petty capitalist merchant class emerged under conditions of commercial capitalism. This class began to deal directly with U.S. importers in the distribution of textiles in the 1970s and consolidated their position in the 1980s, incorporating weavers from the neighboring communities of Santa Ana, San Miguel del Valle, and Díaz Ordaz. While the merchant class of the 1980s came primarily from a weaver and subsistence farming background and there was some fluidity in terms of who could become a merchant, with the advent of NAFTA in the 1990s and a neoliberal economic model in Mexico, class relations became less fluid. The children of the most dynamic merchant households of the 1970s and 1980s inherited wealth and helped to consolidate control of textile reselling and exporting.

The 1990s also brought some significant changes to ways in which the community positioned itself in relation to national politics and a movement for indigenous self-determination inspired by the political opening created by the Zapatista rebellion, and as a home not only for folk art but also for high art, as exemplified by the recognition of the work of a handful of weavers in publications, museums, and elsewhere. The founding of the community museum provided a venue for a local projection of history and identity that contested the ways Teotitecos had been romanticized and often inaccurately described. The simultaneous emergence of the museum with its unified community history and the further entrenchment of class-based difference is a continuation of tensions that existed in the community in the 1980s. The tension between a unified local ethnic history and economic stratification is a key part of the frame within which gender relations and identity formation were played out.

CHAPTER 7

From Contract to Co-op

Gender, Commercialization, and

Neoliberalism in Teotitlán

The relatively egalitarian gender relations that seemed to prevail in subsistence farming and weaving households in Teotitlán eroded as merchant households accumulated capital and contracted laborers in significant numbers. Increased stratification and the solidification of class differences between merchants and weavers in the 1980s resulted in significant differences between women based on the position of their household in the relations of production. A significant aspect of this stratification that also affected gender relations was an increase in more direct involvement by U.S. importers with Teotiteco merchants, resulting in the subcontracting of weavers to reproduce designs and colors in mass quantities for sale in places like Santa Fe, New Mexico (see Wood 1997). Women on the receiving end of these subcontracting relations felt they had little power and had to sell their work very cheaply. Nevertheless, gendered class relations in the areas of production and ritual continued to be mediated by an idiom of kin-based community solidarity that was expressed during ritual events, in community assemblies, and in the community museum.

In the late 1980s and 1990s, weaving women in the middle and poorer sectors of the community began to organize a series of weaving cooperatives in an effort to challenge the increasing class stratification that often relegated them to serving as contract laborers or pieceworkers for merchant families—a position they shared with many weavers in neighboring Santa Ana (see Cohen 1999, 54). In an attempt to bypass local merchant control of the textile industry and to gain political and cultural rights in their community and in the global market as independent artisans, these women pioneered a new era in gender relations in Teotitlán. Several of the founders of the first women's cooperatives were returning migrants who had spent time outside the community and began to question the kinds of restrictions they lived under in accordance with local gendered traditions that restricted women's movements, discouraged them from acting independently, and kept them from participating in formal political processes in the community.

The explicit goal of these cooperatives is to undercut the monopoly held by local merchants and U.S. importers over the textile market and to allow producers to sell their goods collectively so that they can market their textiles directly to consumers. Cooperatives have become a recognized part of community government as well. Their members are formally invited to community assemblies and they have earned the support of local authorities for their activities. The weaver gets a greater economic return for her textiles and enjoys greater visibility and recognition. These findings are consistent with the ongoing work of June Nash, who has focused on ways in which indigenous peoples have challenged neoliberalism (2001) and have drawn on both local traditions and new forms of organization to devise innovative structures, including cooperatives, to preserve their economic and cultural autonomy (1993a, 1993b).

WOMEN'S CRAFT COOPERATIVES IN LATIN AMERICA

An important literature on women's folk art and craft cooperatives in Latin America and elsewhere emerged in the 1990s, emphasizing cooperatives as a way for individual artisans to have some power in determining the nature of their participation in global markets; to gain decision-making power and leadership in the production, distribution, and marketing of folk art and crafts; and to increase their economic and political importance locally and regionally. Many participants in cooperatives in the 1990s were negotiating the transition from producing for use and trade at the local level to producing for sale to national and international buyers (Grimes and Milgram 2000, 3); weavers in Teotitlán negotiated this transition in the 1960s and 1970s.

The experience of Teotitecas in cooperatives is reflective of many of the benefits and difficulties women have experienced elsewhere (see especially Nash 1993a, 1993b; Tice 1995; Grimes and Milgram 2000; Eber and Kovich 2003). Analyses of women's weaving cooperatives tend to offer at least some positive outcomes for their participants, including increased participation in local, regional, and sometimes state-level politics (Tice 1995, 107–8; I. Castro Apreza 2003, 203–4); learning new decision-making skills and demonstrating increased leadership and control in production, distribution, and marketing — often resulting in some increase in income (I. Castro Apreza 2003, 199; Eber and Rosenbaum 1993, 169; Nash 1993b, 147; Tice 1995, 110–11; Grimes and Milgram 2000,

5); developing more direct links to markets, including those of alternative trade organizations (ATOS), and short-circuiting merchants (Bartra 2003a, 140; Ehlers 1993, 190–91; Eber and Rosenbaum 1993, 169; Tice 1995, 112–13; Eber 2000, 53; Rosenbaum 2000, 96–99; Grimes 2000; Lynd 2000); escaping confinement to the domestic sphere and forming solidarity with others (I. Castro Apreza 2003, 205). Additional documented benefits include training in searching for markets, labeling products for sale, accounting, marketing (Y. Castro Apreza 2003, 210–11), and learning financial reporting and organizational accountability (Y. Castro Apreza 2003, 213). Many of these discussions about women's cooperatives provide insights from Chiapas and Guatemala.

Detailed and honest discussions of the challenges and difficulties for women in folk art or craft cooperatives are harder to come by, but those challenges have been particularly well documented in relation to the long tradition of women's cooperatives in Chiapas (see Nash 1993a, 1993b; Eber and Rosenbaum 1993; Eber 2000; Eber and Kovich 2003). The most serious consequences have been murder. June Nash (1993b) documents the murder of Petrona López, who was president of a cooperative of women potters in Amatenango del Valle, Chiapas, for over a decade. While many theories were floated locally about the motive for Petrona's assassination, Nash concludes that Petrona's challenge to male authority in a community where "women's production was controlled by their fathers or husbands," and where "all men . . . were threatened by the autonomy women gained in the cooperative," was a factor in her death. Women, too, felt that her sexual conduct—involvement with married men and other lovers—put her beyond the pale of protection.

Because participation in cooperatives often leads women to leave home and community for meetings or to sell their goods, they are automatically challenging the gendered division of labor. Absence from home and asking others to cook the family's meals and care for their children can be very threatening to both men and other women who are not in the cooperative. In addition, men question what women are doing when they leave the house, often implying that the cooperative is merely an excuse for a romantic liaison.

Such ideas can lead to harassment or domestic violence (Eber 2000, 56; Nash 1993a, 1993b). If cooperatives were begun by outside institutions such as the National Indigenous Institute (INI) in Chiapas, state agencies, and political parties, initial and subsequent control may remain in the hands of men (see Y. Castro Apreza 2003, 209). The politics of outside institutions and situations—such as conflicting local alliances between the Zapatista Army of National Liberation (EZLN), the PRI, and other groups in Chiapas—can enter into the life of a cooperative and result in threats and harassment of members. Leaders in J'pas Joloviltik (Women Who Weave), a cooperative of Tzotzil weavers based in San Cristóbal de Las Casas, were harassed and seriously threatened by armed men on several occasions in the mid-1990s (see Stephen 2000; Y. Castro Apreza 2003, 210, 213–14; Eber 2000, 54). Such circumstances can also lead to divisions in organizations. Around 1990 local political divisions became so pervasive in a weaving cooperative in San Pedro Chenalho that some members split and reorganized as an independent group (Eber 2000, 51). Finally, while almost every account of women's participation in cooperatives documents their ability to increase their income at least modestly, some analysts remind us that we shouldn't assume that cooperatives always help the neediest in each community. Lynne Milgram writes, "Cooperatives often benefit the more affluent weavers and traders—the 'not so poor,' those already engaged in trade who usually have enough land to feed their families. . . . Joining collective production and marketing associations does not automatically offer power to all women because different women are able to pursue different channels in their efforts to maximize collaborative opportunities" (2000, 112). Jeffrey Cohen writes that the problem of cooperatives is that "they tend to assist people who are in a fairly strong economic position, or, in other words, the poorest sectors of the community tend to gain little from such projects. Society members argued it made little sense to give money to unproven weavers who would not invest wisely or fail to gain any economic advantage" (2000, 141n).

All authors writing on cooperatives point out the importance of looking at their specific historic, political, and local circumstances. Largely unsuccessful efforts to begin a cooperative in Teotitlán by BANFOCO in the 1960s led to a later buying program by FONART in the 1970s, whereby the Oaxaca FONART office purchased large numbers of weavings. Because this effort in fact incorporated several large merchants, its effect was the opposite of the one intended—it did not provide new markets and better prices for pieceworkers and independent weavers. The success of the women's cooperatives in the 1990s is in part related to the lessons learned from outsiders' earlier efforts to organize Teotitecos into groups. It is significant that the first successes in organizing cooperatives came to women and that they had positive experiences in earning income, marketing their textiles directly, and being actively involved in decision making. The fact that several of the key women in the first cooperative had lived outside of Teotitlán was also significant. All these factors point to the importance of historical location as well as local experience in building a context that would result in at least moderate success for the first cooperative so that others would emerge.

Participation in the cooperatives has changed the way many women view themselves as artisans, as wives and mothers, and as local citizens. For some, the experience has opened up new possibilities for more egalitarian gender relations at home and in the community. For women who remain outside of the cooperatives, such possibilities may come through marriage and relationships formed outside Teotitlán in the process of migration, which offers women more opportunities for independence. Once they return to the community, however, their relationships may become less equal again. Women who do participate in cooperatives offer alternative gender models for all women. They also reveal for all to see, however, the obstacles, difficulties, and challenges women face as they begin to challenge local gender conventions. Nevertheless, most women in the community, whether in cooperatives or not, view them positively. Many cooperative members not only point out the benefits the co-ops offer but the importance of the close friendships and support networks they develop through their work with other women.

GENDER RELATIONS AND THE DIVISION OF LABOR
UNDER COMMERCIAL PRODUCTION

As tourist and export markets for Zapotec textiles grew during the 1970s, the availability of weaving labor became a critical factor in the expansion of production. This growing need for weaving labor was met in three primary ways. First, women and girls began to weave in greater numbers. Now, four generations of women and girls have been socialized as weavers. In 1986, approximately 35–40 percent of the weaving force were female.[1] The 2000 census puts the percentage of female weavers at about 27 percent (INEGI 2001, Empleo 6A). This number seems quite low. Many women weave on and off and may not register weaving as a primary economic activity. Most of the fifty households where I interviewed people in 2001 and 2002 had women and girls who were active weavers, sometimes three or four. Everyone indicated that almost all girls were learning how to weave. Some young women who work in the service sector in nearby communities weave in the evenings. The census notes 57 percent of men and boys aged 15 or older as "economically active" but only 31 percent of girls and women. The figures suggest some serious undercounting of the economic activities of women and girls.

Overall, 1,447 people were registered in the 2000 census as industrial manufacturers in the municipio of Teotitlán. Almost all these people are weavers. They account for about 64 percent of the economically active population of 2,245, which is consistent with figures from my 1986 survey indicating that weaving is the primary income-earning activity for about 68 percent of the population.

Second, the initial demand for more weaving labor in the 1970s was partially met by expanding the number of weavers in other communities. The population of Santa Ana began to weave on a larger scale in the 1970s, when significant numbers of women entered the labor force. The 1990 census found 379 weavers in Santa Ana, 106 female and 273 male (INEGI 1992). While the same census notes that only thirteen weavers worked as contract weavers, Cohen found that weavers' understandings of the category "independent producer" were quite distinct from those of census workers. "Often," he writes, "an informant would describe his or her approach to textile production, saying, 'Of course, I am an independent producer.' The informant would then go on to tell me that he or she worked on a contract with a particular patron in Teotitlán for many years" (1999, 47).

The 2000 census found 368 weavers in Santa Ana, 236 men and 132 women. Fifty-eight were registered as "employees or workers," 263 as independent weavers (INEGI 2001, Empleo 6A, Santa Ana del Valle). These figures suggest that more people in Santa Ana were reporting themselves as contract weavers in 2000 than in 1990, but a majority still registered as independent weavers. Cohen's discussions with weavers in the mid-1990s suggest that many of those who registered as "independent" in fact worked for merchants in Teotitlán (Cohen 1999, 47–48).

The most dramatic increase in weavers came in the neighboring community of San Miguel, which, although it was originally populated by people from Teotitlán, never undertook weaving as a significant economic activity. Helen Clements (1988b, 22–23) reported that in the mid-1980s, about 30 percent of the community were weaving, with equal numbers of males and females participating in the textile boom. The first weavers probably began working in 1974.

Clements's study of weavers in San Miguel reveals a shift in the division of labor similar to that which occurred in Teotitlán during the same time period, with the greatest number of female weavers concentrated at the lower end of the age pyramid. While there were more male than female weavers over the age of 40 in San Miguel when Clements conducted her study, there were as many female as male weavers under the age of 40 and even more in the 15–19 age group. The number of women who learned to weave in San Miguel tripled between 1975 and 1985 (Clements 1988b, 255).

Weaving production in San Miguel and Santa Ana has been dominated by Teotitlán, particularly by key merchant families, who now funnel a majority of the textiles produced to tourist art stores in Mexico and to an ever-expanding group of U.S. importers. Santa Ana continues to struggle to get out of the shadow of Teotitlán and establish an autonomous marketing structure, but it seems unable to do so. Cohen attributes Teotitlán's dominance as much to geography as to anything else, noting that it is the weaving community closest to Oaxaca (1999, 53).

In 1986 the Shan-Dany Museum was opened in Santa Ana in the hope of drawing tourists to the village from Teotitlán (Cohen 1988). This effort was not sufficient, however, to overcome the dominant marketing position of Teotitlán. Cohen reports that despite the fact that the museum also promotes local textile production and has sent a touring exhibit of textiles to many cities in Mexico and California, these programs primarily help well-established independent weavers, not the poorer weavers who seek to draw tourists to their homes and cut their ties to Teotitlán's merchants. Contract weavers who produce primarily for Teotitlán cannot afford to wait the months it can take to get paid by letting their textiles sit in exhibits. In some ways, the current dominance of Teotitlán is reproducing the important commercial and political position it held as the capital of a very large administrative territory. In its capacity as an administrative center until after independence, Teotitlán enjoyed more than two thousand years of political dominance, acting as an authority and mediator among some thirty communities (Stephen 1987a, 38–39).

The third way in which the increased demand for weaving labor was met in the 1970s was by increasing the quantity of machine-spun yarn used to produce textiles, essentially mechanizing a part of the production process. Increased use of machine-spun yarn also freed significant amounts of labor, predominantly women and children, who had been dedicated to spinning and carding. Significant numbers of women and elderly men continue to card and spin, but the bulk of weaving production is now done with machine-spun yarn. Elderly women, probably the most economically marginalized sector in Teotitlán and Santa Ana, continue to card and spin by hand. They say they are not strong enough to weave because of the stress that working the loom would put on their backs and legs. Many also believe they are too old to learn, but there are some notable exceptions. The high end of the textile market in the United States and Europe, which calls for hand-spun yarn, provides a niche for elderly laborers who earn less than weavers, differentiating the gendered labor force by age as well.

THE DAILY LIVES OF WEAVER WOMEN IN THE MID-1980S

The commercialization of weaving production in the 1970s resulted in the long-term incorporation of Teotitlán's women and girls into the weaving labor force. This process was also affected by continued male migration to the United States. Male out-migration appears to have accelerated in the late 1980s and 1990s; some women migrated as well. In this process the social construction of women's work grew to include weaving as well as food processing, child care, animal production, and reciprocal exchanges. Systematic incorporation of women in the weaving labor force appears to have had mixed results for them.

While some are still being excluded from official census categories as weavers, female weavers in Teotitlán have not suffered a local lack of recognition for their work. Women who are spinners and dyers also receive recognition for their work. Most Teotitecos believe that women are good weavers and with enough time and practice will become equal to or perhaps better than men. Several young women have already established reputations as very talented artisans who work on intricate designs. The greatest respect is given to weavers who work on highly complex original designs.

Female weavers in Teotitlán receive wages comparable to men's, though their wages remain lower in other types of craft production. In the embroidery, hammock, Oaxacan clothing, and shawl industries, women's piecework wages are often significantly lower than those of men, sometimes less than 25 percent of the hourly rate of male workers performing different tasks in the same industry (Cook 1984b).

The schedule and rhythm of work for women weavers, however, are different from those for men. Participant observation and structured interviews in Teotitlán revealed that women weave an average of three to six hours a day, while men weave six to ten hours. Women weave about four hours a day no matter what season it is, while men weave considerably longer during the dry season, when they are not engaged in part-time agricultural work. In general, households that engage in heavy weaving production tend to do less farming, even if they have access to land. However, women's weaving workload is not necessarily cut back in the same proportion as men's if the household engages in farming. Many women are expected to keep up their weaving workloads as well as to contribute to farming during the agricultural season if the household has planted crops that year. Thus women may have heavier workloads than men. When women are left in Teotitlán by migrating husbands, they tend to give up farming and try to keep up with weaving production because it pays more than farming, which often operates at a loss. They farm only if their husbands or sons send home enough money to hire a wage laborer to work their fields. If they do receive funds from husbands or sons, they are more likely to use them to purchase wool, yarn, and dyes to continue in weaving production. The time that individuals allot to weaving is also affected by their ceremonial responsibilities. Members of weaving households often raise cash for ritual consumption by weaving longer hours. If women are alone, they must therefore adjust their production schedule to their ritual obligations.

Men often weave in uninterrupted sessions, but most women sandwich their weaving in between meal preparations, animal care, and child care. They weave in the morning after preparing the morning meal and before beginning the afternoon meal. They weave again in the late afternoon when they have finished cleaning up from the midday meal. They can continue until about 7:00 P.M., when evening coffee must be prepared. They may weave more later at night. Many complain that since they have begun weaving they are working longer hours and no one is relieving them of their responsibilities. "When you get married you feel the strain of weaving," remarked Josefina, age 40. "With that first child a lot of women who weave feel a lot of pain because the loom mistreats your belly. It's hard to stand up so long. Then later you have a child to take care of as well. No one helps with the children."

Children also affect women's ability to weave. Women with babies rarely weave. Daughters can free a mother's time for weaving by taking on domestic chores. Many older women continue to do domestic chores while their daughters weave. Young women often end up with quite heavy workloads, which get worse when they marry.

Those of us who started weaving in our parents' houses are usually already tired by the time we get married. Like me. I would weave early in the morning, go to the market to sell for a while, and go home and weave again. I also helped to take care of my brothers and sisters. Now that I'm married it's the same, except it's my children I have to take care of. I have some regrets about not staying with my parents. If I hadn't gotten married so soon, I might have been able to complete junior high school. (Ana, age 27)

THE DIFFERENTIATION OF WOMEN UNDER COMMERCIALIZATION IN THE 1980S

An integrated approach to analyzing the changing authority roles of women in production suggests that women's positions be evaluated both within the household and in relation to the formal power structures in the community. In their study of women who do assembly work in their Mexico City homes, Lourdes Benería and Martha Roldán (1987, 11–114) suggest that the concept of the household/family entity be taken apart in order to uncover the underlying structures that incorporate hierarchies of class, gender, and age. June Nash (1993b, 6–7) suggests such an approach as well in her exploration of how women's increased autonomy in craft production and in cooperatives has threatened the traditional structure of the family and even marriage traditions as some young women choose not to marry and are supporting themselves and others with their earnings or use their earnings to elope and set up an independent household. Such an approach reveals the negotiation process between men and women within the household, highlighting decision-making power struggles between household members, and permits analysts to recognize women as individual social and political actors with gendered agendas within the household as well as in extradomestic structures. Such an approach helps to illuminate gender conflicts in relation to class and the construction of ethnicity. For example, as we shall see in chapter 8, women's control of resources and labor for ceremonial purposes often brings them into conflict with their husbands, who may want to use the same resources for weaving production or farming. Here I am advocating an approach that frames women as independent-minded social actors.[2] This approach brings a gendered dimension to our analysis but, of course, is also reflective of age, ethnicity, class, and other kinds of concerns that influence individual action. The point is to demonstrate how women can have separate ideas and agendas from those of "the household," an analytical unit made up of social actors of differing genders, ages, and concerns who often enter into processes of negotiation and accommodation. The household does not have a life of its own as a unit.

In the 1980s, as households accumulated capital and achieved employer status, women lost authority in the sphere of production.

Women in merchant households described themselves as managers or laborers working primarily in their husbands' businesses. Like women weavers who complained of double workloads related to weaving, merchant women complained of the management work they had to do for their husbands on top of their heavy domestic workload. Luisa, the wife of one of the wealthiest merchants in Teotitlán, continued to make tortillas for her husband, care for six children, supervise four to six weavers who worked at her house, and deal with pieceworkers.

> My husband still wants me to make tortillas every day so I can save the pesos I'd spend to buy them. I don't like to make tortillas. It's hot, I get burned, my eyes are full of smoke, and I get really tired doing this and feeding my children and the workers who come here. I do it to make him happy. . . . He makes the decisions about what to buy. I don't buy yarn or anything. I don't know how to buy it. Every week my husband tells me what he wants me to do. He tells me how to plan my time and divide my work, including overseeing the workers. I try to do everything he asks, but usually there just isn't enough time.

Scott Cook and Leigh Binford (1986) describe similar findings in the weaving community of Xaaga, where "male-run household enterprises appropriate value from unwaged female labor-power ideologically construed as 'helping out' (*ayuda*) rather than 'work' (*trabajo*)."

In the mid-1980s in Teotitlán, a few younger women married to men who had recently acquired merchant status had a more equal part in business decision making, partly because of their higher levels of education. They had all finished the sixth grade. Younger, more educated girls and women in merchant households were also beginning to take an active stand in community politics, and it appears that class-based authority, along with their increased confidence due to their education and commercial experience, was an important factor in their political consciousness. This trend continued in the 1990s, although merchant women still were limited in their ability to leave the community to attend to their business dealings. Those with an interest in increasing their participation in the formal political system in the community began to have something in common with nonmerchant women who formed a wide range of weaving cooperatives in the late 1980s and 1990s. Some women in the weaving cooperatives were also interested in participating in the formal political system.

Young girls may grow up with expectations of participating more equally in household businesses and community politics, but they realize that their independence is limited by their roles as wives and mothers. According to local custom, a woman's first responsibility is to take care of her husband and children, then to see to the family business. Even younger merchant women who did have considerable control in family businesses were often excluded from trips to sell large lots of rugs in Mexico City and the United States. Their daily responsibilities of feeding their families, shopping, and getting children off to school as well as fears of their husband's jealousy prevented them from initiating even short trips.

> Even if women do go to school more, it doesn't mean they can be merchants. They can't manage everything because they can't leave the house. If they have sons, then the sons will manage for them. Women have a lot of responsibilities at home that make it difficult for them to leave. . . . As long as women have a lot of things to do around the house, they can't run businesses equally with men. . . . And men are jealous. A lot of men get jealous when their wives are gone for a long time. Even when I go to the market and have to run around looking for change, I lose time. When I come home I always feel a little something. Even though my husband doesn't say anything, I always explain to him. . . . The only women who can go where they want and when they want are widows. (Graciela, age 35)

When women in employer households discussed their subordinate position in production decision making in the 1980s, they attributed it to a lack of skills needed to conduct business. While many women did maintain control over a small pot of money for making purchases of household items, when a household accumulated capital and began a business, this money was often kept in a separate pot controlled by men. In contrast to their husbands and sons, who have often spent several years working in the United States, most women had little experience interacting with North Americans in the 1980s. Many believed that their husbands learned how to deal with North Americans and accumulated capital while they labored in the United States, first as braceros and then as illegal immigrants. "It's very hard for women to leave the house and carry on a business because of their responsibilities," said Chavela, age 28. "It's even more difficult for them to get together the money to start a business. They can't go to the United States to work and save some money. They usually have responsibilities."

In large part, the lack of female participation in production and business decisions in the mid-1980s seems to have stemmed from unequal access to education. Most women did not have the same educational opportunities as men. Discussions with older women indicated that most parents in the 1940s, 1950s, and even 1960s believed that women did not need education in their roles as wives and mothers because they seldom left the community. Because women operated primarily in the sphere of the local community or in regional markets where Zapotec is spoken, they did not need Spanish for daily use.

In addition, under Spanish colonial custom and later under independence, women were excluded from roles that called for literacy. Women did not migrate to the United States until the 1970s. By the time large numbers of former weaving households had begun merchant activity, women who had not migrated were not able to catch up with the educational skills of men who had. This situation began to change by the late 1980s, when about as many girls as boys completed primary school and girls began to attend junior high school. Merchants often work with large amounts of capital and their dealings with clients require at least a knowledge of spoken and written Spanish, skills in math, and minimal accounting, which is taught in the later years of primary school. They must also deal with licensing and export procedures. Knowledge of English, usually gained by migrating to the United States, is also helpful.

A questionnaire administered in 1986 to the male and female heads of fifty-four merchant households in Teotitlán revealed important differences between men's and women's linguistic skills and levels of education. While 43 percent of merchant women surveyed had been to school for one year or less and 33 percent were monolingual in Zapotec, only 2 percent of merchant men surveyed were monolingual and 21 percent had been to school for one year or less. A full 54 percent of merchant men had more than three years of education, compared to 25 percent of merchant women. Many merchant men were also able to augment their literacy and language skills in the United States. These differences were important in running a business in the mid-1980s.

While rates of monolingualism were similarly high among weaver women (45 percent of women surveyed, 3 percent of men surveyed), who, like merchant women, had little education (45 percent with one year or less compared to 18 percent of men), these skills were not as necessary for producing weavings sold within the village (N = 100 weaver women, 100 weaver men). Most transactions involved in the local weaving process could be carried out orally in Zapotec.

Data from another question included in the 1986 survey support the

TABLE 16 Male and female education levels in merchant households, 1986

	0–1 year	2–3 years	> 3 years	Missing data
Men (*N* = 54)	21%	21%	54%	4%
Women (*N* = 54)	43	28	25	4

Source: Random stratified household survey conducted by Lynn Stephen, 1986.

TABLE 17 Languages spoken by male and female heads of merchant households, 1986

	Spanish only	Zapotec only	Spanish and Zapotec	Missing data
Men (*N* = 54)	0%	2%	94%	4%
Women (*N* = 54)	1	33	62	4

Source: Random stratified household survey conducted by Lynn Stephen, 1986.

contention that women did not have a high level of participation in managing the financial aspects of business in merchant households. This question was asked of men and women together: Who controls the key to business cash and allocates it for business expenses? They had little trouble agreeing on the answer (table 18). No corresponding figures are available for weaver women because in weaver households expenses for weaving, ritual, and consumption all come out of the same pot. General household money in weaver households is managed as shown in table 19. This information was also solicited from both men and women, who had little trouble agreeing. It was based on who controlled the key and could give out cash. As reflected in table 18, a majority of merchant households surveyed (67 percent) stated that men managed business finances. Participant observation supports this view. In contrast, a majority of weaver households reported that the household pot was managed by both men and women (62 percent). It was also stated that a significant portion of weaver women also managed the pot alone (35 percent). "My wife, María

TABLE 18 Management of business finances reported in merchant households, by gender, 1986 (*N* = 54)

Men alone	Men and women	Women alone
67%	29%	4%

Source: Random stratified household survey conducted by Lynn Stephen, 1986.

TABLE 19 Management of household money reported in weaver households, by gender, 1986 (*N* = 100)

Men alone	Men and women	Women alone
3%	62%	35%

Source: Random stratified household survey conducted by Lynn Stephen, 1986.

Elena, has control of the money," said Eduardo, age. 60. "She guards it and keeps the key, but we both know how much there is. When we need to buy something, like more yarn, or pay some construction workers, we both anticipate that and know we have to put it aside. She usually does the paying." The differences between weaver and merchant women's input into financial management were reflected in other areas of production as well.

In contrast to merchant women, women in pieceworker and independent weaver households repeatedly characterized the production process as a team effort with their husbands and children. They had major control over production decisions such as the allocation of household labor (particularly of children), the timing of weaving production, the number of pieces to be produced, and the negotiation of selling prices with local merchants. "I make a lot of decisions about weaving. I buy the yarn, the dyes, and I sell the serapes," said Hortensia, age 36. "I also handle all the money we make from selling weavings and from my pigs. I also decide about buying food, and what fiestas we will go to, and what to purchase for them. While I decide, I always tell my husband and he agrees." Said María, age 28: "We both decide what to do in our work and on what we buy. I go and sell what we weave to merchants and bring home the money. Then we both talk about how to spend it, what we need."

In the long run, however, women in pieceworker and independent weaver households in the 1980s appeared to face contradictory results from the commercialization of weaving. On the one hand, they retained significant control in relation to the production process. On the other hand, their households as a whole were not reaping the material benefits from commercialization that merchant households were. The preceding analysis of women's roles in production therefore underscores the importance of examining the impact of commercialization on men and on women in conjunction with class. In the late 1980s and 1990s, some women in pieceworker and independent weaving households began to challenge their marginalized position in the relations of production by forming cooperatives to sell their textiles directly to tourists and other consumers. Significantly increased levels of education for women as well as much higher rates of bilingualism were important factors that distinguished weaver women in 2000 from those in 1986. Other important factors were related to women's migration experiences as well as changes within Mexican economic policy and its impact on people in Teotitlán.

WOMEN'S WEAVING COOPERATIVES, 1986–PRESENT

In the mid-1980s, a group of younger women, many of whom sold textiles for their families in the local artisan market, spoke out against their exclusion from the committee that regulated the market and from community assemblies. This public criticism was pivotal in beginning ongoing change in gender roles in women's political participation in Teotitlán and the kind of organizational spaces they created to be able to market their textiles in the local, regional, and international markets. In 1986 some of their protest was taken up by several women who had returned to the community after living in such places as Mexico City and Oaxaca, where their roles as women were not so restricted.

Some young women joined the men who were leaving Teotitlán in an effort to increase their families' incomes. Some spent time working in the homes of middle-class and upper-middle-class families in Mexico City caring for their children, cleaning their houses, and cooking. Others went to work for relatives in Tijuana and Rosarito in folk art stores. And some went to live in communities of Teotiteco migrants in the Los Angeles area, such as Santa Ana, Oxnard, and Moore Park. They worked cleaning houses, caring for children and the elderly, in assembly plants, in restaurants, and in other service jobs. Their work lives required them to have much greater independence than they had had at home. In addition to going to paid jobs every day, they were often required to run errands, shop, obtain medical care, attend school conferences, walk children to and from school, and navigate a wide range of agencies connected to raising their families. Some were able to continue their educations. All of these experiences gave them a different perspective on what their lives were like at home in Teotitlán, where they seldom left the community, were excluded from community political assemblies, usually needed their husband's or mother-in-law's permission to leave the house, and had no possibility of challenging the labor relations of textile production, which often relegated them to contract labor.

In 1986, organizing for the first women's weaving cooperative in Teotitlán was driven in part by the energies of one woman. When Aurora Contreras Lazo returned from ten years in Mexico City she was struck by some of the major differences between life for women there and in Teotitlán. She commented in the summer of 2001:

> The idea behind the group was to find a way for women and girls to leave their homes and the community if they wanted to. In the city you can leave, do what you like. Even though you have to ask permission, you can go. Here it was different. A woman alone can't leave the community or go out at all. They say, "What is she going to do? What is she looking for?" Women didn't have the possibility of leaving this community to sell their textiles. The idea was to look for exhibits and expositions. We started getting women together for a group. We started with about fifty women and girls and we were able to officially constitute ourselves and start to get support. We were called Te Gunah Ruinchi Laadti [Women Who Weave]. This group still exists."

Women Who Weave not only aspired to help women sell their own goods but set out to circumvent the strong control exercised by local merchants working with U.S. importers over the sale of textiles. While everyone in Teotitlán has benefited from the successful commercialization and export of textiles since the late 1970s, some have benefited much more than others, particularly as subcontracting increased in the 1980s. About six or seven extended merchant families still control most business, either by buying finished pieces from independent weavers or by directly contracting weavers as laborers, giving them materials, designs, and the dimensions of textiles to produce. The increased ability of people in Teotitlán to export since the initiation of NAFTA in 1994 has primarily benefited the merchant families who work directly with U.S.-based businessness (see Wood 2000a, 2000b, 2001). They have continued

Figure 8. Aurora Contreras Lazo, cofounder of the Gunah Ruinchi Laadti/Women Who Weave cooperative. Photo by the author.

Figure 9. Women of Teotitlán's first cooperative in Oaxaca, 1987. Photo by the author.

to do well, while others have lost ground, as have many others in rural Mexico.

A series of measures aimed at privatization of government enterprises, a loosening of federal regulations to permit and encourage foreign investment and ownership, and the individualization of property and social relations between the state and its citizens found their logical conclusions in the 1990s in NAFTA. The purpose of NAFTA was to facilitate the entrance of U.S. capital into the Mexican economy. It did so through the privatization of national industry—airlines, telephones, mining, railroads, banks—and the lowering of trade barriers to let U.S. companies into all sectors. In order to allow U.S. products to compete in the Mexican market, Mexico eliminated price supports and subsidies to basic food items. This move resulted in a decrease in the value of real wages as people had to pay more for basic goods and their wages remained the same. Overall, NAFTA led to the acceleration of corporate-led economic integration between Mexico and the United States, which benefited a few, but not most.

In Teotitlán del Valle, the 1990s brought considerable hardship to many independent and contract weavers. Prices for basic goods went up, and prices for textiles remained stagnant or declined as the neighboring communities of Santa Ana and San Miguel began to produce more and compete more intensely with Teotitlán. As we have seen, U.S. and European textile designers and importers who worked in the community began to commission knockoffs of Zapotec rugs in other parts of the world where labor was cheaper. The bitterness of some of the women who have joined the cooperatives about how little merchants paid them for their textiles is an indication of how difficult things were. Most telling is the fact that the number of merchants in the community has decreased since the 1980s and almost all of those who are merchants today come from merchant families. In other words, very few new households have been able to enter the merchant sector. Probably at least twenty smaller merchant enterprises collapsed in the 1990s.

The neoliberal economic model of the 1990s produced results in Teotitlán similar to those elsewhere in Mexico (on popular response to NAFTA in Mexico see Gutmann 2002). More highly capitalized merchant households increased and consolidated their wealth and passed on their wealth to their children, who continued their businesses. Smaller merchant households with little reserve capital were squeezed out of the market and their members returned to being independent or contract weavers. The weaver majority in the community lost some of their power in labor relations and purchasing power. By August 2002, the Secretariat of Social Development reported that 53.7 percent of all Mexicans lived in poverty, defined as an income of less than U.S.$1.50 a day in the countryside (U.S.$548 a year) and U.S.$2.10 in urban areas (U.S.$767 a year). A report from that entity notes that the 1990s were characterized by "stagnation in terms of social progress," leading to an increase of 4.7 million people living in extreme poverty. The poverty level was at 52.6 percent in 1992, but rose to 69.6 percent after the 1995 peso crisis (Mexico Solidarity Network 2002). Loss of income and the diminished possibility of weavers to participate in the market as independents in the 1990s were factors in the formation of cooperatives.

The objective of all the cooperatives formed in Teotitlán since 1986 has been to gain economic, political, and cultural rights in the community, in regional artisan associations, in relation to government institutions, and in the global market as independent artisans. Most of the groups have at one point or another received support from government institutions such as the INI and FONART, small business support organizations, political parties, and nonprofit organizations. In the end, however, almost all cooperatives cut their ties with support groups after the groups tried to involve the cooperatives in nonweaving activities, to recruit them as members of political parties, or somehow to change their original focus. Most cooperatives now engage in short-term projects with outside agencies geared to specific training activities and work with Oaxaca state agencies to promote their crafts through exhibitions and special stores. Some have joined larger federations of artisans that may group up to three hundred people from twenty or more communities that produce a wide range of crafts and folk art. Working with federations has given individual cooperatives more bargaining power in working with state agencies.

Members consistently expressed their long-term goals as trying to help out their families through earning income, receiving respect and reasonable wages for their work, being able to sell their textiles directly to consumers without merchant intermediaries, providing support for one another in their daily struggles, and working together to promote their work in as many places as possible. Reina, a longtime co-op member, commented about the importance of maintaining her independent status as an artisan: "I decided that I'm never again going to sell my work to a reseller. When I need to buy something, I'll think of another way to get money. I never want to be working on contract again. My textiles are mine and I'll save them so we can sell them [in the cooperative]. . . . I'm

Figure 10. Two women of the Gunah Shaguia/Women of Teotitlán
cooperative in front of their display in Oaxaca. Photo by the author.

very proud of this. I never again want to fall into working on contract."
Independence is an important part of Reina's identity as a co-op member. Not all co-op members are able to avoid contract labor relations or
selling their textiles to a merchant for a reduced price, but that is their
goal. Almost all of the fifty women interviewed from 2001 to 2003 who
are co-op members said that they did earn some income through the cooperatives and that the way they earned it—through direct sales of their
signed textiles—was important to them.

   The primary activities of the cooperatives include exhibiting their textiles for sale in the city of Oaxaca and elsewhere during key tourist seasons and holidays; working together with outside consultants and agencies in workshops to learn new dyeing and weaving techniques, how to
combine different materials, how to create new designs, how to market
their wares and work as businesses; regular meetings to plan future activities, evaluate past ones, and provide ongoing support to members.
A few of the cooperatives rent locations in Oaxaca either seasonally or
permanently to sell their wares to tourists.

   Most groups become more active during the tourist seasons. In order
to set up and staff their exhibits, cooperatives organize their members
into teams of two to three people who are responsible for caring for the

exhibit, selling textiles, and keeping track of sales. They usually sleep in the exhibit overnight, never abandoning the group's merchandise. One person will go to get food for the team, but someone is always present. The exhibit is usually one of dozens of artisan booths in long rows lining the Zócalo, Oaxaca's central plaza, one of the city's parks.

In July 2003 the Oaxaca city government decided to suspend the exhibitions of artisans around the Zócalo during the high summer tourist season. City officials met with artisans from Teotitlán and other craft-producing communities to inform them that they were going to clean up the Zócalo and that the artisans would have to relocate their exhibits to the outskirts of the city by the baseball stadium. Fearful of losing the opportunity to exhibit and sell their textiles in Oaxaca in the future, members of three of Teotitlán's cooperatives went along with the change and dutifully tended to their booths for two weeks. It was an economic disaster. Francisca Ruiz García described the move to the stadium in these words:

> Well, they said they were going to "sweep the Zócalo." We thought they literally meant clean. But then we saw that they continued to let other people be there, like the teachers and the other merchants who walk around selling *ropa típica* [locally produced cotton clothing with a peasant flavor]. So when they were talking about "cleaning the Zócalo" we then saw that they meant us. They thought about us like some kind of infestation of pests. They really meant they wanted to clean us up. . . .
>
> . . . So they sent us to the stadium. They told us not to worry, that they'd bring the tourists there in a bus. Well, we were there for two weeks. We didn't sell a thing. The only people who came were those from the nearby poorer *colonias*. It was so bad that even the doughnuts didn't sell. Never mind the ropa típica or our textiles. It was equally terrible for everyone.

Francisca's group then merged with another new cooperative to sell their textiles in Teotitlán. Two other groups that were formed that year did as well. By the end of the summer of 2003, there were eleven cooperatives in Teotitlán that worked on similar principles when they sold their goods, whether in Teotitlán, Oaxaca, or elsewhere in Mexico.

At the cooperative's exhibit booth, each textile is marked with the weaver's name and the price. Those staffing the exhibit keep a list of earnings and give the money from sales to the weavers whose work was sold. Each group requires its members to pay a monthly fee, which is used to pay for space rental, signs, transportation, and other costs associated with the exhibits. Sometimes groups pool their money to buy materials

Figure 11. Francisca Ruiz García (far right) with her cooperative, Dgunaa Gulal Ni Ruin Laadti/Traditional Women Weavers, 2002. Photo by the author.

Figure 12. Four women of the second incarnation of Gunah Ruinchi Laadti/ Women Who Weave, including several founders of the first cooperative of the same name. Photo by the author.

for weaving or to pay for training. Most groups have had at least one or two experiences in producing large orders for export or for sale inside Mexico. Often these experiences have been difficult; the exporters reject some products, fail to pay the prices agreed upon, or change the conditions of sale.

One member of Women Who Weave suggested that the group could learn from the experience. "We didn't hold up our part of the contract, either. We didn't turn in everything in the colors they asked for. Then the goods will be rejected by the large businesses that ordered them. We're thinking about that now in a group of us who are working on exporting. They only want one color so we're looking at ways to come up with uniform dyes for the yarn used in the textiles we export."

While ideally all the cooperatives would like to find an exporter who would work with them, they have had more positive experiences selling within Mexico or in two cases traveling to the United States to sell their work themselves directly to consumers. In 2003, several groups were preparing material for a shared Web page to market their products electronically. They had not worked out the details of actually running an on-line business, but individual members of several groups were trying to get training in Web technologies and information about the requirements for an export license.

The initial participants in Women Who Weave were pivotal in modeling alternative gender roles for women, particularly increased mobility within the community and outside it, renegotiating the division of household labor so that husbands and children took on some domestic responsibilities when women left to go to meetings or exhibitions, and establishing women's presence in community assemblies. Women Who Weave disintegrated over internal disagreements in 1988, but some of the initial members formed a second cooperative that has remained active.

Many of the original members of Women Who Weave who no longer work together have gone on to found other organizations. These women artisans have taken on key leadership roles in Teotitlán. With five active women's cooperatives in the mid-1990s involving up to seventy-five women and their families, it was no longer unusual for women to go together to Oaxaca and stay overnight to sell the wares of their group in exhibit stalls. Women from the cooperatives marched in the local parades on national holidays, met weekly or biweekly in one another's homes, and developed extended support networks. For women who managed to stay active in the co-ops for years on end, a big area of change was their relations with their husbands, in-laws, and children. Initially, they had to battle constantly to go to meetings, prepare food ahead of time for their families if they left, and were called whores for selling their wares outside of town. Mariana described the scene in the summer of 2002:

> It was really hard for us in the community because women never leave. They devote themselves to housework. It was hard for our children and our husbands to let us leave. We had to get up really early to prepare all the food that was needed that day and get our husband's permission to leave. . . . It was hard for us at home and in the community because there was no history of organized groups like this. People were jealous. They saw us as bad women who were out on the street in a group.

It has always been easier for widows and unmarried women to participate in the cooperatives. For significant numbers of married women in the cooperatives, getting family members to understand and appreciate what they were doing was very important. Marcelina Ruiz, who was a member of the original cooperative and now leads another one, related how getting her husband to help her and the group has been a key gain:

> It was a huge battle with our husbands. We had to break our chains with them there in the community. Thanks to all our struggles, now they help us. Our husbands understand us. They understand that what we're doing isn't just for women, but for the whole family. When we first started, it was a huge battle. The fact that we were leaving the community was really looked down upon. . . . Later when our husbands saw what we were doing, that in fact we sold more than the men who came to Oaxaca did, they let us alone. . . . Now they're happy to help us.

From 1986 through 2004, thirteen cooperatives of weavers have formed involving more than 125 households, or about 600 people out of a population of 4,500. As table 20 shows, they include two men's cooperatives and a few that involve both men and women, but most members of cooperatives are still women. With about 15 percent of the households in the community participating in cooperatives, the groups have come to have a significant presence in the community. Their impact on the political life of the community and women's place in it has been primarily through their formal recognition as a part of the government structure of the community and the invitation of women from the cooperatives to participate as voting members in community assemblies. The cooperatives have created a space where women enjoy greater independence as artisans and gain a sense of respect and appreciation for their economic contributions and efforts on behalf of their families.

Figure 13. Moisés Lazo,
one of the founders of
a mixed cooperative of
men and women, Laadti
Guede/Washed Blanket,
founded in 2000. Photo
by the author.

CONCLUSIONS

As commodities intended for use were transformed into folk art, the relations of production, the gendered division of labor, and local ethnic identity were all affected. A new petty capitalist merchant class emerged under conditions of commercial capitalism. This class now works directly with U.S. importers in the production and distribution of textiles. Within this sector women had been consistently marginalized because they lacked experience and education and were limited by their social roles as wives and mothers. Younger women merchants who came of age in the 1980s and 1990s may participate more actively in business decision making and a few of them run their own businesses, but they still are hampered by gender role expectations that make it difficult for women to leave their homes and the community. Women over 45, who grew up during a time when women were not thought to need Spanish in their daily lives and who did not receive exposure to U.S. culture and basic business skills, have been further limited in their ability to participate

TABLE 20 Cooperatives in Teotitlán, 1986–present

Years in existence	Cooperative	Contact
1986–88, 1992–present	Gunah Ruinchi Laadti/ Mujeres Que Tejen (Women Who Weave)	Josefina Jiménez Avenida Juárez no. 86 Teotitlán del Valle Tlacolula, Oaxaca C.P. 70420 Mexico Joker213@brownpride.com
1988–90, 1994–present	Gunah Shaguia/Mujeres de Teotitlán (Women of Teotitlán)	Guadalupe Ruiz Soza Calle Cuáutemoc no. 4 Teotitlán del Valle Tlacolula, Oaxaca C.P. 70420 Mexico Tel. 951-524-4391
1993–2004	Serapes, Arte y Tradición (Serapes, Art, and Tradition) (men)	
1995–present	Galbain Cuy/ Vida Nueva (New Life); formerly Consejo para Integración de la Mujer (Council for the Integration of Women)	Pastora Gutiérrez Reyes Cenetario no. 1 Teotitlán del Valle Tlacolula, Oaxaca C.P. 70420 Mexico estrelladelvalle@hotmail.com Tel. 951-524-4250
1996–present	Dgunaa Gulal Ni Ruin Laadti/Mujeres Antiguas Que Hacen Tapetes (Traditional Women Who Weave)	Isabel Hernández Pino Suárez Teotitlán del Valle Tlacolula, Oaxaca C.P. 70420 Mexico

TABLE 20 *continued*

Years in existence	Cooperative	Contact
2000–present	D'Gunaa Shiguie Nee Sian/Mujeres Unidas de Teotitlán (United Women of Teotitlán)	Francisca Ruiz García Pino Suárez no. 26 Teotitlán del Valle Tlacolula, Oaxaca C.P. 70420 Mexico Tel. 951-524-4364
2000–present	Laadti Guedi/Tapete Lavado (Washed Blanket) (men and women)	Moisés Lazo Avenida Juárez no. 74 Teotitlán del Valle Tlacolula, Oaxaca C.P. 70420
2000–present	Beni Ruinchi Laadti/Tejedores Zapotecos (Zapotec Weavers) (men, some women)	Federico Chávez Sosa Francisco I. Madero no. 28 Teotitlán del Valle Tlacolula, Oaxaca C.P. 70420 Mexico tapeteschavez@hotmail.com Tel. 951-524-4078
2001–present	Gunaa Ghezbetza/Mujeres Piedra Hermana (Sister Rock Women) (women, some men)	no contact available
2002–present	Shini/El Amanecer (The Dawn) (women and men)	Aurora Contreras Avenida Juárez no. 4 Teotitlán del Valle Tlacolula, Oaxaca C.P. 70420 Mexico shiniartrugs@hotmail.com Tel. 951-524-4119

TABLE 20 *continued*

Years in existence	Cooperative	Contact
2003–present	Ghiabetz/Hermano Piedra (Brother Rock) (men and women)	Aurora Bazan López Pino Suárez no. 28 Teotitlán del Valle Tlacolula, Oaxaca C.P. 70420 Mexico shini54@latinmail.com Tel. 951-524-4162
2003–present	Xguia Morad/Piedra Morada (Purple Rock)	Miguel Chávez Sosa Francisco I. Madero no. 28 Teotitlán del Valle Tlacolula, Oaxaca C.P. 70420 Mexico Lucy_10_1@hotmail.com

in business. Many women in merchant families, whether young or old, still are obliged to shop in the market each morning, prepare meals, wash clothing, care for animals, and take care of household ceremonial needs. Even if a woman's household achieves merchant status, many of her domestic obligations continue and perhaps increase, as in the case of Angela, whom we met in chapter 3. Younger women in both merchant and weaver households are receiving more education now. It has become more socially acceptable to educate girls, and many parents even see it as a necessity. The possibility of participating in the family business has encouraged more families to educate daughters.

Merchants have continued to use the idiom of kinship to reinforce the relations of production, placing weavers' relations with merchants in the same arena with compadrazgo and ritual reciprocal labor exchanges at the same time that they function as subcontractors for U.S. importers. At the same time, a continued claim of Zapotec ethnic identity or a pan-indigenous identity (see Wood 2001) is the basis on which Zapotec weavings now achieve the status of folk art in export consumer markets.

Merchants are aware of this fact and represent themselves as the bearers of traditional Zapotec or generic "Indian" authenticity to foreign importers and U.S. and European consumers. Since the 1990s, participants in cooperatives have used this discourse of Zapotec authenticity to promote their crafts directly to consumers and tourists. Internally, the representation of a unified local ethnic identity is in conflict with class identity —merchants are increasingly acquiring political authority, which stands in opposition to the authority sanctified by ritual experience and age.

Commercialization of textiles and the development of subcontracting relations with U.S. importers pushed women into the weaving labor force in significant numbers not only in Teotitlán but also in surrounding communities such as Santa Ana and San Miguel. While women weavers appear to receive the same pay as men for their work and equal occupational recognition—something that most working women in Mexico still lack—weaving has added to the number of hours most women must work in order to complete all of their daily chores. As some women (usually those in weaver households) left the community to work elsewhere in Mexico or in the United States, they began to recognize some of the limits imposed on their movements and ability to earn income in Teotitlán as a result of traditional gender norms. In addition, both returning migrant women and others who remained in the community questioned their status as piecework labor for local merchants working with U.S. importers.

The emergence of twelve weaving cooperatives since 1986, most of them run by women, has begun to change the way some weaver women's work is structured and rewarded at home, in the community, and in the larger textile market. Another effect of the cooperatives has been a limited reordering of gender relations in the homes of co-op members, particularly when they leave home to go to meetings and exhibitions. Then husbands, children, and others have had to assume some of their domestic chores. Some men have also left their work temporarily to accompany their wives to Oaxaca and elsewhere to help set up and maintain exhibit booths. Such an effort represents a significant change in gender relations in the households of co-op members. Nevertheless, a majority of weaver women still remain outside of the cooperatives. For them, many of the customs that dictate the gendered division of labor and restrict women's freedom of movement remain in force. The weaving cooperatives may have had a more direct effect on all women's lives by opening up formal political participation for women, as we shall see in chapter 10.

The overall impact of commercialization on women and on the entire community of Teotitlán has been contradictory. The community's economic success from the 1950s through the 1980s seems clearly tied to a history of independence, particularly with regard to defending Teotitlán's economic claim on textiles. The town first resisted government monitoring of production in the 1930s and 1940s and then avoided heavy participation in craft development projects that put the state in the position of middleman. Because they were successful on their own, Teotitecos avoided participation in government programs. This independent stance emerged again in the 1970s as local merchants developed links to U.S. importers and again in the 1980s and 1990s with the formation of cooperatives.

From 1970 to 1985, it seemed that the average level of income had gone up in Teotitlán. All Teotitecos agreed then that their material life had improved significantly. Because of the rapid development of a petty capitalist merchant class, its consolidation, and ties to U.S. capital, increases in income were not being evenly distributed. People within the community as well as outside it were aware of the heightened differences between merchants and the rest of the population that marked the 1980s. Because most of the town's wealthy merchants in the mid-1980s began as poor farmers and weavers, many people in the community, including young women, believed it was possible to move into the merchant sector. This picture changed in the 1990s.

The economic crisis of 1995 was deeply felt in Teotitlán. Levels of tourism decreased somewhat in the late 1990s and they declined further after September 11, 2001. Cooperative weavers noted that they were selling significantly less in the local market and in Oaxaca markets than they had even in the late 1990s. Thus the marked increase in social stratification brought on throughout Mexico in the 1990s as a result of neoliberal economic policies was also felt in Teotitlán. While the final outcome of such policies on the local economy and gender relations is not clear, one result in combination with the experience of returning migrants and increasing levels of education among women and men was the initiation of weaving cooperatives, which created new kinds of economic, cultural, and political spaces for weavers who were further marginalized in the local and global economies of the 1990s.

CHAPTER 8

Changes in the Civil-Religious Hierarchy and Their Impact on Women

> Being a mayordoma is important. It means everyone will
> respect you because you are supporting the town and working for
> the town. We call mayordomos the same as we call the saints and
> the Virgins. Women mayordomas are *nãn*, like the Virgins. Men
> mayordomos are *dad*, like the saints. They are the same words.
> They both work for the town. For example, if it isn't raining,
> then the mayordomos pray to the gods for rain. They do
> it for everyone. Because they do this, people
> listen to them and respect them.
> —Cristina, age 40

The political life of Teotitlán del Valle still is tightly bound to local ritual institutions. From the late 1800s until the 1960s, the religious cargo system was the primary engine of community ceremonial life and a major arena for the development of prestige and local political authority.[1] Both women and men actively participated in the mayordomías of the religious hierarchy and received authority and prestige for doing so. The eventual divorce of the civil from the religious cargo system in Teotitlán and a major decline in the celebration of mayordomías have had a large impact on women's political and ceremonial lives. Always excluded from formal municipal politics and then further marginalized from political relations when mayordomía sponsorship declined, women have increasingly turned to the idea of authority based on age and ritual experience as a way of participating politically in the community.

BREAKING TRADITIONAL IMAGES OF CIVIL-RELIGIOUS HIERARCHIES

Anthropological descriptions of political life in indigenous communities in the states of Oaxaca and Chiapas have focused heavily on civil-religious cargo systems and on *cacique* (strongman) political machines.

Some caciques have integrated themselves and their supporters into local civil-religious hierarchies (Wasserstrom 1983). Initial anthropological literature on civil-religious cargo systems described them as intertwining hierarchies of civil and religious offices that allowed individual men to advance their civil-political careers as they took on religious sponsorship of celebrations for the cults of the saints and Virgins honored in the church. This original view has been amended through time by refocusing on two dimensions of civil-religious hierarchies. First, as the work of ethnohistorians has shown, the "classical" civil-religious hierarchies described by so many anthropologists are historically specific institutions that operated roughly from Mexican independence until the 1950s. Second, while civil offices were held by men, the mayordomía offices of religious hierarchies were held by pairs of men and women who received equal prestige and authority.

Ethnohistorical work (e.g., Chance 1990; Chance and Taylor 1985; Earle 1990; Wasserstrom 1983) has shown that local government in indigenous communities during the early colonial period was structured only as a civil hierarchy. Religious activities were centered in *cofradías*, religious corporations founded to pay for the cults of saints. Cofradías owned land and herds, the proceeds of which paid for cult celebrations. Only after the church expropriated cofradía property and the state imposed sanctions against religious festivals did individual households begin to sponsor cult celebrations (Stephen and Dow 1990). Individual sponsorship of cult celebrations probably began during the eighteenth century and eventually resulted in the marriage of religious and civil hierarchies in many communities.

John Chance's (1990) comparison of twenty-three ethnographic sources and other recent studies of cargo systems show that, in fact, the civil-religious hierarchy has undergone a structural shift in response to increasing integration of community political structures with those of the state and national governments. In his extended period of study in Zinacantán, Frank Cancian (1990) has also noted that as entrepreneurial opportunities and social stratification increased, often in relation to state development programs, interest in sponsoring cargos declined dramatically.

Ethnographic literature describes several contemporary forms or readaptations of the religious side of former civil-religious hierarchies. Chance (1990) focuses on what he calls "religious cargo systems," which maintain a hierarchy of public offices for the express purpose of serving the saints. He finds this to be the dominant trend in current literature on cargo systems.

Three other possibilities are also described in the literature. One is the complete disappearance of any type of cargo system. Another variety reflects back on communal support for cult celebrations offered by cofradías during the earlier colonial era. Stanley Brandes (1981, 1988) and Catharine Good Eshelman (1988a) describe a system of community-wide collections, usually carried out by specially appointed committees, which support community celebrations in association with particular saints, essentially replacing household-sponsored mayordomías. In some communities, church committees put in place as early as the 1920s as part of the municipal government structure are also instrumental in taking up collections and organizing community rituals that were formerly planned and organized by mayordomos (Stephen 1990a). The final form involves a significant decrease in mayordomía activity and transference of the prestige and ritual forms and content associated with mayordomías to life cycle rituals.

In all these forms that reorganize civil-religious hierarchies, the formal political authority of cargo holders in relation to the state has been steadily undermined. Even in those communities that preserve a prestige system built on holding offices in a religious hierarchy, such prestige may not be sufficient to qualify people to hold elective office and does not hold outside the community. Kate Young vividly describes changes in the basis of political authority as village elders in a Oaxacan sierra community lost control of the municipal government to men who were more oriented toward national culture. Since then, she writes (1976, 260), "the emphasis on youth, education, and wealth is in direct opposition to the former emphasis on age, service to the gods, and the fulfillment of obligations to the community."

James Greenberg (1981, 191) describes a similar situation in contemporary Oaxaca, but concludes that the political authority of elders, rather than eroding, has come to coexist with the formal government of elected civil officials. A "sub rosa structure of authority" not accessible to bureaucratic manipulation by the state is sometimes able to help communities resist pressures from mestizo-dominated political and economic institutions by causing trouble in the state's bureaucratic system (Greenberg 1990). While Greenberg's case provides an interesting and notable example, in most contemporary forms of religious ceremonial systems the political authority of cargo holders or fiesta sponsors has been undermined by the state and often by competing local systems of political authority based on class relations (Stephen 1990a).

The separation of religious from civil hierarchies in indigenous communities and the increasing secularization of formal political decision making have had important effects on the nature of women's political participation. Slowly, beginning in the 1920s and 1930s, holders of civil offices in Oaxaca municipios have been elected by village assemblies, as specified by the 1917 Mexican constitution (Chance 1990). Elderly informants in Teotitlán, Santa Ana, Maquilxóchitl, and San Miguel stated that, by tradition, such assemblies were attended only by men. Recently women have begun to attend municipio assemblies.

One of the consequences of the divorce of religious hierarchies from civil ones is that women lost their most formal remaining link to institutional community politics. As documented by Holly Mathews in Oaxaca (1985), the elimination of religious sponsorship as a requirement for political service in civil cargo systems and the emphasis on individual skills such as fluency in Spanish and experience with state bureaucrats as the basis for selection for community political posts has eliminated many women from consideration. In addition, the responsibilities of many former mayordomos and mayordomas are now part of male civil cargos in the church committees that were mandated by Calles in the 1920s (Stephen 1990).

In many Zapotec communities, household heads, both male and female, accrued and continue to accrue status and social position by taking on the sponsorship of mayordomías. While mayordomía titles are formally held by men in accordance with the Spanish custom of registering only male household heads in the census, mayordomía titles are clearly understood to be held by male-female pairs as documented in Chiapas (Nash 1970) and in Oaxaca (Chance 1990; Chiñas 1973; Mathews 1985; Stephen 1991c; Young 1978). Within the mayordomía system as well as in other formal ritual situations, both men and women have particular responsibilities and obligations that are complementary: rituals cannot be properly completed without the participation of both.

Both mayordomas and mayordomos were important in shaping local political opinion. According to elderly male and female informants in Teotitlán, such opinion was articulated in many areas of the community and became policy under the direction of male elders who held the highest civil cargo posts. In Teotitlán, older women emphasized the importance of women with religious authority in formulating such policy.

This discussion offering two correctives about essential features of civil-religious cargo systems has important implications for our understanding of the political and ceremonial roles of indigenous women in Mexico. The historical specificity of civil-religious cargo systems can be linked to a particular type of political authority rooted in age, ritual experience, and community service. Under this system, ritual and politics were integrated. Respect and authority that stemmed from ritual were readily transferred to politics. Women's participation in mayordomías as community ritual leaders gave them a source of authority that allowed them to have an impact on community politics as well.

The ritual-political system that dominated politics in Teotitlán until the 1960s directly linked social reproduction—that is, the ritual reproduction of social actors—to politics. While this is still partially the case today, through life cycle rituals and the authority they give to women, the direct link between mayordomías and the civil hierarchy provided a more formal validation of women's authority. In order to understand the implications of this historical trajectory for women's contemporary political and ceremonial life in Teotitlán, we shall first look at the community's civil-religious hierarchy and the changes it went through after the Mexican Revolution.

TEOTITLÁN'S CIVIL-RELIGIOUS HIERARCHY: WHEN MAYORDOMOS WERE MAYORDOMOS

At the turn of the twentieth century, Teotitlán's mayordomía system—the basis of the religious hierarchy—was intertwined with the civil cargo system. Male and female mayordomos worked together to move up the religious hierarchy; only men, as representatives of their households, moved up the hierarchy of political offices, jumping from religious to political offices. Their wives remained outside of the formal civil cargo system, politicking through the extended kin and compadrazgo networks that operated in the arena of social reproduction, similar to the way in which many women continue to participate politically in the community today.

The prerevolutionary civil cargo system in Teotitlán had about forty cargos linked to approximately nineteen mayordomías in the community's ritual calendar. After the Revolution, more positions were added to the civil cargo system when the state implemented national development plans that called for new local committees such as those for schools and ejidos. A religious branch of the cargo system took over a lot of the work previously done by mayordomos and mayordomas.

According to elderly people in Teotitlán, the purpose of the civil cargo system was to guard local customs, keep public order, adjudicate local disputes, allocate community resources, and manage the community's relationship with the government. All male heads of households were and still are required to serve in civil cargo posts throughout their adult lives. Households were obligated to provide men for cargo positions and for communal labor. Women also contributed labor to civil cargo functions on many occasions and did so every day by making up for male household labor lost to civil cargos.

According to Teotitecos, the civil cargo system is divided into two main branches: *ayuntamiento* (governmental) and *juzgado mayor* or *alcaldía* (judicial).

The officials elected to the ayuntamiento include a president, a *síndico* (legal adviser to the president and the ayuntamiento), and three *regidores* (councilmen, each dealing with a specific area, such as the cemetary or water resources). Each of these positions has a *suplente* (alternate), who remains in the municipio building on a rotating basis when the primary officials are absent. Other cargos stemming from the ayuntamiento include two employees, a secretary and treasurer, an assistant to the president and the síndico, ten policemen (*topiles*), two police captains (*mayores de vara*), and five section heads (*jefes de sección*). Teotitlán is divided geographically into five sections or neighborhoods. Communal labor is assigned by section. In the late 1990s, the topiles were replaced by *policía municipal* or municipio police.

Each section was also previously policed by officials called *gulap* in Zapotec, who are no longer part of the cargo system. No one in the community knows the Spanish name for them. They were supervised by a *comuín* and a second in command, or *primer vara*. They policed the community for sexual involvements between young boys and girls and had ritual responsibilities in the month of February.

The judicial branch of the cargo system, the juzgado mayor, includes two *alcaldes* (judges or justices of the peace), four suplentes (alternates, two for each alcalde), and two assistants, one for each judge. These local judges were the district judges while Teotitlán was the district seat. They adjudicated property transfers, sales, local disputes over land and livestock, family disagreements, and other conflicts. Today local judges in Teotitlán adjudicate similar issues.

During the colonial era, as today, local authorities were responsible for keeping order in the community and served as the links between the community and higher levels of government. All orders were passed down through the national bureaucracy to the state bureaucracies to the level of the district and municipio. Because Teotitlán was a district seat for so long, local authorities also had to monitor the activities of other municipios. The community archives have clear records of legal transactions and disputes dating back to 1580. Because the district territory of Teotitlán was so extensive, the power of local officials was probably much broader during the colonial era than it is today.

In addition to these principal civil cargo positions, eleven or more committees monitor community projects, resources, and public works. Membership is elective and is considered part of the civil cargo system. The majority of cargos are found in these committees. Each committee usually includes a president, sometimes a vice president, a treasurer, a secretary, and four to five committee members.

These committees include the parents' committees for the secondary (junior high) school, primary school, and kindergarten, and the committees for the (government-run) health center, for the Secretariat of Education (SEP), for running water, for the dam (in charge of irrigation), for communal lands, to fight fires, for electricity, and to carry out activities for national holidays. The president can set up additional committees to take on public works projects or explore new issues as they arise.[2]

Today men representing particular households are elected to civil cargo positions by a large assembly (*junta*). Before the Revolution, they were probably appointed by a group of elders. The oldest people in Teotitlán mention a group of elders who appointed both mayordomos and officials for the civil cargo system. Such practices are reported for the Sierra Juárez before 1917 (Young 1976, 159), for Juquila, Oaxaca (Greenberg 1981, 66–67), for highland Guatemala (Brintnall 1979, 94–99), and elsewhere in Mexico. According to some women, older women and mayordomas had a great deal of influence on this group of elders.

Until recently, age was a dominant factor in structuring the power relationships of local politics. Men entered the civil cargo system at an early age as helpers and slowly worked their way up to the highest positions in the system. It probably took at least twenty to twenty-five years to work through the hierarchy. Most senior officials were in their fifties or sixties. Respect and prestige were closely tied to age, which in turn determined what level an individual and household were at within the cargo system. The cargo career of Manuel Martínez, who was 60 in 1985, illustrates the movement of men up the ladder of civil and religious hierarchies, shifting between the two systems:

1952–53: *šruez* (servant to mayor; no longer exists)
1955–56: Topil (paid someone to do his labor while working in the United States)
1957–58: Mayordomo for the Virgin of Guadalupe
1959–60: Jefe de sección
1961–62: Member of temporary committee to celebrate the opening of a new dam
1963–66: Member of parents' committee for schools
1970–71: *Padrino del niño Jesús*, minor religious cargo
1973–76: President of committee for communal lands
1982: Adviser to the municipio president (no longer exists)
1985–86: President of church committee
1988–89: Mayordomo of Our Lord of the Precious Blood

This pattern is not followed so strictly by younger men. During the twentieth century, the basis for local political power changed considerably as a result of structural changes imposed by the national government and changes in local cultural values related to wealth (see Stephen 1990; Young 1976).

The pantheon of saints, apparitions and attributes of the Virgin, locally significant crosses, and other holy events to be commemorated is long. Teotitecos associate each of them with a pre-Christian divinity or supernatural being, and mayordomías were once linked to most of them:

January 15: El Cristo de Esquipulas
February 2: La Vírgen de la Candelaria
March 19: San José
May 3: La Santísima Cruz (on sacred xiabets mountain)
40 days after the end of Lent: El Asunción de la Vírgen
May (movable feast): El Espíritu Santo
8 days after El Espíritu Santo: La Trinidad
Corpus Cristi (Dadvid Jesús)
June 24: San Juan
June 29: San Pedro
July 1: Nuestro Señor de la Preciosa Sangre
July 16: La Santa Cruz
July 22: Santa Magdalena
August 4: Santo Domingo

August 10: San Jacinto
September 8: La Natividad de la Vírgen Bendita
September 15: Nuestra Señora de los Dolores
September 14: La Exaltación de la Santísima Cruz
First Sunday in October: El Santo Rosario
December 6: San Nicolás
December 12: La Vírgen de Guadalupe
December 18: Nuestra Señora de la Soledad

Under the past mayordomía system, each saint was cared for by at least one and often two sets of mayordomos. Each male-female pair of mayordomos, usually but not always husband and wife, organized and carried out rituals and festivities associated with the saint or Virgin in their charge. The importance of the particular mayordomía is reflected in the amount of money that is spent on the celebration.

The mayordomías of Teotitlán are ranked in a hierarchy. During the 1960s, according to elderly informants, the top-ranked and still active mayordomías included, in order of importance, Nuestro Señor de la Preciosa Sangre, El Cristo de Esquipulas, Guadalupe, Natividad, Trinidad, San Juan, and Santísima Cruz. In the past, households began with a relatively small mayordomía as their initial ritual expenditure. They then would try to work up to one of the more expensive ones. In order to cut back on expenses, pairs of mayordomos (i.e., two male-female couples) took up sponsorship of most of the celebrations. Informants remembered the pairing system going back to the years before the Revolution.

The importance of both male and female contributions in the mayordomía system is still described today by older men and women who have worked their way through two or three mayordomías. The system includes a fairly extensive group of offices, each of which has male and female aspects. The ritual party of the mayordomos includes five to six *diputados* (former high-ranking mayordomos) and their wives, an *escríbano* (scribe) and his wife, and a couple called *bizcochos*, a male-female pair who always accompany the mayordomos. Each man and woman has specific functions. The man's usually pertain to the church-related functions of the mayordomía, while the woman's are related to planning, organizing, preparing food, and supervising activities based in the household of the mayordomo.

While most elderly people emphasized the equal importance of men's and women's work, some women gave greater emphasis to the female component. "Of course you need both men and women, but the women's work is more important," declared Juana, age 35. "The men kill chickens and hang them up, but the women always work more. They work during the fiestas of the mayordomía and beforehand. They make chocolate, prepare a lot of spices, and spend weeks getting ready. If there were no women, there wouldn't be any mayordomías. Of course the men work, but not as much." According to Carmen, age 62, "The men's work was important, but it was always the women who worked harder. The men would get drunk and then they couldn't do anything." As on other types of ceremonial occasions, both in the past and in the present, women have performed most of the labor necessary to carry out three to five days of communal meals and dancing. The gendered division of labor and the sequence of events in mayordomías are similar to those currently seen in the life cycle events described in chapter 9.

The mayordomas' sponsorship involved not only work but an important change in their status in the community. The change is reflected in the terms used to address both men and women who have been mayordomos. Having completed a major mayordomía, men are called *dad*, equivalent to "sir," and women are called *nãn*, an honorific "ma'am." A male saint is also referred to as *dad* and the Virgin as *nãn*. Completion of mayordomía sponsorship gives men and women a linguistic association with the holy ones. "Since I have been a mayordoma everyone respects me," said 55-year-old Lucía. "They admire me now. All of them say *ščãŋ* to me now and they call me Nãn Lucía.³ They never used to." Like the saints and the Virgin, mayordomos are viewed as watching out for the welfare of the community. They may literally intercede for the community by praying for rain or asking for a cure. The only people other than mayordomos who are called *dad* and *nãn* are the elderly, *bɛngul*, who are deemed to have given a lifetime of service to the community. "If you see someone who is under sixty years of age and they are called *nãn* or *dad*, then it's because they were a mayordomo," explained Antonio, age 70. "The only way to be called this as a person who is not old is to sponsor a saint. Otherwise, you have to wait until you're old to be respected. And rich people and poor people make the expenditures to be mayordomos. So it's possible for rich or poor people to have these titles either by being a mayordomo or by waiting until they're very old."

The terms *dad* and *nãn* are strongly associated with respect granted to mayordomos and elderly people. According to informants, the amount of *respet* depends on the size and quantity of expenses involved in the cult celebration. All but the two largest mayordomías, that of Nuestro

Figure 14. A mayordomo lights candles for Nuestro Señor de la Preciosa Sangre in the local church in 1989. Photo by the author.

Señor de la Preciosa Sangre, celebrated in July, and that of the Cristo de Esquipulas, celebrated in January, have been phased out. The smallest mayordomías were medium-sized feasts lasting three days with fifteen to twenty-five couples in attendance. The most extravagant mayordomía in Teotitlán, dedicated to Nuestro Señor de la Preciosa Sangre, involves three major expenditures and smaller monthly fiestas. At the largest celebrations in July, more than two hundred invited guests attend, and a cow, twenty-five to thirty pigs, and hundreds of chickens and turkeys are consumed, along with large quantities of liquor. In addition to sponsoring several large fiestas, mayordomos pay for masses and take care of their saint's altar: they provide oil for lamps constantly burned, change the flowers, and repair the altar and the saint's clothing. Larger altars involve the purchase of twelve dozen gladiolas each week as well as considerable amounts of oil. Care for an altar usually requires one to spend four to five hours working in the church each weekend.

The sponsorship of major mayordomías often requires all of a household's labor for at least a year. Many years of financial sacrifice are also necessary to pay for the high level of ritual consumption maintained throughout the period of celebration. A mayordomía celebrated in Teotitlán in 1988 and 1989 is estimated to have cost at least 60 million pesos, or U.S.\$24,000, to host four large fiestas as well as monthly smaller fiestas.[4]

Reciprocal labor exchanges or *xɛlgɛʐ šte majŕdõ* are the backbone of the mayordomía system. Work parties to gather firewood and to prepare candles and decorations precede the extravagant celebrations. Reciprocal labor exchanges based on donation of labor by the invited guests make the celebrations function on their specified days. Genealogical and fictive kinship ties provide the network of people drawn together to perform the labor for mayordomías. In addition to reciprocal labor, yearlong contracts were made with two butchers, a family of candle makers, and at least one twenty-piece band.

In a survey of a random stratified sample of 154 households in 1986, only about 20 percent had sponsored one mayordomía. About 7 percent had sponsored two or more. Before the 1970s, a couple might try to sponsor two or three mayordomías in their lifetime. For example, Jovenal, the 78-year-old holder of the highest ritual post in the community (*fiscal*), described his mayordomía career as follows: "We were mayordomos twice before I was made fiscal. The first time was in 1939. We were mayordomos of the Santísima Cruz. Then in 1949 we were mayordomos for the Santísima Trinidad. We had a lot of guelaguetza for each one. We had a list of things we had left with people, but someone else had to write it for us. There were about seventy people at each celebration. We had music and danced and burned a fireworks castle. We spent a lot of time and money on those mayordomías." His wife, Luisa, age 75, continued the discussion: "We both thought about doing this at the same time. We really didn't have to discuss it much. We decided four years ahead of time what we would do. Jovenal went to the church to visit the Santísima Cruz and made a *promesa* for both of us that we would hold the mayordomía. Then we knew that we had to get ready for it."

While Jovenal and Luisa did not remember any particular motivation for sponsoring their mayordomía, many other mayordomos described making a vow to hold a cult celebration in connection with a major illness or family disaster. Some households combined a pilgrimage with a mayordomía; sponsors traveled to Esquipulas, Guatemala, on foot and by burro before holding the mayordomía ritual in Teotitlán. Many people came to Teotitlán from other communities and ethnic groups to share in a cult figure's miraculous power, particularly the one associated with Nuestro Señor de la Preciosa Sangre.

In discussing the significance of mayordomías, Teotitecos continually focus on the concept of *respet*, which they identify with authority within their community. Until recently, this was the primary criterion for community leadership, extended to both men and women. This situation slowly began to change with the government's effort to eliminate mayordomías and to secularize local political systems beginning in the late 1920s. In Teotitlán, Calles's effort to eliminate mayordomías coincided with local distress at being forced to sponsor them. People in the community did not want to eliminate the mayordomías entirely, but they wanted to participate freely and not be forced to take on sponsorship. Many people, however, believe that the state's efforts, in conjunction with a local move to democratize participation in the mayordomía system, led to its eventual downfall. Both factors are important in understanding the current basis of political authority and the way it affects women's perceptions of themselves as political actors and their strategies for political action.

THE END OF OBLIGATORY MAYORDOMÍAS AND THE STATE'S CAMPAIGN TO SEPARATE RITUAL FROM POLITICAL AUTHORITY

Until 1931, community ritual activities in Teotitlán were organized by a group of mayordomos who were appointed, often against their will, by local elders. By the mid-1920s, mayordomía *a la fuerza* (obligatory mayordomías) had become an extremely volatile issue. Many Teotitecos believe that they continued after the Revolution because economic conditions were still bad. The economic result of obligatory mayordomías was a system of indentured labor and land grabs by a small group of wealthy merchants.

While Teotitecos clearly wanted to end this obligatory system, they still wanted the political authority that stemmed from mayordomías. Such a system of authority also enabled the community to choose its own leaders. Teotitecos opposed only the obligatory nature of sponsorship.

Throughout the 1800s and early 1900s, the presence of mayordomía offices and the political authority that stemmed from them remained outside state control. While the civil offices of the hierarchy were tied to the state through functions such as census taking, tax collection, and negotiations for funds and resources, the religious offices in the hierarchy remained exclusively under community control. Shortly after the Revolution, however, the autonomy of local religious administration was challenged by state intervention. Postrevolutionary state officials could stop the spread of political authority and leadership outside of official administrative structures only by eliminating ritual sponsorship and bringing all aspects of religious leadership under state control.

The 1917 Mexican constitution, which was actively interpreted under the Calles regime, sought to place all local political offices under state control and to regulate strictly how local churches were run. In an effort to loosen the church's ideological control over Mexican citizens, the Calles government launched an all-out attack against it. Strict application of several anticlerical articles was part of this campaign. The enforcement of these articles and additional government decrees obligating communities to organize secular *juntas vecinales* (neighborhood committees) placed community ritual activity directly under state power in 1926 (see Stephen 1990a for a detailed description).

In 1926 Calles sent out a decree mandating that municipios organize juntas vecinales to oversee church activities. This action set up an alternate administrative structure that took over many of the duties carried out by mayordomos. Throughout the late 1920s, Teotitecos refused to name people to the committee; the local archive contains several exchanges in which officials in the governor's office complain that Teotiteco authorities have yet to name the members of their junta vecinal (Archivo Municipal de Teotitlán del Valle 1927, 1928). By the early 1930s, the junta vecinal was formally constituted and became a branch of the local civil cargo system. Now called the church committee (*comité de la iglesia*), it still manages the church and also organizes major celebrations for saints that no longer have mayordomos. It is structured like this:

Fiscales 1 and 2
Presidente
Vicepresidente
Secretario
Tesorero
Vocales 1, 2, 3, 4, 5, 6, 7, 8, 9
Šudaos 1, 2, 3, 4, 5
Padres del pueblo 1, 2, 3, 4, 5
Sacristanos 1, 2, 3, 4, 5
Acólitos 1, 2, 3, 4, 5

The positions of fiscal are reserved for men who have worked their way to the top of the religious cargo system. It is the last position taken before retirement and is primarily ceremonial. The padres del pueblo (town fathers) are in charge of lighting fireworks. The positions of sacristan and acolyte are voluntary, and often are filled by people who want to avoid other cargo services or by young men who are taking their fathers' places in the cargo system.

Attached to the religious branch of the cargo system is the Cofradía de la Santa Patrona, a group headed by a treasurer that is responsible for maintaining lands that belong to the Virgin del Rosario as patroness of Teotitlán. Corn raised on the land is sold and the money used to maintain the Virgin and to pay for religious festivities in her honor. The lands for maintaining the Virgin, previously communal lands behind the church, were set aside in 1914 (Archivo Municipal de Teotitlán del Valle 1914). Since then the committee has served to administer them.

The creation of the juntas vecinales was not directly designed to eliminate mayordomías, but it was combined with a very strong political strategy on the part of several Oaxaca governors to phase them out. Correspondence from the *Periódico Oficial*, my fieldwork in Teotitlán, and Young's (1976) research among the Sierra Zapotecs all point to a coordinated effort on the part of Oaxaca governors and their associates to discourage and undercut mayordomos, often in the name of moral and economic modernity (see Stephen 1990). For example, in accordance with the party line of the Partido Socialista, precursor to the PRI, officials from San Juan Teitipac wrote to Governor Genaro Vásquez to ask his help in eliminating mayordomías. He responded: "I see with satisfaction your proposal to rectify all the customs that produce the ruin or stagnation of our towns' moral and economic patrimony" (Archivo General del Estado 1926b, 27–28).[5]

The breakdown of mayordomía systems and the eventual disengagement of religious hierarchies from civil ones did result in a considerable realignment of local power relations. In Teotitlán this was a slow process that began in the 1920s and was pushed further in the 1960s and 1970s with the commercialization of the weaving industry. In the late 1920s, the outcome of the campaign against mayordomías in Teotitlán differed from that in other communities because the economy of the mayordomía system was heavily tied to local debt peonage.

The larger political economy of forced mayordomías in Teotitlán until 1931 did little to redistribute wealth, but seems to have justified or perhaps even increased economic differentiation. The redistribution of food and entertainment during mayordomías appears to have been far outweighed by the heavy sacrifices made by poor households who had to sponsor large celebrations despite their pitiful economic circumstances.

By the 1920s, economic resources were scarce in the community and people faced certain hardship when they were forced to make the expenditures associated with sponsorship of a cult. Many men who balked at accepting sponsorships they could not afford were thrown in jail until they accepted. "I remember when we were named to a mayordomía," said Rosa, age 89. "We were working and the police came to get my husband. They took him to jail and then wouldn't let him out until we accepted. Then we went to the church to accept our mayordomía. My husband went to Tlacolula to protest this."

The acute poverty of the community during this period made it necessary for many mayordomos to sell or pawn their property in order to pay for their ritual expenses.

> People had to sell their land and their houses to the merchants. Pels Molín, Manuel Bautista, Lorenzo Martínez, Dad Mon, all these people got a lot of land because people borrowed money from them. People would sell their land to these merchants for very little—eighty or a hundred pesos. The rich merchants took advantage of people selling their land. When people were in jail to receive their mayordomía, their family and friends would come and visit them and offer them a little guelaguetza so they could pay their expenses. The poor people who had to be mayordomos, they had to sell their lands to the rich in order to fulfill their obligations. (Pedro, age 75)

If they did not have land or a house to sell, they would borrow money from merchants or other wealthy families and pay off the debt by indenturing their own and their children's labor for many years. "Before they got rid of forced mayordomía, people sold their houses, their land, their oxen, their children, and themselves to work for a few rich people," recalled Luis, age 65. "A lot of people had to pawn their land for money. Some people got a lot of land this way." The mayordomía system guaranteed a stable and cheap source of labor for merchants as long as members of the impoverished majority in Teotitlán were forced to participate in the sponsorship system. By the late 1920s, the forced poverty stemming from obligatory mayordomías had become a major political issue in the community, pitting merchants and community elders who had already sacrificed and sponsored mayordomías against younger people who were candidates for future sponsorship.

In 1926, the Partido Socialista of Oaxaca, which in 1929 became a part of the Partido Nacional Revolucionario (PNR, precursor to the PRI), formed a local branch in Teotitlán. In 1929, the PNR urged all people in

Teotitlán to free themselves from the oppression of church control and called for an end to mayordomías. This demand was in line with state policies (the PNR was the state party) to undercut local political autonomy and eliminate all institutions that remained outside the state's sphere of influence. Although the PNR itself never gained a wide base of support in Teotitlán, the demand to end obligatory mayordomías did.

After 1928, many couples appointed as mayordomos by community elders refused to carry out their sponsorship duties, even if they had to go to jail. This local mayordomía strike continued until 1931, when the municipio president declared an end to obligatory mayordomía appointments. Community elders and local merchant families protested, but they were overruled by the majority of the community (Stephen 1990a).

The end of obligatory mayordomías in Teotitlán did not by any means spell the end of cult celebrations. Most mayordomías had sponsors until the 1960s, when they began to decline in number and frequency. Teotitlán continued to resist government efforts to eliminate mayordomías, maintaining voluntary celebrations. The nature of the community's reworking of Oaxaca state policy designed to limit local political autonomy after the Revolution is important for understanding contemporary community-state interaction (see Parnell 1988 for a comparative discussion) and the participation of contemporary Teotiteco women in community political affairs.

CONCLUSIONS: THE STRUGGLE FOR LOCAL
AUTONOMY AND TEOTITECO WOMEN

The eventual uncoupling of the civil and religious cargo systems in Teotitlán is an illustration of the historical dynamics of state-local interaction and both the structural obstacles and human efforts involved in maintaining local autonomy. In Teotitlán, state efforts to undermine community control of ritual/political institutions created unintended consequences when they operated in conjunction with local opposition to forced mayordomía sponsorship. While Teotitecos wanted to escape from the yoke of forced sponsorship, they did not want to give up control of their political institutions to the state. In spite of the efforts of state officials to wipe out mayordomías entirely, they continued to thrive in Teotitlán on a voluntary basis until well into the 1960s. However, structural changes in the ways in which local government was formed and the state's formal effort to separate ritual and political power probably slowly began to influence conceptions of community authority and respect in Teotitlán. As we shall see in chapter 9, the eventual transfer of mayordomía content to life cycle rituals temporarily insulated a significant part of the community's ritual life from direct outside interference. While this change certainly provided a measure of protection for the intimate ritual life of the community, it also distanced ritual activity from political life. This was an important factor in shaping the way women seek to influence community politics and to realize their own agendas.

When women participated equally with men in mayordomía activities that sanctified community leadership and directly linked ritual *respet* to political authority, their association with the guardians of the community was widely acknowledged and validated. While women still receive respect and titles for their participation in life cycle ceremonies, the focus of such ritual events is no longer on a saint or supernatural power that represents the community. Women's earlier association with the community's holy cult figures was a direct vehicle for authority that also translated into influence on the policy making of local elders.

As the Mexican state modernized and centralized under Lázaro Cárdenas in the 1930s, the role of women was paid lip service but never taken particularly seriously. After 1917, when municipio authorities were supposed to be elected, women did not have the right to vote. They were unable to do so in most states until 1944. Feminist debates until the 1940s revolved around women's ability to vote and to hold elective office (Partido Feminista Revolucionario de Tabasco 1933; Primer Congreso Feminista de Yucatán 1917). However, even after women were formally given the right to vote and could legally hold public office at the municipio level or higher, tradition limited attendance at community meetings to men in many parts of Mexico.

In Teotitlán, the survival of a fairly complete mayordomía system until the 1960s and the ritually based authority system that went with it were indirect mechanisms for establishing independence from the long arm of the postrevolutionary Mexican state. After the 1960s and the decline of mayordomías, this process continued indirectly through women, who used ritual-based authority and respect as a way of claiming legitimacy as political actors in the community. With commercialization of the weaving industry, however, other criteria for *respet* and political authority associated with wealth and class position have emerged. Those women who were most marginalized in the political system continued to use respect as a way of asserting their opinions. As we shall see in chapter 9, the consolidation of class relations under commercial capitalism contradicted the community solidarity expressed in ritual. A new route to respect through wealth ensured that community authority was no longer equally available to all simply on the bases of age, community service, and ritual sponsorship.

CHAPTER 9

Fiesta

The Gendered Dynamics

of Ritual Participation

I was married in 1936. It was a very small fiesta called
sa(ᵖa)ter(t)síl [morning fiesta]. It lasted only one day. About
sixteen people came. We had one meal and I got a trunk, a metate,
and some blouses. There was no music. Back then, only a few very
rich people got married *sa(ᵖa)χúil(i)* [with music], like
when they are mayordomos. —Julia, age 70

I was married in 1953. My husband's mother paid for
the ceremony. She actually didn't have to pay much money
because she had inherited her mother's guelaguetzas. She was able
to call in a lot of things that people owed her mother—turkeys,
corn, and cacao. She used these in the wedding. She could do
this even though her mother was already dead. There were about
fifty people at the wedding. We killed one pig and about twenty
turkeys. I think the party went on for one or two days. There
was no music and no dancing. The presents I got included
a trunk, two metates, and about five or six blouses. . . .
In 1968 my oldest daughter got married. It was a big party.
There were about eighty couples invited and there was a band and
dancing. She got two trunks, a dresser, and about eighteen different metates and some dishes. She got a lot more than I did. . . .
My son was married in 1978. By then everyone had big weddings,
not just the rich. There were 160 people at that wedding. There
was music for two days and they killed three pigs. The bride got a
trunk, a dresser, a glass case for her dishes, and lots of dishes.
It was a big wedding. —María, age 52

These two women's recollections of their own and their children's
weddings document the change in Teotitlán from a ritual life focused on mayordomías to one centered on elaborate life cycle rituals:
weddings, baptisms, asking a woman's hand in marriage, birthdays, and
funerals. In this change, the form and content of mayordomía rituals that
were found only occasionally in the weddings of the rich were adopted

by most of the population as part of various life cycle ceremonies. This pattern is seen in neighboring communities as well.

In Teotitlán, the reinforcement of life cycle rituals with the form and content of the fading mayordomía system is part of a self-generated local Zapotec identity. The major roles that women play in ritual are valued within the community as part of this identity. When women's ritual roles and status are viewed in a larger political and economic context, however, the ritual authority of women appears to be ridden with contradictions in respect to class differences between women and the limited political participation of all women. The interactions of women in ritual events often reflect a conflict between community solidarity and the divisions created by the economic inequalities of merchants and weavers. Although ritual respect is still open to all who can achieve it, the economic realities of the labor and financial costs of fiesta sponsorship may make it easier for merchant women to achieve such status than for weaver women to do so.

RITUAL REPRESENTATION OF ETHNICITY: BEING ZAPOTEC FOR TOURISTS AND BEING ZAPOTEC FOR TEOTITECOS

The construction of Teotiteco ethnicity involves a variety of dimensions that are invoked according to particular situations. One of the strongest influences on how local ethnicity is represented is whether or not the context involves people from outside the community, particularly nonindigenous individuals who are not from surrounding Zapotec communities. The varying representations of Teotitlán local identity are also reflected in differences in local ritual activity. One level of ritual involves the maintenance of some ceremonies open to tourists and outsiders, including Zapotecs from surrounding communities. The other involves a series of life cycle rituals and a limited number of closed religious fiestas that activate reciprocal exchanges of labor and goods. The significant role of women in the ongoing construction of Teotiteco identity is concentrated at the second tier of ritual activity, where the most intensive ceremonial life of the community is now focused. Ritual-based respect, which women still pursue as a path to community authority, is also concentrated here in the face of a decline in mayordomías.

The first level of ritual activity, the maintenance of saint-related ceremonies open to tourists and outsiders, has largely been taken over by men as an extension of the state-ordained church committee. The days of the community ritual calendar originally attached to mayordomías are still celebrated in Teotitlán today, but instead of being financed and organized primarily by the men and women who served as mayordomos, most celebrations are run on a small scale by the church committee. They are paid for collectively by small contributions from all households in the community.

While many former mayordomía-sponsored rituals are still celebrated in the community, they are structured in a way that makes them available for outside nonindigenous consumption as well. Before, when saints' days were celebrated as mayordomías, the primary activities took place in the mayordomos' home with a large final dance open to all in the community. This culminating activity took place late at night when few outsiders were likely to be present. According to elderly informants, very few tourists were ever present at these final dances because there was no place for them to stay overnight in the community. Even today, most leave at sunset. Thus the ritual activity for mayordomías took place within the space of the sponsor's compound, with the exception of the final dance.

Beginning in the 1960s in Oaxaca and throughout Mexico, the state promoted indigenous ritual life as a major tourist attraction in conjunction with craft production.[1] In a sense, Teotitecos have facilitated, on their own terms, the state's promotion of Indian cultures by turning several local celebrations into performances. In Teotitlán, the celebrations for saints' days, formerly mayordomías, are now conducted largely in the public plaza, in the same community space as celebrations of national holidays such as Mexican Independence Day, Mother's Day, and Revolution Day. Both saints' days and secular ceremonies reflect a fusion of national culture and politics with local ritual tradition. Secular holidays, which draw a significant number of people, are run by school officials in conjunction with municipio officials. Regional dances, poems, and choral readings are performed by schoolchildren in Spanish. Celebrations of saints' days are still run by Teotitlán officials, but are now often attended by outsiders, particularly during Holy Week and during the main fiesta in July. The major attractions at these ritual events are performances by the local dance troupe, which acts out an unusual version of the Conquest story.

By facilitating the celebration of national holidays in community space and permitting outsiders to attend the celebrations of saints' days, Teotitecos have given up local control over part of their ritual sphere. In doing so they have succumbed to pressure to create indigenous ritual for outsiders and to accept the dissemination of national culture in local schools. "People come from all over to see our *danzantes*," said Luisa, age 35, proudly. "They know that in Teotitlán we have the best dancers. During the day you can see lots of tourists here watching. For us, we can only go late in the afternoon for a little while after our chores are finished. We don't have time to go to watch. We're too busy working. We like to go to watch the end of the dance and visit the church." While such ritual may reflect several elements of Indianness encouraged by the state, Teotitecos have nonetheless participated in its formulation and dissemination. In this way, they have consciously added to their local Zapotec identity a dimension other than weaving production that is available for widespread consumption.

The majority of meaningful ritual content and form in Teotitlán, however, does not appear in rituals carried out in the town square. It has been transferred from mayordomías to life cycle rituals carried out in household compounds, an area not readily accessible to tourists but open to the community. As mayordomías were slowly abandoned, the ritual content, forms, and consumption associated with them (drinking, huge feasts, dancing, ornate decorations) were gradually transferred to rituals focused on the developmental cycle, with weddings taking on many of the characteristics and high levels of consumption formerly associated with mayordomías. Thus the meaningful content of mayordomías was transferred almost completely intact to formerly simple life cycle celebrations, with the exception of an extravagant form of wedding ceremony, *sa(ᵖa)xúil(i)*, which was always celebrated by a few wealthy households. By incorporating the core ritual form and content of mayordomías in other rituals, the community transformed individual life cycle rituals into semipublic celebrations that pull together large networks of kin, compadres, and neighbors.

Life cycle ceremonies have become larger and larger. Teotitecos pride themselves on their high levels of ritual consumption and readily admit that occasions such as weddings have turned into contests of one-upmanship.

> Even young people who go to the United States always return. Even if a young man meets a young woman from another community they also return here to follow the custom of the wedding. If people don't follow the custom of a big wedding, others will talk about them, saying bad things— that they don't have any money. Because of what others say, people always

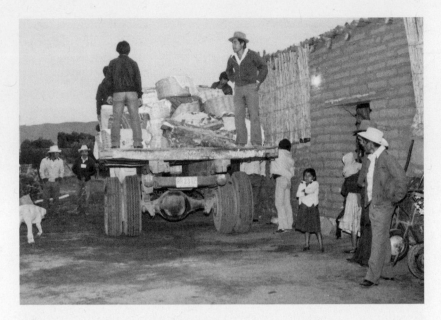

Figure 15. The amount of food and candles given at local engagement ceremonies is now so great that the gifts have to be transported from the house of the prospective groom to the house of his future bride in a truck. Photo by the author.

try to carry on with the custom. People especially don't want others to think they are poor so they will always have a big fiesta. The weddings used to be smaller, but now people spend a lot of money. They practically have a competition to see who can have the biggest one. (Octavio, age 52)

While some younger sectors of the community, particularly merchants, say they want to stop spending so much time and money on fiestas, they acknowledge that social pressure to keep up the costumbre is very strong.

The household compound, which was the location of most mayordomía rituals and is now the site of life cycle ceremonies, becomes a public space during a ritual event. While it is not public in the sense that anyone can walk in, by bringing together a large kin-compadrazgo network, the household compound becomes a focal point for a cross section of the community physically assembled for days on end. The group contains both weavers and merchants and brings them together in ritual relationships that reshuffle some of the inequities implied in the relations of production. Their physical presence transforms the household compound into a semipublic ritual arena while ceremonial activities are taking place. For people within the community, the household plot now provides a secure space for public ritual, temporarily protected from the presence of outsiders.

RESOLVING RELIGIOUS DIFFERENCES IN THE 1990S

Teotitlán has been Catholic at least in name since the sixteenth century. The religious faith practiced here blends local indigenous rituals and traditions with noninstitutional folk Catholicism. The community has no resident priest, and while the sixteenth-century Catholic church is an important center for ritual life in the community, it operates under the control of the local church committee elected through the civil cargo system. Throughout the 1980s, a small group of Protestants more or less quietly coexisted with the Catholic majority. Their ideology taught individual responsibility for achieving economic independence, abstinence from alcohol, personal salvation, and freedom from communal obligations. Christine Eber writes of Protestants in a Tzotzil municipio in highland Chiapas:

> Protestants seem to find justification in the Bible for freedom from a traditional system of personal restrictions and communal obligations which are not only idolatrous, but costly and time consuming. Seeing feasts for Catholic saints and Maya ancestor Gods as idol worship, Protestants no longer serve religious cargos nor assist cargo holders in fiestas. They have also stopped offering feasts at the graves of deceased relatives. . . . In rejecting traditional ideas about collective and personal well-being, Protestants pass on a very different idea of living to their children. (Eber 2000, 17)

A similar assessment could be made of Protestants of the Iglesia de Dios (Church of God) in Teotitlán.

In 1993 the Protestants built a church, funded largely by one successful merchant family. Members told me that the Church of God is based in Tennessee. In the late 1990s, this church split into two and another congregation was formed. At this time, members of the two Iglesias de Dios became more assertive in the community. They began to protest community requirements for participation in the civil cargo system, objected to the community celebration of Catholic religious festivals, refused to pay the required household contributions for expenses associated with celebrations of saints' days, and refused to do communal labor for Catholic rituals and occasions. The leaders of the two churches steadfastly refused to serve on the church committee or to take on any other civil cargos. Their refusal was based on religious objections, although many of the civil cargos had no religious content. They maintained that participation in the civil cargo system was not part of their religion and that the religious ceremonies celebrated in the community were not found in the Bible and therefore not legitimate. They also stressed the benefits of not spending their money on lavish outlays for traditional fiestas as contributing to private capital accumulation (see Eber 2000, 217). One of the key leaders of the Iglesia de Dios was a very successful merchant who had built a large house for himself and another for his children.

When the father of a key Protestant religious leader died at the age of 85, the family refused to burn candles, sound church bells, or take bread, chocolate, and mescal to the house of the deceased. When the family went to the community cemetery, the committee in charge of maintenance and burials referred them to the *presidente municipal* for permission to bury their father there. The presidente municipal said he would have to speak with the people. He called the people together to discuss the matter. The discussion at the assembly got very confrontational and centered on the conflict between the rights granted to community members who carry out their responsibilities and therefore can be buried in the cemetery and the human rights of those who follow a different religion. Rigoberto, who attended the community assembly, described it this way:

> So the family came and said they wanted permission to bury the deceased in the cemetery. But then many people from the town started shouting, "No! They're Protestants. They don't provide communal labor, they don't make contributions to the community, they refuse to carry out any cargos." They screamed, "Get them out of here!" They wanted to beat them up. They were objecting because the people of this family refused to accept the cargos they were elected to. . . . So those Protestants went to Oaxaca to bring the human rights people here, from the Oaxacan government human rights office. They brought some lawyers from Oaxaca. The people were still in a meeting. When they got here the people said, "Who says these lawyers are in charge of our community?" They kicked them out of the meeting. They ran them out of town. They left. That was the day they got rid of the human rights people.

By that time the deceased had been dead for four days. The Protestant family then decided to bury him in a grave at their own church and took the body there. But that solution, too, was unacceptable to the towns-people. Outraged community members and some local officials went to the church leader's house and told him that if he buried the deceased in the courtyard of the Iglesia de Dios, they would all be kicked out of town. To bury the body away from all the community ancestors was un-thinkable. Who knew what the dead would do if this body was buried in the wrong place?

The body was returned to the home of the church leader. Five days had gone by and the body was in an advanced state of decomposition. At the end of the fifth day, the son of the deceased went to the municipio presi-dent to ask forgiveness and begin negotiation of different understand-ings of rights. The two of them, each representing a wider constituency, reached an interesting compromise that allowed room for both the indi-vidual rights that the Protestants associated with freedom of religion and the collective responsibilities that come with living in Teotitlán. The first step was to make restitution for past injuries. The Protestants agreed to pay all the contributions they owed for community fiestas for the past five years. They then agreed that they would do the required labor and ac-cept civil cargo positions that did not involve religious obligations. They are not required to carry out mayordomías or the cult celebrations for saints. On day six, the deceased was buried in the community cemetery.

The State Commission of Human Rights has not received any more calls from people in Teotitlán. Restitution helped to lay the ground-work for new and better ways of living together and negotiations pro-vided unique, culturally appropriate local solutions (Brown 2003, 233). The Protestants agreed to take on some of the responsibilities required for life in their community, but maintained the ability to opt out of some forms of cargos and labor that were directly linked to local Catholic tra-dition and make their collective contributions in other ways. They thus maintained some individual distinctiveness that can be defined as their individual right to worship in their own way but also agreed to continue with some historically defined collective responsibilities.

THE GENDERED DIVISION OF LABOR IN LIFE CYCLE CEREMONIES

A careful look at current secular and religious events performed for com-munity and tourist consumption in Teotitlán provides a clue to the im-portance of gender in the intense ritual life hidden behind the walls of individual homes. All ritual space, whether in a home or in the town square, is divided into a male sphere and a female sphere. In the main square, married couples arrive together to view an event, but quickly split up, the woman going to the female section and the man going to the male section.[2] Teotitecos can spot outsiders instantly, not only by how they look but by where they stand. Many tourists and government officials inadvertently stand in the section of the opposite sex. For Teotitecos, spatial separation by gender is a prerequisite to the creation of ritual space. This structural requirement is vividly seen in life cycle rituals.

While many people in Teotitlán may passively observe ritual events open to outsiders, all of the community participates more actively in rituals associated with the developmental cycle of the household. Active participation of all community members in life cycle rituals gives these rituals more importance and value than saints' day rituals, which are no longer attached to mayordomías. Attendance at community activities associated with saints' days is optional and people are often too busy to go. An invitation to a life cycle ritual, however, cannot be turned down. Even men and women from merchant households who try to downplay their participation in fiestas emphasize how hard it is to get out of invitations to life cycle events. Angela, a middle-aged merchant woman, put it this way:

> We don't participate in many customs, but when someone asks you to go to a fiesta, you can't turn them down. When someone sends a *huehuete* [ritual practitioner] to invite you, you have to go. It isn't a law written down, but you have to go. If you don't go, then people will disown you. Rumors would start to be spread about how you thought you were so important that you didn't need anyone. You know, sometimes my husband doesn't have time to go, but I have to. I'm obligated to go and help. If I didn't go, I'd lose a lot of friends and respect here.

An invitation implies a major time commitment. All life cycle rituals have a similar structure; the formal part of the celebration lasts three days but the preparation and cleanup can go on for a month.

Biological, affinal, and ritual kin perform most of the labor necessary to carry off a successful fiesta.[3] Without the labor pool available through extended family and ritual kinship networks, it would be impossible for any household to perform all the activities necessary for sponsoring a successful fiesta.

Work groups for life cycle rituals, as for mayordomías, are completely segregated by gender. After men and women arrive together and offer a formal greeting to the heads of the household, each retires to his or her separate sphere. Women make fun of men who violate the gender segregation. For example, at a wedding, two men came into the kitchen supposedly to help by carrying out a carton of beer. They were taking a long time and had overstayed their time in the women's kitchen. They were quite drunk. The women were very open about making fun of them. "What are you two drunk chickens doing in here? You can't even walk by yourselves. How can you carry that carton? You'll fall over. Look at them, like babies who can't walk. They're so drunk, who could they help? Go back with the men, where you belong."

Within the separate spheres, activities are organized by age. In general, Teotitecos recognize four significant age divisions for men and women. Outside these categories are children between the ages of 7 and 12, who also work. Categories for adults and near-adults include older teenagers (14–20) who are single and those who have recently begun to live as part of a conjugal couple (they may have small children); young people (21–35) who have young children (age 10 and younger) and whose families are growing; middle-aged people (36–60) whose children are of marriageable age; and elderly people whose children are married (60+). This group includes widows and widowers.

Now that the town has running water and trucks, the physical labor required of men during ritual events has greatly diminished. Their primary tasks are procuring and chopping firewood, cleaning up the yard, setting up shaded work areas, hauling water, and butchering animals. The household head and his older male relatives act as bosses, directing the other men. Those men who have already sponsored large fiestas are seen as experts and asked for advice on how to do the work. Younger men and older teenagers do the bulk of the physical labor.

Firewood is secured by a separate work party about thirty days before the main fiesta. The head of the sponsoring household assembles a guelaguetza group. His wife organizes a parallel work party of women to feed the men. "We don't write it down when we go for firewood," explained Eduardo, age 30, "but we remember. For example, if I already went to get firewood for someone, I can ask them to help me with the harvest. They'll remember that I helped them and they won't charge me for the work I ask them to do in my harvest. Usually the people who help one another the most are families or compadres." According to Matilde, age 32,

"The same is true for women who come to make tortillas while the men gather the wood. The women who come to work during a fiesta don't get paid for their work. They are trading labor for the future." The men borrow or rent a truck and return with enough wood to last for the entire fiesta. They don't have to work again until a few days before the fiesta.

Men's work in preparation for a fiesta centers on getting the house and yard ready for upcoming activities. A large patio space has to be cleared and shaded areas must be constructed for the women who will be making tortillas and cooking. Once the activities begin, the women direct five or six men to haul water and firewood as they need them. The men also haul and transport anything that needs to be moved as the fiesta progresses. They help the butcher cut the meat into large chunks. Once this work is finished, they can relax. Overall, about thirty men make active labor contributions during the course of a fiesta.

Most men who are invited to a fiesta spend their time drinking and talking. Not the women. They often arrive earlier than men and work all day. They do not begin drinking until late in the afternoon or until the last day of the fiesta. While five to ten women work from five to ten days in advance preparing for a fiesta, on the actual days when ritual activities take place and meals are prepared, as many as two hundred women may be working together.

Women have mixed feelings about going to fiestas. Most of them associate it with very hard physical work and clearly state that they go to help because someday they will need other women to help them. "I only like to go to fiestas because it means the people will come here and help me," said Lucía, age 28. "It's a lot of work to be a woman in a fiesta. If it's a close friend or compadre who is having the fiesta, then you have to arrive really early, like at four or five in the morning. And you don't get to leave until one o'clock in the morning." As Isabel noted in chapter 3, in the 1990s some wealthier people began to pay people from Maquilxóchitl to do some of the women's work. Families that don't have extra cash continue to invite relatives. And women still complain.

> Women don't really like to go to fiestas that much because it's a lot of work. Tejate is the worst. Tortillas are bad because of the heat. Making them makes my arms hurt and my knees sore. . . . Most people feel this way. Maybe people like my mother don't mind so much because they're older and don't have to work so hard. My mother doesn't have to do the heavy work like making tejate and tortillas. It's those of us who are still young who have to do all the hard work. . . . I think the men enjoy going to fies-

tas more because they only work a little bit. The men respect our work and say that we work hard. They know the food is the most important thing about a fiesta, and we do that. So our work is most important, but it's hard. (Cristina, age 40)

This large female work force is organized into groups by age. Each age group has a specific task. For example, the youngest women, both married and unmarried, grind corn and cacao together for tejate. This is the hardest physical labor performed, often lasting six to eight hours. Other younger and some middle-aged women work in teams of three or four making tortillas. Older middle-aged women prepare the main ingredients—chopping meat, peeling garlic, roasting chiles, and so forth. The female head of the household and her oldest and closest relatives direct the work process.

The oldest women are in charge of cooking huge pots of food and mixing ingredients in the proper amounts and order. Before the meat is cut up, the hostess invites all the older women who have achieved distinction by giving a large fiesta in their own homes to bless the meat. This invitation is a way of acknowledging an older woman's status and paying her respect. Older women's control of the food is an important indication of their authority in ritual events.

The oldest women eat last, not because they are last in the ritual order but because they supervise the amount of food given to each person according to status. "The women who are seated in the kitchen are always the ones who are most respected," explained Mercedes, age 40. "These are the women who have already been mayordomas or who have had a major expense like a wedding. If a woman hasn't given a large fiesta, like a mayordomía or a wedding, and she goes to sit in the kitchen, the women will look at her and later talk about her. They'll say, 'Why was she in the kitchen? She hasn't even given a large fiesta yet!'" When all have been allocated the proper portions, they begin to eat. Men usually eat before women. They act as waiters, carrying full plates of food to the proper persons according to the instructions of the older women. When the meal is over, they return the empty plates to the women who divided the meat.

Women wash the dishes and then begin to seat themselves and eat, the older and middle-aged women eating first, with the exception of those who are dividing the meat. Younger women follow. Once the older women who have supervised the meal finish eating, their work is over. The younger women clean up and finish up the day's work. At the end of the day people either return home or begin to drink.

Figure 16. Working in teams,
young women work ten to
fourteen hours a day making
tortillas when they are invited
to a fiesta. This is guelaguetza
labor. Photo by the author.

Many of the older women stay until quite late, laughing, talking, gossiping, and drinking. They often comment that going to fiestas is how
they find out what is going on in the community. Several commented,
"Going to a fiesta is like listening to the radio. You learn all the news."
Ritual events provide women with a forum for airing opinions, discussing community politics, and demonstrating their influence in subtle
ways. If the occasion calls for dancing, it takes place in the evening. In
that case, women prepare an evening snack of bread and hot chocolate
for everyone. When they have finished, both men and women move to
the main patio to sit, the men in chairs and the women by themselves on
palm mats. Each section of the patio is supplied with a generous supply
of bottles of mescal and cartons of beer. One older relative of the sponsoring family takes on the job of bartender, a man for the men and a
woman for the women. Drinking, talking, and dancing take up the remainder of the evening, often until 4:00 A.M.

When dancing is called for, as during a wedding, a mayordomía, or a

Figure 17. Men spend a significant amount of time drinking at local ceremonies—more than women, because their work is usually finished sooner. Photo by the author.

large birthday party, the oldest male serves as ritual specialist if an actual huehuete is not present. He selects the people who are to dance together, with regular input from the oldest women present. Traditionally, men danced with men and women with women; recently men and women have been assigned to dance together. Some older Teotitecos frown on this practice as lack of respect. The primary dance done in Teotitlán is the *jarabe*, a three-step in which the woman dances backward while the man moves forward; they do not touch. Whether men and women dance together or not, the oldest people always dance first and the youngest last. The order of dancing reiterates the order found in greeting ceremonies and the seating arrangements. The most respected positions are given to the oldest people. Older people are invited first, greeted first, seated in the most honorable positions, do not do physical labor, and are called on as advisers in work and as ritual specialists during ceremonial activities. In life cycle rituals, the oldest person involved in organizing events is often a woman. If so, she has ultimate authority.

COMPADRAZGO

The compadrazgo system works as a hidden web pulling together the major extended families of Teotitlán into lifelong relationships through ritual commitments and continued reciprocal labor exchanges. If extended to its logical limits, compadrazgo could bind all members of the community together. It is a major source of material resources, labor, influence, and support for women in relation to ceremonial activities, politics, and production. But at the same time, the broader class context in which compadrazgo exists can cause divisions among women.

A study done in Oaxaca suggests that compadrazgo ties are inherited — that the selection of godparents is limited by lines of descent between the two households involved in the relationship (Sault 1985b, 2–11). This is often the case in Teotitlán as well. If the heads of a household die, their children are expected to take over their responsibilities, because godparents remain important throughout the life cycle. Children must have godparents in order to pass through each phase of their lives. "You have to have compadres in order to pass through different stages in the church," explained Mario, age 50. "You need them to give testimony in the church. You need one for baptism, for first communion and confirmation. Mostly you need them to get married. You can't get married in the church without them. Before when fewer people were married in the church, not so many people were compadres."

Teotitecos recognize four major categories of compadrazgo relationships, defined by the amount of expenditures involved, the degree of long-term commitment required, and the amount of prestige attached to sponsorship. Teotitecos label compadrazgo in relation to baptism as the heaviest commitment. It entails paying for a child's baptismal clothing and accoutrements. When the child is married, the baptismal godparents must pay for the wedding clothing and offer a large gift. They also often sponsor a large party in their own home. Two lesser compadrazgo categories are tied to the Catholic rituals of confirmation and first communion. Of these, the confirmation godparents are most important. They buy a child's clothing for the confirmation and must also provide a chest or cabinet for their godchild when he or she is married. First communion godparents must give their godchildren large wedding gifts. Compadres of the fourth category, rosary godparents, buy the child a rosary, accompany the godchild to the church, and bless him or her in front of the statue of a particular saint or of the Virgin. The ritual may end with a meal given by the parents for the new godparents. Often the godparents purchase clothing for the child, but further offerings are voluntary, often contingent on how well the godparents get along with the biological parents. The fourth category of compadrazgo also includes sponsorship of children in such one-time events as school graduations.

Asking someone to be a child's compadre is a way of demonstrating respect (Sault 1985b). The majority of compadres are pairs of men and women, usually but not always husband and wife. Mothers and sons and fathers and daughters may be cosponsors of the same child. A male-female pair of compadres usually sponsor all the children of one household, building a strong tie with the biological parents.

As first documented by Fadwa El Guindi (1986) and Nicole Sault (1985a, 1985b, 2001), women are central figures in the institution of compadrazgo. Sault (1987, 7) argues that among the Zapotecs, "godparenthood is fundamentally a relationship between women, creating bonds which unite separate households." She found that while men must be married to begin sponsorship, girls may sponsor either alone or with a close relative. This is the case in Teotitlán.

In an earlier discussion (1985b), Sault discusses the concept of "corporation"—the people that each villager can count on for support and assistance. In Teotitlán, the same idea is conveyed with the broader term *familia*. An individual with a large familia has many kin and compadrazgo ties. For women, these ties are critical in mobilizing labor for ritual events. The larger a woman's kin-compadrazgo network, the more other women she can mobilize for a successful fiesta. As Sault argues, by sponsoring many godchildren, a woman increases her influence and control over others. She has control not only over her godchildren but also over their parents, since a child's godparents hold the superior position in the hierarchical relationship with his or her biological parents. A woman continues to expand and reinforce these hierarchical ties over generations through her children and grandchildren (Sault 1987, 8).

An examination of data from a random sample of 154 households in Teotitlán indicates that most people are active in the compadrazgo system. The mean number of godchildren per household in 1986 was nine. Some had none; one had 246. While there are no data on individual women and their sponsorship of godchildren in Teotitlán, Sault (1985b, 233) found in a neighboring community that the most influential women had sponsored eight to sixteen for baptism within their own community.

TABLE 21 Age and sponsorship of godchildren, 1986

Age of household head (years) (*N* = 151)	Have no godchildren	Have godchildren
20–40 (younger)	50%	50%
41–60 (middle age)	28	72
61–80 (elderly)	3	97

Source: Random stratified household survey conducted by Lynn Stephen, 1986.

If sponsorship outside the village were included, the numbers would be higher. Many influential women in Teotitlán have sponsored up to twenty children for baptism.

The number of godchildren sponsored by men and women who are household heads is likely to increase as they get older. As table 21 shows, while only half of young household heads have godchildren, almost all elderly household heads sponsor godchildren. While sponsorship provides a woman with access to a wide network of laborers, it can also entail considerable expense, not only in the initial sponsorship but also in the later responsibilities when a godchild marries. As we shall see, the class position of a woman's household can become an important factor in allowing her to fully carry out her ritual obligations as a comadre.

As women age, particularly if they are widowed, their incomes may decline, but their ritual responsibilities multiply. An older woman may be placed in a position where she holds a ritual status of great honor yet barely has the cash available to purchase the flowers, liquor, bread, candles, and presents she is required to bring to life cycle events. As a godmother, she is always expected to make large contributions.

Elderly women have varying strategies for fulfilling their ritual obligations. Some borrow money from their children. Others indirectly invoke lower consumption standards associated with earlier times, when ritual consumption was considerably less. For example, instead of bringing cartons of soft drinks or beer, they will bring a Coke bottle filled with local mescal. This is an acceptable substitute for a carton of commercial beer, yet costs about one-tenth as much. Twenty years ago, no one brought beer to rituals, only mescal. Elderly women also end up saving on food because many of them spend a great deal of time attending rituals, where they are fed and provided with additional food to take home. What income they do have goes toward buying ritual consumption goods rather than food. Some elderly women even attend optional rituals such as funerals for more distant kin or compadres (which occur quite frequently) and are fed for weeks on end. Because funerals involve heavy drinking, some elderly women also support drinking habits by attending rituals.

Extended family ties and the compadrazgo system organize the people of Teotitlán into social groups that may function as units for agricultural production, weaving production, and ritual participation. The existence of these units results in a high degree of cohesion between the production and ritual systems. Often the same people work together during rituals and in weaving production. A direct consequence of this overlap is the use of compadrazgo relationships to recruit weaving labor, as we saw in chapter 5. In this frequent situation, the idiom of kinship, which connotes equality and ethnic unity, becomes contradictory.

When a merchant man or woman uses status as a compadre or comadre to recruit godchildren and compadres as laborers, relations of local ethnic solidarity conflict with the class relations of production. While Teotitecos present a unified vision of themselves to outsiders, internally the concept of ethnic unity is often shaken by the reality of labor relations that differentiate people into merchants and weavers. The level of unity achieved in relation to a common Teotiteco identity varies with the context and with the particular economic and political agendas of those involved.

Interviews on the meanings and criteria for choosing compadres also revealed contradictory ideas about the potential equality of all community members versus the idea that some are better comadres or compadres because they are wealthier. People in the poorer half of the community felt that they were recruited less often as compadres than the well-to-do, as reflected in the statement of this poor 38-year-old weaver: "I don't have any hijados, although I have grandchildren. I think a lot of people choose their compadres by the amount of money people have. They go for the rich, not the poor. Because I don't have a husband now, I also have less money and maybe people don't like that. There's one person, though, who asked me to think about being a *madrina*." Wealthier people in the community seem to think they are selected as compadres on the basis of character as well as wealth. "We have twelve ahijados," said María, age 42. "I think most people choose their compadres for money and for character. They want someone with a good reputation. Because my husband has money, people like to ask him." As the basis for political authority and community respect has changed to include wealth as a significant criterion, the criteria for asking people to be godparents are also changing.

Compadrazgo relationships can also be used to exert pressure on invited guests as laborers in a ritual situation. Nicole Sault (1985b) documents cases in which influential Zapotec women were known to overwork their godchildren and comadres in the kitchen because of their superior position in the compadrazgo relationship. Men can use their compadrazgo relations in a similar way to recruit laborers for agricultural work. While compadrazgo may appear to diminish class differences and promote ethnic solidarity, it can also be used to emphasize authority positions in the relations of production through labor recruitment and, more subtly, in the context of a ritual event.

A study by Sault (2001, 127) on the effects on compadrazgo of conversion to a Protestant denomination in a neighboring Zapotec community suggests that men are more likely than women to convert to Protestantism and that some women who did convert maintained their godparenthood ties. Overall, the great majority of Teotitecos remain Catholic and compadrazgo ties continue to be important. Having many godchildren is a source of influence and authority for women and men alike, and having a strong network of godparents is key to getting established as an adult.

GUELAGUETZA AND ECONOMIC CHANGE

The guelaguetza system provides a basic framework for participation in ritual. The continued existence of guelaguetza permits many households to participate in ritual in spite of spiraling inflation in Mexico and the devaluation of the peso. In contrast to the accounting and business aspects of weaving production, which are usually controlled by men, guelaguetza exchange is the province of women. They are the primary investors in this system of goods and labor exchange. More often than not, men act as the agents of women by carrying, weighing, or writing down the details of whatever is exchanged. "Guelaguetza is a good custom because it helps us," explained Filomena, age 54. "You can't always save what you will need for the future in your own house. If you run out of money or someone gets sick, you may have to kill your turkeys and your hens. If you made a guelaguetza with them, then they're safe in someone else's house and they have to bring them when you need them. As long as you have children, you'll need a lot of guelaguetza for them."

While the recording of guelaguetza debts is often done by men because until recently they were more literate than women, women are the ones who plan and prepare for making loans and for calling them in. In fact, many women interviewed could recite their entire guelaguetza notebooks by heart, having made mental accounts of all the transactions. Accounting and planning for loans is a complex and long-term project. Household guelaguetza books contain up to 200 entries for loans made to other people and items received as loans. Here is an excerpt from a guelaguetza notebook documenting what one household owed from the mayordomía of the Vírgen de la Soledad in 1972:

> Tereso Rodríguez: $100 [pesos]
> Mario López: Six dozen eggs
> Salvador Martínez: One turkey at 6 kilos
> Francisco Pérez: 12 kilos of cacao
> Pedro Vicente: Three turkeys that together weigh 20 kilos
> Manuel Pérez: 2 almudes of beans
> Luis Martínez: 6 almudes of corn
> Enrique Bautista: 3 turkeys that together weigh 21.3 kilos
> Manuel del Monte: 10 1/2 almudes of tortillas [amount of corn used]

The notebook documents more than thirty other guelaguetzas that the household owes for past mayordomías and another thirty-seven entries owed to them in preparation for the weddings of their children. Following the colonial custom of recording only male names to represent households, guelaguetza notebooks do not reflect the fact that a majority of the transactions take place between women. Men still have the role of recorder of the transactions, but women seem to be clearly in charge of them.

> Sometimes men don't know what's needed for guelaguetza. I'd go and leave something with someone and then tell my husband so he would write it down. I could go and leave something and he wouldn't know about it. But he could never leave something without my knowing. Sometimes if I decided to leave something for guelaguetza, then I'd need someone to carry it. I'd get my son, a godson, or my husband. If I go, then they carry what we bring and I enter the house and talk to people about the guelaguetza. (Ana, age 60)

Despite the fact that women are not recorded as the transactors of guelaguetza, they know precisely how their accounts stand. In reality, women are often planning for several events simultaneously. In the life cycles of their families women often have to plan for twenty or more major fiestas. The greatest chore in any household-level ritual is food preparation. Women plan ahead, often years in advance, how much of each ingredient they will need (numbers of chickens and turkeys, bushels of corn, chiles, pounds of sugar and cacao, etc.) in order to have a successful feast. A woman may give out more than three thousand tortillas in guelaguetza loans by the time she recalls them for a ritual event. If the people who received the tortillas have to pay back a large debt, a second level of guelaguetza is invoked, with female family members donating labor to help them meet the tortilla debt. "When you have to pay back a large tortilla debt," explained Margarita, age 40, "then you have two options. You can either pay someone to make them with you, which is expensive, or get someone to work with you. When I needed to make a lot of tortillas I had a small work party and got my sisters to help me. I'll have to help them sometime as well."

WOMEN'S ANIMAL PRODUCTION IN GUELAGUETZA

Animals are raised for investment in the reciprocal exchange system of guelaguetza. Most women begin keeping a brood of turkeys and pigs to prepare for their sons' weddings when the boys reach age 10. Both pigs and turkeys are raised for a year or more and either sold or, in the case of guelaguetza, given to another household and recorded as a loan in the household notebook. Because women plan ritual celebrations years before they actually occur, they have long-term animal production plans. For example, a woman knows that she needs to have loaned out twenty-five to fifty turkeys and one or two pigs by the time her son reaches 20 years of age and will probably be getting married. A woman who has no starting capital begins by raising chickens, which are the cheapest animals to buy and feed, although they are high-risk. If she can successfully raise and sell ten to fifteen chickens, she then has enough capital to buy several small turkeys. The turkeys can then be sold to buy piglets, which have the lowest risk in animal production.

Ralph Beals (1970) mentions pig raising as one of the most important forms of savings engaged in by Zapotecs. While the initial investment is low, the pigs require continued care and feeding. Beals describes it as

TABLE 22 Animal production risks and investments (pesos)

	Pigs	Turkeys	Chickens
Initial cost	$3,500–$5,000	$500	$350
Health care	$1,000		
Weekly maintenance	$2,570	$375	$225
Number of weeks to mature	36+	24+	20+
Minimum total investment	$97,036	$9,500	$4,500
Adult selling price	$40,000	$5,000	$2,000
Difference between selling price and total investment	−$57,036	−$4,500	−$2,500
Daily time investment (minutes)	45–90	45–90	45–90
Risk	Low	High	High (fed with turkeys)

Source: Survey of ten households conducted by Lynn Stephen, 1987.
Note: Prices in 1987 pesos (440 pesos to U.S.$1).

"forced savings" (238) because peasants are forced to invest small sums of money on a long-term basis to feed their pigs, rather than spending a little money daily on small luxuries. When the pig is sold, the return is large enough to be used for an investment.

An analysis of pig, turkey, and chicken raising in ten households in Teotitlán in 1986 supports these findings. Women in Teotitlán are aware that raising animals is a low-return venture, yet they consider it to be an effective way of "saving" a little bit of money. Table 22 summarizes the investment and risks involved in animal production. Results are averaged from ten households.

As table 22 makes clear, animal production does not result in a profit. On the contrary, animal production usually results in at least a 50 percent loss of investment between the total amount of income invested in the animal and its final selling price as an adult. This calculation does not take into account the labor invested in the animals. Nevertheless, women in Teotitlán claim that investing small amounts of money on a daily basis in their animals is the most effective means for them to save some money.

The savings notion seems to be particularly important among women in weaving households, who usually have no familiarity with conventional banks and would probably never have enough money available to make it worthwhile to open a savings account in Oaxaca. They are comfortable with animal production as a means of saving and because of their participation in guelaguetza are usually raising animals to pay back debts or to give out as loans.

Merchant women seem to engage in less animal production than weaver women. Merchant households often purchase animals needed for ritual consumption rather than raise them and do not rely on animal production to pay for household emergencies. Younger merchant women who are taking a more active role in running the household business often leave the home periodically to supervise workers or to run errands in Oaxaca. Their need for mobility is incompatible with the task of animal supervision.

Ultimately the production of animals may become an activity undertaken almost exclusively by weaver women. Their households continue to invest heavily in guelaguetza to finance ritual obligations, and their low cash flow is often insufficient to meet unexpected emergencies. Animal production provides women in weaver households with an easy mechanism to save for ritual and household needs. Although the final returns to investment are in fact negative, the fact that low daily labor and financial inputs can yield a substantial sum when converted into cash encourages women to continue with animal production. Merchant women who have a choice of investing their money and labor in other activities choose to engage in higher-yielding activities tied to weaving or in other businesses.

Discussion with women also suggests that animal raising has noneconomic significance for them. While men describe farming as giving them a sense of their Teotiteco identity and providing security for their families, women describe animal production as aiding them in meeting ritual obligations. Animal production is related to women's cultural identity as the organizers and workers in household ritual.

FACTORS IN GUELAGUETZA DECISION MAKING

When, what, and how much to loan out in guelaguetza are usually determined by household income. Many items given as guelaguetza loans, such as cacao, sugar, chiles, and corn, are purchased outright. Animals are purchased when they are young and are cared for until they are big enough to slaughter. Calculations for making guelaguetza loans have to be planned along with other household expenses. "Right now I'm not making guelaguetzas because I don't have much money," said María, age 28. "People with little money don't make many guelaguetzas because they have to buy what they give. . . . I like guelaguetza because it helps out. We couldn't have had our recent fiesta without it. We bought bread and mescal, but we wouldn't have been able to buy everything. The guelaguetza was very necessary. Now we owe a lot." Guelaguetza planning is particularly crucial for households that do not have a large cash flow and are not able to purchase items needed to put on a good fiesta. Instead, they must invest slowly in guelaguetza loans and call them in when they have the fiesta. Wealthier families who have not invested much in guelaguetza loans can purchase more of what they need when they sponsor a ritual event.

Labor is treated more casually than goods in the guelaguetza system. Labor exchanges are recorded only in memory, not in notebooks. Ritual labor guelaguetza comes through invitations to attend other households' ritual events. Invitations include the unstated assumption that the couple, particularly the woman, will come to work for at least three days. The invited guests may be obligated to work longer, depending on how close they are to the hosts. The guests' labor will be reciprocated by the hosts when the guests have their own fiesta.

Most women feel a strong obligation to reciprocate the help they have received from other women. When asked why they go to so many fiestas and how they feel about the hard work they do, many women reply, "It's like a guelaguetza. I go to help at their fiestas so that they will come and help at mine. What will I do when my children get married? If I don't help now, no one will help me when I need it." While the ethics of guelaguetza exchanges imply that all labor will be reciprocated in future ritual events, data from a study of twelve households (table 23) suggest that weavers may invest a greater percentage of their labor time in ritual events than merchants do. Since the sample is quite small and the time frame limited, the data are only suggestive.

I tallied the amounts of adult labor allocated to ritual events, civil cargos and *tequio* (community service), and farming weekly for ten months because they can vary seasonally. I collected data on adult labor allocated to household reproduction (cooking, animal care, yard sweeping, loom repair, etc.) and weaving activities for a six-week baseline period and then checked them periodically throughout the year for accu-

TABLE 23 Percentages and days of adult (over age 16) labor invested in household/agricultural activities, weaving, community service, and ritual (one day = 12 hours of work)

Case no./ total days		Household and agriculture		Weaving		Community service[a]		Ritual	
		%	Days	%	Days	%	Days	%	Days
Merchants									
1[b]	845.5	40	334	48	402	4	33	9	76.5
2	599	44	262.5	36	213	3	18	18	105.5
3	597	38	225	38	228	13	76	11	68
4	477	46	220	33	159	5	26	15	72
5[b]	794	40	315	47	375	1	5	12	99
6	499.5	36	181	41	207	6	30	16	81.5
Weavers									
1	578.5	22	124.5	54	314	1	6	23	134
2	519	63	329	20	105	0	0	16	85
3	511	36	183	49	251	0	0	15	77
4[b]	812	55	446.5	30	243.5	1	8	14	114
5[b]	772	60	467	10	81	0	0	29	224
6[c]	346	34	119	37	128	0	0	29	99

Source: Data collected from twelve case-study households by Lynn Stephen during ten months of 1985. Note: Totals may not equal 100% due to rounding.

[a] Community service = time spent carrying out civil cargos or engaging in *tequio*.

[b] These households had three adult laborers over age 16.

[c] This household had a laborer who became seriously ill.

racy. The amount of labor invested in these activities tends to be stable throughout the year. The six-week data are projected in table 24 for a period of ten months. Because of the irregularity of ritual events, individual percentages registered by households are not as important as the range seen for each group. The ranges are an indication of the spectrum of possible ritual labor allocations for merchant and weaver households.

As a group, merchants seem to avoid working in rituals, which can drain labor away from their businesses. While no ritual labor data are

TABLE 24 Percentages of total adult (over age 16) labor time invested in ritual by merchants and weavers, March–December 1985

	Average time spent in ritual	Range of time spent in ritual
Merchants (N = 6)	13%	9%–15%
Weavers (N = 6)	21	12–29

Source: Data collected from twelve case-study households by Lynn Stephen, 1985.

available for men and women, as a general rule, women work longer than men during ritual events. Many male merchants leave after the first day of a ritual event. Instead of coming personally on the second and third days, they send a child or a servant with an abundant supply of the necessary goods. Merchant women may work at an event for three full days; they are more likely to do so if they are close comadres or relatives of the sponsoring household. However, many do not seem to feel as strong an obligation as weaver women do to fulfill their reciprocal labor obligations if they have a more distant relationship with the hostess.

These patterns suggest that weaver women are probably investing the greatest amounts of guelaguetza labor in life cycle rituals. Since they cannot afford simply to send large supplies of ritual goods with a child or servant, they usually appear personally to fulfill their labor obligations. While guelaguetza goods and labor exchanges are the primary means through which women build up their status in the community, such exchanges nevertheless can also underscore subtle differences of obligation within the system.

GUELAGUETZA AND MIGRATION

During 2001 to 2004, I found that guelaguetza continued to be of major importance in Teotitlán and most women still kept guelaguetza notebooks, primarily in relation to ritual expenses. Mothers whose children were living in California but returned to have their formal marriages in Teotitlán were busy lending out pigs, turkeys, corn, and other items to kin, neighbors, and friends in anticipation of the time when their children would return for the large fiesta that accompanies most weddings.

In many cases, these efforts on the part of women continued over ten to fifteen years. For women who have moved elsewhere and no longer have Teotitlán as their primary place of residence and may be returning temporarily to organize their children's wedding party, it is more difficult to continue with guelaguetza.

Cristina González described to me in 2004 some of the difficulties she faced in trying to prepare for a wedding for one of her daughters while working in California. She was not able to use guelaguetza in her absence and had to raise large amounts of cash.

> LYNN: How did you save money for your daughter's wedding?
>
> CRISTINA: Well, I was working two jobs at once to save money for the wedding. I did this for three years. I took care of kids and then I also had another job. I saved about $10,000. . . .
>
> LYNN: What kind of wedding did you have? Was it a big one?
>
> CRISTINA: Well, the parents of the groom wanted to make it a big, traditional wedding. I accepted this because the groom's family wanted to spend a lot of money and have a big party. I had to do it for them. I came here for two months in 2000 for the wedding.
>
> LYNN: How did it feel to come back to Teotitlán?
>
> CRISTINA: Well, during the wedding I was really happy because they were getting married and I was glad about that. But at the same time this other family was spending a lot of money that I didn't want to. It was hard because I didn't have any guelaguetza. I had to pay for everything.
>
> LYNN: Can you do guelaguetza long-distance?
>
> CRISTINA: You can and people do, but I didn't ask for any guelaguetza. I didn't ask anyone for anything. I had to feed a lot of people at the wedding and it cost me a lot of money.

In general, I found that women in Cristina's position would have lent out some items in anticipation of a child's wedding, but were also depending on cash savings to finance other parts of the fiesta that they had not prepared for with guelaguetza. All of the women who were members of cooperatives continued to keep guelaguetza notebooks if they were heads of independent households and particularly if they remained in Teotitlán. If they left, they might be less vigilant about keeping their guelaguetza ties activated.

TABLE 25 Primary decision makers for sponsoring fiestas, 1986, by gender

	Male	Female	Both
Merchants ($N = 51$)	13%	5%	82%
Weavers ($N = 100$)	12	12	76

Source: Random stratified household survey conducted by Lynn Stephen, 1986.

WOMEN'S CONTROL OF LABOR AND RESOURCES IN LIFE
CYCLE CEREMONIES

Women in Teotitlán are central figures in economic decision making that pertains to household-level ritual. In both weaver and merchant households women decide together with their husbands when to attend and sponsor rituals. Once a decision has been made to attend or sponsor a ritual, women are usually the ones to decide how it will be paid for.

In merchant households, women's strong role in ritual decision making is distinct from the subordinate role they usually have in business decision making. Only in ritual decision making do merchant women seem to have an equal say with their husbands. Weaver women also seem to have a large measure of equality with their husbands in ritual decision making (table 25), as they do in decisions regarding weaving production.

In a questionnaire given to a stratified random sample of households, 82 percent of male and female informants from merchant households stated that decisions regarding the sponsorship of household fiestas are carried out jointly by men and women; 76 percent of the weaver households sampled stated that sponsorship decisions were made jointly by men and women. If we generalize from the sample, it seems that most households perceive the women's role in ritual decision making as equal to that of men. This is an interesting continuity between merchant and weaver households and provides a common experience for women. "It's women who do a lot of the things for fiestas," admitted Emiliano, age 60. "They have to plan months before, buy all the food, tell people what to do to prepare. Also, on the day a fiesta happens, women tell people what to do because they're the ones who know what has to happen."

The strong role all women play in ritual economic decision making at the household level is related to the social networks and economic channels used in ritual consumption. The economics of ritual consumption are conducted by women, largely within the context of the community. Economic transactions for ritual, unlike business transactions, which often require a knowledge of spoken and written Spanish and basic math, are conducted entirely in Zapotec and require no writing. Because ritual economic decision making requires manipulation of economic channels located primarily within the community, women are in a strong position to take advantage of local connections and to use this fact to press their husbands for more control in the decision-making process. In business decisions, women who have little or no education, cannot speak and write Spanish, and have no math skills have little ground to stand on if they want to take a stronger role in dealing with Mexican and U.S. clients. Through planning and organizing ritual events, women are able to take advantage of family and compadrazgo networks, where they can maximize their influence and use their organizational skills to their best advantage.

Extended kin and compadrazgo networks are important to economic transactions in Teotitlán. Just as many merchants tend to employ their relatives, compadres, and ahijados as pieceworkers, women tend to buy from people who are a part of their extended kin and compadrazgo network. They much prefer to purchase turkeys or chiles for a fiesta from a comadre who sells in the market than from someone they are not connected to. The comadre will also give them a better price.

Because of their ritual labor commitments through guelaguetza, women are closely connected to each other in extended kin and compadrazgo networks. Women may work together in rituals more than twenty times a year. The close bonds that women form by working together are also used in procuring the necessary items for a ritual event. Women can often get a better price than men because of their personal links with women who sell ritual goods. They are thus more successful than men in making purchases for ritual purposes. In addition, the strong role that women have in planning and organizing ritual events and the connections they have in the community through extended family and compadrazgo networks reinforce the local guelaguetza system and the use of primarily local vendors for the purchase of ritual goods.

CONCLUSIONS: THE IMPACT OF MERCHANT AND WEAVER
STATUS ON WOMEN'S RITUAL AUTHORITY

Through their roles in the institutions of compadrazgo and guelaguetza, women are the primary sustainers of ritual activity focused on life cycle ceremonies. Through their decisive roles in the household ritual economy, all women effectively channel significant amounts of resources and labor into life cycle rituals. While this gives them status within the community, this status does not hold up outside of Teotitlán and may result in conflicts between women who hold different positions in the relations of production.

Does economic wealth give women an advantage in ritual? Does household wealth make a difference in the ways in which women of weaver and merchant households participate in ritual and the status they derive from that participation? Many, but not all, of the women in Teotitlán who sponsor large numbers of godchildren also are members of merchant households. They are desired as madrinas because they not only have the resources to fulfill the expensive obligations of godparenthood but also may be able to offer more, most notably employment, to their godchildren. Thus when a merchant woman who has many godchildren invites their mothers to a ritual event signaling that they have been recruited as laborers, the consequences of noncompliance for the invited women may not only be that their comadre does not return the favor; she may also be able to withhold other resources or opportunities from them and their families. While such power differences are never overtly stated, a woman almost always complies more quickly with the request of a madrina or comadre than with that of another woman, particularly if the godmother stands in an employer relationship to her or a family member.

A significant number of women who have sponsored many godchildren are not merchants. They were chosen because of their high status in the community as mayordomas and as well-liked people. Nevertheless, as wealth becomes more important in determining political power and access to resources both within and outside the community, merchant women become more desirable as godmothers. In the future, then, comadres may become concentrated among merchants.

Wealth differences also have a very real effect on the cost of obtaining ritual status. While all households have minimal social obligations for both sponsoring and attending ritual events, households vary widely in the money they invest in ritual and the strategies they use to provide

TABLE 26 Cash outflow data for merchant and weaver households,
March–December 1985 (in U.S. dollars)

	Merchants ($N = 6$)	Weavers ($N = 6$)
Average cash outflow	$7,298	$1,332
Range of total cash flow	$3,544–$18,269	$528–$2,227
Average amount allocated to ritual	$292	$253
Average % of total used for ritual expenses	4	19
Range of amount allocated to ritual	$219–$510	$106–$798
Range of % of total used for ritual expenses	3–7	8–45

Source: Data collected from twelve case-study households by Lynn Stephen, 1985.

cash and goods for ritual consumption. I collected data from six merchant and six weaver households to investigate this trend.

I tallied the twelve households' ritual and farming expenses weekly for ten months. Household reproduction (food, clothing, building materials, medical costs, school costs) and weaving expenses (for production and/or business) were collected for a six-week baseline period and then checked periodically throughout the year for accuracy. Weaving and household costs were found to be stable, while ritual and farming costs can vary throughout the year.

The information in the sample suggests that, while the average amounts that weaver and merchant households spend on ritual are similar (approximately U.S.$292 for merchants and U.S.$253 for weavers), weavers spend a significantly greater percentage of their total cash outflow on ritual consumption than merchants do—an average of 19 percent and a range of 8 to 45 percent for weavers and an average of 4 percent and a range of 3 to 7 percent for merchants. While the data are limited, they do suggest possible trends. Table 26 summarizes ritual versus total cash outflow. These differences have important implications for the ways in which women in merchant and weaver households carry out budgeting and labor allocations as they try to meet their ritual responsibilities and build up their status in the community.

Any household that is sponsoring a major fiesta or is invited to attend a series of ritual events must have cash for ritual consumption as well as for household expenses. In merchant households, where cash flow is relatively large, it does not cause a major disruption to the household budget if women divert a relatively small amount of cash for immediate ritual consumption or for guelaguetza goods. The choices are usually different for women in weaving households, who have a much smaller cash flow and less disposable income.

If a woman in a weaving household is going to sponsor a ritual event, she plans well ahead of time and invests as much as she can in the guelaguetza system. However, she is usually not able to plant enough loans to cover all of her ritual consumption needs. If cash is needed for ritual consumption, either immediately or in the future, women in weaving households push household members to speed up production, resulting in a greater number of blankets and rugs for sale. Labor is funneled into weaving activities to build up a cash surplus for ritual consumption.

Often women in weaver households have to push their children and husbands hard in order to accumulate sufficient cash reserves to invest in ritual consumption, particularly for the sponsorship of events such as weddings. Because ritual consumption can eat up such a large percentage of household cash flow in some years, weaver women may find themselves in an ongoing set of confrontations with their husbands as they plan to procure all the necessary items for a large ritual event and must also take care of daily expenses. The ritual status and authority that weaver women achieve through sponsorship of life cycle rituals is the same as that obtained by merchant women, but they have often made greater family and personal sacrifices to get it. Because ritual spending is a much smaller overall percentage of merchant household budgets, merchant women do not engage in domestic struggles to fund their participation in and sponsorship of rituals.

Personal and household struggles to achieve ritual authority can be a source of tension between women as they act in their ritual statuses. While a large ritual event allows the woman who planned and sponsored it to increase her status if it is carried out correctly, such events also underscore the variance in the resources to which individual women have access as a result of their positions in the relations of production. The contradictions of ethnicity and class that are often softened in the ritual sphere can subtly reappear in the close relations women develop as they work together in ceremonial events.

CHAPTER 10

Challenging Political Culture

Women's Changing Political Participation

in Teotitlán

A little while ago I went to a meeting in the kindergarten.
I don't think the men were used to hearing women talk. One
woman got up to nominate a man for a committee. Some men
who were present objected and made fun of her for naming someone. A lot of people still don't think women know how to talk.
Sure, women want to go to more meetings, but they can't. And
when they do, they aren't listened to like men. — Josefina, age 24

As for women's political participation, I think women
are very important in each community and as women we should
also participate. . . . I think we should participate in the municipio government. Maybe we can't participate as police because they
have to get into the middle of fights, but why not as secretary, as
town councilor or *síndico* [trustee]? If women began to participate
in the cargos, then they could even become mayor. They can take
on committee memberships. Women could begin on the health or
education committee and become city councilors. We certainly are
capable of carrying out our responsibilities at home and taking on
cargos. We can combine service to the community with our
obligations at home. — Aurora, former federal deputy
in the Mexican Congress, age 48

Beginning in the 1970s, some feminist and social science scholarship on politics moved away from defining politics purely in terms
of formal political structures and defined the political sphere more
broadly to include other arenas (see Chiñas 1973, for example). In the
1980s, scholarship on gender and women's political participation and
the dynamics of women's conflicts and coalitions in local political life
emphasized women's roles in overtly political institutions such as local
committees in municipios and school committees as well as in other institutions not usually associated directly with politics, such as mothers'
clubs, ritual institutions, and health organizations (see Borque and Warren 1981; Browner 1986a; Carrillo 1988; Deere and León de Leal 1986;

P. Harvey 1988; Nash and Safa 1986; Radcliffe 1988; Salinas 1986; Siebold 1987.) These studies demonstrated that an emphasis on the gendered roles associated with local culture often illuminates instances when women's initial political participation is not through formal institutions but through networks, channels, and events stemming from cultural institutions associated with social reproduction. In Teotitlán kin and compadrazgo networks underlie the activities at hand. Many of the cooperatives include groups of women related through kinship or compadrazgo. Thus these relationships function not only in the sphere of family but simultaneously in the cooperatives as well as in community political and cultural spaces such as holiday parades and public meetings.

In the 1990s and beyond, the scholarship on women and politics broadened to include social movements, nongovernmental organizations (NGOs), and government agencies and institutions, and more overtly to discuss the politicization of religion and cultural processes and events (Alvarez forthcoming; Alvarez, Dagnino, and Escobar 1998; Babb 2001; Eckstein and Wickham-Crowley 2003; González and Kampwirth 2001; Gutmann 2002; Jaquette 1994; Montoya, Frasier, and Hurtig 2002; Naples and Desai 2002; Rodríguez 1998; Stephen 1997). Such an approach avoids the split between "formal" and "informal" political participation and looks at the wider political culture, noting the ways in which gender, class, ethnicity, and other factors can limit participation. Moving our analysis to the arena of political culture in order to understand changes in women's political participation involves exploring the ways in which political subjects—in this case the diversity of Zapotec women—"challenge the boundaries of cultural and political representation and practice" (Warren and Jackson 2002, 28). As Sonia Alvarez and her colleagues have written (1998, 8):

> Every society is marked by a dominant political culture. . . . We define political culture as the particular cultural construction in every society of what counts as "political." . . . In this way, political culture is the domain of practices and institutions, carved out of the totality of social reality, that historically comes to be considered as properly political. . . .
>
> The cultural politics of social movements often attempt to challenge or unsettle dominant political cultures. To the extent that the objectives of contemporary social movements sometimes reach beyond perceived material and institutional gains; to the extent that social movements shake the boundaries of cultural and political representation and social practice, calling into question even what may or may not be seen as political; and to the

extent, finally, that the cultural politics of social movements enact cultural contestations or presuppose cultural differences—then we must accept that what is at stake for social movements, in a profound way, is the transformation of the dominant political culture in which they have to move and constitute themselves as social actors with political pretensions.

In Teotitlán this transformation includes not only having women occupy posts that have traditionally been held by men (such as most civil cargos) but also helping people to imagine the possibility that women can do these jobs as well as men. As Aurora says, "We certainly are capable of carrying out our responsibilities at home and taking on cargos. We can combine service to the community with our obligations at home." Such a statement clearly works to challenge the boundaries that have excluded women from cultural and political representation and practice. By bringing attention to women's ability to produce and sell artistic products and to have important and meaningful opinions in a wide range of public discussions, the cooperatives clearly are opening up the local political culture of Teotitlán (see Babb 2001, 203–39 for examples from Nicaragua).

By challenging conventions of political and cultural representation and practice—particularly of indigenous women—the cooperatives and the women in them are suggesting new ways that women define themselves as cultural citizens, both in their own community and in the larger Mexican nation. Cultural citizenship can be understood as everyday activities through which marginalized social groups can claim recognition, public space, and eventually specific rights (see Flores and Benmayor 1997). First formulated by Renato Rosaldo in the late 1980s, the concept of cultural citizenship suggests an idea of culture "whereby different cultures are equally constitutive of society and expressive of humanity" (Yúdice 2003, 22). Rosaldo emphasizes how legal concepts of citizenship that underscore universal, formal political rights for all members of a nation mask real inequalities that can be observed. He raises key questions that are important for us to consider:

> Begin with difference in gender. Can women disguise their gender in the public sphere? If they must appear as women, and not as universal unmarked citizens, then one can ask, who has the right to speak in public debates? . . . Are men or women more likely to be interrupted with greater frequency? Are men or women more likely to be referred to as having a good idea in these discussions? As much recent sociolinguistic and femi-

nist research has shown, one must consider whether or not certain categories of persons are present in the public sphere. One must consider categories that are visibly inscribed on the body, such as gender, race, and their consequences for full democratic participation. The moment a woman or a person of color enters the public square both differences and inequality come to the surface. (R. Rosaldo 1997, 28–29)

These are very useful questions to keep in mind as we consider the struggles that women have gone through in order to overcome multiple levels of exclusion from a variety of political arenas. In looking at how Teotiteco women began to assert their right to political participation, it is helpful to look closely at the changing structure and culture of politics in Teotitlán and shifting gender roles within these arenas.

Until the 1960s in Teotitlán, the symbolic reproduction of the community through the celebration of mayordomías linked political and ritual authority through the civil-religious hierarchy. As the mayordomía system declined and the population became more formally differentiated between merchants and weavers, the links between ritual and political authority have become more tenuous. As a result, by the 1980s women's roles in the public cultural and political life of the community became less visible and focused primarily on life cycle rituals, which have taken over much of the symbolic content of mayordomías. Despite their distancing from formal politics since the decline of mayordomías, many Teotitecas continue to place great importance on the ceremonial life of the community and the ritual authority that stems from active participation in it. Many continue to use *respet* as a basis for achieving influence and gaining a right to express political opinions and expect to be heard. In the 1980s, the process that separated the population into more permanent groups of weavers and merchants had different effects on the ways women perceived themselves as political actors and the types of strategies they used to achieve their goals within the community. With the emergence of the largely women's cooperatives in the 1990s, some weaver women began to strategize: they could participate in the formal political spaces of the community by establishing a presence and a voice in community assemblies, as leaders serving in public cargos, and as an organized presence in community ceremonial events.

As wealth became a source for the legitimization of authority and a basis for earning *respet* and in some cases political power, merchant and weaver women demonstrated different patterns of political participation and opinions about their ability to participate. Often these differences translated into varying linguistic abilities and experiences in negotiating with outsiders. While the community had a high degree of interaction with U.S. importers and tourists in the 1980s, only people of merchant households, particularly women staffing market stalls and stores, were involved in this interaction. The commercial experience of merchant women gave them an edge over weaver women in feeling comfortable in voicing their opinions, particularly in relation to local and outside authorities.

In the 1990s, this situation began to change as a greater number of women and girls received higher levels of education, left the community in greater numbers to work elsewhere, and returned with new ideas about what kinds of rights and responsibilities they should have in the local system of governance. In addition, a discussion about indigenous rights at the national level in Mexico raised the issue of the role of indigenous women in community decision making (see Hernández Castillo 1997, 2001a; Rovira 2000; Stephen 1998, 2002). With the emergence of women's cooperatives, which gave women a public, organized presence as a group, the visibility of women in the formal political system grew in Teotitlán. They were invited to participate in community assemblies and to a small degree to take on new leadership roles.

While such changes are notable, women who did go to community assemblies and who took on public leadership roles also faced a significant backlash not only from men in their families but also from other women—often their mothers or mothers-in-law criticized them openly for not following tradition. The number of women who hold formal leadership positions at the municipio level is very small. In 1998, women governed only eighty-two, or about 3.4 percent, of Mexico's 2,412 municipios. In Oaxaca, this number was 6 out of 570 municipios in 1998, or 1.05 percent (Massolo 1998, 200–201). Women did somewhat better as regidores or city councilors. In 1998, 12 percent of síndicos (trustees) and regidores were women in Mexico (Rodríguez 2003, 158). In the Oaxacan elections of 2001, ten women were elected as mayors in 570 municipios, or 1.7 percent (*Noticias* [Oaxaca], March 18, 2002).

The work of Margarita Dalton Paloma (2003a, 2003b) on women who have served as mayors in Oaxaca suggests that while recognition of women's leadership in formal political office at the community level may be viewed as a major change in the gendered dynamics of local politics, women in such offices almost always suffer severe consequences that make it very difficult for them to carry out their formal responsibilities and may force them to leave. Dalton's interviews with past and present municipio mayors in Oaxaca revealed that almost all have been harassed, have suffered noncooperation from other local officials, and at worst have been shot at. Women in Teotitlán who have participated in community assemblies and served as authorities in the municipio have also experienced high levels of harassment. Change in women's formal political participation has begun, but the transformation is slow.

THE CHANGING BASIS OF COMMUNITY AUTHORITY AND RESPECT IN THE 1980S

The political scenario in Teotitlán has been increasingly affected by class stratification. In order to measure potential material differences between merchants and weavers, I collected indices of material wealth and consumer goods from seventy-four weaver households and fifty-four merchant households included in a random stratified sample in 1986. I chose house type and land-ownership as primary indicators of wealth. I measured house type by construction material (adobe versus brick) and number of rooms. The divisions were suggested by Teotitecos in discussions of how houses are upgraded. The numbers of other wealth indicators owned are shown in table 29.

A summary of the data in tables 27–30 is provided in table 31. Merchants did not have an absolute monopoly on consumer goods, land, and good-quality housing, but they definitely possessed a greater amount of material wealth in 1986. Significantly, their wealth does not include their rug inventory; merchants were unwilling to provide any information on the amount of merchandise they had stockpiled and other investments. Several had begun to buy up local land and had real estate in Oaxaca and in the cities of Tijuana and Rosarito in Baja California in 1986, when the survey was conducted.

Once I had collected information on material wealth indicators from the merchant and weaver households according to my criteria, I also wanted to see how people of Teotitlán would rank the same households by their own criteria. Three men and three women, both weavers and merchants of varying ages, were asked to rank the merchant and weaver households (along with twenty-six farmer and service households) in groups by wealth. The names of all of the household heads included in a random sample survey of 154 households were put on slips of paper with their Zapotec nicknames on them as well. The six participants then ranked these households in relation to each other. They began by com-

Figure 18. The poorest type of housing in Teotitlán in the mid-1980s. This was the condition of most houses before the commercialization of weaving. A tile roof tops a dirt-floored structure of adobe and cane. Photo by the author.

Figure 19. A newer two-story house of concrete, built with remittances from migrants, photographed in 2003. In front of it is a community basketball court. Photo by the author.

TABLE 27 House types of merchant and weaver households, 1986

	Merchant Households		Weaver Households	
	No.	%	No.	%
1 room adobe without floor	0	0.0	13	17.6
1 room adobe with floor	3	5.6	11	14.9
1–2 rooms, brick	14	25.9	30	40.5
3 rooms, brick	16	29.6	15	20.3
4–5 rooms, brick	15	27.8	4	5.4
6 or more rooms	6	11.1	1	1.4
Total	54	100.0	74	100.0

Source: Random stratified household survey conducted by Lynn Stephen, 1986.

TABLE 28 Land ownership of merchant and weaver households, 1986

	Merchants		Weavers	
	No.	%	No.	%
No land	13	24.1	45	60.8
0.01–1.0 hectare	35	64.8	26	35.1
1.01–2.0 hectares	4	7.4	2	2.7
More than 2.0 hectares	2	3.7	1	1.4
Total	54	100.0	74	100.0

Source: Random stratified household survey conducted by Lynn Stephen, 1986.

paring two households and built their wealth groups up from their initial comparison.

Initially two participants ranked the households in five groups, one participant ranked them in four groups, two participants ranked them in seven groups, and one participant ranked them in three groups. When asked what the minimum number of groups was, all collapsed them into three groups. The six participants' wealth rankings (of high, mid, and

TABLE 29 Consumer goods owned in merchant and weaver households, 1986

	Merchants (N = 54)		Weavers (N = 74)	
	No.	%	No.	%
Television(s)	49	90.7	46	62.2
Truck or car	26	48.1	2	2.7
Refrigerator(s)	35	64.8	15	20.3
Sewing machine(s)	35	64.8	29	39.2
At least 1 bed	53	98.1	48	64.9
Stove	49	90.7	50	67.6

Source: Random stratified household survey conducted by Lynn Stephen, 1986.

TABLE 30 Looms owned in merchant and weaver households, 1986

No. of looms	Merchants		Weavers	
	No.	%	No.	%
0–1	7	13.0	10	13.5
2–3	24	44.4	49	66.2
4–5	15	27.8	12	16.2
More than 5	8	14.8	3	4.1
Total	54	100.0	74	100.0

Source: Random stratified household survey conducted by Lynn Stephen, 1986.

low) for each of the fifty-four merchant and seventy-four weaver households in the sample were averaged and frequencies were run. According to the six participants, the merchant and weaver households in the sample have the average wealth rankings shown in table 32.

The averages of six participant rankings of merchant versus weaver wealth suggest that Teotitecos recognized significant wealth differences between merchants and weavers in 1986. While a sample of six people is

TABLE 31 Merchant and weaver wealth compared, 1986

House type

27% more weavers than merchants live in the poorest-quality housing, adobe structures of one room

32% more merchants than weavers live in the best-quality housing, brick with four or more rooms

Land

37% more weavers than merchants are landless

Consumer goods

45% more merchants than weavers own cars or trucks

45% more merchants than weavers have refrigerators

23% more merchants than weavers have stoves

33% more merchants than weavers have beds

26% more merchants than weavers have sewing machines

29% more merchants than weavers have televisions

Looms

22% more merchants than weavers have more than three looms

TABLE 32 Average wealth rankings of merchant and weaver households by six participants in the 1980s

	Weavers (*N* = 74)		Merchants (*N* = 54)	
	No.	%	No.	%
Low (little money, few things)	46	62	6	11
Middle (neither rich nor poor)	19	26	16	30
High (have money and things)	9	12	32	59

Source: Ranking exercises carried out with six informants by Lynn Stephen, 1986.

certainly not large enough for generalization to the whole population, it does support the idea that Teotitecos identified differences in wealth with merchant and weaver class positions. The fact that the six participants themselves represent different sectors of the class system also helps to ensure a more complete picture.

Participants ranked 59 percent of the merchants in the sample in the highest wealth rank and only 12 percent of the weavers; 62 percent of the weavers in the sample were placed in the lowest wealth ranking in comparison with 11 percent of the merchants. Almost equal percentages of weavers and merchants were ranked in the middle wealth category.

When sorting households into groups, participants always defined high wealth levels in positive terms. The wealthiest in the community were described as having "large, well-built houses," "cars or trucks," "a business," "a large stockpile of weavings to sell," and "good-quality land." The lowest-ranking households were defined completely by negatives such as "They don't have a good house," "They don't have any land," "They have no business," and "They don't have anything to sell." The possessions of the wealthiest set the terms for evaluating everyone else.

Apart from wealth, Teotitecos emphasized *respet* as a way to rank households. When I originally asked people to rank households, they told me that ranking by wealth—*rap (ᵃ)day med(ž)* (they have money); *rap(ᵃ)day kos* (they have things)—was not the only way people were evaluated. People repeatedly emphasized that wealth and *respet* were different, and that one did not necessarily imply the other. "*Respet* and being rich are not the same thing. Even poor people can become important here. They can become mayor or síndico. The people who have the most respect are the elderly. Both they and people with money can have *respet* here," explained Gregorio, age 65. Marcos, age 30, agreed: "We are Teotitecos. We are all united here. We don't have disagreements and fights. Everyone can be respected."

In a second exercise, the same six participants who ranked fifty-four merchant households and seventy-four weaver households by wealth were asked to rank the same set of households in groups by respect. The respect rankings of the six participants were then averaged. When the averaged wealth rankings were correlated with the averaged respect rankings, the resulting Spearman correlation coefficient of 0.44 (with a significance level of .005) suggested that respect was no longer associated simply with age, ritual experience, and service to the community in the minds of the six participants. In addition, extended interviews, linguistic behavior, and the political strategies of several large merchants suggest that wealth has also become a road to *respet*, community authority, and political influence. It is not without contestation, however.

The conceptual overlap between wealth and *respet* expressed in the correlation is indicative of a wider contradictory dynamic that underlies the projected unifying ethnic identity tied to social reproduction and the ability of all community members to receive *respet*. This unifying identity was constantly challenged in the 1980s and continued to be challenged in 2003 by the fact that having wealth in combination with being an employer can give an individual quite a bit of leverage in production relations, ritual relations, and local politics. The conceptual overlap between wealth and *respet* was indicative of the shifting economic and political relations that women navigated every day.

The importance of wealth in relation to respect was also expressed in extending the use of the Zapotec honorific titles of *dad* and *nãn* to a few wealthy merchants in the community who had not sponsored major fiestas or engaged in extensive cargo service in the 1980s. Some people referred to the wealthiest man in town as *dad*, although he was neither a mayordomo nor an old man. "Now people who have a lot of money also get respect, like old people," said Clemente, age 58. "For example, Miguel. They say Dad Miguel to him. I'm the same age as he and I've been a mayordomo and he hasn't, but they still call him Dad Miguel. He has a lot of money and a lot of godchildren. He's very well known. That's why he's called Dad Miguel." "Well," added Margarita, age 32, "I respect the rich people in this town, like Miguel and Luisa. People say Dad to him for his money. Because he has a lot of money he has a lot of godchildren, too. That's why people respect him."

Terms of respect were extended to a few women as well. Merchant men and women who were addressed as *dad* and *nãn* were placed in the same category as elderly couples who had sponsored at least one mayordomía and worked their way through the ranks of the civil cargo system. These linguistic practices of the 1980s that extended honorific titles of respect and forms of speech to persons who had wealth and had not necessarily demonstrated their commitment to the community through an established record of ritual and political service continued in the 1990s.

Picking up on the linguistic symbolism used to legitimate their positions of high respect in the 1980s, some male merchants were trying to manipulate ritual symbolism to reinforce their authority and political positions in the community. While some male merchants were adamantly against ritual expenditures, several of them gave large parties on their birthdays. These parties contained traditional ritual elements such as complicated foods, single-sex jarabe dancing, and band music. The merchants who sponsored these rituals put themselves in the position of ritual leaders without having gone through the proper training and sacrifice. By sponsoring fiestas on secular occasions, merchants demonstrated their material wealth and also attempted to validate their rank by acting in a ritual capacity. "They throw these big parties so they'll be respected and to show how much money they have," sniffed Irene, age 50. "Giving these big birthday parties can be more important than having a big wedding for the purposes of showing off your money. People say, 'How impressive! He had a big party!' You know women don't do that kind of thing. Only men do that for themselves."

Some merchants tried to convert their purchased ritual *respet* into political authority. The wealthiest merchant in town made several attempts to become mayor. He succeeded in the early 1990s. As other Teotitecos indicated, one of the ways in which he wielded great influence in the 1980s (and continues to do so) is through the record number of ahijados he and his wife sponsored. In 1986 he had 246 (see Sault 2001 on the importance of godchildren).

The purchasing of ritual respect in the 1980s indicated a partial realignment of the basis of political authority in the face of a persistent ideology that still gives credence to ritually based *respet* as a basis for influence. In 2002 the trend of selecting mayors who had a background of wealth and ample experience outside of the community was reversed with the selection of a very traditional, highly respected mayor who had worked his way up through all the levels of the civil-religious cargo system and was a highly proficient speaker of traditional Zapotec. Women played a significant role in his selection. For women who had been shut out of the formal political institutions of the community in the 1980s, the traditional arena of age and ritually based respect was an important focus for their efforts to influence community politics. The degree to which they used this strategy, however, was also influenced by their class position and the degree of wealth accumulated by their households. The strong association of great material wealth, a high level of respect, and merchant/employer status in the community was likely to cause merchant and weaver women to have differing political strategies. This was confirmed in the 1990s when it was primarily weaver women who formed cooperatives and used them as a basis for pushing for more participation in the formal political system of Teotitlán.

WOMEN'S EXCLUSION FROM MUNICIPIO MEETINGS
AND CARGO POSITIONS IN THE MID-1980S

In the mid-1980s men held almost all of the formal cargo positions in the ayuntamiento, juzgado mayor, and comité de la iglesia. However, a few women held positions on the kindergarten committee, the health committee, and the committee for the Secretariat of Education (SEP). All the committees in which women held low-level offices or whose meetings they regularly attended were initiated by the government, which actively encouraged women's participation and often required it.

Women's visible attendance at school committees was important in demonstrating that it was possible for them to participate in politics. "I know a lot of women who could go to assemblies," said Cristina, age 37. "They don't go because they only see men going. But now when there are meetings at the school, women go. This is good because they can see that there are women there with good ideas. But in the municipio, since from the beginning only men went, it's hard for women to go." Some women who attended the meetings, however, found there was still a great deal of resistance to women's participation. Rosa, age 34, said, "Of course women have a right to go to public meetings. They go to school meetings. Sometimes, however, when a woman speaks up there, the men say she doesn't know what she's talking about. But she has the right to speak."

The greatest factor preventing women's participation in general municipio assemblies in the mid-1980s was simply custom. When asked whether or not assemblies would be better if women attended, both men and women repeatedly said, "Sí, pueden participar, pero no es la costumbre" (Yes, they can participate, but it's not the custom). Many also pointed out, however, that women's participation in the various school committees had been valuable and signaled their ability to take part in public meetings. Here is an example of how women began to assert their cultural citizenship, albeit in a more traditional public realm—education.

Overall, men and women felt that it would be better for women to participate in all public meetings, but the fact that they were often held at night and that women might attend alone were seen as obstacles.

> Of course, it would be better if women went to municipio assemblies. Once they had a meeting in the afternoon and women went. In this meeting

women had more courage than the men. They're better at working things out than men. Women are more honest when they say things. The problem is that they always have the meetings at night, so women can't go. The problem is that the men are in charge and they have the meetings in the evening. If they had meetings during the day and invited the women, they'd be much better. (Leonora, age 40)

Much of women's political discussion takes place in space that is strongly segmented by gender. Any time men and women come together outside their immediate household, they usually congregate in physically separate spaces. Many political discussions take place during ritual celebrations, in markets, and during reciprocal labor exchanges, the men in their space, the women in theirs. Women acknowledge the importance of these discussions and feel that their experience there is a valid basis for participating in community assemblies.

There are some women in this town who are really articulate. I know they can express themselves very well and would be really good at community assemblies. We always talk about politics at fiestas and that way you can see who the really influential and articulate women are. Often we talk about what the men do and say. It's too bad that the costumbre keeps us from going to community assemblies, because we know how to do things. Fiestas are very important to us because that's where we talk about things, things that men discuss in their community assemblies. A lot of women know how to talk really well, but they're afraid to talk in front of men. (Isabel, age 50)

Even in formal civic functions or community religious festivities that take place in the public square, men and women sit separately. People in Teotitlán defined this custom as an indication of mutual respect. "I'm not sure women are ready to go to meetings with men," said Soledad, age 25. "You can't have men and women together in the same place. It isn't respectful."

In Teotitlán, both men and women are socialized to discuss politics in gendered spheres and in a manner that resembles small discussion groups rather than formal meetings in which a designated leader calls on participants and opinions must be expressed in front of large numbers of people. As greater numbers of men and women attended school for longer periods of time and lived for significant periods outside of Teotitlán, they began to learn alternate ways of thinking about politics and asserting their opinions. This experience sometimes affected the way

TABLE 33 Men's attitudes toward women's attendance at municipio meetings in the 1980s

	Merchant men (N = 25)	Weaver men (N = 40)
Believe meetings would be better if women attended	56%	78%
Do not believe meetings would be better if women attended	44	22
Total	100	100

Source: Random stratified household survey of male and female household heads conducted by Lynn Stephen, 1986.

they saw themselves as political actors and the strategies they chose, as exemplified by women who organized weaving cooperatives.

MERCHANT AND WEAVER MEN'S ATTITUDES TOWARD WOMEN'S POLITICAL PARTICIPATION IN THE 1980S

Male attitudes toward women's political participation in the 1980s depended somewhat on whether they were merchants or weavers. The limitations that merchant men placed on their wives' participation in business were also indicated in their attitudes toward women's political participation. In the questionnaire given to fifty-four merchant households and seventy-four weaver households, a subset of questions concerned women's political participation. Respondents included sixty-seven men and eighty-four women. In three households, both men and women insisted on responding simultaneously, making it impossible to differentiate their responses. In some cases not all of the questions were answered.

In the random sample of merchant and weaver men, only 56 percent of merchant men interviewed and 78 percent of weaver men thought that local assemblies would be better if women participated in them, as table 33 indicates. Extreme comments focused on the idea that community assembly space was traditionally all-male and should stay that way, with women meeting in their own forums, such as fiestas and the market.

TABLE 34 Men's opinions on women's ability to hold cargo posts in the 1980s

	Merchant men (*N* = 25)	Weaver men (*N* = 40)
Believe women are qualified to hold cargo posts	68%	85%
Do not believe women are qualified to hold cargo posts	32	15
Total	100	100

Source: Random stratified household survey of male and female household heads conducted by Lynn Stephen, 1986.

"I think it should just be men," proclaimed Mario, a 54-year-old merchant. "I don't think men and women should be in meetings together. The men would get jealous if their women came. The custom says it's only men. That's how it should be. Women have their own places to go." Francisco, a 60-year-old merchant, said, "I do tell my wife what goes on in the municipio meetings, but women can't go to them. They're not for women. They don't have any reason to get involved with men's affairs — the affairs of the community."

More weaver men (85 percent) than merchant men (68 percent) thought that women were capable of holding civil cargo posts. Merchant men emphasized young women's increased levels of education as qualifying some of them for such posts. In contrast, weaver men often focused on knowledge that women already had as a basis for their participation in community political discussions. "I think there are a lot of women who are capable of holding office," admitted Raul, a 36-year-old weaver, "but their husbands won't let them. It would be better with them there because sometimes we can't work things out alone. They know different things than we do." A few male weavers, such as 48-year-old Pedro, thought women might be even better for cargo posts than men: "Women are capable of carrying out cargos. . . . Women know better than men what goes on here. They have more ideas about what to do. Women don't forget things. If they say they're going to do something, they do it. Men only remember for a little while." Despite the fact that a majority of both

TABLE 35 Women's perceptions of men's sharing of political
information in the 1980s

	Merchant women (N = 25)	Weaver women (N = 59)
Believe men in their household share political information	46%	65%
Do not believe men in their household share political information	54	35
Total	100	100

Source: Random stratified household survey of male and female household heads
conducted by Lynn Stephen, 1986.

merchant and weaver men surveyed thought that women were capable
of holding cargo positions and that community meetings would be improved by their presence, many men did not seem to share political information with their wives and daughters. While only 21 percent of the
men surveyed said that they did not share information with the women
in their households, 42 percent of women surveyed said that men in their
households did not share information with them. The discrepancy may
indicate different perceptions of what political information is and what
constitutes sharing. In several interviews, men and women began to argue about whether or not information was shared. Women maintained
that information was not shared with them or that what was shared was
superficial.

The stronger feeling among merchant men that community assemblies would not be improved by the presence of women was reflected in
the number of merchant women who responded negatively when asked
if their husbands discussed the content of community assemblies with
them. While 35 percent of the weaver women interviewed said that their
husbands did not discuss the business of community assemblies with
them, 54 percent of merchant women responded negatively to the question. Many of the merchant women who indicated that their husbands
did not discuss assembly business with them said they felt distant from
the municipio's political process; they found out what went on by talking with other women in the market the next morning.

THE SELF-PERCEPTIONS AND POLITICAL STRATEGIES OF
MERCHANT AND WEAVER WOMEN IN THE 1980S

Given differing male opinions regarding the desirability of women in
community meetings and women's perceptions of how much men in
their households discuss assembly business with them, we might now
ask: What was the impact of male attitudes and the structure of community assemblies on women's own attitudes and strategies for political
participation?

While a majority of merchant (60 percent) and weaver (56 percent)
women surveyed agreed that community assembly meetings would be
better if both men and women attended, they felt differently about the
capacity of women to hold cargo offices. Eighty percent of merchant
women interviewed believed women were capable of holding such
offices; only 64 percent of weaver women agreed. The difference is not
huge, but it is significant, particularly in view of differences between
merchant and weaver women with regard to linguistic skills and experience in dealing with outsiders. "There are women who could hold these
jobs because now there are women who can read and write," said Godelia, age 58. "It would be good if these women had cargos. They would
say things more correctly and get things done."

As we have seen, education and Spanish literacy have become increasingly important in determining who is qualified to function in the municipio's elective positions. The individuals holding such offices became
the primary political brokers for the community in formal relations with
the state bureaucracy, particularly concerning the use of state funds for
public works. As such they were also crucial in prioritizing the needs of
the community.

More merchant women than weaver women believed women are qualified to fill official positions in the municipio. Many of them expressed
their desire to do so. Several merchant women and one woman from
an independently producing weaving household served as secretaries on
parents' committees for the kindergarten and primary school. Others
have served on the government-mandated health committee. That committee followed the principle of gender separation and had male and
female components. For several young women who served on it, it was
a positive experience. Claudia, a 24-year-old merchant woman, was glad
she had been named to the health committee. "There was a women's
committee and a men's committee. In the process we were able to talk

TABLE 36 Women's opinions about their own ability to attend municipio meetings and hold cargo posts in the 1980s

	Merchant women ($N = 25$)	Weaver women ($N = 59$)
Believe meetings would be better if women attended	60%	56%
Do not believe meetings would be better if women attended	40	44
Believe women are qualified to hold cargo posts	80	64
Do not believe women are qualified to hold cargo posts	20	36

Source: Random stratified household survey of male and female household heads conducted by Lynn Stephen, 1986.

freely about our own ideas and participated equally with men in the project. I learned how to give injections and traveled to some other towns as part of my experience. It was good and I was listened to. . . . But in the kindergarten, where men and women are together, they made fun of a woman because she spoke up."

The influence of women's linguistic abilities on their perceptions of themselves as political actors has been reflected in a relatively small but significant difference in this area between merchant and weaver women. In the 1980s, weaver women who spoke Spanish did not practice it as often as merchant women, who often spoke Spanish every day because they sat in the local artisan market selling to tourists. Weaver women stayed at home more and used Spanish only when they went to Oaxaca to shop. While there were no significant differences in the educational levels of merchant and weaver women, merchant women were more inclined to exercise their minimal literacy skills in their interactions with tourists and importers.

These differences may have had important consequences for when and how merchant and weaver women felt they could be politically effective in the 1980s. The strongest indication of differences in women's perceptions of themselves as political actors could be seen in the strategies they chose, particularly in relation to their age. Several young merchant

TABLE 37 Linguistic skills of merchant and weaver women, 1986

	Weaver women (N = 59)	Merchant women (N = 25)
Monolingual Zapotec	45%	33%
Bilingual Zapotec/Spanish	51	62
Spanish only	1	4
No data	3	1

Source: Random stratified household survey of male and female household heads conducted by Lynn Stephen, 1986.

TABLE 38 Minimum literacy skills of merchant and weaver women, 1986

	Weaver women (N = 59)	Merchant women (N = 25)
One year or less of school	45%	43%
Two years or more of school	53	53
No data	2	4

Source: Random stratified household survey of male and female household heads conducted by Lynn Stephen, 1986.

women and girls (approximately ages 14–24), most of them daughters of prominent merchants, indicated a willingness to confront the structure of the municipio and demand equal participation with men on one of the committees. Many of these young women ran stalls for their families' businesses in the local artisan market. They were bilingual, sometimes trilingual with rudimentary English. Most had completed at least the sixth grade and were interested in questions of accounting and investments. Through their socialization in the public school system, they received an education in Spanish that defined political participation as voting in local and state elections. They were taught that it was important for women to vote.

During the 1980s, decisions regarding local price controls and market policy were made by an all-male market committee attached to the municipio government. Members of the committee were elected in the same all-male community assemblies in which local officials were elected. The fathers of several of the young women who ran market stalls sat on the committee. Few men visited the artisan market every day.

This group of approximately twenty-five young women voiced their criticism of the committee that excluded them. Some also criticized the municipio structure for excluding women. "There's a committee that meets to regulate the serape market where I work with my daughters and a lot of other girls and women," said Concepción, age 35. "We all want to go to the meetings. The problem is that the committee chair is a man, and he only calls the men from the families who sell in the market to the meeting. They call the husbands and fathers who don't know what's going on. We know what's going on in the market because we're there all day. The problem is that men run the meetings." Many of these women voiced their dissatisfaction, and expressed frustration at having to keep silent because of their fathers' authority in the household. Younger men in the community brought up the possibility of including women on more local committees, such as the market committee, at the behest of their young wives.

In the 1980s, these young women of merchant households were in a contradictory position. On the one hand, they had decreasing influence over production and business decision making as their households accumulated capital. On the other hand, they gained significant business expertise by going to school and by their daily interactions with tourists and importers. Because they had the skills that were identified with being able to hold municipio office and participate in national politics, they seemed more willing to question the authority structure that excluded them. In the 1990s they were joined by some weaver women who had come to have similar exposure to life outside of Teotitlán and who had received more education than their 1980s counterparts.

One of the most volatile political issues was a lack of community involvement in the building and administration of the yarn factory. Almost every day locals would question both the quality of production and the price of wool yarn (Stephen 1987a, 159–63). Merchant women were in the forefront of many of these confrontations, talking directly to the manager and the director, threatening them with personal boycotts and action by local authorities. At one point, these confrontations frightened factory workers so badly that they halted production for several days.

Many of the merchant women who confronted factory management purchased significant amounts of yarn (100 to 200 kilos at a time) for their husbands. Their role as important customers as well as their position in the community made factory officials take them seriously. When a formal municipio price-control committee was set up to negotiate with the factory, however, its members were all male.

Weaver women and older monolingual Zapotec merchant women had different strategies in dealing with the factory price increases. They would talk with one another at fiestas, at the market, and at the community wells, advocating a boycott of the factory and urging people to purchase from local yarn merchants. The channels they used to hold political discussions, influence public opinion, and coordinate activity were subtler and did not involve a direct confrontation of officials or threats to disrupt the municipio. Instead they worked through channels and events connected with social reproduction. Older merchant women and many weaver women emphasized the influence they had over public opinion by virtue of their status as mayordomas or the comadres of many ahijados. When they conceptualized their sphere of community influence, it was in reference to the number of people they were connected to through kin and compadrazgo networks. They worked to influence their own kin-based networks of people in a particular direction instead of opting to work through the formal structure of the municipio.

In the 1980s, weaver women, who could not rely on wealth or education as a source of authority, turned to the concept of respect and the institutional links of social reproduction as a source of power. By using this strategy, they were militating against the use of wealth as the sole basis of political authority. They continued this strategy in the 1990s through the formation of cooperatives in an effort to undercut the economic and political influence of merchant households. Like the young merchant women who were pushing for acceptance within the formal political system, they were broadening the boundaries of the political process in the community.

MOVEMENTS FOR INDIGENOUS AUTONOMY,
CHANGE IN OAXACA'S LAWS, AND THEIR IMPACT
ON TEOTITLÁN IN THE 1990S

The 1990s in Mexico were marked politically by the Zapatista rebellion, which gave a significant boost to a range of movements for indigenous rights and culture (see N. Harvey 1998; Rus, Hernández Castillo, and Mattiace 2003; Mattiace 2003; Nash 2001; Stephen 2002). In Oaxaca, groups such as the Isthmus Coalition of Workers, Peasants, and Students (COCEI), founded in the 1970s; the Assembly of Mixe Producers (ASAPROM, later SER, or Services of the Mixe People); and the Union of Indigenous Communities of the Northern Zone of the Isthmus (UCIZONI) had already established a history of militating for indigenous rights in the state. In the 1980s in Oaxaca other indigenous organizations were created that based their claims on the right to maintain themselves as culturally distinct populations. In Zapotec communities such as Villa Alta and the municipio of Guelatao, Zapotec leaders consolidated their positions in local government and began participating in indigenous coalitions as indigenous governors. In the mid-1980s, Mixtec leaders in Oaxaca began to experiment with "forms of associations that combined members from various communities into fronts, which are organizations of associations" (Kearney 1996a, 178). Mixtec and Zapotec migrants in the United States formed hometown associations that raised money for local development projects such as basketball courts, street paving, and refurbishing of churches and public buildings (see Goldring 1998; Guarnizo and Smith 1998; Johnston 2001; Kearney 1995a, 1995b; Massey, Goldring, and Durand 1994; Rivera-Salgado 1999a, 1999b, 2000; Rouse 1992; Robert Smith 1998). In the 1990s, the Mixtec forms of association and other indigenous hometown associations came together to form a multiethnic organization called the Zapotec-Mixtec Binational Front, which then evolved into the Oaxaca Binational Indigenous Front (FIOB), which included other ethnic groups such as Triques, Mixes, and Chatinos.

Thus before the 1994 Zapatista rebellion, indigenous organizations and communities in Oaxaca had engaged in significant political organizing at the regional level. Many of these groups were sympathetic to the initial demands of the Zapatista rebellion: work, land, housing, food, education, independence, liberty, democracy, and justice. Within a short time the Zapatista agenda grew to include calls for indigenous autonomy within the framework of the Mexican nation. In their thirty-two-point document released at the Meetings for Peace and Conciliation in Chiapas in March 1994, they called for self-government with political, economic, and cultural autonomy, an end to discrimination against indigenous peoples, mandatory indigenous language instruction, respect for indigenous culture and traditions, and administration of indigenous justice systems according to customs and traditions and without interference by the government (CCRI-CG 1994, 638–45). This initial document set up a long series of consultations between the EZLN and indigenous and nonindigenous advisers that culminated in the National Indigenous Forum in San Cristóbal de Las Casas in January 1996. This forum included more than four hundred indigenous representatives from throughout Mexico, nonindigenous Mexican writers, academics, and supporters, and visitors from eleven other countries (Nash 2001, 149–50). Through four days of discussions, delegates—including a contingent from Oaxaca—debated the outlines for a set of national agreements on indigenous rights and culture. A month later, Zapatista leaders announced they would sign an initial set of accords with the agreement of 96 percent of thousands of Zapatista base community members who had been consulted (Preston 1996).

The San Andrés Peace Accords were signed by the Zapatista Army of National Liberation and the Mexican federal government in February 1996. The Accords on Indigenous Rights and Culture laid the groundwork for significant changes in the areas of indigenous rights, political participation, and cultural autonomy. Most important, they recognized the existence of political and legal subjects called *pueblos indios* (indigenous peoples/towns/communities) and gave conceptual validation to the terms "self-determination" and "autonomy" by using them in the signed accords. The accords emphasize that the government takes responsibility not only for reinforcing the political representation of indigenous peoples and their participation in legislatures but also for guaranteeing the validity of internal forms of indigenous government. They further note that the government promises to create national legislation guaranteeing indigenous communities the right to (1) freely associate themselves with municipios that are primarily indigenous in population, (2) form associations among communities, and (3) coordinate their actions as indigenous peoples.

What ultimately came to be called "indigenous autonomy" or self-determination in the San Andrés Accords was built on strong recognition of local customs and traditions. The accords specifically recognize the rights of indigenous peoples to "develop their specific forms of social, cultural, political, and economic organization," "to obtain recognition of their internal normative systems for regulation and sanction insofar as they are not contrary to constitutional guarantees and human rights, especially those of women," "to freely designate their representatives within the community as well as in their municipal government bodies as well as the leaders of their *pueblos indígenas* in accordance with the institutions and traditions of each pueblo," and "to promote and develop their languages, cultures, as well as their political, social, economic, religious, and cultural customs and traditions." The accords further specify that the Mexican constitution should "guarantee the organization of their own elections or leadership selection processes within communities or *pueblos indígenas*," "recognize the procedures of cargo systems and other forms of organization, methods of representatives and decision making by assembly and through popular consultation," "and establish that municipal agents or other [municipio] leaders be elected, or, when appropriate, named by the respective pueblos and communities" (San Andrés Accords 1999, 35). These proposals are regarded as the basic framework for indigenous rights in Mexico by a wide network of movements for indigenous autonomy and by many indigenous community leaders, including many I interviewed in Teotitlán. Many of these ideas are now part of Oaxaca's constitution and state law.

While the propositions finally adopted by the Mexican Congress as a constitutional amendment for "indigenous rights and culture" in 2001 were a greatly watered-down version of the San Andrés Accords, in Oaxaca many of the core ideas of the accords were adopted. The idea of Oaxacan communal autonomy is based in collective institutions such as tequio or communal work obligations, methods of selecting local authorities, and the preservation of language and ritual. In 1995, the Oaxaca state legislature approved a change in the state constitution to allow the election of municipio authorities through traditions and customs in recognition of the indigenous autonomy movement. In 1998, the Oaxacan Congress approved a legislative plan that gives indigenous communities the right to name their municipio authorities without the intervention of political parties in accordance with local traditions, thus implementing the changes made to the state constitution in 1995. This legislative recognition of local systems of governance and definitions of local citizenship according to locally defined rights and responsibilities in Oaxaca has been an important part of the context in which local politics are currently played out. In Teotitlán, local officials frequently cite the Oaxaca constitution as guaranteeing local self-determination, autonomy, and respect for internal decision-making processes. The final (never-implemented) legislative proposal of the San Andrés Accords prepared by the Commission of Concord and Pacification (COCOPA) in 1996 ensures the right of indigenous peoples "to elect their authorities and exercise their own forms of internal government in accordance with their norms . . . guaranteeing the equal participation of women" (Stephen 2002, 196–97). The Oaxaca legislation of 1998 on indigenous rights makes no mention of women. However, numerous

Figure 20. Aurora Bazán
López in her garden. Photo
by the author.

indigenous female leaders of Oaxaca participated in the processes that
led up to the signing of the accords and were involved in trying to get
the Mexican Congress to adopt the COCOPA legislative proposal. An extended national discussion about the rights of indigenous women and
the emergence of the women's cooperatives in the 1990s were key factors
in beginning to change the nature of women's formal political participation in Teotitlán.

   One influential community member in Teotitlán, Aurora Bazán López, served as a state representative to the national house of representatives from 1997 to 2000. As a part of her legislative work, she served as a
member of the COCOPA and was deeply involved in efforts to try to get
the Mexican government to legislate the San Andrés Accords. She had
strong feelings about women's political participation. We discussed the
matter in the summer of 2002:

   LYNN: In the COCOPA draft for legislation of the San Andrés Accords, it
   says that within customs and traditions the rights of women to participate

in local governance should be honored. But are there customs that dictate that women shouldn't participate in community assemblies and be elected as leaders?

AURORA: Well, there are good customs and bad customs and I think we should save the good customs and get rid of the bad ones. I say this because we women are citizens of our communities. We are citizens and we are also governed by our authorities, aren't we? . . . I see more participation by women now than I did before. Young women and girls are a lot more interested in participating and I don't think it will be long before this will start.

LYNN: How long do you think it will take for this to happen?

AURORA: Let's say a year to a year and a half or less. If the women begin to participate now, if we give ourselves the task of going to the meetings.

LYNN: Now?

AURORA: Well, it's important for us to go so we can realize what kind of subjects are being discussed so we can participate.

RIGHTS AND RESPONSIBILITIES OF TEOTITECO CITIZENSHIP

Belonging to *šxía* (Zapotec for Teotitlán, written in Spanish as Xaquiya) is both self-designated and acknowledged by others through linguistic labels in Zapotec, such as *bɛ:n(i) šxía* (a person from Teotitlán), *bɛ:n(i) lo' getš* (person of the community), *bɛ:n(i) reh>* (person from here). If one inquires in Zapotec about what qualifies a person for one of those linguistic labels, the response usually includes the following elements:

Being born in the community.

Having grown up in a household that participated in community institutions.

As an adult being part of a household that has taken part in community institutions.

Specifically, "belonging to Teotitlán" and being considered a citizen or *bɛ:n(i) šxía* entails a set of responsibilities and rights:

1. Participation of men and increasingly some women in the local system of civil cargos, comprising more than 250 unpaid jobs—mayor, judge, police, school committees, committee for irrigation, firefighter, committee regulating the use of communal land, committee to care for the local Catholic church, and more. Slates of people are proposed by outgoing officials and confirmed or contested through a recorded voice

vote in community assemblies conducted in Zapotec. Such assemblies
are attended primarily by men, but by some women as well. Women are
also named to some of the volunteer governance and staffing positions
or cargos. The contributions of women to the civil cargo system were
and continue to be recognized also informally as supporting the community through the work they do when their husbands are absent carrying
out their jobs. While individuals are named to specific cargo positions,
it is understood that the entire household is supporting the community
through the sacrifices they make to have one person devote his time to
community needs instead of to the household. The most labor-intensive
job is that of presidente municipal. His household is understood to be
acting on behalf of the entire community as they support the mayor.

2. Participation of men and women in the religious cargo system
bound up in the celebration of mayordomías. From the 1880s until the
1960s, both men and women actively participated in the mayordomías of
the religious hierarchy and received authority and prestige for doing so as
mayordomos. Until the 1960s some twenty-one mayordomías were celebrated annually; by 2003 only two or three were sporadically sponsored.
During this period, the civil cargo system of governance was linked to
the religious cargo system. Offices of the civil cargo system were held by
men; the mayordomía sponsorships of the religious cargo system were
held by pairs of men and women, both of whom received authority and
prestige. Currently many of the activities carried out by mayordomos
who sponsored celebrations for the saints are carried out on a smaller
scale by the church committee, which is elected as part of the civil cargo
system in community assemblies.

3. Participation of men and women in communal labor or tequio. Such
assignments are apart from obligations to participate in the civil and
religious cargo systems. Households are notified of their obligation to
commit a worker to a specified number of days for a particular community project.

4. Payment by men and women of specific amounts of money for community projects or celebrations. Specially appointed committees named
by the presidente municipal circulate through the community to collect specific amounts of money to pay for new community infrastructure
projects (roads, bridges, markets) or to support local celebrations such
as the Fiesta Patriótica on September 16. Some religious celebrations are
financed this way as well.

Consistent and responsible participation in civil and religious cargos, tequio, and payment of community quotas entitles a Teotiteco to the following rights:

A. Access to communal land for farming or house construction. The right to communal land for house construction has become the most important right for poor members of the community who lack the means to purchase land for house construction.

B. Access to community forests, water, sand, minerals, plants, and wild animals within the communal lands that stretch up behind the community for miles into the Sierra Juárez, to the border of the mountain community of Rancho Benito Juárez. Access to these communal resources provides firewood used in daily cooking, large fiestas, and the preparation of dyes for dying wool yarn; sand and gravel for construction projects; lumber for construction projects; deer, rabbits, and other local animals to supplement the local diet; plants used as dyes, as medicinal remedies, and as ritual decorations; and water for irrigation of land and household use. A large dam channels mountain streams into irrigation channels and into the community water system. Many houses have now been connected to a potable water system.

C. The right to burial in the community cemetery, which is under the care and maintenance of the local government. This walled burial ground contains the remains of the community's ancestors and is a ritual center not only during individual funerals but also on the Día de los Muertos, or All Souls' Day (November 2), when families congregate in the cemetery to eat and drink with their dead, who return to be with their loved ones.

D. The right to express opinions and vote in the decision-making process that takes place in community assemblies. Election of local government officials in the civil cargo system and discussions and decisions about many aspects of community life take place in community assemblies in the municipio building. Such discussions can cover topics ranging from the qualifications of people proposed to occupy civil cargo positions to debates about the construction of new infrastructure projects or whether or not the community should patent its weaving designs. Community assemblies are announced by a roving loudspeaker hooked up to a car, by official notices posted around town, and finally by the ringing of the church bell shortly before they begin. All men and women who have reached adult status in the community either through marriage or through participation in the civil cargo system are eligible to attend.

In addition to these rights and responsibilities, citizenship is expressed through the speaking of the Zapotec of Teotitlán and through claims of being the first weavers of wool in Oaxaca as well as coming from an origin population of importance. Because of the various levels through which Teotiteco identity is manipulated, the common heritage of a united community of weavers bonded by kinship has been used by various sectors of the population in different ways throughout history.

WOMEN'S POLITICAL PARTICIPATION IN TEOTITLÁN, 1990–2004

The primary reason offered for women's absence from community assemblies and from civil cargo posts is costumbre: "*Se hizo costumbre*" (It became the custom), "*Costum shte re*" (It's the custom here). Women who wanted to go to assemblies and felt qualified to hold cargo posts commented that it was not only costumbre, but in fact it was also machismo (their word) and a lack of confidence in women. The growing number of women in the weaving cooperatives in the late 1980s and 1990s began to establish the presence of women in community politics, both formally and informally understood. They were actively struggling to change local political culture and were also picking up on national calls for extending formal political participation to all indigenous women.

Members of the Women Who Weave cooperative began to attend community assemblies at the invitation of the mayor in 1989. These women were the first to set foot in the all-male assemblies. They remember it as very difficult. Cristina Ruiz commented, "We received a lot of criticism. They said, 'What are you doing? You'd be better off going back to your kitchens.' We even got this kind of comment from the men in the municipio who were the elected authorities. . . . We had to be really tough to go back." The women from the cooperative entered the meetings as a group and sat together on a bench in the front of the assembly. Dozens of women I interviewed acknowledged the importance of this breakthrough.

When Women Who Weave split and its members stopped being active between 1988 and 1990, their attendance at community assemblies dropped off. It was not until other cooperatives were formed that women began to attend the meetings again in small groups of five to ten. Josefina Jiménez, who is a member of the second incarnation of Gunah Ruinchi Laadti/Mujeres Que Tejen (Women Who Weave), began to go to community assemblies with about eight other women from her cooperative

Figure 21. Josefina Jiménez and Lynn Stephen in front of Josefina's loom. Photo by the author.

in 1995. She described how difficult it was and how many years had to pass before women began to go to community assemblies in large numbers:

> LYNN: Do you think the fact that there are so many women in weavers' cooperatives now is going to affect their political participation in the community? Do you think that if women are going to community assemblies they will eventually start to take on more of the cargos?
>
> JOSEFINA: Yes, I think this could happen, or the more that women participate in the assemblies, the more this idea [of women holding civil cargos] could come true. This is the idea, that we go, that we be treated equal to the men, and more than anything that they give us the right to vote, to have an opinion. Because we are human beings and we think the same way as men. We shouldn't be excluded anymore because of our culture. Before when we went to the first meetings, both women and men shouted at us, "These women should go home and make their tamales." They used to stand outside the meeting in front and say to us, "These women should go make tamales. They should go make tortillas." In other words, to tell us that we had nothing to do with what went on there, that we should return home to our housework, that's what they told us then. . . .
>
> LYNN: It sounds really hard.

JOSEFINA: It was very hard because they would scream at us. Then the women and girls in the group would say, "We're not going to go again." I would tell them, "Come on, let's participate." They'd reply, "No, we don't want to because then the men will scream at us." When there was a new mayor, we went to talk with him. As you know, all the groups go to present themselves to the new mayor. He asked us how much we were going to participate in the assemblies. We said, well, first, it's really late at night when the meetings get out, and second, the men are going to scream at us. We told him that the time at night wasn't convenient for us and that we couldn't come because we also had husbands and if we went then that could cause problems with them. The mayor and other authorities told us, "Well, we invite you. Think about it and if you can come, you are very welcome." So after that we didn't go to the assemblies or only went once in a while.

LYNN: Because of the pressure.

JOSEFINA: Yes, because of the pressure. It was the same way in the parades. They would invite us to march in the parade for the sixteenth of September [Mexican Independence Day] and then everyone would shout at us, "There go the artisan women" and point.

LYNN: So what happened with this?

JOSEFINA: Well, this ended and now the women are going to the assemblies. For example, the mayor who was just elected was named by the women because the majority of the votes for him were women's votes . . . the women's groups were there in the meeting.

For almost eight years, between 1993 and 2001, women's attendance at community assemblies was sporadic. Women in the co-ops decided instead to concentrate their energies on promoting their textiles in Oaxaca and elsewhere in Mexico. The presence and activities of the women's cooperatives, however, seemed to have a subtle impact elsewhere as well. Sometime in the early 1990s, women became a part of the municipio's marketing committee and by the mid-1990s began to serve as elected officers of the market committee, such as treasurer and vice president. By 2001 women were well represented on the market committee and were gaining administrative experience that may allow them to move on to other cargos as well.

The experience of those few women who have served in formal political roles has not been an easy one. Reina Martínez was asked to serve as municipio secretary in 1989, when she was 23 years old, single, and living with her parents. Three secretaries are named to provide support for the mayor, the treasurer, and the city council.

Reina was a member of the first women's weaving cooperative, formed in 1986. She joined Women Who Weave when she was 20 years old and served as its secretary. In this role she developed skills in working with government agencies and drafting documents, and learned how to obtain credit and support. She was honored to be named to serve her community as the secretary in city hall, and began her job with great enthusiasm. Her commitment to her job left her no time for the women's cooperative, so she left the group. She learned how to get along with the men she worked with every day, but suffered from community gossip, which eventually undermined a planned marriage. She said in 2001:

> It was a real accomplishment for me to serve in our government. I learned how to get along with the guys in the city hall. When I was done with my cargo, people said I was romantically involved with the treasurer. They said I only went there in order to go out with him. They said, didn't I feel bad about going there and being with all those men? They said my father drank too much and that my parents let me go out and nobody said anything. I wasn't going to be able to survive this kind of talk. I felt really bad. I was going to get married, but my fiancé left. He said, "Look, if they're going to talk badly about you, then I can't be with you. They say you've already been with men." We ended it. What I didn't feel bad about was everything I learned. I learned a lot about the community and the kinds of problems we face.

In 1994 and 1995 she was asked to serve again as undersecretary. The rumors started up again. This time they said she was having an affair with the mayor and had gotten pregnant. She stuck out the term of her service and as a result of her position in the municipio she met the state governor at the time, Heladio Ramírez. The governor suggested that she form an organization and affiliate with the Confederación Nacional Campesina (CNC)/National Peasants' Confederation, which could offer support. The CNC is a national organization affiliated with the PRI. The group Reina formed, Dgunaa Gulal Ni Ruin Laadti/Mujeres Antiguas Que Hacen Tapetes (Traditional Women Who Weave), was formally incorporated in 1996. In 1998, when the cooperative had a disagreement with their CNC sponsors about the kinds of products they were to produce, the group became independent. Reina continues to work with the group and is optimistic that women will come to assume more public roles (as she did) as they continue participating in community assemblies and gain political experience.

In discussing why women have not taken on more elective cargos, several co-op members pointed out that it can be difficult for women to find someone to take on their domestic responsibilities if they are absent from home. "It's hard for women to leave the house, have someone take on their chores, and also find jobs where they can make money outside the home," pointed out one person. This perspective suggests the importance of family and spousal support behind anyone who takes on an unpaid cargo position. Replacing women's lost labor might be difficult, and if women are not doing their housework, it is often assumed that someone else will have to be paid to do it—make tortillas, wash clothes, cook, tend to the animals, take on all her other chores. This point was seriously discussed when women tried to explain why it is that women may not take on public cargos, even if they want to and feel qualified.

Another founding member of Women Who Weave also emerged as a community and national leader. Aurora Bazán López studied for three years in a nursing program in Oaxaca before she left to get married in 1976, at age 22. She joined Women Who Weave in 1986. In the late 1980s, representatives of Women Who Weave would go down to the beach resort of Huatulco and sell their textiles in the lobby of the Sheridan Hotel. There she met the leader of what was called the Alianza Ecologista de México (Ecological Alliance of Mexico). In 1993 this group was constituted as a political party, the Partido Verde Ecologista (Green Party). The Green Party has maintained significant links with the PRI. In 2004 it was part of a PRI alliance for the governor's race in Oaxaca, which the PRI won.

Aurora went to meetings and was part of the group of people who founded the party in Oaxaca in 1993. She served as president of the Partido Verde Ecologista in Oaxaca from 1993 to 1997. In 1997 she was asked to be the Green Party's candidate for the Third District open opposition seat for the federal house of representatives. She won and served as a federal representative in the Mexican Congress from 1997 to 2000. In her capacity as a state representative she served on the Commission for Indigenous Affairs, the Commission for Artisans, and the Commission of Concord and Pacification (COCOPA), which mediated the Chiapas peace negotiations between the EZLN and the Mexican government. Aurora was one of the first few indigenous women to be members of the COCOPA. Her experience on the COCOPA brought her into contact with the EZLN and its advisers, a wide range of indigenous leaders, and many indigenous communities in Chiapas and elsewhere in Mexico. In 1998 she was invited by Mary Robinson, United Nations high commissioner of human rights, to go to Spain, Bolivia, and Peru to exchange ideas and experiences with other indigenous legislators. She also traveled to Colombia, Guatemala, Brazil, Switzerland, Great Britain, and France in political, human rights, and indigenous rights delegations. Aurora also participated in many forums in Mexico focused on indigenous rights and attended congresses of the National Indigenous Congress (CNI) and worked with the National Plural Indigenous Assembly for Autonomy (ANIPA).

Before being elected, she had never been out of the state of Oaxaca. She described the initial experience of arriving in the Congress as "a brutal 90-degree change" from her life in Oaxaca. When she returned from her three years as a congresswoman, she had to readjust to life in Teotitlán. After flying around the world on global business, she had to ask her husband's permission when she wanted to leave the house. She also had to face the limits that women encountered in their political participation in the community. She was rumored to be a candidate for mayor in the fall of 2001. Was it possible for a woman to be mayor? That was a real challenge to local political culture.

> AURORA: There was an interesting discussion before the election of this most recent mayor . . . I don't know what this means, but they talked about electing me mayor.
>
> LYNN: Oh, yeah?
>
> AURORA: Well, in the corn mill, at the fiestas, lots of women made comments like, "How is a woman going to be mayor? She's a woman. . . . How is she ever going to climb up the mountains?" Because as mayor you have to climb up to check out the boundaries we have with other towns. They said, "How is she going to be able to do that?" Other women said, "Yes, yes, of course she can do that."
>
> LYNN: Did the men say that?
>
> AURORA: No, these were women. They would say, "Only the men can do that." Then they would ask me, "How are you going to climb up the mountains there?" So there are a lot of women who think we still can't do these kinds of jobs like mayor. I think we can do them. We have to find a way to do them. We have to participate.

In August 2004, Aurora worked for a gubernatorial candidate who was running on a PRI–Green Party coalition ticket. He won the vote, but the victory was contested. Aurora's support for the PRI was contingent on its support for several issues related to the women's cooperatives.

Women in the cooperatives are now invited as groups to attend community assemblies. Written invitations are often delivered before the assemblies to the presidents of the various cooperatives or a messenger goes to invite them. All of the committees that are part of the municipio government structure receive invitations to come to the community assemblies. Inclusion of all the cooperatives is formal recognition of their existence as a valid part of the community governance structure. As such they are being recognized by the costumbres of the town.

The cooperatives are formally recognized again by the granting of space to sell their textiles to tourists at times when the town is full of them, such as Holy Week and the guelaguetza celebrations in July. In the summer of 2003, when some of the cooperatives that had traditionally been granted space in the Zócalo in Oaxaca were denied space there, they were granted space in the community. Many who participated in selling their textiles in the community felt that this was an important arena of recognition and a novel one.

From 2001 on, women's participation in community assemblies seems to have increased. In the fall of 2001, at the meeting where the new mayor was elected, more than 250 women attended, invited by the outgoing mayor. Some of the women who attended were in cooperatives; others were affiliated with government programs such as PROGRESA (Education, Health, and Nutrition Program), now called Opportunities. Some people referred to the mayor from 2001 to 2004 as "the mayor the women elected" because so many voted for him. He is deeply respected and is considered one of the few remaining elders who has a deep knowledge of local history, customs, language, and farming techniques. Women who attended the meeting recalled it as "impressive" to see that many of those present were women and that they all voted. Although attendance at subsequent meetings has not been so high, women have established a consistent presence at community assemblies since that time. In the fall of 2004 they once again voted in large numbers for a new mayor. In addition, in the politicking that goes on at the market, at fiestas, and elsewhere, a few women have been seriously mentioned as candidates for civil cargo positions—something I never heard in the 1980s. Nevertheless, while women are making headway in establishing a formal political presence in the community, those who have been pioneers in initiating women's presence at assemblies and who have taken on leadership roles have endured significant harassment from community members and may face battles with their relatives.

At the same time, however, a new generation of young men are supportive of women's participation in community political life and want to work with them. In 2003, several new cooperatives were formed by men and women working together. The leadership of these cooperatives was often mixed. Men and women who worked together in them talked about their commitment to working together, and not only in the co-operative. The traditional female committee associated with the Sistema Nacional para el Desarollo Integral de la Familia (DIF)/Integral Development (Services) of the Family, a federal agency that has a committee in every municipio, has been another avenue to official recognition. While many local DIF committees are responsible only for administering programs for school breakfasts and lunches and low-cost milk for families with young children, the Teotitlán DIF committee from 2002 to 2004 was involved in a great many initiatives to improve the community. In 2003, Pastora Gutiérrez Reyes, chair of the local DIF committee, was extremely enthusiastic about the committee and the support that local male authorities were giving it. Pastora was 31 years old in 2003. She has always been a community leader. She was one of the founding members of the first women's cooperative, Women Who Weave, joining at the age of 14. She has been the leader of two other cooperatives, but by 2002 was devoting herself primarily to the DIF.

Pastora and her DIF committee go to community assembly meetings, accept invitations to outside meetings and workshops along with the community authorities, have been working on providing birth certificates, retirement documents, and other forms of identification to people who never had any, and are learning a great deal about interacting with men in and outside of the community. She becomes quite animated when she describes all she is learning and doing as a part of the DIF committee. One of the many things she has been learning about is institutional racism and the way indigenous people are treated in government offices in Oaxaca.

> My experience in meeting with officials in Oaxaca comes from going to governmental offices. I have gone as a representative for my cooperative and for our DIF committee. A lot of times I've had to face people ignoring me, making me wait, the humiliations that people in these offices put indigenous people through. They tell you the person you're looking for isn't there, that they'll be there later, that they didn't come today, they tell you to come back tomorrow. That's what we have to go through when we have to bring some paperwork from our community to Oaxaca. In order to bring those papers we have to go through a lot of humiliating experiences. I have really felt this when people tell you, for example, "Just wait twenty

Figure 22. Pastora Gutié-
rrez Reyes goes over paper-
work as part of her duties
as president of the local
DIF committee. Photo by
the author.

minutes," and you end up sitting there for hours without eating, with just a little bit of water and you're waiting all day for a person who never shows up. Then you see that person walking by talking into their cell phone and they still tell you, "Now, they just went to leave some paper," or "They're with another group," or "They'll be here any minute." But then you see another person who arrives and is well dressed or who arrives dangling their car keys from their hand, and they say, "Come on in, come on in," and they take care of them. . . . This is very humiliating for us when we have to go through this to go to government offices, which I have to do a lot. . . .

I guess more than anything, I am learning, learning, learning. I've had to learn to talk with all kinds of people, people who hold positions superior to mine, for example, those people they call secretaries who work for other people. Sometimes they leave you just sitting there and waiting. When I go to these offices and I have the opportunity to speak to the people who supervise these secretaries, I express my feelings. I tell the supervisor how these secretaries have treated us. I say, "Why do they act this way? Why have they made us lose so much time, as if we don't have our own important work to do? We come from far away, but it isn't right for them to treat us that way." I feel that when I tell the superiors these things, then it's a way of getting even, of taking out those bad feelings and at least calling it to the attention of people who are nice, who listen and have some respect for us.

Pastora has been humiliated not only in the Oaxaca offices she has to visit regularly as part of her work as chair of the Teotitlán DIF committee, but also in her own community, as some men still have a hard time accepting women's presence on the committee in community assemblies. Part of her struggle in the DIF committee is working with other women to help them overcome their fear and resistance to going to public meetings after being insulted. She told me the following story to make this point:

> As I was telling you, we in the DIF now get official invitations so that we attend the community assemblies, and this one time we went. I don't remember if it was November or December, but we went to the assembly. A man from the Committee for Potable Water who was half drunk and half crazy began to make comments like "Here come the milk women." But when he'd say "milk women," he'd make this sign with his hands signifying breasts. Well, for us, the nine poor women who were there, we felt really insulted. Two of them were ready to leave. With another woman from the group we called out to them and said we shouldn't pay any attention to them.... This guy went into the office of the Committee for Potable Water, he left, made his insinuations, and left again, saying there wasn't going to be an assembly. All my friends from the group wanted to leave, but I said more people were coming and we should wait. The meeting hadn't even begun and this man who insulted us left. Well, we stayed until the assembly ended. It was midnight when it was over. I told my friends, "See? This man couldn't even stay and we are women and we're still here."

In the summer of 2003, Pastora felt that she was prevailing in her efforts and that the DIF committee had congealed into a strong, united group of women. They had marched in the annual parade on September 15 and 16 to honor Mexican independence, frequently left to go to other communities to attend workshops on a wide range of topics from literacy to human reproduction, and were a growing presence in community assemblies. Pastora's experience with this group convinced her of the value of pushing women to participate and also to leave the community. She believes that when women get experience in participating in public meetings they will speak up. She gave an example from a recent meeting of *comuneros*, those who are actively using communal land for which they have received use rights:

> In this one meeting, there was a case in which a woman's husband had a problem and he was implicating another couple, the man and the woman. So the man and the woman were talking in the meeting about this problem. The women were also listening and taking in what was said. They gave their opinion and each one spoke about the problem of this couple and how it might be solved. They each gave their view about how to solve the problem. It had to do with the border between two plots of land that houses are on. So the women gave their opinion on how to reach an agreement and they did. They came up with a good solution. . . . These kinds of spaces give experience.

The broadening horizons of the DIF committee and their greater recognition and inclusion in the formal structure of governance in the community indicate a shift taking place in the kinds of spaces where women are conducting politics. Women are moving from fiestas, the markets, and public gatherings to the more formalized political spaces of the community, expanding local political culture and claiming their cultural citizenship. Like the cooperatives, the DIF committee is being included in the recognized structure. While the individual experiences of women in this process can be quite difficult and varied, such a change is public recognition of the growing importance of women's political roles, experiences, and leadership in Teotitlán—contested, but present.

CONCLUSIONS

My research suggests that women will push to be formally included in the structure of government, yet also continue to use the institutions of social reproduction as a basis for defining their cultural citizenship. By 2004, women in Teotitlán had gained access to community assemblies, were voting and occasionally speaking where fifteen years ago they had not been present. The space of the cooperatives helped to provide entry into formal politics, but also remained bound to kin and compadrazgo ties as women not only produced textiles together but also discussed with one another how they could gain local and national recognition for their artistic ability and ethnic heritage as weavers. In the 1980s, my in-depth questionnaire and discussions suggested that not all women were likely to have the same perceptions of themselves as political actors or be at-

tracted by the same institutional possibilities or strategies. Their strategies for change tend to reflect the positions they hold in the relations
of production and corresponding levels of literacy and language skills,
which have become vital in determining formal political authority at the
level of the municipio. This was true in the 1980s, and continued to be
true in the 1990s as poorer weaver women used the strategy of the cooperatives not only to try to improve their economic situation but also
to gain access to community assemblies and challenge the local political culture. The ethnography of Teotitlán underlines the importance for
women of class/ethnic conflicts that are reflected in changing ideas of
respect and ongoing processes of differentiation. In the 1980s, local criteria of respect and the ranking of community participants in accordance
with these criteria helped to determine political authority and influence.
In situations where broader popular movements are not reordering traditional, male-run political structures, disenfranchised women who did
not have language and literacy skills or wealth generated through entrepreneurial activities used the networks, events, and institutions such as
guelaguetza, compadrazgo, and kinship to influence community political agendas and to mobilize people to take specific action. In this process, they were indirectly militating against the use of wealth and occupation as the sole criteria for determining political participation. Their
strategy was continued by women who formed weaving cooperatives and
used their group membership and its validation in the community governance structure as a way to gain a political voice, the right to vote, and
the possibility of being named to cargo positions. The contradictory experiences of women who have participated as leaders and in community
assemblies suggest that we cannot yet talk about the full participation
of women in formal politics, only of a shaky beginning.

After Words

On Speaking and Being Heard

Address of Comandante Esther,
in Juchitán, Oaxaca, February 25, 2001:

Brothers and Sisters:
Good afternoon to all of you in the name of my fellow insurgents, our militia; our bases of support, men and women, boys and girls. The EZLN speaks through my voice. We have suffered exploitation and invisibility for more than 500 years, they pay no attention to us because we speak in our native tongue and use our traditional clothing. The great powers wanted to make us disappear; but they couldn't succeed. Here we are.

Primarily it is we women who are triply exploited. First, for being indigenous women. And because we are indigenous, we don't know how to speak Spanish and are scorned. Second, because we are women who they say don't know how to speak, they say we're fools, that we don't know how to think. We don't have the same opportunities as men. Third, for being poor women. We're all poor because we don't have adequate nutrition, decent housing, education, and we're not in good health. Many of our children die in our arms of curable diseases.

Because of this triple exploitation, all indigenous women must raise our voices, join hands so that we'll be heard and listened to and our rights will be guaranteed. I am calling out to all of you, let us fight without stopping until we have achieved a place of honor as women and as indigenous peoples. (http://www.ezln.org/marcha/20010225d.es.htm)

When I spoke with Aurora Bazán López in August 2003, she told me about the time women in cooperatives spoke on the radio for the first time to invite people to visit Teotitlán:

... They were really afraid. They said, "What am I going to say, what am I going to do if they ask me something and I won't know how to answer?" I told them, "Let's just go." I tried to give them confidence. They were able to go on the air and invite people to come visit. It was the first time that Señora Marta went on the radio. The same for Señora Gloria and Señora Rosario, too. These are women who never imagined that one day they would be speaking into a microphone for a radio program. When we left they were really happy. I said, "See, we can all do this. It wasn't so difficult." I was really moved because it's a big accomplishment to take a woman out of her kitchen, have her face being in a cooperative with other people, and then come to speak on the radio representing the cooperative. At first Señora Marta said no. I said, "Come on, let's go. It's your turn to come." She said, "What am I going to say? I don't know how to speak." I said, "Well, speak in Zapotec." So she did. She gave her message in Zapotec. . . . When we left [the radio station], we were all really happy. This was because we all left with the accomplishment of what we had done, of everyone getting to this place to where they could do this. They were afraid to do it before we went and they left saying, "This isn't so hard! When can we come back again?"

On the evening of February 25, 2001, Tzeltal Zapatista Comandante Esther addressed a huge crowd in front of the city hall of Juchitán, Oaxaca. Juchitán has a long history of indigenous autonomy and fierce independence (see Rubin 1997). More than 15,000 men, women, and children from the Zapotec, Huave, Chinantec, Zoque, Mixe, Chontal, and Mazatec ethnic groups received Comandante Esther and 23 other EZLN commanders representing the Tzeltal, Tzotzil, Tojolabal, and Chol ethnic groups. Each comandante received a necklace of flowers and was addressed by representatives in the languages of all the Oaxacan native groups present. The ceremony of necklace presentation was done without a word of Spanish. The Zapatista comandantes and the Oaxacan indigenous representatives who presented the necklaces spoke in their own languages. Subcomandante Marcos took up the subject of speaking in his address before Esther addressed the crowd. "The struggle for constitutional recognition of indigenous rights and culture is the struggle for respect for our languages. Again and again, the false gods of money have wanted to take our languages away from us because they know that without our languages, we would not be who we are and they could take everything away from us" (Ramírez Cuevas 2001).

In her address, Comandante Esther emphasized that inability to speak Spanish is equivalent to silence, to not being heard—to being denied a political voice and cultural recognition. When Señora Marta said, "I don't know how to speak," it was Spanish she meant. In her mind, if she could not speak Spanish on the radio, then she could not be heard.

Marta's concept of speaking and Esther's reminder to thousands of indigenous listeners in Juchitán that indigenous women who don't speak Spanish are not respected captures the struggle in which indigenous women in Mexico as well as elsewhere in the world are engaged: to be heard, respected, and granted rights as indigenous women—to stake their claims to cultural citizenship. What some people in Mexico call "indigenous feminism" (see Hernández Castillo 2001b; Sierra 2002; Speed forthcoming) attempts to protect ethnic rights and women's rights all at once. The experience and analysis of leaders like Aurora Bazán and Comandante Esther begin at the level of lived experience for indigenous women in Oaxaca and Chiapas and link it to wider political struggles in Mexico. Many people see "ethnic" or "indigenous" rights as collective rights and women's rights as pertaining to the individual, but indigenous women activists see no dichotomy and emphasize that ethnic and gender rights potentially unite collective and individual rights and can function together in an expanded sense of citizenship. For example, the right to speak in an indigenous language and to have that language legitimized in legal, educational, and official political arenas involves both the right of the individual to speak and the collective right to have the language recognized. Zapotec and other indigenous languages also have forms of speech that involve a particular style, tone, vocabulary, and terms of address for women and for men. Thus the issue of the right to speak is a complex one that involves individual and collective ethnic claims as well as gendered dimensions.

Discussions of indigenous women's rights in Mexico emphasize economic autonomy, access to and control over means of production (including land); political autonomy, basic political rights; physical autonomy, the right to make decisions concerning one's own body, the right to a life without violence; and sociocultural autonomy, the right to assert one's specific identity as an indigenous woman (Hernández Castillo, 1997, 112). In Teotitlán women have become increasingly assertive about the importance of economic autonomy for women, particularly in relation to weaving and controlling the fruits of their labor. They have asserted the right to attend municipio assemblies and assemblies for people with rights to communal land, and the right to formal recognition of their cooperatives as part of the governance structure of Teotitlán. Issues of domestic violence are increasingly coming to the fore as well as discussions of women's reproduction and reproductive health in spaces such as the DIF as well as in informal discussions in cooperative meetings. Thus women in Teotitlán are very much in tune with the kinds of demands being articulated by indigenous women elsewhere in Mexico.

DIFFERENT PATHS TO SPEAKING AND HEARING

An ongoing question in the study of women's articulation of rights is how different kinds of women may be relating to rights discourses that often join larger national discourses such as that of indigenous autonomy in Mexico and transnational discussions of rights such as universal human rights and the rights of human security under conditions of global neoliberalism. As Carmen Deere and Magdalena León have suggested in their comparative work on women's land and property rights in Latin America, it is often not clear whether demands for different types of women's rights come from the grassroots or circulate primarily at the level of women leaders and their feminist advisers (2001, 154), or perhaps both. Other writers have suggested that the circulation of rights discourses usually operates on multiple levels simultaneously and the context for local discussions about rights contains global, national, state, and local elements that contradict, compete, collide, and may or may not reinforce one another (Merry 1997, 2003a; Stephen 2005). We can also view the globalization of rights discourses as "extensions of particular localisms" that serve to broaden and modify local political cultures (Jensen and de Sousa Santos 2000, 12).

In Teotitlán, women who have participated in cooperatives or in the local DIF committee have often interacted repeatedly with indigenous women leaders from outside their communities as well as with the staffs of nongovernmental organizations or government agencies who work with programs aimed at "improving" the position of indigenous women. There, discussions of domestic violence, reproductive rights, the right to choose one's sexual partner and husband, and other issues surface from time to time. Some of these issues get woven into the hushed discussions women have always had among themselves. Many women in the community, however, are not in the position of Aurora Bazán or in the orbit of the discussions and workshops of which women in the cooperatives and the DIF committee are a part.

For some women, as for those who formed the first women's cooperative, leaving home and moving away from Teotitlán, away from their parents, is their path to experiencing some of the rights discussed at home — particularly the right to control over their bodies and choice of sex partners. Not long ago I spoke with Luis, one of my compadres in Teotitlán, by phone. He was visiting the United States with his wife, María, and was calling from Southern California. He and my comadre were about to get on a bus to go to Portland, where his youngest daughter, Isabel, has been living for some months. Isabel is my goddaughter. She has a baby a few months old named Nanci, who was born in the United States.

Like many girls her age, Isabel—now 20—completed eighth grade in Teotitlán. There is no high school in Teotitlán. She had hoped to go to secondary school in Oaxaca, but was not able to get into the morning session. Taking the bus home at night and having to walk the four kilometers down the road from the Pan American Highway to Teotitlán seemed dangerous. For several years she stayed at home and worked at weaving with her father and sister for a nearby merchant. Never overly enthusiastic about weaving, Isabel settled into a predictable existence at the loom, helping to care for animals, helping her mother and sister with housework, and going to church once a week. After some time she became very bored and desperate for a change.

She took a job working at Suburbia, a large department store in a shopping mall on the outskirts of Oaxaca. Isabel took the bus to and from Teotitlán to Oaxaca. She was home by 4 P.M., and both she and her parents were pleased with the arrangement. After working for some time, she began to date her future husband, who was finishing a university degree in Oaxaca, one of the few young people in Teotitlán who were able to do so. Isabel and Jorge became formally engaged and began to go through the steps of formal marriage. Because he couldn't find a job in Oaxaca, Jorge went to the United States. Isabel waited for him to return, but finally crossed the border herself and joined him. They did not complete the formal process of marriage before their daughter was born. As Isabel explained it, "We were in love, we wanted to be close, and it just happened. We don't think it should matter that we're not married. We'll do that. But our parents care a great deal." Living independently in the Pacific Northwest, Isabel has been able to take control of her sexuality, her partnership, and establish herself as an independent adult, something she could not have done in Teotitlán. Isabel now is educated about birth control and the functioning of her own body. She is conversant with a set of issues and definitions of her rights in relation to those issues that parallel discussions she might have had in Teotitlán. The processes of globalization and the circulation of the discourse of rights have been a part of the experiences of both leaders such as Aurora and now the migrant Isabel.

GENDERED CONTRADICTIONS OF GLOBAL
ECONOMIC RESTRUCTURING

One of the key lessons from an analysis of economic change in Teoti-tlán since the 1980s involves the gendered contradictions of the global restructuring of capital. The strengthening of production relations between U.S. importers and merchants in Teotitlán resulted in a significantly higher level of subcontracting of weaving labor, much of it female. Ultimately this same set of shifting structural economic relations also gave rise to cooperatives in which women worked self-consciously to jump over local merchants and sell their goods directly to consumers. In the process, their assertion of ethnic pride and the right to political participation and recognition in their community also emerged. Thus the transnationalization of the production process led to changes in production roles for women that connected with other experiences, such as increased women's migration, also generated by the economic restructuring of the 1980s. Both of these changes linked to globalization opened up new possibilities for some women that challenged the older gender order in Teotitlán. As Lisa Lowe has written in a more general sense:

> One of the distinct features of the global restructuring of capital is its ability to profit not through homogenization but through the differentiation of specific resources and markets that permit the exploitation of gendered and racialized labor within regional and national sites. . . . Ironically, the very processes that produce a racialized feminized proletariat displace traditional and national patriarchies, [thus generating] new possibilities precisely because they have led to a breakdown and reformulation of the categories of nation, race, class, and gender. (Lowe 1996, 161–62, as cited in Naples 2002, 8)

In a globalized Teotitlán, women weavers in the cooperatives are linking community-based economic development projects with a local understanding of global interdependence. Many demonstrate a sophisticated understanding of global political, economic, and cultural relations, as suggested by their projects to create Web sites that can advertise their products directly to consumers and that emphasize their cultural distinctiveness as Zapotec women. Women weavers outside the cooperative sector—still the majority—are observing the cooperative process and often discuss the advantages and disadvantages of participating. The cooperatives tend to sell most of their work in spurts: Christmas, Holy

Week, the summer tourist season. Some women say that the cooperatives may work some of the time, but "we still have to sell our work all year round. We can't wait for Christmas or Holy Week to sell something."

Some women, such as the five Ruiz Santiago sisters, express concerns about the cooperatives' lack of control over larger economic circumstances. Ranging between the ages of 35 and 22, none of the sisters have married. To them it seems better to make a reasonable living working together and living with their parents than to risk marriage. A few years ago they built a small house on the road leading into town in the hope of attracting tourists and selling to them directly—essentially the same objective as a cooperative. The five of them work as one unit with their grandmother, mother, and father to make a living together as weavers. I spoke with the sisters in August 2003:

> HERMELINDA: We've been here at the new house on this road for four years. This year has gone really badly for us. We've hardly sold anything. The first year went really well. The second year was OK, and then it started to get worse. Now it isn't working at all for us here.
>
> LYNN: What would it be that caused your sales to decrease?
>
> GLORIA: It was the war there . . . since August 11.
>
> BLANCA: You mean September 11.
>
> GLORIA: OK, September 11, 2001. That's when things began to go downhill. We had someone in town who used to buy from us, in addition to what we sold here. We'd take him four or five weavings every two weeks. Now he hasn't come for more than three months.
>
> HERMELINDA: Well, he still wants to buy from us, but the problem is he wants to pay us practically nothing for our work. It doesn't work out for us to weave for him. We can't even afford the materials to start a new weaving with what he pays us.
>
> GLORIA: We used to sell at least about ten weavings a month here, but now we've sold nothing. This summer we've sold only a few very small pieces. Practically nothing.
>
> HERMELINDA: We don't even take the bus to go from the village to way out here. We walk now because we don't have money for the bus. We make tortillas, but we have to go for our own firewood. We can't afford to buy it. We have to buy our corn for our tortillas because we didn't plant this year. The price of corn has gone up, too.
>
> LYNN: Well, other women I've talked to about the same things tell me they're going to the other side [to the United States] to work.
>
> MARINA: Yes. A lot of girls are talking about going. We can make weav-

ings here, but if we don't sell them, what can we do? They are leaving to go to the United States to work. A lot of girls and women are doing that. . . .

HERMELINDA: Well, it's the war in the United States that caused tourism to decline here.

ANGELA: And why did this war happen?

LYNN: Well, it's a complicated story. . . .

GLORIA: Well, no matter what it was for, now there aren't many people going on vacation. If things are going well in the United States, then things go well here. When things go badly there, they go badly here. I think people there don't have enough money now for airplane tickets. They don't come to buy our products here. We are very connected.

As Gloria says, we are very connected. Since 1983, I have been connected with many of the people whose lives are chronicled in this book, not only as an individual who regularly visits and interacts with people in Teotitlán but also in my role as an American citizen, consumer, and participant in the linked economies of the United States and Mexico. A few Teotiteco families live in my home state of Oregon, some of whom I see regularly. Our lives, intertwined personally, politically, economically, and socially, emphasize what I have written about elsewhere as always being "in the field"—in the larger field of the U.S.-Mexican political economy as well as in a field of ongoing personal relationships (Stephen 2002, 8–9). It is my sincere hope and expectation that I will continue to be bound through my personal relationships as well as the larger place I hold along with Teotitecos in the field of the larger Americas for many years to come.

Notes

CHAPTER 1: ETHNICITY AND CLASS

1 In the *Prison Notebooks* (1971, 242, as cited in Buci-Glucksman 1980, 92–93) Gramsci wrote: "Educative and formative role of the state. Its aim is always that of creating new and higher types of civilization [*civiltà*]; of adapting 'civilization' and the morality of the broadest masses to the necessities of the continuous development of the economic apparatus of production."

2 I use the words "Indian" and "Indianness" here to conform with the way various Mexican officials use them. In Spanish, *indio* usually has a derogatory meaning. Few people refer to themselves as indios. Whenever possible, they use the ethnic name.

3 These activities are explained in detail in chapters 8 and 9.

4 Absolute delineations are difficult because there are always some households that resell other people's weavings while also engaging in independent production or doing piecework for someone else. Since the 1990s, some households have also established themselves in transnational spaces and networks where they try to work independently as weavers and exporters, marketing their goods directly in the United States. Most households today, however, continue to categorize themselves as weavers, merchants, or independent weavers, whatever they view as their primary economic activity.

CHAPTER 2: KINSHIP, GENDER, AND GLOBALIZATION

1 See Beals 1970, 234; Cohen 1999, 85–93; Cook and Diskin 1976, 11; de la Fuente 1949, 120–23; Diskin 1986, 34–39; R. González 2001; Leslie 1960; Martínez Ríos 1964; Nader 1964, 1990; Parsons 1936; Sault 2001; Vargas-Barón 1968, 80–82.

2 In her further discussion of social reproduction Benería defines it as "structures that have to be reproduced in order that social reproduction as a whole can take place" (1979, 205). She offers as an example such structures as inheritance, which controls the transmission of resources from one generation to another.

CHAPTER 3: SIX WOMEN'S STORIES

1 Cristina is referring to a ceremony in which a young man's family formally asks for a young woman's hand in marriage—*contentar* in Spanish. The request is accompanied by a gift of candles, fruit, and chocolate. While formerly the gifts were quite limited, as in Cristina's experience, now such ceremonies involve up to sixty candles and truckloads of fruit, chocolate, and bread.

2 Angela is referring to a cave where the Virgin Mary is said to have appeared about 400 years ago. Locals go there to ask for miracles and for things they want in life. Most of the community can be found there on New Year's Day. People signal their requests by producing small models of what they want, such as a house or a horse.

3 A checkpoint on a highway there is usually staffed by immigration officers. All cars are stopped; passengers who appear to be Mexican are asked to produce documentation of their legal presence in the United States.

4 Hiring women from poorer neighboring towns to make tortillas for weddings, baptisms, mayordomías, and other celebrations appears to be a relatively new practice in Teotitlán. In the 1980s, even rich merchants who sponsored ritual events usually expected the female guests to prepare meals for up to two hundred people.

CHAPTER 4: SETTING THE SCENE

1 The 570 municipios in Oaxaca are grouped together in thirty districts or *distritos*. The distrito is an administrative unit of federal and state tax collection and the lowest level of the national court system. Each municipio unit is made up of a municipal seat and municipal agencies and police agencies.

2 *Comunidades agrarias* is a term that came into use in the 1970s. Most of this land constitutes a significant part of the holdings of indigenous communities and is based on historical claims, usually dating to pre-Columbian or colonial times. In many cases, these communal lands are known as *comunales*. For details on the legal and legislative history of comunidades agrarias in the twentieth century, see Stephen 2002, 63–64.

3 These topics include ritual systems and civil-religious cargo systems (El Guindi 1986; Mathews 1985; Peterson Royce 1975); participation in local market systems (Cook and Diskin 1976; Malinowski and de la Fuente 1982); peasant economics (Benítez Zenteno 1980; Clements 1988b; S. Cook 1982b, 1984b; Cook and Binford 1986; Turkenik 1976); farming and food (R. González, 2001); social values (Selby 1974); legal systems and dispute settlement (Nader 1964, 1990; Parnell 1988); aggression (Fry 1988; O'Nell 1979, 1981, 1986); intercommunity conflict (Dennis 1987); general ethnography (de la Fuente 1949; Kearney 1972; Parsons 1936); ethnohistory (Chance 1978; Chance and Taylor 1985; Taylor 1972, 1979); history (Oudijk 2000; Whitecotton 1977); compadrazgo (Sault 1985b, 2001); pre-Hispanic Zapotec civilization and urbanization (Marcus and Flannery 1996; Miller 1995); local politics and social movements (Campbell 1993, 1994, 2001; Rubin 1997); gender and sexuality (Chiñas 1973, 1987, 1995; Henestrosa 1993; Marcus 1998; Ruiz Campbell 1993; Rymph 1974; Sousa 1997); and Zapotec migration (Hirabayashi 1983, 1993, 1994; Hulshof 1991). This is not a comprehensive list, but it indicates the richness of Zapotec ethnography.

4 Census information is broken down only to the level of the municipio,

so many figures in this and other chapters include the agencia of Santiaguito, which has a population of 998. Table 1 includes estimates only for Teotitlán.

5 One hectare is equal to 2.47 acres.

CHAPTER 5: CONTESTED HISTORIES

1 While the restructuring of local governments as "free" municipios was supposed to increase the autonomy of indigenous communities, in reality it severely limited their control over local political and economic decisions (see Greenberg 1990; Stephen 1990).

2 The documents known as *copiadores de oficios* contain copies of all official correspondence received from the government and the community's response as written by municipio authorities. The archives of Teotitlán have a complete set of this correspondence for the entire twentieth century and before.

3 Teotitecos were adamant in their insistence that there were no factories in Teotitlán. While homes with more than several looms might have been considered factories by the state, they were never reported as such. Factories were required to pay taxes on their production. Textile manufacturers fought throughout the late 1920s and early 1930s to reduce federal taxes on production (Secretaría de la Economía Nacional 1934).

4 The recorded Spanish reads, ". . . *adornados con grecas y hidolos significación histórica de Mitla y Monte Albán incluyendo figuras Zapotecas y Toltecas. . . .*"

5 Susan Borque and Kay Warren (1981, 118–19) also found that women and men in Peru had different perceptions of women's work in relation to community ritual and production activities. Men had more limited perceptions of what women did.

6 It is unclear exactly when Maquilxóchitl dropped out of weaving and shifted into full-time subsistence agriculture. Census data suggest it may have been shortly after the Mexican Revolution, in the 1920s. In the late 1980s, however, increasing numbers of households in the community took up weaving again to take advantage of the booming commercial market.

7 Oral histories collected from collaborators roughly corroborate census data from 1945 on. Collaborators were asked to name all merchants in Teotitlán during a particular year. Local collaborators also recalled viajeros.

8 The Dirección de Asuntos Trabajadores Migratorios (DATUM) of the Secretaría de Relaciones Exteriores and officials of the Secretaría de Gobernación and the Secretaría del Trabajo y Previsión Social.

CHAPTER 6: WEAVING AS HERITAGE

1 Richard Salvucci (1987, 61) maintains that the obrajes did not represent protoindustry or protofactories. He instead refers to them as rational, if inefficient, textile manufacturers that responded well to the needs and limitations of

the colonial economy. One of the key reasons he declines to call them factories is that the workers resided in them (1987, 32–33).

2 It should be noted, however, that most women now supplement their metates with electric blenders. No Teotitlán kitchen is complete without one; a blender is one of the most popular wedding presents.

3 The three government agencies that funded the Lanera de Oaxaca included the Secretaría de Industria y Comercio, the Secretaría de Programas Estatales de Oaxaca, and La Financiera Nacional.

4 See Nagengast 1990 for a discussion of how prosperous Polish households benefit from unequal nonmonetary and monetary exchanges with "relatives."

5 Zapotec terminology in the narrative of this book has been rendered uniformly, in accordance with the International Phonetic Alphabet. People in the Zapotec community, however, do not write Zapotec uniformly: in most cases, they try to approximate their terminology according to the Spanish phonetic system and alphabet. Thus, there are some inconsistencies between how I have chosen to indicate certain Zapotec terms and how various cooperative groups and the Teotitlán museum indicate the same terms in the names of their groups and in their writings. When referring to the cooperatives by proper name I have honored the spellings the groups themselves use, and when citing writings posted by the museum I have retained their original spellings.

CHAPTER 7: FROM CONTRACT TO CO-OP

1 This figure came from a random stratified sample of 154 households carried out in 1986. The percentage is probably higher now, as younger girls continue to enter weaving production as early as age 10 or 11.

2 This approach is not to be confused with advocating that women be treated as economistic individuals engaged in rational choice.

CHAPTER 8: CHANGES IN THE CIVIL-RELIGIOUS HIERARCHY

1 See Cancian 1965 for a thorough and sophisticated discussion of civil-religious cargo systems. Cancian was one of the first to raise questions about the relationship between social and economic stratification and cargo sponsorship.

2 See Segura 1979 and 1980 for more detailed descriptions of the cargo system of Teotitlán.

3 *Ščay* is a ritual greeting that connotes a great deal of respect. It is used ceremonially on all occasions when people enter ritual space. It is also used on the street to demonstrate respect for someone. It implies a subordinate relationship between the person who initiates the greeting and the one who receives it. When the word is spoken, the initiator offers his or her hands face up to the person receiving the greeting. The person receiving the greeting touches the initiator's hands with his or her own hands palms down, connoting a superior position.

The greeting is always offered by children and young adults to an older person and by others to people to whom they want to demonstrate respect.

4 This figure should be compared with average annual cash outflows for merchants and weavers. In 1985, the average annual cash outflow for six merchants of various sizes was U.S.$7,857. For six weaver households measured the same year, it was U.S.$1,600. The family sponsoring the mayordomía in 1989 was a small-scale merchant household.

5 "Vé con satisfacción los propósitos que tienen de rectificar todas las costumbres que en nuestros pueblos producen la ruina o el estancamiento de su patrimonio moral y económico."

CHAPTER 9: FIESTA

1 Volkman (1984, 1985) discusses a similar process in Toroja, Indonesia.

2 See El Guindi (1986) for rich, detailed descriptions of Zapotec ritual space and ritual speech and their symbolic meanings.

3 The term "ritual kin" is used here instead of the more commonly used "fictive kin" in order to emphasize the genuine equality of this kin relationship — as real as blood kinship. The ritual kinship of compadrazgo, as well as adoptive forms of kinship and those connections derived through marriage, can be seen as kin relations. As Gailey (1985b, 12) notes, the content of kinship can be seen as broadly reciprocal claims to labor and products, mutual responsibility, and balanced or generalized sharing.

Glossary of Spanish and Zapotec Terms

Zapotec words are spelled in accordance with the International Phonetic Alphabet.

agencia   a population center under the control of a municipio

agricultores   agriculturists (usually with land)

ahijadas/hijadas   goddaughters

ahijados/hijados   godsons; godchildren in general

a la fuerza   obligatory

alcaldes   judges

alcaldes mayores   regional administrative offices of the crown during the colonial period

almud   dry measure that when filled with corn is equivalent to two kilos

artesanía   artisanry, crafts

artes populares indígenas   indigenous folk arts

atole   corn-based drink

ayuntamiento   town council

BANFOCO (Banco de Fomento de Cooperativas)   Bank for the Promotion of Cooperatives

bɛngul   an elderly person

bɛnguna   women

bɛ:n(i) lo'getš   people of Teotitlán

bɛ:n(i) reh   person from here

biuχ   cochineal-dyed wool cloth worn as a skirt

bracería   program to recruit Mexicans to work in the United States under contract; the body of people so employed

bracero   contract worker under a U.S. program for Mexican workers; by extension, any person who migrates to the United States to work as a manual laborer

cacique   political boss

cargo   civil or religious office within the community government or church committee

cliente   regular customer

CNC (Confederación Nacional Campesina)   PRI-controlled peasant union

COCEI (Coalición de Obreros, Campesinos, y Estudiantes del Istmo)   Coalition of Workers, Peasants, and Students of the Isthmus

COCOPA (Comisión de Concordia y Pacificación)   Commission of Concord and Pacification

cofradía   religious corporation established to pay for ceremonies sponsored by the cult of a saint

comadre   a child's godmother in relation to the biological parents

comité de la iglesia   church committee

compadrazgo   ritual kinship

compadre   a child's godfather in relation to the biological parents

concuño   sister-in-law's brother

contentar   to go to appease the

heart of a bride's parents, part
of the ceremony of a marriage
proposal

coordinadora   coordinating body

copiador de oficios   official record
of documents received and responded to by municipio officials

corregimientos   local administrative
units of the crown, later called
alcaldes mayores

costumbre   custom

cruz   cross

cultura   culture

dàd   honorific title for a man who is
elderly or has been a mayordomo,
indicative of respect; also applied
to a male saint

danzante   Teotitlán's ritual dance
troop, which is a religious cargo
of community service; *lit.* dancer

daχn   mountain

DICONSA (Distribuidora CONASUPO
S.A.)   CONASUPO Distribu-
tor; Mexican food distribution
program

diputado   formerly a high-ranking
mayordomo

distrito   district administrative unit
that ranks above municipio

ejidatario   member of an ejido

ejido   land given to a community
at the time of agrarian reform,
whose ultimate owner is the state,
unless ejidatarios vote to allow
individual members to privatize
the land they are entitled to use

escríbano   scribe

EZLN (Ejército Zapatista de Liberación Nacional)   Zapatista Army
of National Liberation

familia   family; related by blood,
marriage, adoption, or ritual
kinship

fiscal   top religious cargo rank

FONART (Fondo National de Artesanía)   National Fund for Artisanry

gañanes   migrant laborers paid by
the day

guelaguetza   exchange of goods or
labor. *See also* xɛlgɛz

χolbats   hand ax

historia   history

(h)lats   flat farmland; countryside

huaraches   sandals

huehuete   ritual specialist

huipil   indigenous blouse

hurɛšlat(ši)   merchant or seller of
textiles

indio   Indian

industria de alimentación   food
production

INI (Instituto Nacional Indigenista)   National Indigenous
Institute

invitados   guests; people invited to
a party to share in the work and
celebration

ir a medias   to go halves

jaχ   wood

jarabe   traditional Zapotec dance to
brass band music

jefe de sección   neighborhood sec-
tional chief

jornalero   day laborer

junta   assembly or community
gathering

juntas vecinales   neighborhood
  committees
juzgado mayor   judicial office

Lanera de Oaxaca   Oaxaca Wool
  Yarn Factory

madrina   godmother
manta   traditional cochineal-dyed
  wool cloth worn by women; can
  also mean cotton
mayor de vara   police captain
mayordomía   sponsorship of a cult
  celebration for a saint or the
  Virgin
mayordomo/a   sponsor of a cult
  celebration
mescal   strong alcoholic beverage
  made from the maguey cactus
mestizo   a person of mixed Indian
  or black and Spanish ancestry (a
  historically constructed category
  and historical racial category)
metate   mortar and pestle for grinding
molendera   female corn grinder
monte   mountain, mountainside
mozo   hired worker; *lit.* servant
municipio   administrative unit
  equivalent to a township

NAFTA   North American Free Trade
  Agreement
nãn   term of respect for a woman
  who is elderly or has been a
  mayordoma, or for a female saint
  or apparition of the Virgin (e.g.,
  the Vírgen de Guadalupe)
novia/novio   sweetheart; girl-
  friend/boyfriend
Nuestro Señor de la Preciosa Sangre   Our Lord of the Precious

Blood, patron saint of Teotitlán
  del Valle

padres del pueblo   town fathers;
  men assigned a symbolic religious
  cargo
padrino   godfather
PAN (Partido Acción Nacional)   National Action Party
pelusa   blanket woven of animal
  hair and cotton
petate   reed mat
posada   celebration before Christmas commemorating Mary and
  Joseph's search for shelter; *lit.*
  inn
PRD (Partido de la Revolución
  Democrática)   Party of the
  Democratic Revolution
presidente/a   mayor or chair of a
  group or committee
PRI (Partido Revolucionario Institucional)   Institutional Revolutionary Party
promesa   vow; promise to sponsor a
  cult celebration

quehaceres de la casa   housework

rap(ᵃ)daŋ kos   they have things
rap(ᵃ)daŋ ḿed(ʒ)   they have money
raza cósmica   cosmic race; indi-
  genes
regatones   merchants or resellers
regidor   town councilor in charge of
  a specific area or resource, such as
  water or forest
respet   respect
ricos   the rich
rúnčilàt(ši)   weaver; *lit.* maker of
  textiles
ruʔóř(n)   oven mouth river

sa(ᵖa)χúil(i) fiesta with music; an elaborate five-day ceremony

sa(ᵖa)tɛr(t)síl morning fiesta; a small-scale fiesta

SARH (Secretaría de Agricultura y Recursos Hidráulicos) Ministry of Agriculture and Water Resources

ščãŋ ritual greeting denoting respect

serranos people from surrounding communities in the Sierra Juárez; *lit.* mountain people

síndico adviser, legal counsel to mayor; *lit.* trustee

škalbao clever, lucky you

šruɛz servant to the mayor

šudao bearer of religious symbols; a religious cargo title

suplente alternate

šxía Zapotec name for Teotitlán; *lit.* Under the Rock

tejate refreshing drink made of corn, cacao, and sugar

tejedoras female weavers

tejedores male weavers; weavers in general

temporal unirrigated farmland

teŋgjuwɛʔɛñĩ(ŋ)? Is it a boy?

Teotiteco/Teotiteca native of Teotitlán

težapɛʔɛ(nɛn) It's a girl.

típico typical

topil policeman

valles centrales five valleys in the central region of the state of Oaxaca

viajero trader, traveling merchant

vocal committee member

xɛlgɛz guelaguetza; exchange of goods or labor

xɛlgɛz daχn labor exchange for corral construction, planting, weeding, and harvesting on communal land

xɛlgɛz (h)lats(v) labor exchange for planting, weeding, and harvesting on flat land, mostly privately held

xɛlgɛz šte majŕdõ exchanges of labor or goods by the mayordomos of a fiesta

xɛlgɛz xed jaχ exchange of wood gathering

x̌iabets Brother Rock, mountain above Teotitlán

zacate fodder; applied to grass, hay, straw, dried cornstalks

Bibliography

Acuña, René, ed. 1984. *Relaciones geográficas del siglo XVI, Antequera*. Vol. I. Mexico City: Universidad National Autónoma de México, Instituto de Investigaciones Antropológicas.

Adams, Richard. 1967. Nationalization. In *Handbook of Middle American Indians*. Vol. 6, *Social Anthropology*, ed. M. Nash. Austin: University of Texas Press.

———. 1988. Ethnic Images and Strategies in 1944. Prepublication working paper of the Institute of Latin American Studies, University of Texas at Austin, Paper no. 88–06. Austin: University of Texas, Center for Latin American Studies.

Aguirre Beltrán, Gonzalo. 1975. *Obra polémica*. Mexico City: SEP-INAH.

Alvarez, Sonia. Forthcoming. *Contentious Feminisms: Cultural Politics, Policy Advocacy, and Transnational Activism in Latin America*. Durham: Duke University Press.

Alvarez, Sonia, Evelina Dagnino, and Arturo Escobar. 1998. *Cultures of Politics/ Politics of Cultures: Re-visioning Latin American Social Movements*. Boulder: Westview.

Appadurai, Arjun. 1996. *Modernity at Large: Cultural Dimensions of Globalization*. Minneapolis: University of Minnesota Press.

Appel, Jill. 1982. A Summary of the Ethnohistoric Information Relevant to the Interpretation of Late Postclassic Settlement Patterns Data, the Central and Valle Grande Survey Zone. In *Monte Albán's Hinterland*, pt. 1, *The Prehispanic Settlement Patterns of the Central and Southern Parts of the Valley of Oaxaca, Mexico*, ed. R. Blanton, S. Kowalewski, G. Feinman, and J. Appel. Memoirs of the Museum of Anthropology, University of Michigan, no. 15. Ann Arbor: University of Michigan Press.

Archivo General del Estado de Oaxaca. 1890. Padrón general de población, Teotitlán del Valle.

———. 1926a. Sección de gobernación. *Diario oficial* 34(2): 1–4.

———. 1926b. Sección de gobernación. *Periódico oficial* 8(4): 27–28.

Archivo Municipal de Teotitlán del Valle. 1863–1984. Registro de difunciones.

———. 1868. Padrón general de población.

———. 1890. Padrón electoral.

———. 1900. Padrón general de población.

———. 1914. Copiador de oficios.

———. 1918. Copiador de oficios, no. 48.

———. 1920. Padrón general de población.

———. 1925. Noticia mensual de la casa del pueblo de Teotitlán del Valle (February–April).

———. 1927. Copiador de oficios, no. 17.

————. 1928. Copiador de circulares, no. 14.

————. 1930–39. Copiadores de oficios.

————. 1931a. Copiador de oficios, July 13.

————. 1931b. Copiador de oficios, August 31.

————. 1932. Copiador de oficios, no. 113, February 17.

————. 1938. Copiador de oficios.

————. 1981. Censo del pueblo.

Arizpe, Lourdes. 1985. *Campesinado y migración*. Mexico City: Secretaría de Educación Pública.

Arizpe, Lourdes, and Josefina Aranda. 1981. The "Comparative Advantage" of Women's Disadvantages: Women Workers in the Strawberry Export Agribusiness in Mexico. *Signs* 7(2): 453–73.

Atl, Dr. [Gerardo Murillo]. 1922. *Las artes populares en México*. Mexico City: Secretaría de Industria y Comercio.

Babb, Florence E. 1986. Producers and Reproducers: Andean Market Women in the Economy. In Nash and Safa 1986.

————. 1989. *Between Field and Cooking Pot: The Political Economy of Marketwomen in Peru*. Austin: University of Texas Press.

————. 1998. *Between Field and Cooking Pot: The Political Economy of Marketwomen in Peru*. Rev. ed. Austin: University of Texas Press.

————. 2001. *After Revolution: Mapping Gender and Cultural Politics in Neoliberal Nicaragua*. Austin: University of Texas Press.

Baizerman, Suzanne. 1988. Tourist Art, Ethnicity, and Economic Development: Hispanic Weavers in Northern New Mexico. Paper prepared for the Latin American Studies Association 14th International Congress, March 17–19, New Orleans.

————. 1991. Textile Tourist Art: Can We Call It Traditional? In *Mesoamerican and Andean Cloth and Costume*, ed. M. Schevill, J. Berle, and E. Dwyer. San Francisco: Garland.

Barabas, Alicia, and Miguel Bartolomé. 1986. La pluralidad desigual en Oaxaca. In *Ethnicidad y pluralismo cultural: La dinámica étnica en Oaxaca*, ed. A. Barabas and M. Bartolomé. Mexico City: Instituto Nacional de Antropología e Historia.

Barlow, R. H. 1949. *The Extent of the Empire of the Culhua Mexica*. Ibero Americana, no. 28. Berkeley: University of California Press.

Barth, Fredrik. 1969. Introduction. In *Ethnic Groups and Boundaries*, ed. F. Barth. London: Allen and Unwin.

Bartolomé, Miguel Alberto. 1979. Conciencia étnica y autogestión indígena. In *Indianidad y descolonización en América Latina: Documentos de la Segunda Reunión de Barbados*. Mexico City: Nueva Imagen.

Bartra, Eli. 2000. Of Alebrijes and Ocumichos: Some Myths about Folk Art and Mexican Identity. In *Primitivism and Identity in Latin America: Essays on Art,*

Literature, and Culture, ed. Erik Camayd-Freixas and José Eduardo González. Tucson: University of Arizona Press.

———. 2003. Engendering Clay: Women Potters of Mata Ortiz. In Bartra 2003.

———, ed. 2003. *Crafting Gender: Women and Folk Art in Latin America and the Caribbean*. Durham: Duke University Press.

Beals, Ralph. 1970. Gifting, Reciprocity, Savings and Credit in Peasant Oaxaca. *Southeastern Journal of Anthropology* 26(3): 231–41.

Benería, Lourdes. 1979. Reproduction, Production and the Sexual Division of Labour. *Cambridge Journal of Economics* 3:203–25.

———. 1992. The Mexican Debt Crisis: Restructuring the Economy and the Household. In *Unequal Burden: Economic Crises, Persistent Poverty, and Women's Work*, ed. Lourdes Benería and Shelly Feldman. Boulder: Westview.

Benería, Lourdes, and Martha Roldán. 1987. *The Crossroads of Class and Gender: Industrial Homework, Subcontracting, and Household Dynamics in Mexico City*. Chicago: University of Chicago Press.

Benería, Lourdes, and Gita Sen. 1986. Accumulation, Reproduction and Women's Role in Economic Development: Boserup Revisited. In *Women's Work: Development and the Division of Labor by Gender*, ed. E. Leacock and H. Safa. South Hadley, Mass.: Bergin and Garvey.

Benítez Zenteno, Raul, ed. 1980. *Sociedad y política en Oaxaca, 1980: Quince estudios de caso*. Oaxaca: Instituto de Investigaciones Sociológicas, UABJO.

Benjamin, Thomas. 1996. *A Rich Land, A Poor People: Politics and Society in Modern Chiapas*. Albuquerque: University of New Mexico Press.

Bennholdt-Thomsen, Veronika. 1980. Toward a Class Analysis of Agrarian Sectors: Mexico. *Latin American Perspectives* 7(4): 100–114.

Binford, Leigh, and Howard Campbell. 1993. Introduction. In *Zapotec Struggles: Histories, Politics, and Representations from Juchitán, Oaxaca*, ed. Howard Campbell, Leigh Binford, Miguel Bartolomé, and Alicia Barabas. Washington, D.C.: Smithsonian Institution Press.

Blanton, Richard E. 1978. *Monte Albán: Settlement Patterns at the Ancient Zapotec Capital*. New York: Academic Press.

Bonfil Batalla, Guillermo. 1981. Utopía y revolución: El pensamiento político contemporáneo de los indios en América Latina. In *Utopía y Revolución*, ed. Guillermo Bonfil Batalla. Mexico City: Nueva Imagen.

Borque, Susan C., and Kay B. Warren. 1981. *Women of the Andes*. Ann Arbor: University of Michigan Press.

Bossen, Laurel Herbenar. 1984. *The Redivision of Labor*. Albany: State University of New York Press.

Bourgois, Philippe. 1988. Conjugated Oppression: Class and Ethnicity among Guaymi and Kuna Banana Workers. *American Ethnologist* 15(2): 328–48.

Brandes, Stanley. 1981. Cargos versus Cost Sharing in Mesoamerican Fiestas with Special Reference to Tzintzuntzan. *Journal of Anthropological Research* 37(3): 209–25.

———. 1988. *Power and Persuasion: Fiestas and Social Control in Rural Mexico*. Philadelphia: University of Pennsylvania Press.

Brenner, Anita. 1929. *Idols behind the Altars*. New York: Payson and Clarke.

Briggs, Charles. 1996. The Politics of Discursive Authority in Research on the Invention of Tradition. *Cultural Anthropology* 11(4): 435–69.

Brintnall, Douglas. 1979. *Revolt against the Dead: The Modernization of a Mayan Community in the Highlands of Guatemala*. New York: Gordon and Breach.

Brito de Martí, José. 1982. *Almanaque de Oaxaca*. Oaxaca: Gobernador del Estado.

Brown, Michael. 2003. *Who Owns Native Culture?* Cambridge: Harvard University Press.

Browner, Carol. 1986a. Gender Roles and Social Change: A Mexican Case Study. *Ethnology* 25(2): 89–105.

———. 1986b. The Politics of Reproduction in a Mexican Village. *Signs* 11(4): 710–24.

Buci-Glucksman, Christine. 1980. *Gramsci and the State*. Trans. David Fernbach. London: Lawrence and Wishart.

Buechler, Judith Maria. 1986. Women in Petty Commodity Production in La Paz, Bolivia. In Nash and Safa 1986.

Bukh, Jette. 1979. *The Village Woman in Ghana*. Uppsala: Scandinavian Institute of African Studies.

Bullock, William. 1825. *Catalogue of the Exhibition, called Modern Mexico; containing a panoramic view of the city, with specimens of the natural history of New Spain, and models of the vegetable produce, costume, etc.* London.

Bunster-Burotto, Ximena. 1986. Surviving beyond Fear: Women and Torture in Latin America. In Nash and Safa 1986.

Burgoa, Fray Francisco de. 1934. *Geográfica descripción*. 2 vols. Mexico City: Archivo General de la Nación.

Butler, Judith. 1993. *Bodies That Matter: On the Discursive Limits of "Sex."* New York: Routledge.

Campbell, Howard. 1993. Class Struggle, Ethnopolitics and Cultural Revivalism in Juchitán. In *Zapotec Struggles: Histories, Politics, and Representations from Juchitán, Oaxaca*, ed. Howard Campbell et al. Washington, D.C.: Smithsonian Institution Press.

———. 1994. *Zapotec Renaissance: Ethnic Politics and Cultural Revivalism in Southern Mexico*. Albuquerque: University of New Mexico Press.

———. 2001. *Mexican Memoir: A Personal Account of Anthropology and Radical Politics in Oaxaca*. Westport: Bergin and Garvey.

Cancian, Frank. 1965. *Economics and Prestige in a Mayan Community*. Stanford: Stanford University Press.

———. 1990. The Zinacantán Cargo Waiting Lists as a Reflection of Social, Political, and Economic Changes, 1952–1987. In Stephen and Dow 1990.

Carrillo, Teresa. 1988. *Working Women and the "19th of September Mexican Garment Workers Union": The Significance of Gender.* Cambridge: Harvard/MIT Women in Development Group Papers.

———. 1990. Women and Independent Unionism in the Garment Industry. In Foweraker and Craig 1990.

Castile, George P. 1981. Issues in the Analysis of Enduring Cultural Systems. In *Persistent Peoples: Cultural Enclaves in Perspective*, ed. George P. Castile and Gilbert Kushner. Tucson: University of Arizona Press.

Castro Apreza, Inés. 2003. Contemporary Women's Movement in Chiapas. In Eber and Kovic 2003.

Castro Apreza, Yolanda. 2003. J'pas Joloviletik-Jolom Mayaetik-K'inal Antzetik: An Organization Experience of Indigenous and Mestiza Women. In Eber and Kovic 2003.

CCRI-CG (Comité Clandestino Revolucionario Indígena, Comandancia General del Ejército Zapatista de Liberación Nacional). 1994. EZLN Demands at the Dialogue Table. In *The Mexico Reader: History, Culture, Politics*, ed. Gilbert M. Joseph and Timothy J. Henderson. Durham: Duke University Press.

Chance, John. 1978. *Race and Class in Colonial Oaxaca.* Stanford: Stanford University Press.

———. 1990. Changes in Twentieth-Century Mesoamerican Cargo Systems. In Stephen and Dow 1990.

Chance, John K., and William B. Taylor. 1985. Cofradías and Cargos: An Historical Perspective on the Mesoamerican Civil-Religious Hierarchy. *American Ethnologist* 12(1): 1–26.

Chávez, Leo R., Esteban Flores, and Marta López Garza. 1989. Migrants and Settlers: A Comparison of Undocumented Mexicans and Central Americans in the United States. *Frontera Norte* 1(1): 49–75.

Chayanov, A. V. 1966. *The Theory of Peasant Economy.* Ed. Daniel Thomer, Basile Kerblay, and R. E. F. Smith. Homewood, Ill.: Irwin.

Chibnik, Michael. 2003. *Crafting Tradition: The Making and Marketing of Oaxacan Wood Carvings.* Austin: University of Texas Press.

Chiñas, Beverly. 1973. *The Isthmus Zapotecs: Women's Roles in Cultural Context.* New York: Holt, Rinehart and Winston.

———. 1987. Women: The Heart of Isthmus Zapotec Ceremonial Exchange. Paper presented at the Annual Meeting of the American Anthropological Association, November 18–22, Chicago.

———. 1995. Isthmus Zapotec Attitudes toward Sex and Gender Anomalies. In *Latin American Male Homosexualities*, ed. Stephen O. Murray. Albuquerque: University of New Mexico Press.

CIA (Central Intelligence Agency). 2003. *CIA World Factbook.* Electronic version found at http://www.cia.gov/cia/publications/factbook/geos/mx.html#Econ (accessed November 3, 2003).

Clements, Helen. 1988a. Mujeres, trabajo y cambio social: Los casos de dos comunidades oaxaqueños. In *Las mujeres en el campo*, ed. Josefina Aranda Bezaury. Oaxaca: Instituto de Investigaciones Sociológicas de la Universidad Autónoma Benito Juárez de Oaxaca.

———. 1988b. Buscando la Forma: Self-Reorganization in Craft Commercialization. Paper presented at the 46th International Congress of Americanists, July 4–8, Amsterdam.

Cohen, Jeffrey. 1988. Zapotec Weaving: Performance Theory, from Verbal to Visual Art. Paper prepared for the American Ethnological Society Annual Meeting, March 24–27, St. Louis.

———. 1999. *Cooperation and Community: Economy and Society in Oaxaca*. Austin: University of Texas Press.

———. 2000. Textile Production in Rural Mexico: The Complexities of the Global Market for Handmade Crafts. In Grimes and Milgram 2000.

———. 2001. Transnational Migration in Rural Oaxaca, Mexico: Dependency, Development, and the Household. *American Anthropologist* 103(4): 954–67.

Collier, George, with Elizabeth Lowery Quaratiello. 1994. *Basta! Land and the Zapatista Rebellion in Chiapas*. San Francisco: Food First Books.

Collier, Jane Fishburne, and Sylvia Junko Yanagisako, eds. 1987. *Gender and Kinship: Essays toward a Unified Analysis*. Stanford: Stanford University Press.

Comaroff, Jean, and John L. Comaroff. 1992. *Christianity, Colonialism, and Consciousness in South Africa*. Vol. 1 of *Of Revelation and Revolution*. Chicago: University of Chicago Press.

———. 1995. *The Dialectics of Modernity on a South African Frontier*. Vol. 2 of *Of Revelation and Revolution*. Chicago: University of Chicago Press.

Comaroff, John L., and Jean Comaroff. 1992. *Ethnography and the Historical Imaginations*. Boulder: Westview.

Cook, Maria Lorena. 1990. Organizing Opposition in the Teachers' Movement in Oaxaca. In Foweraker and Craig 1990.

Cook, Scott. 1982a. Craft Production in Oaxaca, Mexico. *Cultural Survival Quarterly* 6(4): 18–20.

———. 1982b. *Zapotec Stoneworkers*. Lanham, Md.: University Press of America.

———. 1984a. Peasant Economy and the Dynamics of Rural, Industrial Commodity Production in the Oaxaca Valley, Mexico. *Journal of Peasant Studies* 12(1): 3–40.

———. 1984b. *Peasant Capitalist Industry: Piecework and Enterprise in Southern Mexican Brickyards*. Lanham, Md.: University Press of America.

———. 1988. Crafts and Class: Thoughts about How the Production and Exchange of Craft Commodities Differentiates Society. Paper presented at the 46th International Congress of Americanists, July 4–8, Amsterdam.

———. 1993. Craft Commodity Production: Market Diversity and Differential Rewards in Mexican Capitalism Today. In Nash 1993a.

Cook, Scott, and Leigh Binford. 1986. Petty Commodity Production, Capital

Accumulation, and Peasant Differentiation: Lenin vs. Chayanov in Rural Mexico. *Review of Radical Political Economics* 18(4): 1–31.

————. 1988. Industrial Commodity Production and Agriculture in the Oaxaca Valley. Paper presented at the 46th International Congress of Americanists, July 4–8, Amsterdam.

————. 1990. *Obliging Need: Petty Rural Industry in Mexican Capitalism*. Austin: University of Texas Press.

Cook, Scott, and Martin Diskin. 1976. The Peasant Market Economy of the Valley of Oaxaca in Analysis and History. In *Markets of Oaxaca*, ed. S. Cook and M. Diskin. Austin: University of Texas Press.

Crummet, Maria de los Angeles. 1987. Rural Women and Migration in Latin America. In Deere and León 1987.

Dalton Paloma, Margarita. 2003a. Las presidentas municipales in Oaxaca y los usos y costumbres. In *El municipio: Un reto para la igualdad de oportunidades entre hombres y mujeres*, ed. Dalia Barrera Bassols and Alejandra Massolo. Mexico City: Grupo Interdisciplinario sobre Mujer, Trabajo y Pobreza, A.C./Instituto Nacional de las Mujeres.

————. 2003b. Democracia y equidad de género: La voz de las presidentas. Manuscript.

da Silva Ruiz, Gilberto. 1980. *Examen de una economía artesanal en Oaxaca*. Estudios de Antropología e Historia 21. Oaxaca: Centro Regional de Oaxaca, Instituto Nacional de Antropología e Historia.

Deere, Carmen Diana. 1978. The Differentiation of the Peasantry and Family Structure: A Peruvian Case Study. *Journal of Family History* 3:422–38.

————. 1979. Changing Relations of Production and Peruvian Peasant Women's Work. In *Women in Latin America*. Riverside, Calif.: Latin American Perspectives.

————. 1987. The Latin American Agrarian Reform Experience. In Deere and León 1987.

Deere, Carmen Diana, and Alain de Janvry. 1979. A Conceptual Framework for the Empirical Analysis of Peasants. *American Journal of Agricultural Economics* 61:601–11.

————. 1981. Demographic and Social Differentiation among Northern Peruvian Peasants. *Journal of Peasant Studies* 8(3): 335–66.

Deere, Carmen Diana, and Magdalena León. 1986. Rural Women and Agrarian Reform in Peru, Chile, and Cuba. In Nash and Safa 1986.

————. 2001. *Empowering Women: Land and Property Rights in Latin America*. Pittsburgh: University of Pittsburgh Press.

————, eds. 1987. *Rural Women and State Policy: Feminist Perspectives on Latin American Agricultural Development*. Boulder: Westview.

de Janvry, Alain. 1981. *The Agrarian Question and Reformism in Latin America*. Baltimore: Johns Hopkins University Press.

de la Fuente, Julio. 1949. *Yalalag: Una villa zapoteca serrana*. Serie Científica. Mexico City: Museo Nacional de Antropología.

del Paso y Troncoso, Francisco, ed. 1981. *Relaciones geográficas de la Diócesis de Oaxaca: Manuscritos de la Real Academia de la Historia de Madrid y del Archivo de Indias en Sevilla, años 1579–1581*. 1890. Mexico City: Inovación.

Dennis, Phillip. 1987. *Inter-Village Conflict in Oaxaca*. New Brunswick: Rutgers University Press.

Departamento de la Estadística National. 1925–28. *Censo general de habitantes, 30 de Noviembre 1921*. Mexico City: Talleres Gráficos de la Nación.

Diamond, Stanley. 1951. Dahomey: A Proto-State in West Africa. Ph.D. diss., Columbia University.

Díaz Polanco, Héctor. 1981. La teoría indigenista y la integración. In *Indigenismo, modernización y marginalidad: Una revisión crítica*, ed. H. Díaz-Polanco et al. Mexico City: Centro de Investigación para la Integración Social.

Dirección General de Estadística. 1897–99. *Censo general de la República Mexicana verificado el 20 de octubre de 1895*. Mexico City: Secretaría de Fomento.

———. 1906. *Censo general de la República Mexicana verificado el 29 de octubre de 1900*. Mexico City: Secretaría de Fomento.

———. 1918–20. *Tercer censo de población de los Estados Unidos Mexicanos verificado el 27 de octubre de 1910*. Mexico City: Secretaría de Hacienda, Departamento de Fomento.

———. 1936. *Quinto censo de población, 15 de Mayo 1930*. Mexico City: Secretaría de la Economía Nacional.

———. 1946. *Sexto censo de población, 1940*. Mexico City: Secretaría de Industria y Comercio.

———. 1954. *Séptimo censo de población, 1950*. Mexico City: Secretaría de Industria y Comercio.

———. 1963. *Octavo censo general de población, 1960*. Mexico City: Secretaría de Industria y Comercio.

———. 1973. *Noveno censo general de población, 1970*. Mexico City: Secretaría de Industria y Comercio.

Dirlik, Arif. 2000. Place-Based Imagination: Globalism and the Politics of Place. In *Places and Politics in an Age of Globalization*, ed. Rozann Praznick and Arif Dirlik. Lanham, Md.: Rowan and Littlefield.

Diskin, Martin. 1986. La economía de la comunidad étnica en Oaxaca. In *Etnicidad y pluralismo cultural: La dinámica étnica en Oaxaca*, ed. A. Barabas and M. Bartolomé. Mexico City: Instituto National de Antropología e Historia.

Dore, Elizabeth. 1997. *Gender Politics in Latin America: Debates in Theory and Practice*. New York: Monthly Review Press.

Dörner, Gerd. 1962. *Folk Art of Mexico*. Trans. Gladys Wheelhouse. New York: A. S. Barnes.

Dow, James. 1977. Religion in the Organization of a Mexican Peasant Economy. In *Peasant Livelihood: Studies in Economic Anthropology and Cultural Ecology*, ed. Rhoda Halperin and James Dow. New York: St. Martin's Press.

Earle, Duncan. 1990. Appropriating the Enemy: Maya Religious Organization and Community Survival. In Stephen and Dow 1990.

Eber, Christine. 2000. That They Be in the Middle, Lord: Women, Weaving, and Cultural Survival in Highland Chiapas, Mexico. In Grimes and Milgram 2000.

Eber, Christine, and Christine Kovic, eds. 2003. *Women of Chiapas: Making History in Times of Struggle and Hope*. New York: Routledge.

Eber, Christine, and Brenda Rosenbaum. 1993. "That we may serve beneath your hands and feet": Women Weavers in Highland Chiapas, Mexico. In Nash 1993.

Eckstein, Susan Eva, and Timothy Wickham-Crowley. 2003. *Struggles for Social Rights in Latin America*. New York: Routledge.

Edholm, Felicity, Olivia Harris, and Kate Young. 1977. Conceptualizing Women. *Critique of Anthropology* 3:101–30.

Ehlers, Tracy Bachrach. 1993. Belts, Business, and Bloomingdale's: An Alternative Model for Guatemalan Artisan Development. In Nash 1993.

El Guindi, Fadwa. 1986. *The Myth of Ritual*. Phoenix: University of Arizona Press.

Engels, Frederick. 1972. *The Origin of the Family, Private Property, and the State*. Ed. Eleanor B. Leacock. New York: International Publishers.

Escobar, Arturo, and Sonia Alvarez. 1992. *The Making of Social Movements in Latin America: Identity, Strategy, and Democracy*. Boulder: Westview.

Espejel, Carlos. 1978. *Mexican Folk Crafts*. Trans. Pablo Shekelton. Barcelona: Blume.

Feijoo, Carmen, and Monica Gogna. 1987. Mujeres, cotidianeidad y política. En *Ciudadanía e identidad: Las mujeres en los movimientos sociales latino-americanos*, ed. E. Jelin. Geneva: Instituto de Investigaciones de las Naciones Unidas para el Desarrollo Social (UNRISD).

Fernández-Kelly, María Patricia. 1983. *For We Are Sold, I and My People: Women and Industry in Mexico's Frontier*. Albany: State University of New York Press.

Fernández-Kelly, María Patricia, and Saskia Sassen. 1995. Recasting Women in the Global Economy: Internationalization and Changing Definitions of Gender. In *Women and Development in the Third World*, ed. E. Acost-Belén and C. Bose. Philadelphia: Temple University Press.

Field, Les W. 1999. *The Grimace of Macho Ratón: Artisans, Identity, and Nation in Late-Twentieth-Century Western Nicaragua*. Durham: Duke University Press.

Fischgrund Stanton, Andra. 2000. *Zapotec Weavers of Teotitlán*. Santa Fe: Museum of New Mexico Press.

Fitzgerald, David. 2000. *Negotiating Extra-territorial Citizenship: Mexican Migration and the Transnational Politics of Community*. Monograph Series, no. 2. La Jolla: Center for Comparative Immigration Studies, University of California, San Diego.

Flannery, Kent V., and Joyce Marcus. 1983. The Changing Politics of A.D. 600–900. Editor's introduction to "The Changing Politics of A.D. 600–900." In *The Cloud People: Divergent Evolution of the Zapotec and Mixtec Civilizations*, ed. K. Flannery and J. Marcus. New York: Academic Press.

Flores, William V., and Rina Benmayor. 1997. Introduction: Constructing Cultural Citizenship. In *Latino Cultural Citizenship: Claiming Identity, Space, and Rights*, ed. W. V. Flores and R. Benmayor. Boston: Beacon.

Fomento Cultural BANAMEX. 2001. *Great Masters of Mexican Folk Art*. New York: Harry Abrams.

Foster, George. 1953. Cofradía and Compadrazgo in Spain and Spanish America. *Southwestern Journal of Anthropology* 9:1–28.

———. 1969. Godparents and Social Networks in Tzintzuntzan. *Southwestern Journal of Anthropology* 25:261–78.

Foweraker, Joe, and Ann L. Craig, eds. 1990. *Popular Movements and Political Change in Mexico*. Boulder: L. Rienner.

Fox, Jonathan, Gaspar Rivera-Salgado, and Lynn Stephen. 1999. Indigenous Rights and Self-Determination in Mexico. *Cultural Survival Quarterly*, April.

Friedlander, Judith. 1975. *Being Indian in Hueyapan: A Study of Forced Identity in Contemporary Mexico*. New York: St. Martin's Press.

Fry, Douglas. 1988. Intercommunity Differences in Aggression among Zapotec Children. *Child Development* 59(4): 1008–1019.

Gailey, Christine Ward. 1985a. The State of the State in Anthropology. *Dialectical Anthropology* 9:65–89.

———. 1985b. The Kindness of Strangers: Transformations of Kinship in Precapitalist Class and State Formation. *Culture* 5(2): 3–16.

———. 1987a. *Kinship to Kingship: Gender Hierarchy and State Formation in the Tongan Islands*. Austin: University of Texas Press.

———. 1987b. Culture Wars: Resistance to State Formation. In *Power Relations and State Formation*, ed. C. Gailey and T. Patterson. Washington, D.C.: American Anthropological Association.

Gamio, M. 1946. La identificación del indio. *América Indígena* 6:99–103.

García Canclini, Néstor. 1982. *Las culturas populares en el capitalismo*. Mexico City: Nueva Imagen.

———. 1989. *Culturas hibridas: Estrategias para entrar y salir de la modernidad*. Mexico City: Grijalba.

García y Griego, Manuel. 1981. *The Importation of Mexican Contract Laborers to the United States, 1942–1964: Antecedents, Operations and Legacy*. La Jolla, Calif.: Center for U.S.-Mexican Studies.

Gay, José Antonio. 1881. *Historia de Oaxaca*. Mexico City: Dublán.

Gerhard, Peter. 1972. *A Guide to the Historical Geography of New Spain*. Cambridge: Cambridge University Press.

Glick Schiller, Nina, Linda Basch, and Cristina Blanc-Szanton, eds. 1992. *To-*

wards a Transnational Perspective on Migration: Race, Class, Ethnicity, and National-ism Reconsidered. New York: New York Academy of Social Sciences.

Goldring, Luin. 1996. Gendered Memory: Reconstructions of Rurality among Mexican Transnational Migrants. In *Creating the Countryside: The Politics of Rural and Environmental Discourse*, ed. E. Melanie DuPuis and Peter Vandergest. Philadelphia: Temple University Press.

———. 1998. Power and Status in Transnational Social Fields. In *Transnationalism from Below*, ed. Michael Peter Smith and Luis Eduardo Guarnizo. New Brunswick, N.J.: Transaction.

———. 2001. The Gender and Geography of Citizenship in Mexico-U.S. Transnational Spaces. *Identities* 7(4): 501–37.

González, Roberto J. 2001. *Zapotec Science: Farming and Food in the Northern Sierra of Oaxaca*. Austin: University of Texas Press.

González, Victoria, and Karen Kampwirth. 2001. *Radical Women in Latin America: Left and Right*. University Park: Pennsylvania State University Press.

González de la Rocha, Mercedes. 1994. *The Resources of Poverty: Women and Survival in a Mexican City*. Oxford: Blackwell.

Good Eshelman, Catharine. 1988a. *Haciendo la lucha: Arte y comercio Nahua de Guerrero*. Mexico City: Fondo de la Cultura Económica.

———. 1988b. Crafts, Commerce, and Cultural Identity: A Case Study of Nahua Economic Enterprise in Guerrero, Mexico. Paper presented at the Latin American Studies Association, 14th International Congress, March 17–19, New Orleans.

Graburn, Nelson. 1982. The Dynamics of Change in Tourist Arts. *Cultural Survival Quarterly* 6(4): 7–14.

Gramsci, Antonio. 1971. *Selections from the Prison Notebooks*. Ed. and trans. Quintin Hoare and Geoffrey Nowell Smith. London: Lawrence and Wishart.

Greenberg, James. 1981. *Santiago's Sword*. Berkeley: University of California Press.

———. 1989. *Blood Ties: Life and Violence in Rural Mexico*. Tucson: University of Arizona Press.

———. 1990. Sanctity and Resistance in Closed Corporate Indian Communities. In Stephen and Dow 1990.

Grimes, Kimberly M. 2000. Democratizing International Production and Trade: North American Alternative Trading Organizations. In Grimes and Milgram 2000.

Grimes, Kimberly M., and B. Lynne Milgram. 2000. Introduction: Facing the Challenges of Artisan Production in the Global Market. In Grimes and Milgram 2000.

———, eds. 2000. *Artisans and Cooperatives: Developing Alternative Trade for the Global Economy*. Tucson: University of Arizona Press.

Guarnizo, Luis Eduardo, and Michael Peter Smith. 1998. The Locations of Transnationalism. In *Transnationalism from Below*, ed. Michael Peter Smith and Luis Eduardo Guarnizo. New Brunswick, N.J.: Transaction.

Gutiérrez, David. 1995. *Walls and Mirrors: Mexican Americans, Mexican Immigrants, and the Politics of Ethnicity*. Berkeley: University of California Press.

————, ed. 1996. *Between Two Worlds: Mexican Immigrants in the United States*. Wilmington, Del.: Scholarly Resources.

Gutmann, Matthew. 1996. *The Meanings of Macho: Being a Man in Mexico City*. Berkeley: University of California Press.

————. 2002. *The Romance of Democracy: Compliant Defiance in Contemporary Mexico*. Berkeley: University of California Press.

————. 2003. *Changing Men and Masculinities in Latin America*. Durham: Duke University Press.

Hall, Stuart. 1988. New Ethnicities. ICA Document 7, 27–31. London: Institute for Community Arts.

————. 1996. Introduction: Who Needs 'Identity'? In *Questions of Cultural Identity*, ed. Stuart Hall and Paul du Gay. London: Sage.

Hamilton, Nora. 1982. *The Limits of State Autonomy: Post-Revolutionary Mexico*. Princeton: Princeton University Press.

Harris, Olivia, and Kate Young. 1981. Engendered Structures: Some Problems in the Analysis of Reproduction. In *The Anthropology of Pre-Capitalist Societies*, ed. Joel S. Kahn and Josep R. Llobera. London: Routledge and Kegan Paul.

Harvey, David. 1989. *The Condition of Postmodernity: An Enquiry into the Origins of Cultural Change*. Cambridge, Mass.: Blackwell.

Harvey, Neil. 1989. Corporatist Strategies and Popular Responses in Rural Mexico: State and Unions in Chiapas, 1968–1988. Ph.D. diss., University of Essex.

————. 1998. *The Chiapas Rebellion: The Struggle for Land and Democracy*. Durham: Duke University Press.

Harvey, Penelope. 1988. Muted or Ignored? Questions of Gender and Ethnicity in the Politics of the Southern Peruvian Andes. Paper presented at the Latin American Studies Association, 14th International Congress, March 17–19, New Orleans.

Heath Constable, Maria Joy. 1982. *Lucha de clases: La industria textil en Tlaxcala*. Mexico City: El Caballito.

Henestrosa, Andrés. 1993. The Forms of Sexual Life in Juchitán. In *Zapotec Struggles: Histories, Politics, and Representations from Juchitán, Oaxaca*, ed. Howard Campbell, Leigh Binford, Miguel Bartolomé, and Alicia Barabas. Washington, D.C.: Smithsonian Institution Press.

Hernández Castillo, Rosalva Aída. 1997. Between Hope and Adversity: The Struggle of Organized Women in Chiapas since the Zapatista Rebellion. *Journal of Latin American Anthropology* 3(1): 102–20.

————. 2001a. The Hopes and Challenges of the Women of Chiapas. In *The Other Word: Women and Violence in Chiapas Before and After Acteal*, ed. R. A. Hernández-Castillo. Copenhagen: International Working Group for Indigenous Affairs.

————. 2001b. Entre el esencialismo feminista y el esencialismo étnico: Génesis de un feminismo indígena en México. *Debate Feminista* 12(24), October.

Higgins, Michael. 1990. Martyrs and Virgins: Popular Religion in Mexico and Nicaragua. In Stephen and Dow 1990.

Higgins, Michael, and Tanya Coen. 2000. *Streets, Bedrooms, and Patios: The Ordinariness of Diversity in Urban Oaxaca: Ethnographic Portraits of the Urban Poor, Transvestites, Descapacitados, and Other Popular Cultures*. Austin: University of Texas Press.

Hirabayashi, Lane Ryo. 1983. On the Formation of Migrant Village Associations in Mexico: Mixtec and Mountain Zapotec in Mexico City. *Urban Anthropology* 12(1): 29–44.

————. 1993. *Cultural Capital: Mountain Zapotec Migrant Associations in Mexico City*. Tucson: University of Arizona Press.

————. 1994. Mountain Zapotec Migrants and Forms of Capital. *PoLAR (Political and Legal Anthropology Review)* 17(2): 105–16.

Holloman, Regina Evans. 1969. Developmental Change in San Blas. Ph.D. diss., Northwestern University.

Howe, James. 1986. *The Kuna Gathering: Contemporary Village Politics in Panama*. Austin: University of Texas Press.

Howell, Jayne. 1993. Education, Employment, and Economic Growth: New Directions for Rural Oaxacan Women. Ph.D. diss., State University of New York, Stonybrook.

Hu-DeHart, Evelyn. 1995. Chinese. In *The Encyclopedia of Mexico: History, Society, and Culture*, ed. Michael S. Werner. Chicago: Fitzroy Dearborn.

Hulshof, Marje. 1991. *Zapotec Moves: Networks and Remittances of U.S.-Bound Migrants from Oaxaca, Mexico*. Amsterdam: University of Amsterdam.

INEGI (Instituto Nacional de Estadística, Geografía e Informática). 1984. *Décimo censo general de población y vivienda, 1980*. Estado de Oaxaca. 2 vols. Mexico City: Dirección General de Integración y Análisis de la Información.

————. 1986. *La industria textil y del vestido en Mexico, 1976–1985*. Mexico City: Secretario de Programación y Presupuesto.

————. 2000. XII Censo General de Población y Vivienda 2000, Oaxaca. http://www.inego.bog.mx/difusioin/espanol/poblacion/definitivos/oaxa/indice.html (accessed May 11, 2003).

————. 2001. Encuesta Nacional de Empleo, 2000. Aguascalientes, Ags. http://www.inegi.com (accessed May 11, 2003).

Jackson, Jean. 1995. Culture, Genuine and Spurious: The Politics of Indianness in Vaupés, Colombia. *American Ethnologist* 22(1): 3–27.

Jaquette, Jane. 1994. *The Women's Movement in Latin America: Feminism and the Transition to Democracy*. Rev. ed. Boulder: Westview.

Jelin, Elizabeth. 1990. *Women and Social Change in Latin America*. London: Zed.

Jenson, Jane, and Boaventura de Sousa Santos. 2000. *Globalizing Institutions: Case Studies in Regulation and Innovation*. Burlington, Vt.: Ashgate.

Jeter, James, and Paula Marie Juelke. 1978. *The Saltillo Serape: An Exhibition Orga-nized by the Santa Barbara Museum of Art*. Santa Barbara, Calif.: New World Arts.

Johnston, Paul. 2001. The Emergence of Transnational Citizenship among Mex-ican Migrants in California. In *Citizenship Today: Global Perspectives and Practices*, ed. T. Alexander Aleinikoff and Douglas Klusmeyer. Washington: Carnegie Endowment for International Peace.

Kearney, Michael. 1972. *The Winds of Ixtepeji: World View and Society in a Zapotec Town*. New York: Holt, Rinehart and Winston.

———. 1991. Borders and Boundaries of States and Self at the End of Empire. *Journal of Historical Sociology* 4(1): 52–74.

———. 1995a. The Effects of Transnational Culture, Economy, and Migration on Mixtec Identity in Oaxacalifornia. In *The Bubbling Cauldron: Race, Ethnicity, and the Urban Crisis*, ed. Michael Peter Smith and Joe R. Feagin. Minneapo-lis: University of Minnesota Press.

———. 1995b. The Local and the Global: The Anthropology of Globalization and Transnationalism. *Annual Review of Anthropology* 24:547–65.

———. 1996a. *Reconceptualizing the Peasantry: Anthropology in Global Perspective*. Boulder: Westview.

———. 1996b. Transnationalism in California at End of Empire. In *Border Iden-tities: Nation and State at International Frontiers*, ed. Thomas Wilson and Hasting Donnan. Cambridge: Cambridge University Press.

Kemper, Robert. 1982. The Compadrazgo in Urban Mexico. *Anthropological Quarterly* 55:17–30.

Kirkby, Anne V. T. 1973. *The Use of Land and Water Resources in the Past and Present Valley of Oaxaca, Mexico*. Memoirs of the Museum of Anthropology, Univer-sity of Michigan, no. 5. Ann Arbor: University of Michigan Press.

Kiser, George, and Martha Woody Kiser. 1979. The Second Bracero Era (1942–1964). Introduction to *Mexican Workers in the United States*, ed. G. Kiser and M. W. Kiser. Albuquerque: University of New Mexico Press.

Kowalewski, Stephen A. 1976. Prehispanic Settlement Patterns of the Central Part of the Valley of Oaxaca, Mexico. Ph.D. diss., University of Arizona, Tucson.

Kumar, Krishna, ed. 2001. *Women and Civil War: Impact, Organizations, and Action*. Boulder: Lynne Rienner.

Labra, Armando. 1996. La migración hace Estados Unidos: El caso oaxaqueño. *Momentos Económicos* 86(1): 34–39.

Laclau, Ernesto, and Chantal Mouffe. 1985. *Hegemony and Socialist Strategy: Towards a Radical Democratic Politics*. Trans. Winston Moore and Paul Cammack. Lon-don: Verso.

Lenin, V. I. 1967. *Selected Works*. 3 vols. Vol. 3. New York: International Pub-lishers.

———. 1974. *The Development of Capitalism in Russia*. Moscow: Progress.

Leslie, Charles. 1960. *Now We Are Civilized: A Study of the World View of the Zapotec Indians of Mitla, Oaxaca.* Detroit: Wayne State University.

Levitt, Peggy. 2001. *The Transnational Villagers.* Berkeley: University of California Press.

Lewis, Laura. 1997. African Mexicans. In *The Encyclopedia of Mexico: History, Society, and Culture,* ed. Michael S. Werner. Chicago: Fitzroy Dearborn.

Leyva Solano, Xóchitl, and Gabriel Ascencio Franco. 1996. *Lacandona al filo del agua.* Mexico City: Centro de Investigaciones y Estudios Superiores en Antropología Social/San Cristóbal de Las Casas: Centro de Investigaciones Humanísticas de Mesoamérica y el Estado de Chiapas/Tuxtla Gutiérrez: Universidad de Ciencias y Artes del Estado de Chiapas/Mexico City: Fondo de Cultura Económica.

Lind, Amy. 1992. Power, Gender, and Development: Popular Women's Organizations and the Politics of Needs in Ecuador. In Escobar and Alvarez 1992.

Livas, Raúl, and Rafael Gamboa. 1998. The Local Response to the Decentralization of Infrastructure in Oaxaca. In *Integrating Regions: North America Faces Globalization,* ed. James W. Wilkie and Clint E. Smith. Guadalajara: Universidad de Guadalajara UCLA Program on Mexico, Centro Internacional Lucas Alemán para Crecimiento Económico.

Lomonitz, Larissa. 1977. *Networks and Marginality: Life in a Mexican Shantytown.* Stanford: Stanford University Press.

López, Felipe H., Luis Escala-Rabadan, and Raúl Hinojosa-Ojeda. 2001. Migrant Associations, Remittances, and Regional Development between Los Angeles and Oaxaca, Mexico. Research Report Series no. 10. Los Angeles: North American Integration and Development Center, School of Public Policy and Social Research, UCLA. http://naid.sppsr.ucla.edu

López, Felipe, and David Runsten. 2004. Mixtecs and Zapotec Working in California: Rural and Urban Experiences. In *Indigenous Mexican Migrants in the United States,* ed. Jonathan Fox and Gaspar Rivera-Salgado. La Jolla: Center for U.S.-Mexican Studies and Center for Comparative Immigration Studies, University of California, San Diego.

López, Rick. 2002. The Morrows in Mexico: Nationalist Politics, Foreign Patronage, and the Promotion of Mexican Popular Arts. In *Casa Mañana: The Morrow Collection of Mexican Popular Arts,* ed. Susan Danly. Albuquerque: University of New Mexico Press.

Lowe, Lisa. 1996. *Immigrant Acts: On Asian American Cultural Politics.* Durham: Duke University Press.

Lozano, Rafael Cruz, and María Teresa Vargas. 1982. Análisis para la creación de un centro de convenciones en la ciudad de Oaxaca. B.A. thesis, Instituto Tecnológico de Oaxaca.

Lynd, Martha. 2000. The International Craft Market: A Double-Edged Sword for Guatemalan Maya Women. In Grimes and Milgram 2000.

Malinowski, Bronislaw, and Julio de la Fuente. 1982. *Malinowski in Mexico: The*

Economics of a Mexican Market System. Ed. Susan Drucker-Brown. London: Routledge and Kegan Paul.

Mallon, Florencia. 1995. *Peasant and Nation: The Making of Postcolonial Mexico and Peru.* Berkeley: University of California Press.

——. 1996. Constructing Mestizaje in Latin America: Authenticity, Marginality, and Gender in the Claiming of Ethnic Identities. *Journal of Latin American Anthropology* 2(2): 170–81.

Marcus, Joyce. 1998. *Women's Ritual in Formative Oaxaca: Figurine-Making, Divination, Death, and the Ancestors.* Vol. 11 of *Prehistory and Human Ecology of the Valley of Oaxaca,* ed. Kent V. Flannery. Ann Arbor: University of Michigan Museum of Anthropology.

Marcus, Joyce, and Kent V. Flannery. 1996. *Zapotec Civilization: How Urban Society Evolved into Mexico's Oaxaca Valley.* London: Thames and Hudson.

Margolis, J. 1979. El papel de la mujer en la agricultura del Bajío. *Iztapalapa* 1(1): 158–69.

Marroquín, Alejandro D. 1977. *Balance del indigenismo: Informe sobre la política indigenista en América.* Mexico City: Instituto Indigenista Interamericano.

Martínez del Campo, M. 1985. *Industrialización en México: Hacia un análisis crítico.* Mexico City: Colegio de México.

Martínez Ríos, Jorge. 1964. Análisis funcional de la "Guelaguetza Agrícola." *Revista Mexicana de Sociología* 26(1): 79–125.

Marx, Karl. 1881/1967. *Capital.* 3 vols. New York: International Publishers.

Massey, Douglas, Luin Goldring, and Jorge Durand. 1994. Continuities in Transnational Migration: An Analysis of Nineteen Mexican Communities. *American Journal of Sociology* 99(6): 1492–1533.

Massolo, Alejandra. 1998. Women in the Local Arena and Municipal Power. In Rodríguez 1998.

Mathews, Holly F. 1982. Sexual Status in Oaxaca, Mexico: An Analysis of the Relationship between Extradomestic Participation and Ideological Constructs of Gender. Ph.D. diss., Duke University.

——. 1985. "We Are Mayordomo": A Reinterpretation of Women's Roles in the Mexican Cargo System. *American Ethnologist* 17:285–301.

Mattiace, Shannan L. 2003. *To See with Two Eyes: Peasant Activism and Indian Autonomy in Chiapas, Mexico.* Albuquerque: University of New Mexico Press.

M'Closkey, Kathy. 2002. *Swept under the Rug: A Hidden History of Navajo Weaving.* Albuquerque: University of New Mexico Press.

Medina Hernández, Andrés. 1983. Los grupos étnicos y los sistemas tradicionales de poder en México. *Nueva Antropología* 5(20): 5–29.

Mercado García, Alfonso. 1980. *Estructura y dinamismo del mercado de tecnología industrial en México.* Mexico City: Colegio de México.

Merry, Sally Engle. 1997. Legal Pluralism and Transnational Culture: The *Ka Ho'okolokolonui Kanaka Maoli* Tribunal, Hawai'i, 1993. In *Human Rights, Cul-*

ture, and Context: Anthropological Perspectives, ed. Richard A. Wilson. London: Pluto.

———. 2003a. Human-Rights Law and the Demonization of Culture. *Anthropology News* 44(2): 4–5.

———. 2003b. Hegemony and Culture in Historical Anthropology: A Review Essay on Jean and John L. Comaroff's *Of Revelation and Revolution. American Historical Review* 108(2): 460–70.

Mexico Solidarity Network. 2002. Weekly News and Analysis, August 12–18, 2002. http://www.mexicosolidarity.org/ (accessed August 19, 2002).

Mies, Maria. 1982. *The Lace Makers of Narsapur: Indian Housewives Produce for the World Market*. London: Zed.

Milgram, Lynne B. 2000. Reorganizing Textile Production for the Global Market: Women's Craft Cooperatives in Ifugad, Upland Philippines. In Grimes and Milgram 2000.

Miller, Arthur. 1995. *The Painted Tombs of Oaxaca, Mexico: Living with the Dead*. Cambridge: Cambridge University Press.

Mintz, Sidney W., and Eric Wolf. 1950. An Analysis of Ritual Coparenthood (Compadrazgo). *Southwestern Journal of Anthropology* 6:341–65.

Molyneux, Maxine. 2003. *Women's Movements in International Perspective: Latin America and Beyond*. London: Institute of Latin American Studies.

Montoya, Rosario, Lessie Jo Frazier, and Janise Hurtig, eds. 2002. *Gender's Place: Feminist Anthropologies of Latin America*. New York: Palgrave Macmillan.

Morris, Walter F. 1986. Crafts, Crap, and Art: The Marketing of Maya Textiles in Highland Chiapas, Mexico. Unpublished manuscript.

Munck, Ronaldo. 1985. *Politics and Dependency in the Third World*. London: Zed.

Murphey, Arthur D., and Alex Stepick. 1999. *Social Inequality in Oaxaca: A History of Resistance and Change*. Philadelphia: Temple University Press.

Nader, Laura. 1964. *Talea and Juquila: A Comparison of Zapotec Social Organization*. University of California Publications in American Archaeology and Ethnology, vol. 48, no. 3: 195–296. Berkeley: University of California Press.

———. 1990. *Harmony Ideology: Justice and Control in a Zapotec Mountain Village*. Stanford: Stanford University Press.

Nagengast, Marian Carole. 1990. *The Polish Paradox: Rural Class, Culture, and the State*. Boulder: Westview.

Naples, Nancy. 2002. Changing the Terms: Community Activity, Globalization, and the Dilemmas of Transnational Feminist Praxis. In Naples and Desai 2002.

Naples, Nancy, and Manisha Desai, eds. 2002. *Women's Activism and Globalization: Linking Local Struggles and Transnational Politics*. New York: Routledge.

Nash, June. 1970. *In the Eyes of the Ancestors: Belief and Behavior in a Maya Community*. New Haven: Yale University Press.

———. 1986. A Decade of Research on Women in Latin America. In Nash and Safa 1986.

————. 1989. *From Tank Town to High Tech: The Class of Community and Corporate Cycles*. New York: Columbia University Press.

————. 1993a. Introduction: Traditional Arts and Changing Markets in Middle America. In Nash 1993.

————. 1993b. Maya Household Production in the World Market: The Potters of Amatenango del Valle, Chiapas. In Nash 1993.

————. 2000. Postscript: To Market, to Market. In Grimes and Milgram 2000.

————. 2001. *Mayan Visions: The Quest for Autonomy in an Age of Globalization*. New York: Routledge.

————, ed. 1993. *Crafts in the World Market: The Impact of Global Exchange on Middle American Artisans*. Albany: State University of New York Press.

Nash, June, and Helen Safa, eds. 1986. *Women and Change in Latin America*. South Hadley, Mass.: Bergin and Garvey.

Novelo, Victoria. 1976. *Artesanías y capitalismo en México*. Mexico City: SEP-INAH.

————. 1988. Las artesanías en México. Paper presented at the 46th International Congress of Americanists, July 4–8, Amsterdam.

Novo, Salvador. 1932. Nuestras artes populares. *Nuestro México* 1(5): 56.

Nutini, Hugo. 1984. *Ritual Kinship: Ideological and Structural Integration of the Compadrazgo System in Rural Tlaxcala*. Vol. 2. Princeton: Princeton University Press.

Nutini, Hugo G., and Betty Bell. 1980. *Ritual Kinship: The Structure and Historical Development of the Compadrazgo System in Rural Tlaxcala*. Vol. 1. Princeton: Princeton University Press.

Nutini, Hugo, and Timothy Murphy. 1970. Labor Migration and Family Structure in the Tlaxcalan-Pueblan Area, Mexico. In *The Social Anthropology of Latin America*, ed. Walter Goldschmidt and Harry Hoijer. Los Angeles: Latin American Center, University of California.

Oaxaca, Estado de. 2002. Atlas Agrario: Estado de Oaxaca. Oaxaca: Secretaría de Asuntos Indígenas, Secretaría de la Reforma Agraria, Instituto Nacional Indigenista.

Oles, James. 2002. Business or Pleasure: Exhibiting Mexican Folk Art, 1830–1930. In *Casa Mañana: The Morrow Collection of Mexican Popular Arts*, ed. Susan Danly. Albuquerque: University of New Mexico Press.

Omi, Michael, and Howard Winant. 1986. *Racial Formation in the United States: From the 1960s to the 1980s*. New York: Routledge and Kegan Paul.

O'Nell, Carl W. 1979. Nonviolence and Personality Dispositions among the Zapotec. *Journal of Psychological Anthropology* 2:301–22.

————. 1981. Hostility Management and the Control of Aggression in a Zapotec Community. *Aggressive Behavior* 7:351–66.

————. 1986. Primary and Secondary Effects of Violence Control among the Nonviolent Zapotec. *Anthropological Quarterly* 59(4): 184–203.

Ong, Aiwa. 1999. *Flexible Citizenship: The Cultural Logics of Transnationality*. Durham: Duke University Press.

Oudijk, Michel. 2000. Historiography of the Bènizàa: The Postclassic and Early

Colonial Periods (1000–1600 A.D.). Leiden: Research School of Asian, African, and Amerindian Studies, University of Leiden.

Paddock, John. 1982. Confluence in Zapotec and Mixtec Ethnohistories: The 1580 Mapa de Macuilxóchitl. In *Native American Ethnohistory* 2:345–58. Papers in Anthropology, Department of Anthropology, University of Oklahoma.

Parnell, Phillip. 1988. *Escalating Disputes: Social Participation and Change in the Oaxacan Highlands*. Tucson: University of Arizona Press.

Parrish, Timothy. 1982. Class Structure and Social Reproduction in New Spain / Mexico. *Dialectical Anthropology* 7:115–36.

Parsons, Elsie Clews. 1936. *Mitla: Town of Souls*. Chicago: University of Chicago Press.

Partido Feminista Revolucionario de Tabasco. 1933. *Tabasco feminista* (March). In the permanent collection of the Bancroft Library, University of California, Berkeley.

Peterson Royce, Anya. 1975. *Prestigio y afiliación en una comunidad urbana: Juchitán, Oaxaca*. Mexico City: Instituto Nacional Indigenista.

————. 1982. *Ethnic Identity: Strategies of Diversity*. Bloomington: Indiana University Press.

Portes, Alejandro. 1984. The Rise of Ethnicity. *American Sociological Review* 49(3): 383–97.

Preston, Julia. 1996. Mexico and Insurgent Group Reach Pact on Indian Rights. *New York Times*, February 1, A12.

Primer Congreso Feminista de Yucatán. 1917. *Primer congreso feminista de Yucatán convocado por el governador y comandante militar de Estado Gral. D. Salvador Alvarado, 13–16 enero de 1916*. Mérida: Ateneo Peninsular. In the permanent collection of the Bancroft Library, University of California, Berkeley.

Radcliffe, Sarah. 1988. Así es una mujer del pueblo: Low-Income Women's Organizations under APRA, 1985–87: The Case of the Domestic Servants. Paper presented at the Latin American Studies Association, 14th International Congress, March 17–19, New Orleans.

Raisz, Katherine. 1986. Wooing Industry to Oaxaca: A Long-Term Project. *Mexico City News*, January 13, 39.

Ramírez Cuevas, Jesús. 2001. En mitín de pueblos diferentes, indígenas oaxaqueños sellan pacto con los rebeldes. Desbordante recibimiento en Juchitán. *La Jornada* (Mexico City), February 1. http://www.jornada.unam.mx/2001/feb01/010226/005n1pol.html (accessed February 3, 2005).

Redfield, Robert, and Sol Tax. 1952. General Characteristics of Present-Day Mesoamerican Indian Society. In *Heritage of Conquest*, ed. Sol Tax. Glencoe, Ill.: Free Press.

Relaciones geográficas de la Diócesis de Oaxaca. 1981. *Papeles de Nueva España, segunda serie. Geografía y estadística: Relaciones Geográficas de la Diócesis de Oaxaca — Manuscritos de la Real Academa de la Historia de Madrid y del Archivo de Indias en Sevilla, años 1579–1581*. Mexico: Editorial Innovación.

Reyes Morales, Rafael, and Alicia Silvia Gijón Cruz. 2002. Migration, Remittance, and Economic Development between Oaxaca and California (Preliminary Version). Oaxaca: Instituto Tecnológico de Oaxaca.

Rivera-Salgado, Gaspar. 1999a. Mixtec Activism in Oaxacalifornia: Transborder Grassroots Political Strategies. *American Behavioral Scientist* 42(9): 1439–1458.

———. 1999b. Welcome to Oaxacalifornia: Transnational Political Strategies among Mexican Indigenous Migrants. Ph.D. diss., University of California, Santa Cruz.

———. 2000. Transnational Political Strategies: The Case of Mexican Indigenous Migrants. In *Immigration Research for a New Century: Multidisciplinary Perspectives*, ed. Nancy Foner, Rubén G. Rumbaut, and Steven J. Gold. New York: Russell Sage Foundation.

Rivera-Sanchez, Liliana. 2004. Expressions of Identity and Belonging: Mexican Immigrants in New York. In *Indigenous Mexican Migrants in the United States*, ed. Jonathan Fox and Gaspar Rivera-Salgado. La Jolla: Center for U.S.-Mexican Studies and Center for Comparative Immigration Studies, University of California, San Diego.

Robbins, Edward. 1975. Ethnicity or Class? Social Relations in a Small Canadian Industrial Community. In *The New Ethnicity: Perspectives from Ethnology, 1973 Proceedings of the American Ethnological Society*, ed. John W. Bennet. New York: West.

Rodríguez, Victoria E. 2003. *Women in Contemporary Mexican Politics*. Austin: University of Texas Press.

———, ed. 1998. *Women's Participation in Mexican Political Life*. Boulder: Westview.

Romero Frizzi, María de los Angeles. 1988. Epoca colonial (1519–1785). In *Historia de la cuestión agraria mexicana: Estado de Oaxaca*, ed. Leticia Reina. Oaxaca: Universidad Autónoma Benito Juárez de Oaxaca.

Rosaldo, Michelle Zimbalist. 1974. Woman, Culture, and Society: A Theoretical Overview. In *Woman, Culture, and Society*, ed. M. Z. Rosaldo and Louise Lamphere. Stanford: Stanford University Press.

Rosaldo, Renato. 1997. Cultural Citizenship, Inequality, and Multiculturalism. In Flores and Benmayor 1997.

Roseberry, William. 1989. *Anthropologies and Histories: Essays in Culture, History, and Political Economy*. New Brunswick: Rutgers University Press.

Rosenbaum, Brenda. 2000. Of Women, Hope, and Angels: Fair Trade and Artisan Production in a Squatter Settlement in Guatemala City. In Grimes and Milgram 2000.

Rothstein, Frances Abrahamer. 1982. *Three Different Worlds: Women, Men, and Children in an Industrializing Community*. Westport, Conn.: Greenwood.

———. 1999. Declining Odds: Kinship, Women's Employment, and Political Economy in Rural Mexico. *American Anthropologist* 101(3): 579–93.

————. 2005. Challenging Consumption Theory: Production and Consumption in Central Mexico. *Critique of Anthropology* 25(1).

Rouse, Roger. 1992. Making Sense of Settlement: Class Transformation, Cultural Struggle, and Transnationalism among Mexican Migrants in the United States. *Annals of the New York Academy of Sciences* 645 (July): 25–52.

————. 1994. Questions of Identity: Personhood and Collectivity in Transnational Migration to the United States. *Critical Anthropology* 15(5): 351–80.

Rovira, Guiomar. 2000. *Women of Maize: Indigenous Women and the Zapatista Rebellion.* Trans. Anna Keene. London: Latin American Bureau.

Rubin, Jeffrey W. 1997. *Decentering the Regime: Ethnicity, Radicalism, and Democracy in Juchitán, Mexico.* Durham: Duke University Press.

Ruiz Campbell, Obdulia. 1993. Representations of Isthmus Women: A Zapotec Woman's Point of View. In *Zapotec Struggles: Histories, Politics, and Representations from Juchitán, Oaxaca,* ed. Howard Campbell, Leigh Binford, Miguel Bartolomé, and Alicia Barabas. Washington, D.C.: Smithsonian Institution Press.

Rus, Jan, Rosalva Aída Hernández Castillo, and Shannan L. Mattiace. 2003. *Mayan Lives, Mayan Utopias: The Indigenous Peoples of Chiapas and the Zapatista Rebellion.* Lanham, Md.: Rowan and Littlefield.

Rymph, David. 1974. Cross-Sex Behavior in an Isthmus Zapotec Village. Paper presented at the annual meeting of the American Anthropological Association, Mexico City.

Sacks, Karen Brodkin. 1988. *Caring by the Hour: Women, Work, and Organizing at Duke Medical Center.* Urbana: University of Illinois Press.

Safa, Helen. 1983. Women, Production, and Reproduction in Industrial Capitalism: A Comparison of Brazilian and U.S. Factory Workers. In *Women, Men, and the International Division of Labor,* ed. June Nash and M. Patricia Fernández Kelly. Albany: State University of New York Press.

————. 1995. *The Myth of the Male Breadwinner: Women and Industrialization in the Caribbean.* Boulder: Westview.

Salinas, Gloria Ardaya. 1986. Women's Equality and the Cuban Revolution. In Nash and Safa 1986.

Salomon, Frank. 1981. Weavers of Otavalo. In *Cultural Transformations and Ethnicity in Modern Ecuador,* ed. Norman E. Whitten Jr. Urbana: University of Illinois Press.

Salvucci, Richard J. 1987. *Textiles and Capitalism in Mexico: An Economic History of the Obrajes, 1539–1840.* Princeton: Princeton University Press.

San Andrés Accords. 1999. San Andrés Accords on Indigenous Rights and Culture. Trans. Lynn Stephen and Jonathan Fox. *Cultural Survival Quarterly* 12(1): 33–38.

Sapir, Edward. 1956. Culture, Genuine and Spurious. In *Language, Culture, and Personality: Selected Essays,* ed. David G. Mandelbaum. Berkeley: University of California Press.

Sault, Nicole. 1985a. Zapotec Godmothers: The Centrality of Women for Compadrazgo Groups in a Village of Oaxaca, Mexico. Ph.D. diss., University of California, Los Angeles.

———. 1985b. Baptismal Sponsorship as a Source of Power for Zapotec Women in Oaxaca, Mexico. *Journal of Latin American Lore* 11(2): 225–43.

———. 1987. Godparenthood in Latin America, Joining Kinship and Gender. Paper presented at the Annual Meeting of the American Anthropological Association, November 18–22, Chicago.

———. 2001. Godparenthood Ties among Zapotec Women and the Effects of Protestant Conversion. In *Holy Saints and Fiery Preachers: The Anthropology of Protestantism in Mexico and Central America*, ed. James W. Dow and Alan R. Sandstrom. Westport, Conn.: Praeger.

Scher, Phillip. 2003. *Carnival and the Formation of a Caribbean Transnation*. Gainesville: University of Florida Press.

Secretaría de Agricultura y Recursos Hidráulicos, Oaxaca. 1977, 1978, 1982, 1983. Datos definitivos de cultivos cíclicos. Dirección General de Economía Agrícola, Departamento de Estadística Agropecuaria Nacional Producción y Cultivos.

Secretaría de la Economía Nacional. 1934. *La industria textil en Mexico: El problema obrero y los problemas económicos*. Mexico City: Talleres Gráficos de la Nación.

Secretaría de Programación y Presupuesto. 1979–85. Cuestionario de inscripciones, inicio de cursos. Dirección General de Estadística. Oaxaca.

———. 1981. Carta de precipitación total anual. Mexico City.

Segura, Jaime Jesús. 1979. Vinculación estado y sistema de cargos en una comunidad: Teotitlán del Valle. B.A. thesis, Centro de Sociología, Universidad Autonóma Benito Juárez de Oaxaca.

———. 1980. El sistema de cargos en Teotitlán del Valle, Oaxaca. In *Sociedad y política en Oaxaca, 1980*. Barcelona: ICARIA.

Selby, Henry. 1974. *Zapotec Deviance: The Convergence of Folk and Modern Sociology*. Austin: University of Texas Press.

Sider, Gerald. 1976. Lumbee Indian Cultural Nationalism and Ethnogenesis. *Dialectical Anthropology* 1(2): 161–71.

———. 1986. *Culture and Class in Anthropology and History: A Newfoundland Illustration*. Cambridge: Cambridge University Press.

Siebold, Katharine. 1987. Women's Networks in Choquecancha, Cuzco, Peru. Paper presented at the Annual Meeting of the American Anthropological Association, November 18–22, Chicago.

Sierra, María Teresa. 2002. The Challenge to Diversity in Mexico: Human Rights, Gender, and Ethnicity. Working Paper no. 49. Halle: Max Planck Institute for Social Anthropology.

Silverblatt, Irene. 1987. *Moon, Sun, and Witches: Gender Ideologies and Class in Inca and Colonial Peru*. Princeton: Princeton University Press.

Silverman, Sydel. 1966. An Ethnographic Approach to Social Stratification: Prestige in a Central Italian Community. *American Anthropologist* 68: 899–921.

Smith, Carol. 1984. Does a Commodity Economy Enrich the Few while Ruining the Masses? *Journal of Peasant Studies* 12(3): 60–95.

Smith, Richard Chase. 1985. A Search for Unity within Diversity: Peasant Unions, Ethnic Federations, and Indianist Movements in the Andean Republics. In *Native Peoples and Economic Development*, ed. Theodore Macdonald Jr. Cambridge, Mass.: Cultural Survival.

Smith, Robert. 1996. Immigration, Race, and Social Location: An Analysis of the Contingent Futures of Mexicans in New York City. In *Latinos in New York: Communities in Transition*, ed. Gabriel Haspil-Viera and Sherrie L. Baver. South Bend: University of Notre Dame Press.

———. 1998. Transnational Localities: Community, Technology, and the Politics of Membership within the Context of Mexico and U.S. Migration. In *Transnationalism from Below*, ed. Michael Peter Smith and Luis Eduardo Guarnizo. New Brunswick, N.J.: Transaction.

Sousa, Lisa Mary. 1997. Women and Crime in Colonial Oaxaca: Evidence of Complementary Gender Roles in Mixtec and Zapotec Societies. In *Indian Women of Early Mexico*, ed. Susan Schroeder, Stephanie Wood, and Robert Haskett. Norman: University of Oklahoma Press.

Speed, Shannon. Forthcoming. Rights at the Intersection: Gender and Ethnicity in Neoliberal Mexico. In *Dissident Women: Gender and Cultural Politics in Chiapas*, ed. Shannon Speed, R. Aida Hernández, and Lynn Stephen. Austin: University of Texas Press.

Spicer, Edward. 1971. Persistent Cultural Systems: A Comparative Study of Identity Systems That Can Adapt to Contrasting Environments. *Science* 174: 795–800.

Spooner, Brian. 1986. Weavers and Dealers: The Authenticity of an Oriental Carpet. In *The Social Life of Things: Commodities in Cultural Perspective*, ed. Arjun Appadurai. New York: Cambridge University Press.

Starr, Frederick. 1899. *Catalogue of a Collection of Objects Illustrating the Folklore of Mexico*. London: Folklore Society.

———. 1899–1900. Notes upon the Ethnography of Southern Mexico. *Proceedings of the Davenport Academy of Sciences* 8.

Stavenhagen, Rodolfo. 1975. *Social Classes in Agrarian Societies*. Trans. Judith Adler Hellman. Garden City, N.Y.: Anchor/Doubleday.

Stephen, Lynn. 1987a. Weaving Changes. Ph.D. diss., Brandeis University.

———. 1987b. Zapotec Weavers of Oaxaca: Development and Community Control. *Cultural Survival Quarterly* 11(1): 46–48.

———. 1988. Production, Social Reproduction, and Gender Roles in Zapotec Craft Production. Paper presented at the 46th International Congress of Americanists, July 4–8, Amsterdam.

————. 1989a. Anthropology and the Politics of Facts, Knowledge, and History. *Dialectical Anthropology* 14:259–69.

————. 1989b. Popular Feminism in Mexico. *Z Magazine* 2(12): 102–6.

————. 1990. The Politics of Ritual: The Mexican State and Zapotec Autonomy, 1926–1989. In Stephen and Dow 1990.

————. 1991a. Culture as a Resource: Four Cases of Self-Managed Indigenous Craft Production. *Economic Development and Cultural Change* 40(1): 101–30.

————. 1991b. Export Markets and Their Effects on Indigenous Craft Production: The Case of the Weavers of Teotitlán del Valle, Mexico. In *Textile Traditions of Mesoamerica and the Andes: An Anthology*, ed. Margo Blum Schevill, Janet Catherine Berlo, and Edward Dwyer. New York: Garland.

————. 1991c. Zapotec Gender Politics: Gender and Class in the Political Participation of Indigenous Mexican Women. Working Papers on Women in International Development, no. 216. East Lansing: Office of International Development, Michigan State University.

————. 1993. Weaving in the Fast Lane: Class, Ethnicity, and Gender in Zapotec Craft Commercialization. In Nash 1993.

————. 1996. Too Little Too Late: The Impact of Article 27 on Women in Oaxaca. In *The Reform of the Mexican Agrarian Reform*, ed. Laura Randall. Armonk, N.Y.: M. E. Sharpe.

————. 1997a. *Women and Social Movements in Latin America: Power from Below*. Austin: University of Texas Press.

————. 1997b. Redefined Nationalism in Building a Movement for Indigenous Autonomy in Mexico: Oaxaca and Chiapas. *Journal of Latin American Anthropology* 3(1): 72–101.

————. 1997c. The Zapatista Opening: The Movement for Indigenous Autonomy and State Discourses on Indigenous Rights in Mexico, 1970–1996. *Journal of Latin American Anthropology* 2(2): 2–39.

————. 1998. Gender and Grassroots Organizing: Lessons from Chiapas. In Rodríguez 1998.

————. 2000. The Construction of Indigenous Suspects: Militarization and the Gendered and Ethnic Dynamics of Human Rights Abuses in Southern Mexico. *American Ethnologist* 26(4): 822–42.

————. 2002. *Zapata Lives! Histories and Cultural Politics in Southern Mexico*. Berkeley: University of California Press.

————. 2005. Defining Indigenous Rights and Human Rights at the Local Level: Conflicts and Lessons from Oaxaca. *Political and Legal Anthropology Review* 28(1): 133–50.

Stephen, Lynn, and James Dow, eds. 1990. *Class, Politics, and Popular Religion: Religious Change in Mexico and Central America*. Washington, D.C.: American Anthropological Association.

Stern, Alexandra. 1997. Eugenics. In *The Encyclopedia of Mexico: History, Society, and Culture*, ed. Michael S. Werner. Chicago: Fitzroy Dearborn.

Stern, Steve J. 1982. *Peru's Peoples and the Challenges of Spanish Conquest: Huamanga to 1640.* Madison: University of Wisconsin Press.

———. 1987. New Approaches to the Study of Peasant Rebellion and Consciousness: Implications of the Andean Experience. In *Resistance, Rebellion, and Consciousness in the Andean Peasant World, 18th to 20th Centuries,* ed. S. Stern. Madison: University of Wisconsin Press.

Tamayo, Jorge L. 1960. *Oaxaca: Breve monografía geográfica anexa a la carta municipal.* Mexico City: Instituto Panamericano de Geografía e Historia.

———. 1982. *Geografía de Oaxaca.* Mexico City: Comisión Editora de El National, Cooperativa de Talleres Gráficos de la Nación.

Taylor, Robert B. 1960. Teotitlán del Valle: A Typical Mesoamerican Community. Ph.D. diss., University of Oregon.

———. 1966. Conservative Factors in the Changing Culture of a Zapotec Town. *Human Organization* 25(2): 116–21.

Taylor, William B. 1972. *Landlord and Peasant in Colonial Oaxaca.* Stanford: Stanford University Press.

———. 1979. *Drinking, Homicide, and Rebellion in Colonial Mexican Villages.* Stanford: Stanford University Press.

Tice, Karin E. 1995. *Kuna Crafts, Gender, and the Global Economy.* Austin: University of Texas Press.

Turkenik, Carol. 1976. Agricultural Production Strategies in a Mexican Peasant Community. Ph.D. diss., University of California, Los Angeles.

United Nations Secretariat. 1984. Population Distribution, Migration, and Development: Highlights on the Issues in the Context of the World Population Plan of Action. In *Population Distribution, Migration and Development, International Conference on Population.* New York.

U.S. Embassy, Mexico City. 2001. The U.S. and Mexico at a Glance: General Information. http://www.usembassy-mexico.gov/eataglance1.htm (accessed May 14, 2003).

van den Berghe, Pierre L. 1981. *The Ethnic Phenomenon.* New York: Elsevier.

Varese, Stefano. 1982. Restoring Multiplicity: Indianities and the Civilizing Project in Latin America. *Latin American Perspectives* 9(2): 29–41.

———. 1988. Multi-ethnicity and Hegemonic Construction: Indian Projects and the Global Future. In *Ethnicities and Nations: Processes of Interethnic Relations in Latin America, Southeast Asia, and the Pacific,* ed. Remo Guidieri, Francesco Pellizzi, and Stanley J. Tambiah. Austin: University of Texas Press.

Vargas-Barón, Emily. 1968. Development and Change of Rural Artisanry: Weaving Industries of the Oaxaca Valley, Mexico. Ph.D. diss., Stanford University.

Vasconcelos, José. 1979. *The Cosmic Race: A Bilingual Edition.* Trans. Didier T. Jaén. 1925. Baltimore: Johns Hopkins University Press.

Velasco Ortiz, Laura. 2002. *El regreso de la comunidad: Migración indígena y agentes étnicos.* Tijuana: El Colegio de la Frontera Norte.

Vogt, Evon A. 1969. *Zinacantán: A Maya Community in the Highlands of Chiapas.* Cambridge: Harvard University Press.

Volkman, Toby Alice. 1984. Great Performances: Torojo Cultural Identity in the 1970s. *American Ethnologist* 11(1): 152–69.

————. 1985. *Fiestas of Honor: Ritual and Change in the Toroja Highlands.* Urbana: University of Illinois Press.

Walter, Lynn. 1981. Social Strategies and the Fiesta Complex in an Otavaleño Community. *American Ethnologist* 2:172–85.

Warren, Kay B., and Jean E. Jackson. 2002. Introduction: Studying Indigenous Activism in Latin America. In *Indigenous Movements, Self-Representation, and the State in Latin America*, ed. K. Warren and J. Jackson. Austin: University of Texas Press.

Wasserstrom, Robert. 1983. *Class and Society in Central Chiapas.* Berkeley: University of California Press.

Weist, R. E. 1973. Wage-Labour Migration and the Household in a Mexican Town. *Journal of Anthropological Research* 29(3): 236–47.

Welte, Cecil. 1965. *Mapa de las localidades del Valle de Oaxaca.* Oaxaca: Oficina de Estudios de Humanidad del Valle de Oaxaca.

Whitecotton, Joseph W. 1977. *The Zapotecs: Princes, Priests, and Peasants.* Norman: University of Oklahoma Press.

Williams, Brackette. 1989. A Class Act: Anthropology and the Race to Nation across Ethnic Terrain. *Annual Review of Anthropology* 18:401–44.

Williams, Raymond. 1977. *Marxism and Literature.* Oxford: Oxford University Press.

————. 1987. Changing Power and Authority in Gender Roles. Ph.D. diss., Indiana University.

————. 1994. Selections from *Marxism and Literature.* In *Culture/Power/History*, ed. Nicholas B. Dirks, Geoff Eley, and Sherry Ortner. Princeton: Princeton University Press.

Winter, Marcus. 1977. El impacto teotihuacano y procesos de cambio en Oaxaca. In *Los procesos de cambio: XV Mesa Redonda.* Guanajuato: Sociedad Mexicana de Antropología.

Wolf, Eric. 1959. *Sons of the Shaking Earth.* Chicago: University of Chicago Press.

————. 1986. The Vicissitudes of the Closed Corporate Peasant Community. *American Ethnologist* 13(2): 320–25.

Wood, William Warner. 1995. Zapotec Artisans: The Genealogy of an "Other." Paper presented at the Annual Meeting of the American Anthropological Association, November 15–18, Washington.

————. 1996. Teotitlán del Valle: A Maquiladora in Oaxaca, Mexico. Paper presented at the Annual Meeting of the American Anthropological Association, November 19–23, San Francisco.

————. 1997. To Learn Weaving below the Rock: Making Zapotec Textiles and Artisans in Teotitlán del Valle. Ph.D. diss., University of Illinois.

————. 2000a. Flexible Production, Households, and Fieldwork: Multisited Zapotec Weavers in the Era of Late Capitalism. *Ethnology* 39(2): 133–48.

————. 2000b. Stories from the Field: Handicraft Production and Mexican National Patrimony: A Lesson in Translocality from B. Traven. *Ethnology* 39(3): 183–203.

————. 2001. Rapport Is Overrated: Southwestern Ethnic Art Dealers and Ethnographers in the "Field." *Qualitative Inquiry* 7(4): 484–503.

————. 2003. Textiles oaxaqueñas: Arte indigena "falso" y la "invación" mexicana a la Tierra del Encanto. *Cuadernos del Sur* 9(19): 19–33.

Wright, Erik Olin. 1979. *Class Structure and Income Determination*. New York: Academic Press.

————. 1985. *Classes*. London: Verso.

Young, Kate. 1976. The Social Setting of Migration. Ph.D. diss., London University.

————. 1978. Modes of Appropriation and the Sexual Division of Labour: A Case Study from Oaxaca, Mexico. In *Feminism and Materialism: Women and Modes of Production*, ed. Annette Kuhn and Ann Marie Wolpe. London: Routledge and Kegan Paul.

Yúdice, George. 2003. *The Expediency of Culture: Uses of Culture in the Global Era*. Durham: Duke University Press.

labor, 175, 200–201, 220; control of the means of production, 42–43; direct dealings with U.S. importers, 134, 167–69, 187, 199, 211; financial management, 213–14, 214*t*; gendered roles, 150, 152, 209–15; growth under commercial capitalism, 132, 143–44, 144*t*, 152, 172, 198–99; *guelaguetza* exchanges, 274–75, 275*t*; inherited assets, 174, 199; *mayordomía* obligations, 124–25; mercantile capital, 34–36; paid labor, 88, 124–25, 145, 152, 175, 260–61, 334 n.4 (ch. 3); piecework system, 7, 42–43, 145, 175; ritual life, 34, 88, 260–61, 277–81, 277*t*, 334 n.4 (ch. 3); three types, 173–74; transitions from weaver class, 64–68, 176–77; unpaid labor, 75, 175, 210, 225–28; wealth and status, 34, 287–94, 289–91*t*; women's oral histories, 72–76; on women's political participation, 297–304, 297–99*t*, 301–2*t*; yarn dyeing, 181
Merry, Sally Engle, 17–18
mescal, 341
mestizos, 24–25, 341
metates, 156, 198, 337 n.2 (ch. 6), 341
Mexican Arts Association, 162
"Mexican Indian" images. *See* Indianness
Mexico. *See* state-level government
Mies, Maria, 149
migration, 11, 96–98, 330–31; accumulation of capital, 176–77; border crossings, 78, 82, 334 n.3 (ch. 3); *bracero* program, 11, 36–37, 97, 122–23, 145–50, 335 n.8, 339; cars and trucks, 92; ethnic identity, 18–20, 25, 30–31; *guelaguetza* exchanges, 275–77; home-building in Teotitlán, 102, 311; hometown associations, 60, 305; Immigration Reform Act of 1986, 148; NAFTA,

96; respect, 48; returns to Teotitlán, 97–98, 200, 204, 215–16; ritual life, 253–54, 275–77; role of women as weavers, 207–15; of women, 7, 150–51, 200, 204, 215–16; women's oral histories, 78–85. *See also* transnationalism
Milgram, Lynne, 203
Mitla, 112–13, 142
mixed cooperatives, 224, 225*f*, 227*t*, 319
Modern Mexico exhibit, 157–58
molenderas, 128, 341
monte, 341
Monte Albán, 31
Monte Albán period, 26
Montenegro, Roberto, 158–59
Morrow, Dwight and Elizabeth, 161–63
Mouffe, Chantal, 40
mozo, 341
Mujeres Que Tejan. *See* Gunah Ruinchi Laadti
Mujeres zapotecas (Stephens), 1
municipio, 341. *See also* local-level government
Murillo, Gerardo, 159
museum. *See* community museums
The Myth of the Male Breadwinner (Safa), 60

NAFTA (North American Free Trade Agreement), 13, 121, 341; impact on agriculture, 96; impact on class relations, 199; impact on migration, 96; impact on textile industry, 7; origins of weaving cooperatives, 216–19. *See also* neoliberal economics
nán, 240, 293, 341
Nash, June, 60, 201–2, 209
national factors. *See* state-level government
National Indigenous Congress (CNI), 194, 317

LYNN STEPHEN is a Distinguished Professor of Anthropology
and the Chair of the Department of Anthropology at
the University of Oregon.

LIBRARY OF CONGRESS CATALOGING-

IN-PUBLICATION DATA

Stephen, Lynn.
Zapotec women : gender, class, and ethnicity in globalized Oaxaca /
Lynn Stephen.— 2nd ed.
p. cm.
Includes bibliographical references and index.
ISBN 0-8223-3603-0 (cloth : alk. paper)
ISBN 0-8223-3641-3 (pbk. : alk. paper)
1. Zapotec women—Mexico—Teotitlán del Valle—
Social conditions. 2. Zapotec women—Mexico—Teotitlán del
Valle—Economic conditions. 3. Zapotec textile fabrics—Mexico—
Teotitlán del Valle. 4. Textile industry—Mexico-Teotitlán del Valle.
5. Social structure—Mexico—Teotitlán del Valle. 6. Teotitlán del
Valle (Mexico)—Social life and customs. I. Title. F1221.Z3S74 2005
305.48'89768—dc22   2005009919